W9-BWR-791

The Family Handyman

Home Improvement 2005

Handyman

Home Improvement 2005

by The Editors of *The Family Handyman* magazine

THE FAMILY HANDYMAN HOME IMPROVEMENT 2005
Executive Editor: Spike Carlsen
Managing Editor: Mary Flanagan
Contributing Designers: Bruce Bohnenstingl, Teresa Marrone, Barbara Pederson
Contributing Copy Editors: Donna Bierbach, Dinah Swain Schuster
Marketing Director: Michael J. Kuzma

Editor in Chief: Ken Collier
Vice President, General Manager, North American Publishing Group: Bonnie Bachar

Warning: All do-it-yourself activities involve a degree of risk. Skills, materials, tools, and site conditions vary widely. Although the editors have made every effort to ensure accuracy, the reader remains responsible for the selection and use of tools, materials, and methods. Always obey local codes and laws, follow manufacturer's operating instructions, and observe safety precautions.

ISBN 0-7621-0650-6

Address any comments about *The Family Handyman Home Improvement 2004* to:
Editor, Home Improvement 2005
2915 Commers Drive, Suite 700
Eagan, MN 55121

To order additional copies of *The Family Handyman Home Improvement 2005,* call 1-800-344-2560.

For more Reader's Digest products and information, visit our Web site at www.rd.com.
For more about *The Family Handyman* magazine, visit www.familyhandyman.com

Printed in the United States of America.
1 3 5 7 9 10 8 6 4 2

ABOUT THIS BOOK

and *The Family Handyman* magazine

The home improvement/reality TV craze keeps right on raging, so watch your step. Swap houses with your neighbor for a little reciprocal redecorating, and you may come home to a bedroom with moss stapled to the walls. Go away with your buddies for a fishing weekend and you could return to a basement converted into a disco. Tired of that boring backyard? Well for $100—and the assistance of 15 skilled landscapers hired by the production company—you can have a yard that looks like the grounds of Hearst Castle. Reality TV makes it all look so simple, fast, cheap and fun, but projects and repairs rarely fall into place so neatly, with such little hassle, and they never fit into a half-hour time frame.

Well, here's some information based on real reality—*The Family Handyman Home Improvement 2005*. It organizes the best articles and departments found in *The Family Handyman* magazine (from December of 2003 through November of 2004) into a single, easy-to-use volume. It's created to help you tackle projects and repairs with information that's "really real." We know there's no such thing as a perfectly square house, one trip to the hardware store or a project that's as easy as one, two, three. So we present information in a way that's useful, down-to-earth and easy to understand, using step-by-step photos, illustrations, tips, buying information and the wisdom of the best experts around.

Our advice? Turn on your television if you're looking for entertainment, but turn to this book if you need real home improvement advice.

Best of luck in all your projects. Really.

—The entire crew at *The Family Handyman* magazine

Contents

Safety 8

1 WALL, CEILING & FLOOR PROJECTS

You Can Fix It: Drywall Repairs . .10
Handy Hints 14, 26
Wall & Trim Makeover 15
Ask Handyman 20
Working Alone with Drywall . . .22
Great Goofs 29
You Can Fix It: Floor Squeaks . .30
Trim Tricks for Bad Walls 34
8 Tips for a Neater Paint Job 40
Using Tools: Drywall Sanding . . .44

2 KITCHEN, BATHROOM & LAUNDRY ROOM PROJECTS

10 Simple Cabinet Repairs 48
Fridge Repair for Rookies 52
Great Goofs 56
Handy Hints 57
Gallery of Ideas 60
Ask Handyman 62
New Laminate Countertops
and Kitchen Sink 64
You Can Fix It: Bath Fan Motor . .72

3 WIRING & ELECTRICAL

You Can Fix It: Lamp Fixes 74
Ask Handyman 78
4 Ways to Hide Speaker Wire . . .80
Troubleshoot a Dead Outlet 82
Surface-mounted Wiring 86
Using Tools:
Tips for Safer Wiring 92
Handy Hints 95
Great Goofs 94, 96

4 PLUMBING, HEATING & APPLIANCES

Stop Faucet Drips 98
Ask Handyman 102
Handy Hints 106
Great Goofs 109
Using Tools:
Leakproof Solder Joints 110

5 INTERIOR PROJECTS, REPAIRS & REMODELING

Stop Dust! 114
You Can Fix It: Subborn
Bifold Doors 118
Ask Handyman 121
Using Tools: Leveling Tips 122
Home Theater 126
Gallery of Ideas 128
Handy Hints 131
Burglar-Proof Your Door 134
Great Goofs 139

WOODWORKING PROJECTS & BUILT-INS

Adirondack Chair & Love Seat . . 142
Workshop Tips 148
Leaning Tower of Shelves 150
Gallery of Ideas 155
Super-Strong Glue Joints 158

WORKSHOP TOOLS, TIPS & STORAGE

Using Tools:
Driving Concrete Screws 164
10-Minute Workshop:
Storage Projects 168
Tips for Tough Cuts 172
Budget Workbench 177
Control Shop Dust 178
Workshop Tips 184

EXTERIOR MAINTENANCE & REPAIRS

Stop Peeling Paint 190
Ask Handyman 196
Handy Hints 199
Pointing Brick 202
Using Tools:
Finishing Concrete 206
You Can Fix It: Deck Repairs . . 210

OUTDOOR STRUCTURES & LANDSCAPING

7 Steps to a Lush, Green Lawn . . 216
Ask Handyman 224
Retaining Walls 226
Handy Hints 232
Backyard Stream & Waterfalls . . 234
Gallery of Ideas 240
You Can Fix It: Fixing Pond Leaks . . 246
Low-Maintenance
Garden Borders 248
Wordless Workshop 252

AUTO & GARAGE

Clear Your Garage Floor 254
Handy Hints 259
Auto Fast Fixes 260
Ask Handyman 266
Great Goofs 268
Handy Hints 269

SPECIAL FAMILY HANDYMAN BONUS SECTION

Handy Hints Hall of Fame 272
5 Simple "One-Hour" Gifts 276
15 Amazing PVC Pipe
Tips and Tricks 281

Index 284
Acknowledgments 288

SAFETY

Tackling home improvement projects and repairs can be endlessly rewarding. But, as most of us know, with the rewards come risks. DIYers use power tools, climb ladders and tear into walls that can contain big and hazardous surprises.

The good news is, armed with the right knowledge, tools and procedures, homeowners can minimize risk. As you go about your home improvement projects and repairs, stay alert for these hazards:

Aluminum wiring

Aluminum wiring, installed in about 7 million homes between 1965 and 1973, requires special techniques and materials to make safe connections. This wiring is dull gray, not the dull orange characteristic of copper. Hire a licensed electrician certified to work with it. For more information visit www.inspect-ny.com/aluminum.htm.

Asbestos

Texture sprayed on ceilings before 1978, adhesives and tiles for vinyl and asphalt floors before 1980, and vermiculite insulation (with gray granules) all may contain asbestos. Other building materials, made between 1940 and 1980, could also contain asbestos. If you suspect that materials you're removing or working around contain asbestos, contact your health department or visit www.epa.gov/asbestos for information.

Backdrafting

As you make your home more energy-efficient and airtight, existing ducts and chimneys can't always successfully vent combustion gases, including potentially deadly carbon monoxide (CO). Install a UL-listed CO detector.

Buried utilities

Call your utility companies to have them mark underground gas, electrical, water and telephone lines before digging. In many areas it takes just one call.

Five-gallon buckets

Since 1984 more than 200 children have drowned in 5-gallon buckets. Store empty buckets upside down and store those containing liquids with the cover securely snapped.

Lead paint

If your home was built before 1979, it may contain lead paint, which is a serious health hazard, especially for children six and under. Take precautions when you scrape or remove it. Contact your public health department for detailed safety information or call (800) 424-LEAD to receive an information pamphlet.

Spontaneous combustion

Rags saturated with oil finishes like Danish oil and linseed oil, and oil-based paints and stains can spontaneously combust if left bunched up. Always dry them outdoors, spread out loosely. When the oil has thoroughly dried, you can safely throw them in the trash.

Mini-blind and other window covering cords

Since 1991, more than 160 children have died of strangulation from window covering cords. Most accidents occur when infants in cribs near windows become entangled in looped cords or when toddlers looking out windows or climbing furniture lose their footing and becoming wrapped up in cords. Recalls, regulations, new products and new designs have lessened the dangers, but older existing window covering cords still pose a threat, and some experts maintain that no corded window treatment—old or new—is completely safe. In addition, some older vinyl blinds present a lead poisoning threat. For more information visit www.windowblindskillchildren.org or the Consumer Product Safety Commission at www.cpsc.gov. or (800) 638-2772.

1 Wall, Ceiling & Floor Projects

IN THIS CHAPTER

You Can Fix It 10
Drywall repairs

Handy Hints 14
Mark drywall with lipstick, renew a knife blade and more ...

Wall & Trim Makeover 15

Ask Handyman 20
Stop radon, carpet a basement, size a ceiling fan

Handy Hints 26
Focus on paint

Great Goofs 29

You Can Fix It 30
Fixing floor squeaks

Trim Tricks for Bad Walls 34

8 Tips for a Neater Paint Job 40

Using Tools: Drywall Sanding 44

You Can Fix It™

3 DRYWALL REPAIRS

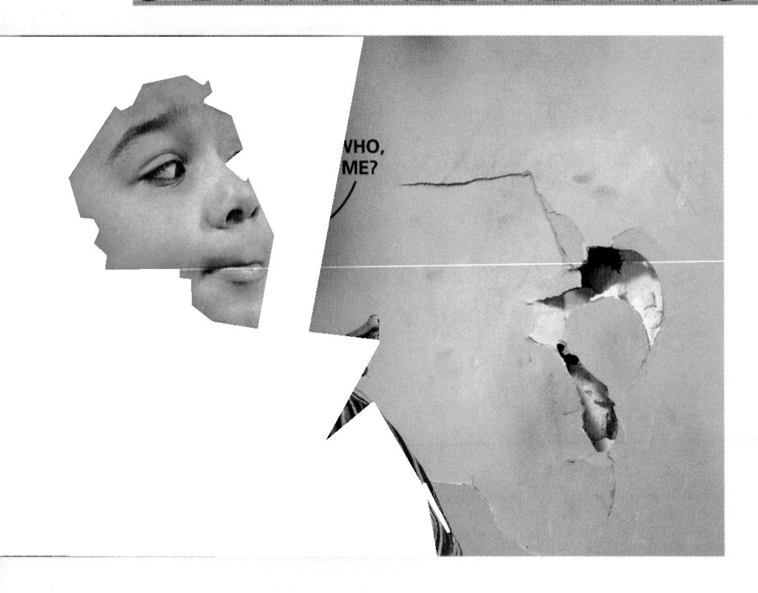

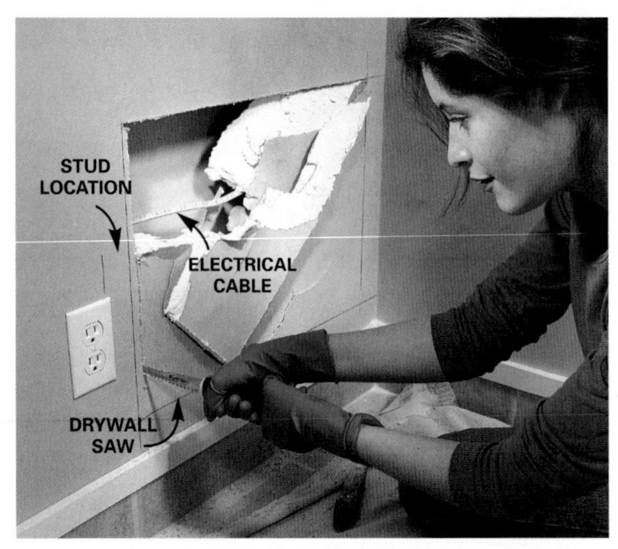

1 DRAW a rectangle around the break with a straightedge or square. Look or put your hand through the break to feel for wires or other obstructions. Then cut out the section with a drywall saw or utility knife.

1: LARGE HOLES

Don't melt down if a doorknob, misguided chair or an impromptu hockey game knocks a big hole in your wall. With a little patience, even a novice can complete a near-invisible repair. While the total time commitment isn't great, the process stretches over three to four days to allow coats of drywall compound and paint to dry.

Before cutting out the damaged area, check the wall for obstructions. Often you'll find a wire, pipe or duct (**Photo 1**). If so, work carefully around them with a drywall or keyhole saw. Or make a shallow cut by repeatedly scoring the line with a sharp utility knife.

It's easier to add backer board than to try to cut the drywall over studs (**Photo 2**). Cut the backer boards about 4 in. longer than the height of the hole. Pine or other soft wood works well. Hold them tight to the backside of the drywall when fastening them. Hold the boards carefully so the screw points won't prick your fingers if they pop out of the back side. The drywall screws will draw the boards in tight. Sink the screwheads slightly below the drywall surface.

Measure the thickness of the drywall (most likely 1/2 in.), and look for a large enough scrap from a damaged piece at a home center, rather than buy a full 4 x 8-ft. sheet. Cut it to size and screw it into place, spacing the screws every 6 in.

Taping the edges of the patch to make it invisible is the trickiest part of the job (**Photos 3 and 4**). Buy a gallon tub of drywall compound ($4) and a roll of paper tape ($1.50).

2 INSERT 1x4 backer boards at each end of the hole and drive a pair of 1-1/4 in. drywall screws through the drywall into the boards to anchor them. Fit and screw a drywall patch to the boards.

You can use mesh tape, but it isn't as strong. If you have a lot of repairs, also buy a sack of 20-minute setting compound ($5 a bag). It hardens quickly and doesn't shrink, so it's ideal for filling cracks and gaps before applying the

3 LAY a 1/8-in. thick bed of drywall compound over the joints and press paper tape into the compound with a flexible 6-in. knife. Immediately apply a thin layer of compound on top of the tape. Allow to dry.

4 APPLY a second coat of compound, drawing it at least 6 in. beyond the edge of the first coat to taper the edges of the repair. Let dry, then add a third coat to smooth any remaining uneven areas.

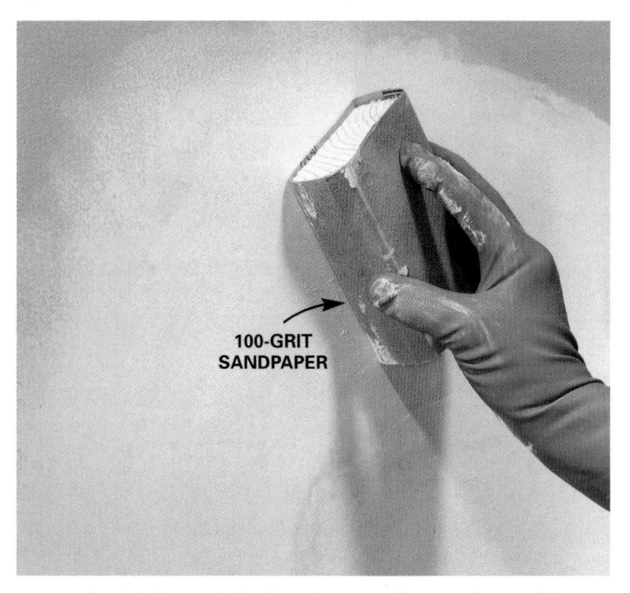

5 SAND the dry compound lightly with 100-grit sandpaper to remove ridges and blend edges. Prime and paint.

20-MINUTE SETTING COMPOUND

Twenty-minute setting compound is a great product for filling deep holes and gaps and for your first taping coat because, unlike regular joint compound, it hardens quickly without shrinking. That means less time spent filling. And you can apply a second coat of compound as soon as the first hardens. You don't have to wait for it to dry completely.

For most uses, buy the lightweight type. It comes as a powder in sacks ($5 for 18 lbs.). Mix only what you can use in about 10 minutes. It hardens quickly, often in your pan if you're too slow! Completely clean your pan and knife before mixing a new batch. Otherwise it'll harden even faster! To avoid clogging the sink drain, throw leftover compound into the trash.

joint tape. For smoothest results, also pick up flexible 6- and 10-in. taping knives ($7 each).

Apply a coat of compound and tape to each joint (Photo 3). Thin the compound a bit with water to help embed the tape. Smooth the tape with the 6-in. knife, pulling out from the center toward each end. Squeeze some, but not all, of the compound out from under the tape so you don't create a big hump on the wall. Immediately apply a light coating to the topside of the tape, tapering it out onto the wall.

The second and third coats are to blend and smooth the taped joints so they'll be invisible when painted. After each coat is dry, set a straightedge against the wall to check for obvious dips and bumps. Knock off bumps and ridges with your taping knife. Add more coats as needed. Then sand, prime and paint.

When possible, leave a few inches of drywall at corners so you won't have to spread taping compound onto adjacent walls or ceilings and repaint them as well!

2: SMALL HOLES

Small holes caused by screws or hooks, wall fasteners or drywall fasteners that pop up are simple to repair, but again time consuming because you almost always have to repaint the walls. Nail pops are common and particularly irritating, because you're likely to have more than one. But drywall screws sometimes pop up too, as a result of damp framing that dries out and shrinks during the first year or two in new construction.

The first step of the fix is to drive nails back down using a nail set (**Photo 1**). If you have screws, dig the drywall compound from their heads with a utility knife and turn them in tight with a screwdriver.

Then dimple the hole slightly concave with a hammer to indent any raised edges. But take care not to crush the drywall core. In addition, cut away any paper tears with a sharp utility knife. This is a good technique to use with old wall fasteners as well. It's usually easier to tap them into the wall slightly rather than pull them out.

Two coats of drywall compound, applied with two swipes of the knife in an "+" pattern, should fill the holes (**Photo 3**). The first coat will shrink a bit, leaving a slightly smaller dent to be filled by the second coat. Scrape the excess off the surrounding wall so you don't build up a hump. Sand lightly to blend with the surrounding wall. Be sure to prime the spot. Otherwise the topcoat will absorb into the patch and make the area look different from the surrounding paint. And use a roller when priming to help raise the surface texture to match the surrounding wall.

1 DRIVE a popped nail below the surface of the drywall with a hammer and a nail set. Cut away loose joint compound and paper shreds.

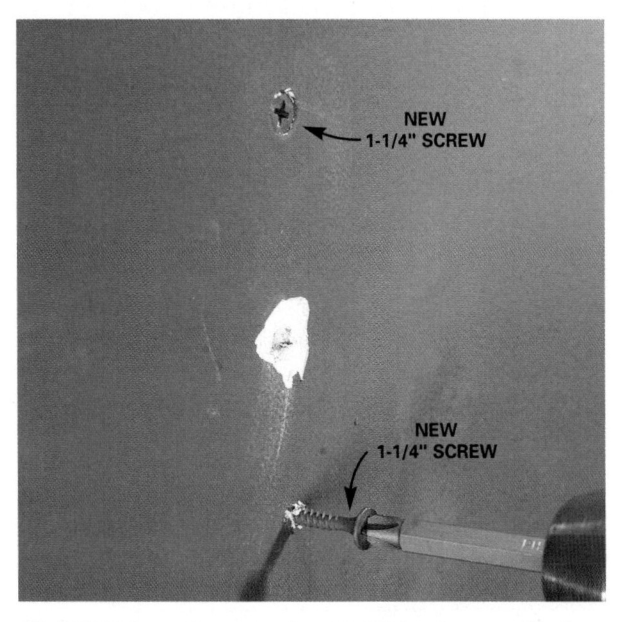

2 DRIVE drywall screws about 1-1/2 in. above and below the popped nail. Sink the screwhead just below the surface of the drywall.

3 FILL the holes with joint compound, swiping first across the holes, then down. Let dry, apply a second coat, then sand, prime and paint.

3: CRACKED CORNERS

Every home settles unevenly as it ages. This sometimes causes inside corners to crack or ripple. Often the crack will run from floor to ceiling. Once you spot this problem, watch it for two to three months for continued movement and fix it after all movement stops.

The key to renewing the strength of the corner is to remove all loose tape and drywall compound (**Photo 1**). If the drywall below has crumbled, cut it away with your utility knife and fill the gap with setting compound. (See "20-Minute Setting Compound," p. 11.)

Retape the joint following the techniques shown on p. 11. Crease the paper tape down the middle so it fits into the corner easily (**Photo 2**).

It's difficult to spread compound smoothly on one side of the corner without marring the other side. The trick is to apply compound for the second and third coats only on one side at a time. Let the one side dry, then do the other side.

Finally, buy a fine-grit sanding sponge ($3) to smooth the corners (**Photo 4**). It'll do a nice job without gouging.

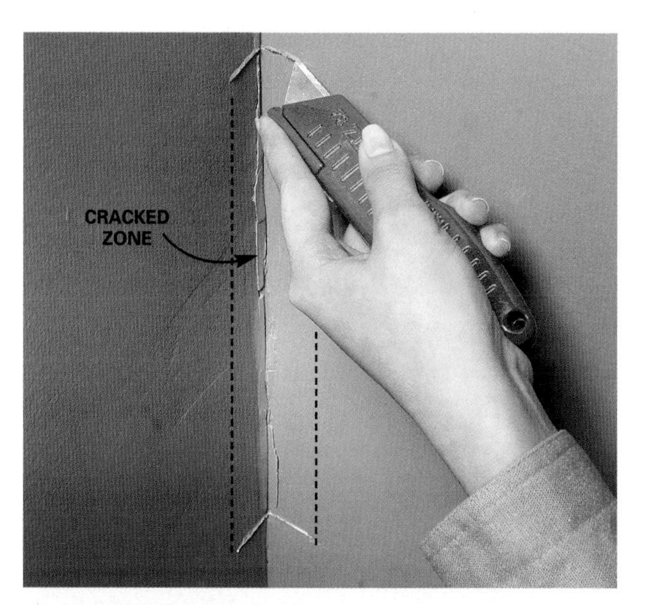

1 CUT through the tape at the ends of the cracked area and slice, scrape and tear away all loose tape and compound.

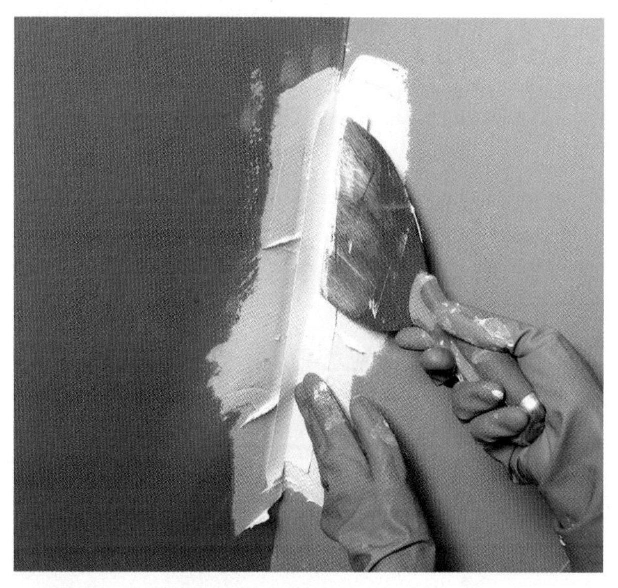

2 APPLY a 1/8-in. layer of joint compound, then fold and press paper tape into it. Stroke the length of the tape, squeezing compound out on both sides. Let dry.

3 APPLY second and third coats to smooth the joint, tapering the compound about 6 in. out. Let one side dry before applying compound to the other side.

4 LIGHTLY SAND the finished repair using a fine-grit sanding sponge to make a crisp corner. Prime and paint to match the existing wall.

Handy Hints® from our readers

COPE MOLDINGS WITH A DRUM SANDER

Use a drum sander in a hand drill to quickly create perfectly coped inside corners on molding. First, nail one molding piece in the corner so the end meets flush with the wall. Next, cut a 45-degree miter (if the corner is 90 degrees) on the corner end of the second molding piece, then clamp it to a steady work surface. With a coarse-grit sanding sleeve in an electric drill, sand away the mitered end. Be careful to sand only to the line, running the drum back and forth along the joint line to ensure a smooth contour.

FINISH-SAND TO LINE WHILE BEVELING UNDERCUT SLIGHTLY

If your molding has intricate curves, use a rotary tool with a small drum sander to finish these areas. Test-fit, resand as necessary and nail on the second piece.

STAY-FRESH COMPOUND

Here's a slick, long-term storage method to keep premixed compounds from drying out. Wipe the lip and lid of the container clean, removing any residue. Pour a cup or so of water on top of the compound, then stretch a piece of plastic wrap over the container. Pound the lid tight, and then flip the container upside down. This will keep air out of the compound and fresh until needed again.

RENEW A KNIFE BLADE

Utility knife blades often dull near the tip long before the rest of the blade loses its edge. To get more mileage out of a blade, put on a pair of safety glasses and snap off the tip with a pliers. Presto! You've got a new sharp tip.

SPECIALTY DRYWALL KNIFE

If you have to drywall a room with a cathedral ceiling and a lot of odd angles, trim off the end of a 6-in. knife to make it easier to apply joint compound in the corners.

TOO-TIGHT CEILING PANELS

The panels in a suspended ceiling often fit tight in the rails, so every time you have to get behind them, you can't get the panels to drop back into place. The solution? Hold your shop vacuum nozzle against the offending corners and use the suction to pull them right into place.

MARK DRYWALL CUTOUTS WITH LIPSTICK

When hanging drywall, smear lipstick on electrical boxes. Then position the sheet and press it into place to create a perfect cutout pattern.

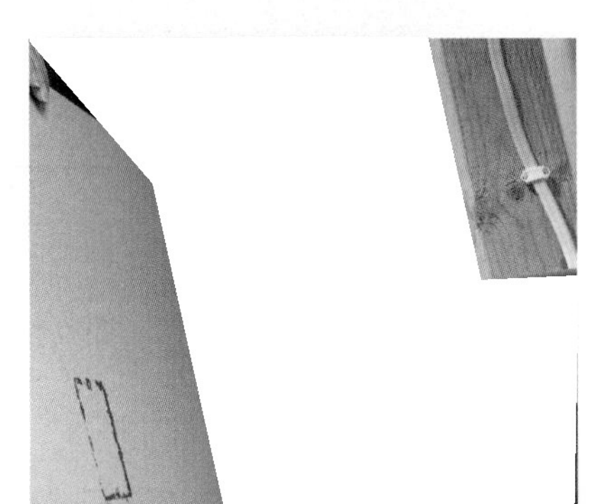

WALL & TRIM **MAKEOVER**

Give any room a face-lift with two simple projects: Venetian plaster wall texture and urethane moldings

by **David Radtke**

Maybe you've decided that red bedroom walls just aren't you. Maybe you think your 2-year-old could have sponge-painted better than the previous owners. Whatever the case, if you're ready for a new look in your bedroom, bath, dining room—or just about any other room in the house—we'll show you how to redo it in a weekend with two simple projects.

The first is a new decorative wall technique called Venetian plaster. Once a difficult project tackled only by pros, Venetian plaster is now easy to apply in a simple multistep process. With this solid-color product in a can, you can add a rich visual texture with highlights and shadows. It's as simple as patching and painting walls, and inexpensive, too. For a project like ours in an average-size bedroom, you'll spend $30 for the plaster and $10 on basic tools.

The second project is an easy-to-install urethane molding that you can cut with a handsaw (no power miter box necessary) and then glue and nail to the walls. The molding is a durable product with the crisp details and shapes you'd expect from solid wood, but it's a lot easier to work with. For an average-size bedroom, figure on spending about $75 for chair railing. If you plan to trim the windows and doors with moldings similar to those shown, add $80 per unit. For more information on the plaster and moldings, see pp. 17 and 19.

PART ONE: VENETIAN PLASTER

Getting started

Before you start, choose a color from the brochure available at your home center (or go to the company's Web site, www.behr.com, if the product isn't available locally). The supplier will mix and blend the colored plaster just like ordinary paint so it's ready to use right out of the can. Don't be fooled when you open the can and see just a solid color. The subtle color differences you see in the final job are part of the process of applying, sanding and tooling the plaster.

Prep the room just as you would for any paint job by cleaning walls and filling holes. Mask the areas you don't want painted such as around windows, doors and baseboards. You can plaster over any paint that's sound, but if the paint is glossy or semigloss, wipe it down with a deglosser (available at paint stores).

You can create a two-color wall like ours or use the Venetian plaster product from floor to ceiling with dramatic effects. If you want two colors, paint the top first and allow it to dry so you won't drip paint on the Venetian plaster below. When figuring the proportions for a wainscot, keep in mind that it'll look best about one-third of the way up from the floor to the ceiling. You can go a bit higher up the wall, but keep from going as far as halfway up. This will divide the room into a distinct top and bottom and look odd.

With the room prepped, mask off the wall just above where you'll be plastering. Measure up from the floor in several locations and mark a level line with a straightedge. Use a 2- to 3-in. wide strip of tape so you can stroke freely and not be tempted to make smaller strokes at the top. Also, open a window in the room. Although this product has very low odor, adequate ventilation is necessary until it dries.

Trowel it on

When you're at the home center, pick up a drywall mud pan like the one shown in Photo 2 to hold the colored plaster while you're spreading it on the wall. The long top edges have a sharp rim to wipe your drywall knife clean. Also buy a 5-in. flexible drywall knife to spread the product on the walls. You could use a 4-1/2 in. or a 6-in. knife instead, with slightly different effects. I found it helpful to practice on a scrap of painted drywall to get the hang of it. Your home center paint department may also have small boards available to practice on.

Before you start, sand the corners of the drywall knife to round them slightly to keep the tool from leaving sharp ridges and digging into the wall. Start applying the plaster to the wall in a corner and work your way along the wall as shown in Photo 3. Don't try to do the whole wall in one coat. You'll find it easiest to trowel an even coat on a 3- to 4-ft. section with your knife at a less than 45-degree angle and then go back and do random strokes with the knife, alternating left to right and right to left. You'll see the original color of the wall show through on the first coat but this is good. If you don't see some of the wall beneath, you're putting the plaster on too thick. After a couple of sections, stop and examine the wall. Tool any section with heavy ridges and even it with a clean trowel before it dries, then move along.

Fill the voids with the second coat

Wait for the first coat to dry, from two to four hours, then apply the second. Load your knife and fill in the voids with strokes of your knife. Repeat the randomness of the first coat and the combination of the two coats will add up to a great-looking, varied texture later. Hold the drywall knife at a bit steeper angle, at least 45 degrees to the wall. Look for the spots where the first coat didn't cover and apply plaster in those areas. Again, after a couple of sections, go back and

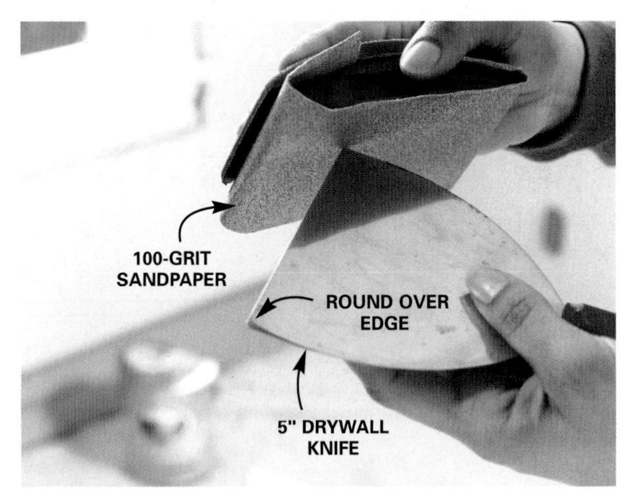

1 ROUND the corners of a standard 5-in. drywall knife to prevent the tool from digging in.

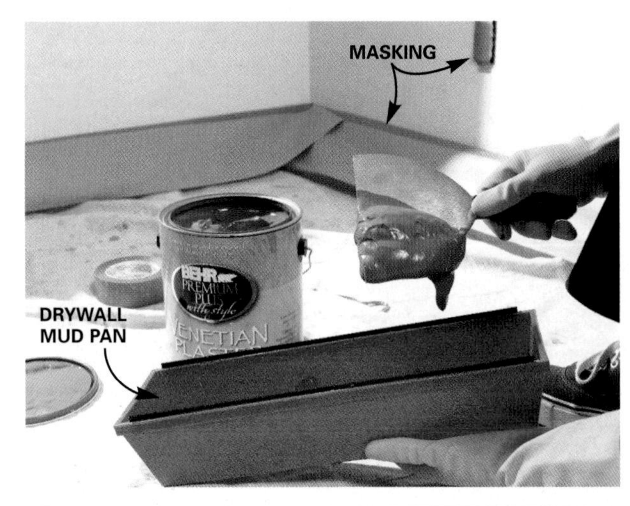

2 TRANSFER the Venetian plaster mix to a drywall pan so it's easier to scrape the excess off the knife. The plaster is a bit thinner than drywall compound but thicker than paint.

3 APPLY the colored plaster mix with your drywall knife in random strokes back and forth at less than 45 degrees to vertical. Avoid heavy buildup.

4 **FINISH one wall section at a time. Go back after each section and remove any blotches thicker than 1/8 in. before they dry.**

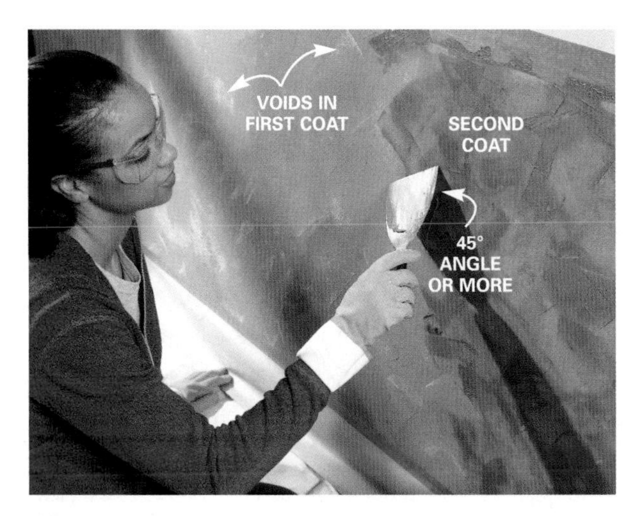

5 **TROWEL on the second coat once the first is thoroughly dry. Again using random strokes, fill in the voids where the undercoat shows, turning the knife from left to right and then from right to left.**

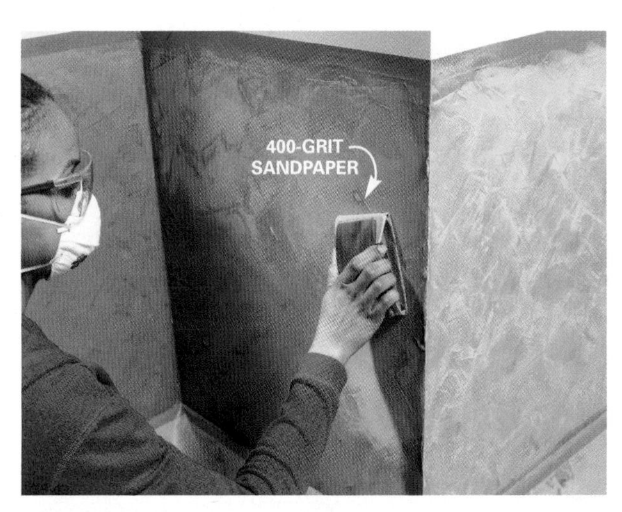

6 **SAND the second coat with 400-grit sandpaper once it has dried (24 hours) to remove heavy ridges. Each area the size shown needs about one minute of vigorous sanding. Rub down the entire surface with clean, dry cotton cloths.**

check your work, making sure the wall is adequately covered and the wall color behind doesn't show through. The plaster should be about 1/8 in. thick in the thicker areas and thinner elsewhere, so judge your job accordingly. Remember, the finished job will have more visual texture than actual texture.

You'll find that outside corners can build up quickly, so try to keep them as even as the rest of the wall. If the plaster is too thin, you can always go back and dab corners with a small paint brush later. When you've finished the room, let this coat dry for 24 hours before moving to the next step. The job will look a bit sloppy at this stage, so don't be disappointed. The final steps will bring the walls to life.

Sanding and burnishing create visual depth

Sand the walls with 400-grit sandpaper clamped into a stiff rubber sanding block (Photo 6). Just fold a full sheet into thirds and then put it into the block. As you sand (wear a dust mask), you'll see the character in the finish develop as the foreground appears lighter and the background stays a bit darker. Keep sanding until you get a uniform appearance. Don't worry about sanding through the plaster finish, because the paper is very fine. Change sandpaper as the sheets wear out or clog. You'll need about four sheets for an entire room. Wipe all the sanded areas with clean, dry

Venetian plaster

Venetian plaster is available in gallon containers, which cover approximately 150 sq. ft. for the two coats shown. You can choose from more than 20 stock colors to fit almost any decorating scheme. For our project, we chose Italian Cypress, color No. VP40. For more information on Behr Venetian Plaster, go to www.behr.com and look under "Faux Finishes." For added durability in high-traffic areas, you can apply a water-based polyurethane topcoat.

cloths to remove the residue and then vacuum the floor and sanded areas with the brush attachment.

Now it's time to burnish the surface (Photo 7) with your steel drywall knife. Start anywhere, holding the knife at about a 30-degree angle to the wall. Pull the knife blade along the wall firmly with long, bold strokes. The direction isn't particularly important; just be sure you go over each square foot of wall several times. The high spots of the thin texture will get a bit darker and polished as you move along the wall from one end to the other. You'll start to see three distinct levels of color from the background to the foreground. Once you've finished the wall, remove the masking tape slowly and get ready to apply your chair rail molding.

7 PULL the knife briskly over the surface in long, bold strokes to smooth the high spots and create a luster as well as darken areas to develop contrast and character.

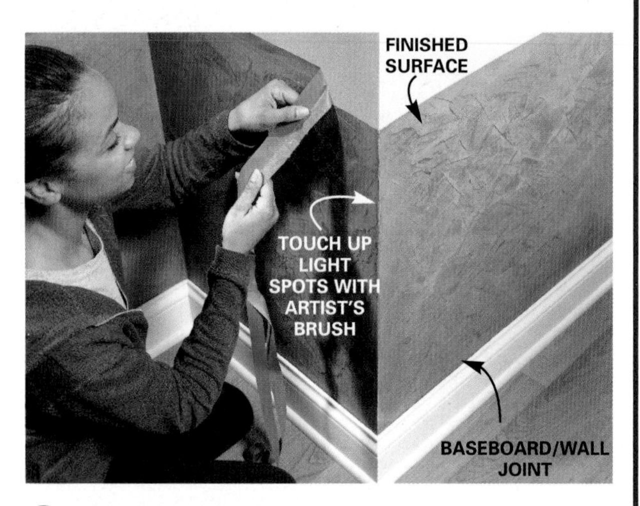

8 PULL the painter's masking tape gently from the wall to avoid lifting the paint beneath. Using your utility knife, carefully cut the texture along the joint where the baseboard meets the wall. This will allow you to easily peel back the tape.

PART TWO: URETHANE CHAIR RAIL

Urethane chair rail and moldings

Urethane moldings are both lightweight and easy to apply, making them a great alternative to wood molding. In this story, we used them for chair rail and window trim.

The manufacturer recommends cutting the molding about 1/4 in. overlong for long runs (12 to 16 ft.) to help make up for seasonal wall expansion. It'll compress slightly and snap into place. Shorter lengths to 8 ft. should be cut about 1/8 in. overlong and anything less than 4 ft. should be cut to fit. The company also recommends butting crosscut ends together when splicing long lengths instead of bevel-cutting moldings at mid-wall joints. The molding is applied just like wood molding except that it cuts and nails easier.

Set the molding into your miter box (screw the miter box down to your sawhorse or work table) and cut it on your mark with slow, steady strokes as you hold the molding firmly with your other hand. Support long ends with additional sawhorses. Don't bother coping joints in corners; just lay the molding on its backside and cut at 45 degrees for inside and outside corners. Nails alone won't do—you must use the polyurethane adhesive caulk to bond it to the wall surface to make up for its low density.

Fill nail holes with spackling compound and then wipe the surface clean with a damp rag (Photo 4). This process will take two coats. Sand urethane molding as little as possible because unlike wood, the factory finish on the urethane molding is thin. Because you'll be painting the molding, you can touch up joints with acrylic caulk and wipe the excess away with a damp rag. You can save yourself a lot of time by prepainting the molding and then touching it up after you've cut and installed it.

Tip

To widen your miter box as shown in **Photo 1**, opposite page, use a hammer to tap the sides free of the original base. Drill pilot holes and screw the sides to the new base. With the wider base, you'll be able to crosscut and bevel-cut the moldings. However, the other miter operations won't be possible, since the precut slots will no longer line up. This won't be a problem for cutting the moldings we show here.

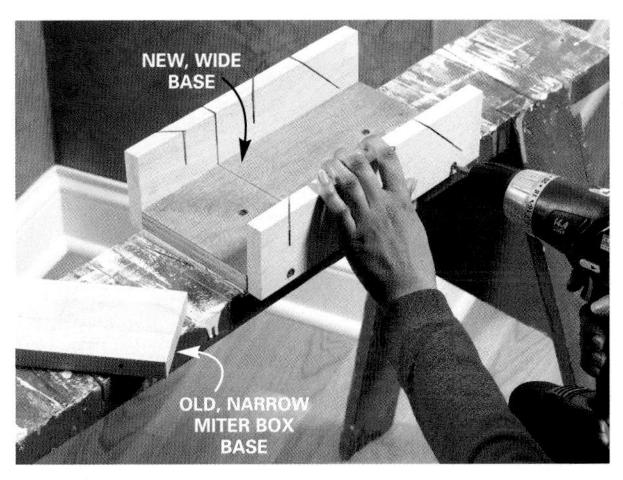

1 **HAND miter boxes and fine-tooth hand saws are best for cutting urethane moldings. The moldings, however, are often wider than the miter box bed. Widen the bed by removing the screws on the side of the box and adding a wider base. See tip on previous page.**

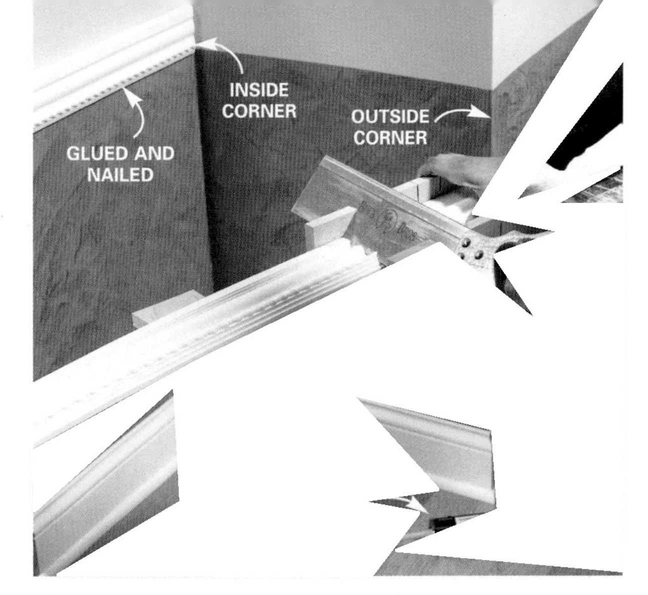

2 **MEASURE the length, then cut the moldings with 45-degree bevel cuts in the corners and glue the backsides and joints with polyurethane molding adhesive.**

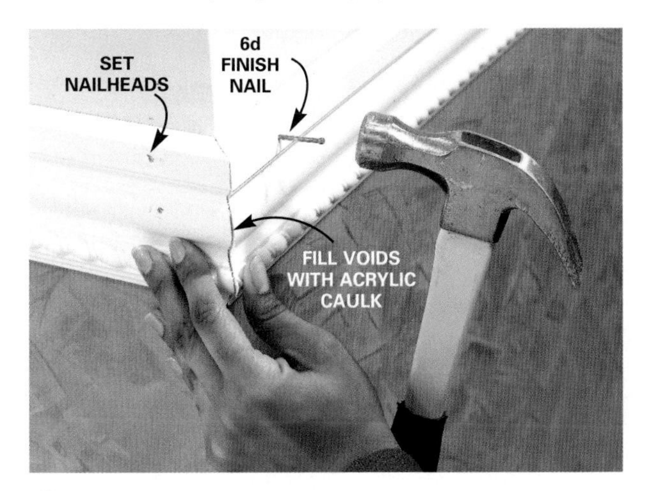

3 **GLUE and nail the moldings to the wall. Make small reference marks along the wall with your level to make sure you keep the molding straight as you nail. Set the nails with a nail set.**

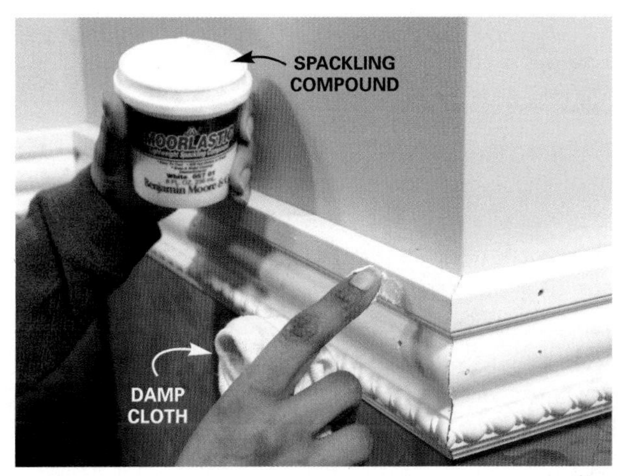

4 **FILL the nail holes with spackling compound and the joints with acrylic caulk, then wipe with a slightly damp cloth. You'll need a second application once the spackling compound and caulk are dry. Wipe smooth or lightly sand, then paint.**

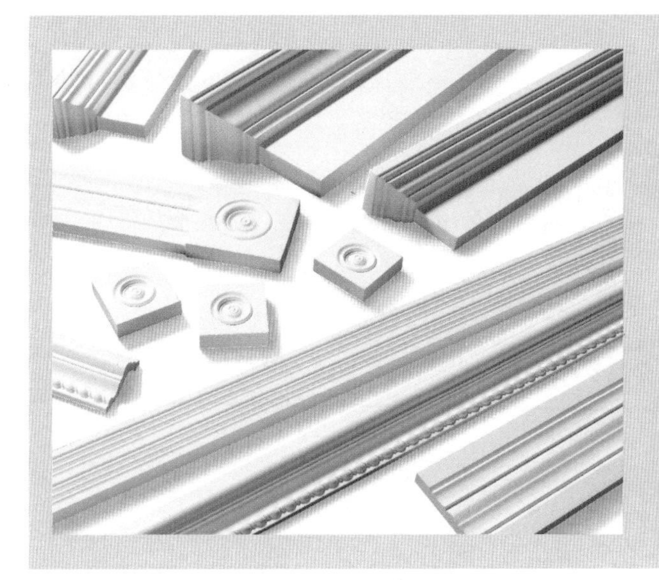

Buying urethane moldings

Home centers and lumberyards carry a limited selection of urethane moldings. They come in a wide variety of preprimed profiles and sizes for windows, doors, crown moldings and decorative panels. They're expensive but cost less than decorative wood moldings with the same profiles. To see all your options, take a look at the manufacturer's catalog. There you can order moldings to suit your taste. The moldings shown here are only a small sample.

For more information on urethane molding options, go to www.stylesolutionsinc.com or call (800) 446-3040. Also check with www.focalpointap.com or call (800) 662-5550 to find a dealer in your area.

Ask Handyman™

STOP RADON

Tests have shown that our house has a radon gas problem. After speaking with a few radon mitigation contractors, we think the process seems easy enough to do ourselves. Know of any good resources that detail this process?

Congratulations on testing your home. Our best advice, if you have high levels of this radioactive gas, is to hire a certified professional radon mitigator. They're trained to perform diagnostic tests to choose the best reduction system for your specific house—based on your foundation design and the entry points for the gas. To get a list of certified pros in your state, call (800) 644-6999. Mitigation to an existing home usually costs $800 to $2,500.

Radon is a naturally occurring radioactive gas that's formed when uranium breaks down in the soil. One way this colorless, odorless soil gas can seep into a house is through cracks and holes (especially at or near a sump pump) in the foundation and crawlspace. If the gas builds up to a level of 4 picoCuries per liter (pCi/L) or higher, you run a long-term risk of getting lung cancer.

Homeowners can take steps to reduce radon gas. For example, you can seal holes and cracks in your basement, place a gas-tight seal over a sump pump hole, and pour concrete over dirt floors or crawlspaces. However, some practices, if applied incorrectly, can actually increase the radon level. If you find and close these major entry routes and another test doesn't show sufficient reductions, hire a pro rather than try to seal all possible minor openings.

One good resource is the Environmental Protection Agency (EPA) Web site: www.epa.gov/iaq/radon. To learn more about radon mitigation standards, visit www.epa.gov/iaq/radon/pubs/mitstds.html. The National Radon Information Line is (800) 767-7236.

EPA Map of Radon Zones

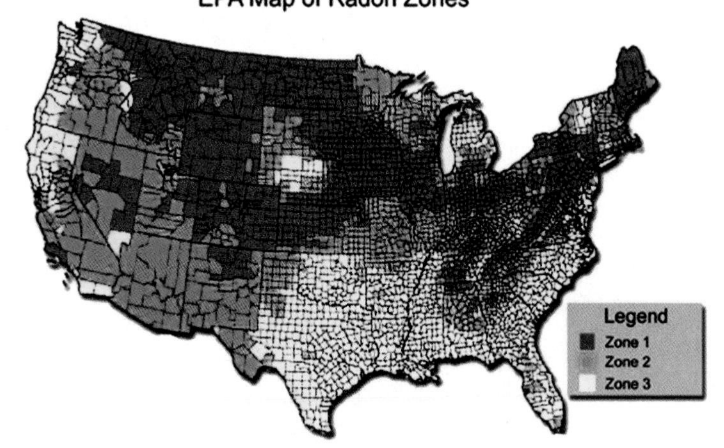

Zone 1: Potential exists for dangerous levels of radon (>4 pCi/L)
Zone 2: Potential for moderate levels of radon (2 to 4 pCi/L)
Zone 3: Predicted low levels of radon (<2 pCi/L)

SIZING A CEILING FAN

I understand ceiling fans can save energy and money for heating and cooling. Is there a rule of thumb for what size fan I need?

Yes, a quick rule of thumb matches the diameter of the fan with the largest dimension of a room. For 12 ft. or less, use a 36-in. fan. For 12 to 16 ft., use a 48-in. fan. For 16 to 18 ft., use a 52-in. fan. And for dimensions larger than 18 ft., install two fans.

Placement of a ceiling fan for adequate air circulation is 7 ft. above the floor with the blades 8 to 10 in. from the ceiling. And to move more air at low speed, a fan with five blades is best.

Regarding energy savings, research has proven that ceiling fans can save energy during the cooling season by creating a gentle breeze. You get your savings then by raising your thermostat by a minimum of 2 degrees. This decreases air conditioning energy used by 10 to 15 percent, or 5 to 8 percent per degree.

CARPETING A BASEMENT FLOOR

My husband wants to finish our basement with carpet and padding directly on the concrete. I feel there should be a wood subfloor to make it warmer on the feet. Which is the preferred method? P.S. During heavy storms, our basement floor occasionally gets wet.

A warmer floor is always the best option, and a wood subfloor helps a little bit. But neither option will work if your floor is damp or if seepage or leakage is likely. Any kind of persistent moisture will allow mold to get a foothold and soon ruin your carpet.

For below-grade slabs like yours, assume that the concrete floor will get damp at some point. You then have two options, depending on your circumstances. And both of the options use the same layers of 1/2-in. plywood, carpet pad and carpet as shown. It's the initial layer that differs.

The solution on the right (Option B) will work on a concrete floor that has no persistent dampness, seepage or leakage. The 6-mil layer of plastic helps to minimize potential moisture migration up into the plywood.

Option A can be applied on concrete where there's a higher risk of some dampness. The initial layer is a durable high-density polyethylene sheet (called Delta-FL) that uses evenly spaced 3/8-in. tall dimples to create air space and a moisture barrier between the concrete and the plywood.

Lay the sheet over the concrete floor (dimples down), overlap adjacent edges and tape the seams. Add the plywood layer on top and anchor it to the concrete with 15 concrete screws (predrilled and countersunk) per 4 x 8-ft. sheet.

You can buy Delta-FL in 4 x 8-ft. sheets or in a 5 x 65-1/2 ft. roll. It costs about 50¢ per square foot plus shipping. Visit www.deltams.com or call (888) 433-5824 to locate a retailer.

Before you proceed, consult a local building inspector to determine specific building codes for this type of project. Also, be sure your basement floor is level. Finally, note that these options will raise your floor by 1-1/4 to 1-1/2 in., so make sure this added height won't create problems.

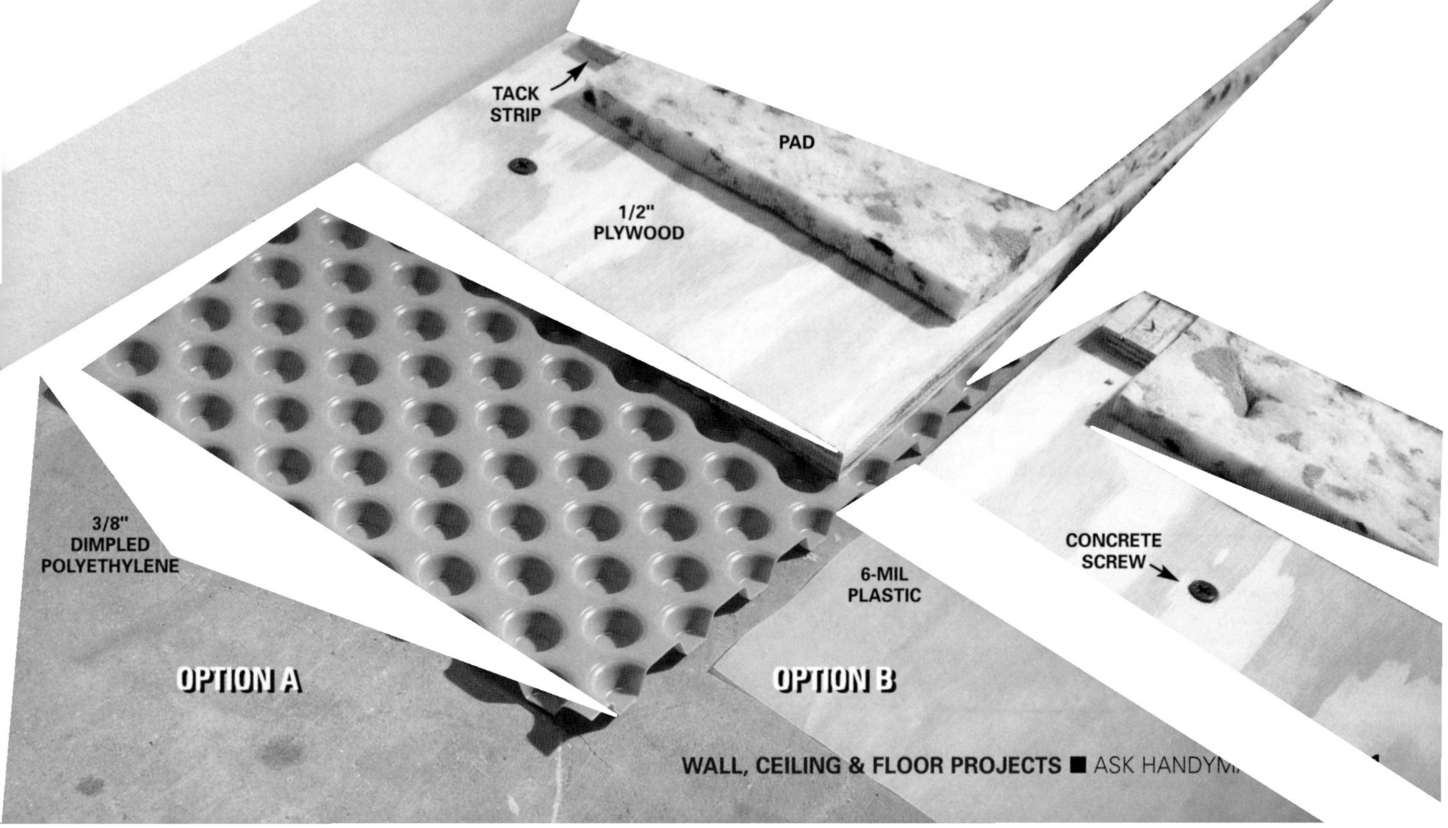

WORKING ALONE **WITH DRYWALL**

With special tools and techniques, one person can hang it as easily as two

by **Eric Smith**

Lifts work for walls, too

A lift works on upper wall sheets just as well as it does on ceilings. After loading the drywall, push the lift to the wall, position the sheet, tip the top edge against the wall and crank it snugly against the ceiling.

Rent a drywall lift for ceiling work

If you have to drywall a ceiling, don't hesitate to rent a lift. It's well worth the $30 to $40 daily rental fee and is by far the best way to get a ceiling up without back strain.

Drywall lifts break down into three parts and fit easily into a midsize car. After you reassemble it, release the catch on the wheel and crank it up and down a few times to make sure it's working smoothly. Then lock the lift and hoist one end of the drywall sheet up to the support hook—finish side down. Now lift the other end of the sheet up and slide it onto the second hook as shown. Lift slowly and smoothly—abrupt or jerky handling can pop the front edge of the drywall off the hook.

Tip the sheet so it's horizontal and lock it down. Then wheel the lift into approximate position. Lifts are stable and maneuverable, so you can fine-tune the placement when you raise the drywall (**Photo**, p. 22). Then crank it tight. You may need to get up on a ladder to nudge the sheet into place. Put in at least eight screws before lowering the lift.

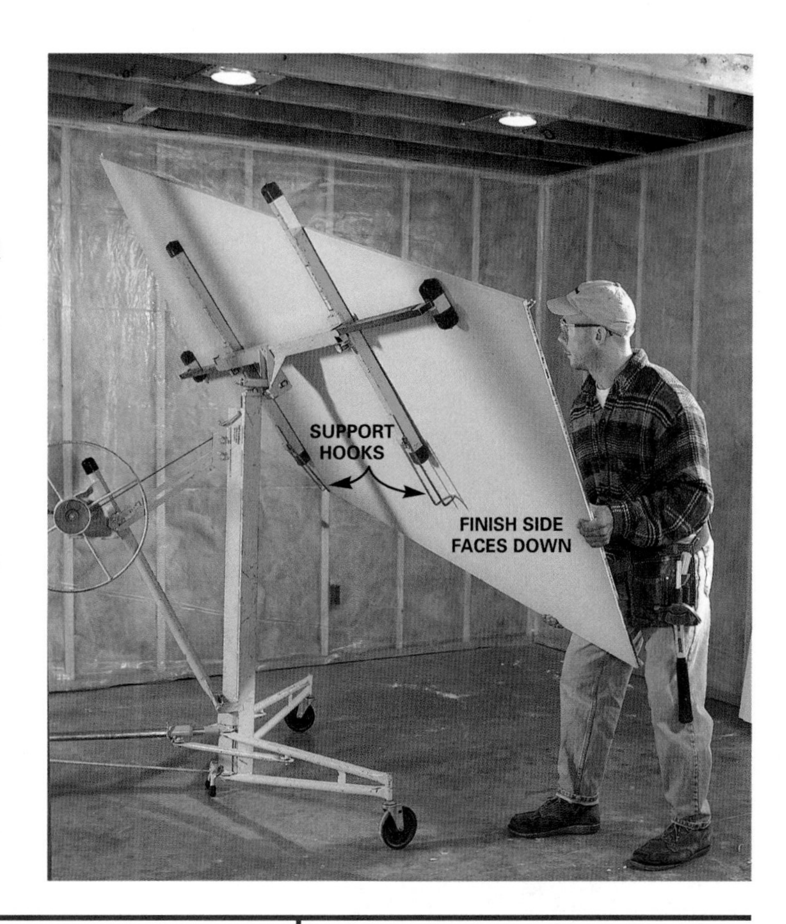

Make cutouts in place

Cutouts for lights and outlets are much faster and easier to make with the drywall in place, saving the trouble of taking the sheet down and recutting it if a precut hole doesn't quite fit. Use a special cutout tool with a drywall bit, available for $60 to $80 at hardware stores and home centers. First, make sure to push electrical wires at least an inch back into the boxes, out of the way of the cutout bit. Next, measure and mark the approximate center points of the electrical boxes on the drywall, before you put it up. Crank the sheet up, and put in just enough screws to hold it in place, keeping the screws at least 12 in. from the cutout. Then punch the drywall cutout tool through the center mark and run it out to the edge until the bit hits the side of the fixture. Ease the bit up and over the edge to the outside of the can or box and slowly cut counterclockwise around it as shown. Drive nearby screws after the cutout is finished.

Preset nails (and use your head)

When you need to hold a piece up in place without the lift, preset a half-dozen drywall nails around the edges at joist or stud locations before you lift the sheet. Hoist it up, support it tightly against the ceiling joists with a hand and your head (a sponge under the hat helps), then drive in the nails to hold the piece in place. Fasten it off with screws.

Ease the strain with a panel lifter

Take the strain off your arms and upper body and make navigating tight spots easier with a $4 plastic panel lifter (shown above), available at home centers. Just hook the panel lifter around the bottom of the sheet at the center point, tip the sheet up and lift, leaving your lifting arm fully extended as if you were carrying a suitcase. Use your other arm to balance the sheet, keeping the drywall close to horizontal. You'll be amazed—you can move drywall with half the effort. But it doesn't work on full flights of stairs. Get a helper for that.

Panel rollers make big jobs small

Have a few dozen sheets to move? For $30, you can get the next best thing to having somebody carry the drywall for you—a heavy-duty panel roller that carries up to two sheets at a time (or anything else that's flat and heavy). Roll drywall almost effortlessly through the house, as we did in this photo, using one hand to control the roller and the other to balance the sheet and steer around corners. The wheels tilt and roll over thresholds, and for bigger obstacles, just grasp the handle and lift the drywall as you would with a panel lifter. You can even tuck a sheet under your arm, a very simple and comfortable carrying position. This lifter doesn't work on a full flight of stairs. Panel rollers are available at drywall and tool suppliers. We used the Troll 49 ($30 plus shipping) from Telpro Inc. (www.telproinc.com, 800-448-0822).

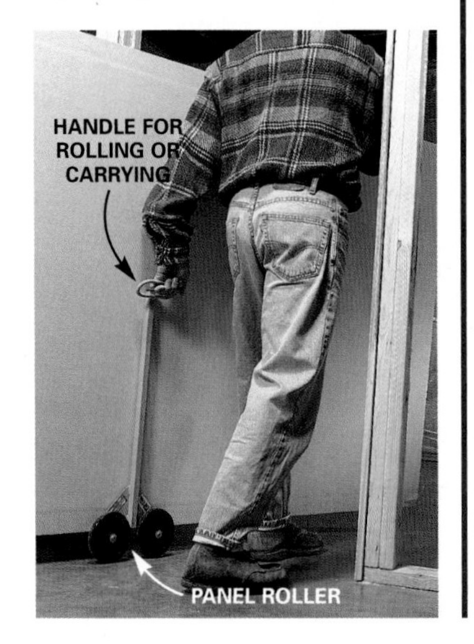

Measure tight but cut loose

Putting drywall up and then taking it down to shave an edge that won't fit is a waste of energy if you're alone. Instead, subtract 1/4 in. from your measurements to make up for rough cuts and wavy walls. It's easier to fill slight gaps with joint compound than to struggle with a tight fit.

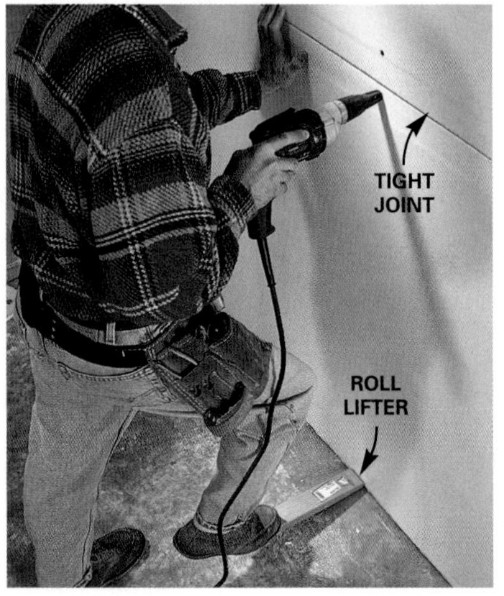

Lever; don't lift

Rather than straining to hold lower sheets up off the floor, lever them up snug against the upper sheet with a pry bar and a block of wood or a roll lifter ($11 at home centers).

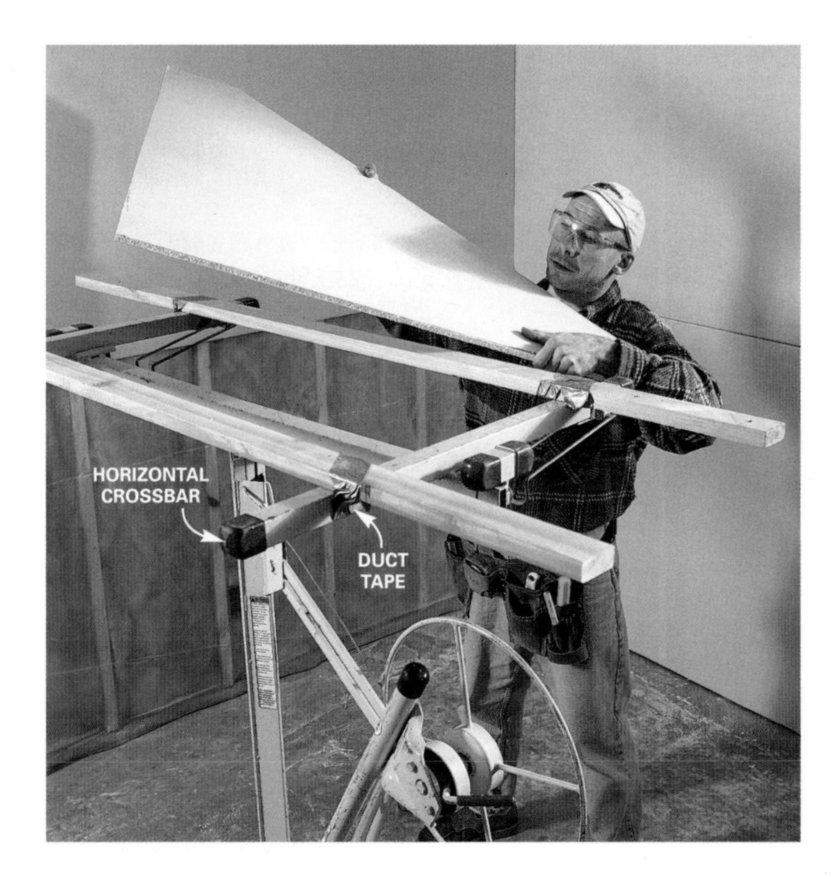

Customize the lift for angled pieces

Modify the lift to hold small or irregular pieces by taping a pair of 1x4s or 2x4s perpendicular to the crossbars as temporary supports. The hooks won't catch, so lock the crossbars down into the horizontal position.

Add nailers instead of recutting

You've wrestled a heavy sheet up, put in half the screws and just noticed that you slightly miscut the sheet. Before you go through the hassle of taking the sheet down and recutting, try these possible fixes:

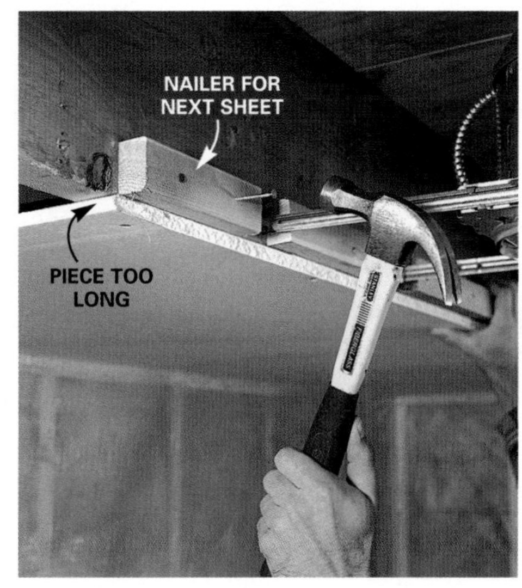

1. Tack a 2x4 to the side of the joist as a nailer for the next piece (photo right)—or for the piece you've just put up, if it's short.
2. Create a floating seam by screwing the unsupported end to a 1x4 that you slide on top of it. Let the 1x4 overlap the end about 1-1/2 in. Then screw the next piece to the 1x4 as well. Cut the 1x4 longer than the piece you're seaming so that adjoining sheets will help support it.

New Product

SMART PACKAGING

Patching compound usually comes in little round hard-to-open plastic containers. The openings are too small to get a putty knife in for loading, and it gets tougher the closer you get to the flat bottom. Next time you have to patch some walls, pick up DAP's new Vinyl Spackling kit. It has a nice wide easy-open top so you can actually get at the stuff, and the rounded bottom makes it easy to scrape out the last little bit. It even comes with a built-in plastic putty knife that stores in the lid. It contains a generous 24 ozs., so you're unlikely to run out in the middle of the job. Buy yours at any home center or hardware store for about $6. DAP Inc., (888) 327-8477. www.dap.com

Handy Hints® focus on painting

MIXING PAINT IN A BAG

When mixing paint with an electric drill and mixing paddle, place the can inside a paper grocery bag. If you spill or splatter (and you will!), you won't get paint on the floor, nearby objects or yourself.

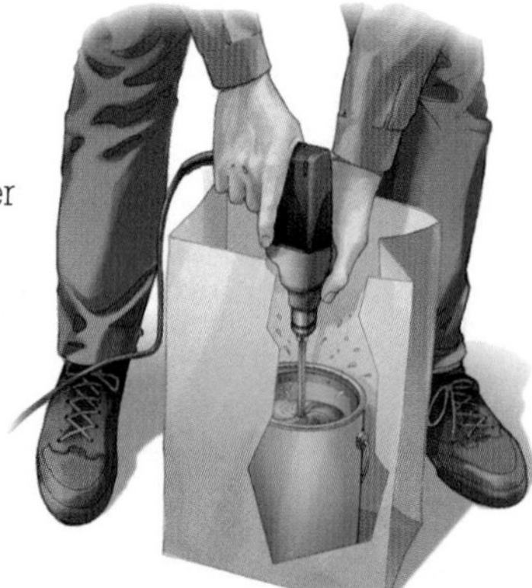

PAINT CAN SCRAPER

When you pour paint from a gallon paint can, a lot of paint stays inside the can. To get all the paint out, cut a notch in the handle end of a wood paint stick. Now you can scrape the inside of the can clean and stop wasting paint.

RELEASE MASKING TAPE WITH HEAT

If masking tape tears as you remove it or pulls off flakes of finish, heat it with a hair dryer. Heat softens the adhesive. Then pull the tape off at a 90-degree angle.

PIMPLE PADS FOR PAINT CLEANUP

Facial cleansing wipes aren't just for pimple prevention. The alcohol in them softens latex paint, but won't harm most surfaces (test first to make sure). They work best on paint that's been dry just a few hours.

PAINT BRUSH RESTORER

Have a paint brush that wasn't cleaned out well the last time it was used? First, loosen the paint by soaking the brush in denatured alcohol. Then hold it against the rim of your work sink and run a stiff wire brush through the bristles to remove the dried paint.

New Product

KING-SIZE MASKING

The Quick Mask system from Homeright is a dispenser, cutter, and masking paper and tape all rolled into one. After you roll out the masking, you just tear it off with the cutting teeth at the top of the dispenser. Unfold the paper to its full 7-in. width and even the widest trim will be well protected from paint drips. Each roll contains 70 ft. of masking and costs 5 to 7 bucks. Contact the manufacturer if you need to find a store near you, or order directly on-line (No. C800132).

Homeright,
(800) 264-5442.
www.homeright.com

GENTLE PAINT REMOVER

Take a tip from artists and use baby oil to remove dried latex or oil-based paint from your skin. It doesn't work as quickly as solvents, but it's safer and gentler.

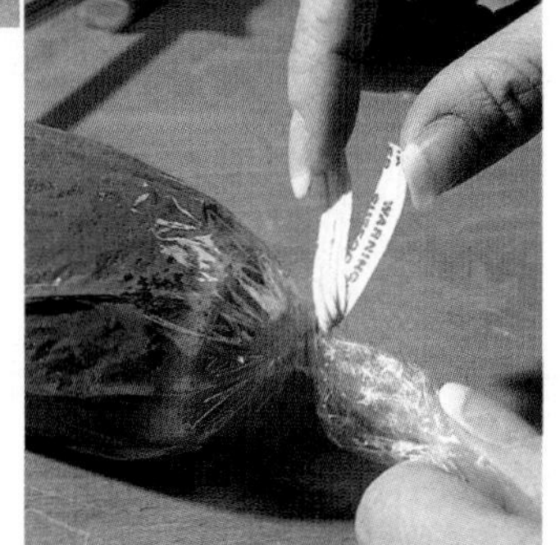

PLASTIC-WRAPPED PAINT ROLLER

You don't have to wash out your paint roller if you'll be using it again tomorrow. Spread a 14-in. long strip of plastic wrap on a flat surface and push the roller over the plastic. Seal the ends with twist ties.

Handy Hints® focus on painting

DOUBLE-DUTY GLOVES

Metal cans of paint, stain and varnish don't always seal airtight. So when you're done applying the finish, add a second seal using the same latex glove you used while finishing. Grab the can with your fingers, then peel the glove off your hand and pull it over the can.

PAINT ROLLER STORAGE

When the painting job's half done but the day is all done, slide your paint roller off the roller frame and store it in a Lay's Stax potato chip container. It's just the right size for a standard 9-in. roller. Once you've slipped the roller cover inside, pop on the lid and the wet roller is sealed and ready for service in the morning.

PEANUTTY PAINT STORAGE

Your painting project is done—now what do you do with the unused half gallon of paint? Store it in peanut butter jars with labels indicating the color and the date used. The paint stays fresh if you fill the jar to the brim, so you won't have to mess with a dried layer of paint during a touch-up job next spring. Plus, you can pick the right color in a second without sorting through a shelf load of bulky, rusting gallon cans.

DOUBLE-DUTY DOOR FLIPPER

You can speed up door painting and staining by driving 3-in. nails into the top and bottom of the doors, then hanging them over two sawhorses. The nails act like handles for flipping the door over, and both sides can dry at the same time—without runs!

Great Goofs™

Shocking wallpaper

Several years ago, I hung metal foil wallpaper in the bathroom and installed a new light fixture on the wall. The next day, my daughter told me that she got a mild shock when she touched the walls. In disbelief, I went into the bathroom and pushed my palms to the wall and yes, I felt a mild current. I quickly called a friend who's an expert at wiring and he pointed out that I'd wired the fixture incorrectly. I'd energized the metal fixture, which in turn energized the foil wallpaper! An occasional ribbing now and then is a good tradeoff for a safe bathroom.

Gone fishing

My husband and I recently bought a real fixer-upper. Since we were newlyweds and a bit short on cash, we started saving our money to do a complete bathroom makeover. To further save money, my handy father said he'd help us out for free.

While we went on a much-needed vacation, my father got right to work installing a new toilet, vanity, sink and floor. He even tackled the wallpaper. When we returned we were elated to see the whole job completed and thanked my dad profusely.

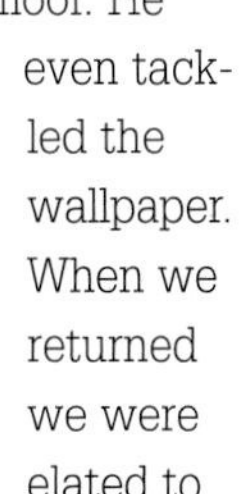

Later the next day, as I looked at the wallpaper, something looked peculiar, but I couldn't put my finger on it. Then it dawned on me. The fish pattern wallpaper was upside down. The fish were all swimming belly side up!

Bleeding paint

Last year my wife and I bought our first house, which unfortunately included the awful pink floral wallpaper in the bathroom. The first order of business, of course, was to strip the wallpaper and then paint. Well, everything went well and our freshly painted walls looked great. But when we tried out our shower for the first time, the humidity from the shower collected on the walls and started to drip, causing the paint to streak and bleed. When the walls dried, the streaks didn't go away! We went to our paint supplier and asked for advice. It turns out that we should have used semigloss paint instead of flat.

Hazy morning

One of the first projects in our new home was to retile the bathroom tub surround. My father-in-law told us how to get started and said he'd be back in a week to help finish the job. After doing all the prep work the first day, and putting up about half the tile the next, I was getting pretty tired, but I decided to keep going. I got all the tile up by midnight. I started to grout and halfway through I noticed there wouldn't be enough. Fortunately, my local home center was open 24 hours, so I left to get more grout.

Unfortunately, I hadn't cleaned any grout off the tile, and it hardened while I was gone. Days later, after we chipped it, scrubbed it and applied several haze-removing products, even my father-in-law thought it looked great.

A cut below the rest

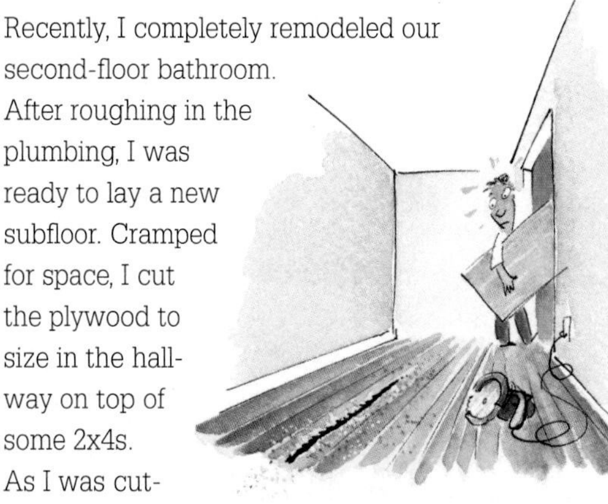

Recently, I completely remodeled our second-floor bathroom. After roughing in the plumbing, I was ready to lay a new subfloor. Cramped for space, I cut the plywood to size in the hallway on top of some 2x4s. As I was cutting, it felt like the saw was working pretty hard and the blade was dull. When I picked up the plywood, I discovered why the saw was laboring. There was a 1/4-in. deep cut about 3 ft. long in the hardwood floor! The bathroom came out great, but until I get around to repairing the hallway floor, I'm constantly reminded to check the depth of the blade before every cut.

You Can Fix It™

FIXING FLOOR SQUEAKS FROM BELOW

Floor squeaks are caused by wood rubbing against a nail, other wood, or even ductwork and piping. Finding the squeak can be difficult, but if the squeaking floor is open from below, you're in luck. You'll have several options to stop it.

To locate the source of the squeak, have a helper spring up and down on the squeaky area while you listen and watch for subfloor movement from below. Also look for loose nails or subfloor seams rubbing against each other. It doesn't take much movement to cause a squeak, especially since your floor amplifies the sound like a giant soundboard.

If you're working alone, measure the squeak's location in relation to a wall or heating register that you can locate from below. Then go downstairs and measure these distances along the subfloor. Or, if your floor is carpeted, you can drive an 8d finish nail through it to mark the squeak source.

Screw hardwood flooring from below

A solid-wood floor is usually fastened with hundreds of nails, so squeaks often occur as the floor ages. But some squeaks aren't caused by nails; they come from one edge of a board rubbing on another. A simple "first" solution is to dust the squeaky area of your floor with talcum powder, working it into the cracks. The talc reduces friction and may solve the problem, at least for one season.
Note: Talc can be slippery. Wipe off the excess.

For a more permanent solution, however, you'll usually have to screw the subfloor to the wood flooring from below. Drill a 1/8-in. pilot hole about 1/2 in. less than the thickness of the entire floor, and buy screws 1/4 in. shorter than the floor thickness so they won't penetrate the surface. You can find your floor thickness by either removing a floor register and measuring the floor where the duct comes through, or by drilling a small hole in an out-of-the-way corner and measuring with a nail.

To maintain a safe margin, mark the desired drilling depth on the drill bit with masking tape. Space your screws about every 6 in. in the area of the squeak. Have someone stand on the floor above while you drive the screws. Set the heads flush with the subfloor. Sinking the head into the subfloor could cause the screw point to break through the finished floor surface.

MARK the depth of the pilot hole on a 1/8-in. drill bit with tape. The depth should be 1/2 in. less than the floor thickness. Drill pilot holes 4 to 8 in. apart. Drive No. 8 wood screws flush to subfloor.

Fill gaps with shims and glue

Finding the exact cause of the squeak, and then choosing the best remedy, isn't always a simple task. Don't be surprised if you have to try several solutions before you stop it for good. Look for gaps between a joist and the subfloor first. Plug in a drop light and examine the area closely; a gap or movement may not be obvious.

If you spot a gap, use the wood shim solution to stop floor movement. Shims are available at any home center or lumberyard. Push a pair of shims in lightly (Photo 1). If you drive them in, you'll widen the gap and potentially create a new squeak. Adding construction adhesive before final assembly makes the fix permanent while filling in irregularities between the wood surfaces.

1 SLIDE a pair of shims into the gap for a snug fit. Draw a line on each shim to mark the depth. Don't wedge the gap wider.

2 ADD a bead of construction adhesive to both sides of each shim. Shove shims back into the gap. Align to the depth line.

3 SCORE the excess shim two or three times with a sharp utility knife and snap it off. Keep off the floor for four hours while the adhesive hardens.

SQUEEZE a thick bead of construction adhesive into the crack along both sides of the squeaky joist and subfloor. Apply adhesive to adjacent joist/subfloor joints as well.

Fill slim cracks with construction adhesive

Sometimes the gapping between the subfloor and joist is too narrow, too irregular or too widespread for shims to be effective. Or perhaps you can't pinpoint the exact source of the squeak. A good solution is to use a bead of construction adhesive to glue the wood together. You don't have to press the gaps closed; construction adhesive fills the space and hardens. The key is to force it as far as possible into the gaps without widening them. Work both sides of the joist for a strong, lasting connection. And glue nearby joists as well in case you can't find the exact squeak source. Keep off the floor for a day until the glue hardens.

CAUTION: Construction adhesive contains a strong solvent. Wear a respirator with an organic-vapor cartridge when working in closely confined areas.

Block underneath squeaky joints

Once in a while, movement in a subfloor joint will cause a squeak. You can stop it by screwing and gluing 2x8 blocking under the joint to give it solid support (**Photos 1 and 2**). First angle-screw through the blocking, up into the joists, to ensure a tight fit. But be sure to drive additional nails or screws to anchor the block. Otherwise it might work loose and cause more squeaks!

1 CUT 2x8 blocking to fit snugly between joists. Add construction adhesive to the top and slide it into place.

2 PREDRILL angled pilot holes with a 1/8-in. bit. Drive 3-in. wood screws to force the block snug against the subfloor seam. Drive an additional pair of screws (or 16d nails) through the joist into the block on each end.

Reinforce the joists

If you spot wide gaps along sagging or damaged joists or see that a subfloor edge is poorly supported (**Photo 1**), add blocking to support the subfloor and stop movement. Also keep an eye out for protruding nails and clip them with diagonal cutters. (You may need a strong grip and a few tries to work your way through the nail!)

Measure and cut a 2x4 block that's 2 ft. longer than the poorly supported area (**Photo 1**). Apply construction adhesive to the side and top of the blocking before installation to add strength. It should squish out when you screw the 2x4 in place. Predrill screw holes (for 2-1/2 in. wood screws) to prevent splitting the block and to make driving easier.

1 MEASURE the length of the subfloor gap for 2x4 blocking. Extend the block about 1 ft. on each end. Cut away protruding nails with diagonal cutters.

2 PREDRILL 3/16-in. clearance holes every 12 in. along the 2x4 at a slightly upward angle for the screws. Then apply construction adhesive liberally to the top and the side of block, press tightly to the subfloor and drive 2-1/2 in. wood screws into the joist.

New Products

TWO WAYS TO FIX SQUEAKY FLOORS

From-down-under fix

If you can get at the squeaky floor from underneath (usually an unfinished basement or crawlspace), the Squeak-Relief kit is one way to go. Have someone spring up and down to activate the squeak while you prowl around downstairs ready to zero in on the rascal. It'll most likely be a nail rubbing on a subfloor that wasn't glued down to the joist. The gap is what allows the subfloor to move independently of the framing. Using the special nail that's included in the kit, tack the bracket to the side of the joist with the top against the bottom of the subfloor. Then run the long screw into the joist and the short screw into the subfloor. Simple, elegant, effective and fast. Order a package of four (item No. 105064) for about $15.
Improvements Mail Order Catalog, (800) 642-2112.
www.ImprovementsCatalog.com.

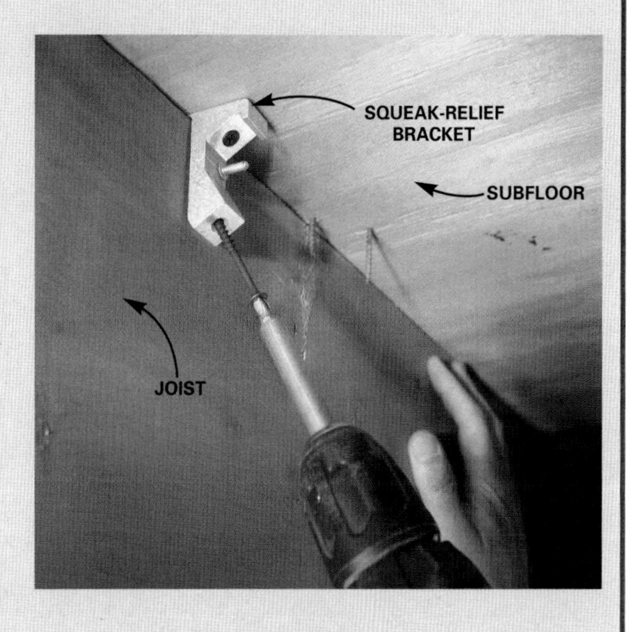

From-the-top fix

If you can't get at a floor squeak from underneath, another good solution is the Squeeeeek No More kit (item No. 110189) designed to send a snap-off screw right through the carpet—without unraveling the fibers. The kit comes with a screw designed to help you find the joist under the squeak. Then you run a specially scored screw through the middle of the depth-control jig, which stops the screw at the right distance from the floor. Use a recess on one of the wings on the jig to snap off the screw just below the floor surface. For $30, you get the jig, the joist-finding screw and 50 of the scored screws, enough to fix all the floors in a haunted mansion.
Improvements Mail Order Catalog, (800) 642-2112.
www.ImprovementsCatalog.com

TRIM TRICKS FOR BAD WALLS

How to install good-looking baseboards on any problem wall

by **Travis Larson**

Every good trim carpenter has a tool apron full of special tricks for cutting and installing baseboards gap free and with tight joints. They need them, and so will you when you trim out that new family room. That's because walls are rarely the perfectly flat surfaces that first meet the eye. On closer inspection, you'll find lumpy mounds of taping compound, corners that are out of square and wavy walls—no matter how well your house was built.

In this article, we'll show you the five most common problems that conspire against you when you're installing base trim and the solutions for each. You'll get first-class results without hours of frustrating effort. While you sometimes only need one of these tips to solve a problem, often a combination of two or more will be required for polished results. But don't worry—they're all easy, fast and free.

PROBLEM 1:
WAVY WALLS AND BUILT-UP CORNERS

When you lay baseboard against a wall and see gaps between the top of the trim and the drywall, it's usually because of a misaligned stud or a built-up ridge of taping compound over a joint. Both will create bulges that cause gaps. You'll also find the problem at outside and inside corners, again caused by built-up taping compound. While you can scrape off small lumps with a putty knife, you can't move studs or sand off the bulge of compound without creating a huge mess. It's almost always easier to adjust the trim rather than to attempt any wall fixes.

SOLUTION 1:
FLEX THIN TRIM AND GLUE IT TO FOLLOW WALL CONTOURS

Most standard baseboards these days are 3-1/4 in. high and 3/8 in. thick, which makes them pretty doggone flexible. First hold the trim against the wall after you cut it to length, and look for gaps. If you see some, cut a few braces from 4- to 6-in. lengths of scrap baseboard and put 45-degree angles on the ends. Then apply construction adhesive at the top and bottom. Nail the trim to the studs and then tack the braces to the trim with 1-in. brads. Force the gaps closed with the scrap and tack the blocks to the trim. Leave it overnight to let the adhesive set, and then pry the blocks free. Fill the little holes when you fill the rest of the nailheads.

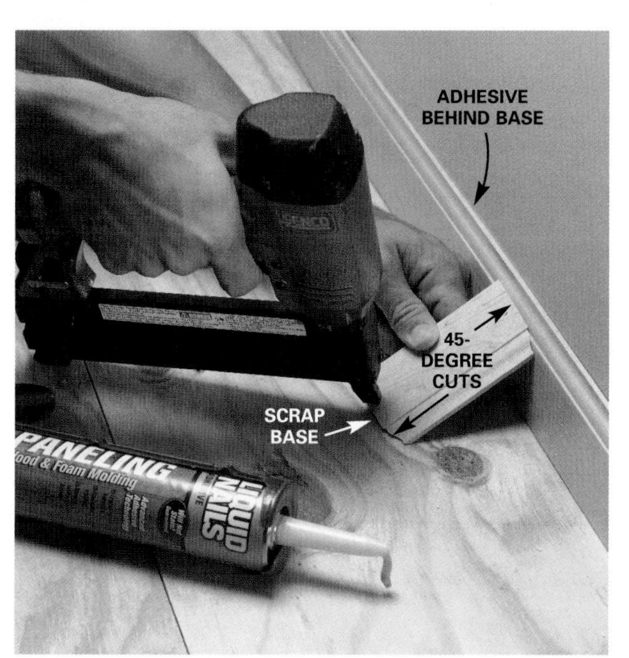

SOLUTION 2:
CAULK GAPS ABOVE THICK TRIM

Thick (3/4-in.) board trim isn't flexible, so it's unlikely you'll be able to flex it against the wall as we show (see Solution 1) nor will glue hold it. The best solution is to simply fill any gaps with caulk. Select a premium acrylic latex caulk ($3 and up per tube) that says "paintable" on the label.

Snip a hole in the spout no larger than 1/8 in. for the neatest job. Force the caulk into the gap and fill it a little higher than the top of the trim. Immediately wipe off the excess with a damp rag. The next day, paint the caulk to match the wall color. You'll be surprised how well even large gaps nearly disappear.

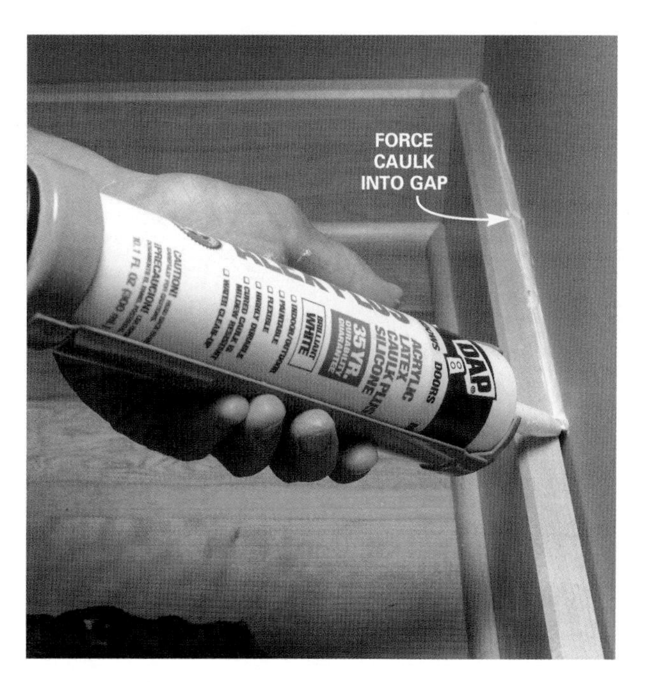

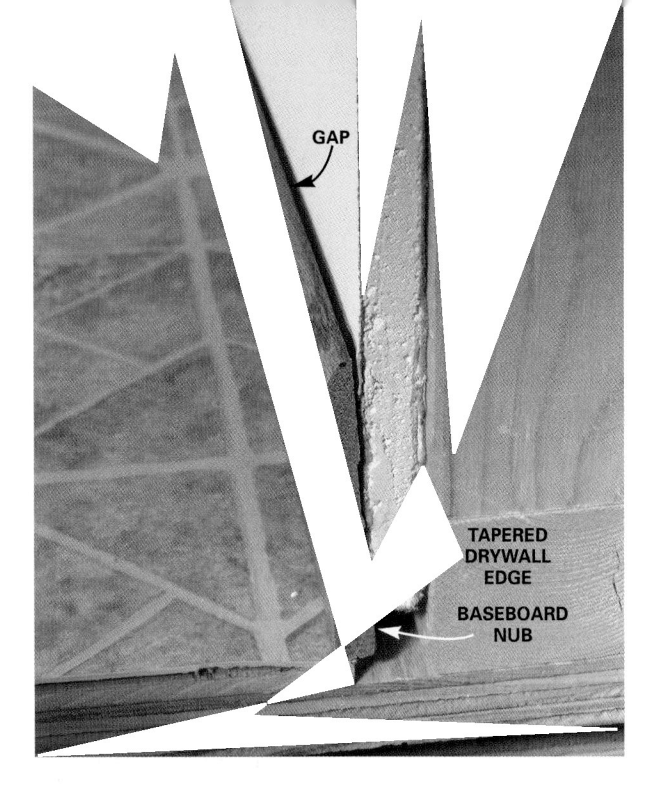

PROBLEM 2: TILTED BASEBOARDS

Baseboards, especially narrow ones, will frequently tilt toward the wall at the bottom. That's because the lower nub on thin trim can fall into the space between the drywall edge and the floor. In addition, the baseboard follows the tapered drywall edge near the floor. Taller baseboards usually aren't affected because they're high enough to rest against the flat drywall surface above. Don't worry about small tilts if they're noticeable only at inside corners (see "Tilted Inside Corners," p. 37). Push the base firmly against the wall with your hand to determine how severe the tilts will be. If gaps appear between the top of the trim and the wall, you'll need to use the solutions we show.

SOLUTION 1: SPACE THE BASEBOARDS ABOVE FLOORS TO BE CARPETED

Carpeting and pad together are at least 1 in. thick, meaning that it covers at least the lower 3/4 in. of baseboard, so there's no reason to rest base right on the floor. You can fix a tilted baseboard by raising it above the drywall gap.

Cut a few 3/8- to 1/2-in. thick spacers (6-in. scraps of standard base will do). Lay them flat on the floor every few feet, and then cut the base to fit, rest it on the spacers and nail it into place. This technique also leaves more of that handsome baseboard showing above the carpet. One more thing: Carpet installers prefer to cut the carpet a little long and tuck the excess into the gap for a neater job.

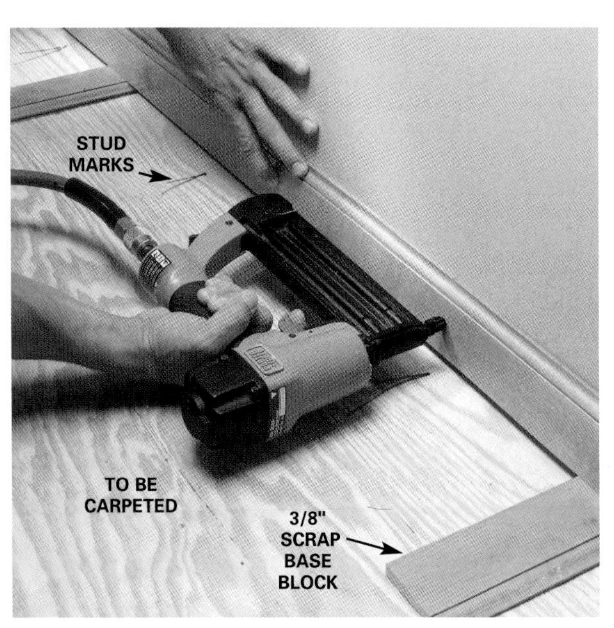

SOLUTION 2: FILL THE GAP WITH BLOCKS ABOVE VINYL OR LAMINATE FLOORS

When you're installing baseboards over vinyl, wood or plastic laminate floors, the best way to handle gaps between the drywall and the flooring is to shim the gap with narrow blocks of 1/2-in. wood.

Any wood will work, but chunks of 1/2-in. scrap plywood are ideal. Cut the blocks and tuck them into the gap every few feet. There's no need to nail or glue them into place; just install the baseboard right over them, tight against the floor. It's best to keep the nails at the bottom of the base above the gap so they go through drywall, not air.

PROBLEM 3:
TILTED INSIDE CORNERS

Trim at inside corners often won't meet evenly despite a perfectly cut cope. That's generally because corner tape joints don't always get filled or sanded all the way to the floor. (I know a few drywall finishers who don't like to bend over.) The tapered drywall edge can also cause tipping.

SOLUTION:
CUT SHORT TEST PIECES TO CHECK, THEN INSTALL AN ADJUSTMENT SCREW

The key to a clean inside corner is to use test pieces to help you prepare the corner for the permanent base. Conduct this test before you nail any base permanently to the wall, because you'll just have to remove it if the corner joint is bad.

Cut a perfect cope on the end of a foot-long chunk of baseboard, then use that and another short piece of base with a square end to check the corner. Be sure to push the pieces tight against the wall (especially at the bottom) to simulate the pressure the nails will exert. If the joint looks good, go ahead with the standard installation. But if there's a gap at the bottom of the joint, set aside the test pieces and drive a 2-in. screw about 1/2 in. above the floor and an inch or two away from the corner behind the square-ended piece. Sink the screw until the head is protruding slightly beyond the drywall, then check the joint again with the test pieces. Adjust the screw in or out and continue adjusting and testing until the joint is perfect. Then go ahead and install the baseboard.

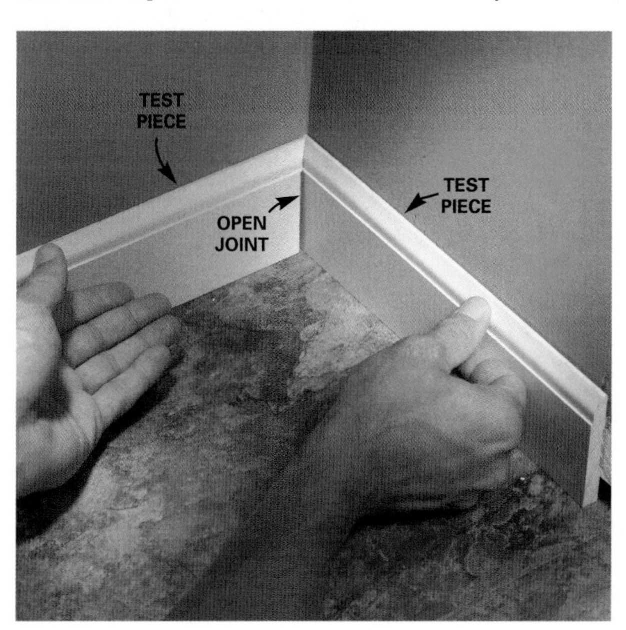

PROBLEM 4:
OUT-OF-SQUARE OUTSIDE CORNERS

Only about half the time can you cut 45-degree miters on baseboards and have them meet perfectly on outside corners. Built-up drywall compound and imperfect corner bead installation or framing generally leave you with something greater or less than an exact 90-degree angle, and standard 45-degree miters won't work. Don't even bother trying to measure the angle with an angle finder. It's easier to find the miter angle simply by testing with scraps.

SOLUTION:
TEST MITERS WITH SHORT TEST PIECES

Start by cutting 45-degree miters on the ends of 10-in. long base scraps. Put them together at the corner to check the fit. Recut both pieces at angles slightly more or less than 45 degrees as required. There's no magic to it—after a few cuts and test fits, you'll find the right angle. After you find the angle, save the miter saw setting and cut the finished base miters. And don't think you have to limit yourself to whole numbers. More often than not, the right angle will fall between the marked degrees on your saw. It's surprising how big a difference even a half-degree adjustment will make. This method also works great for finding miters for corners other than 90 degrees. Just guess an angle to start with, and with a little practice, you'll find the perfect miter angle for any corner in moments.

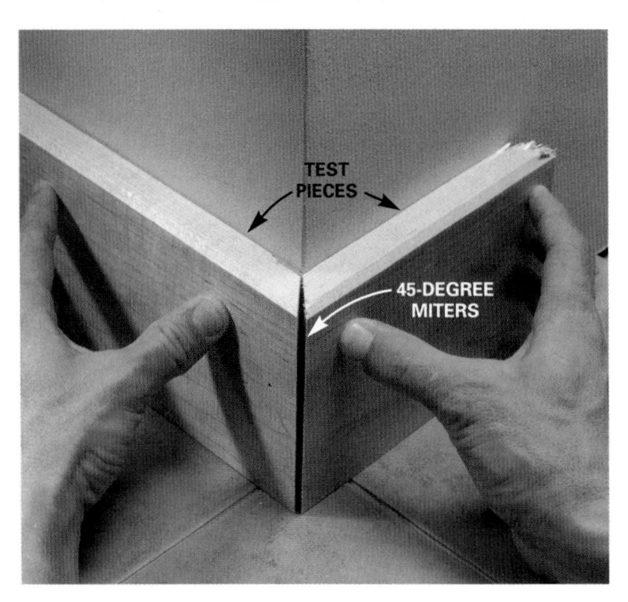

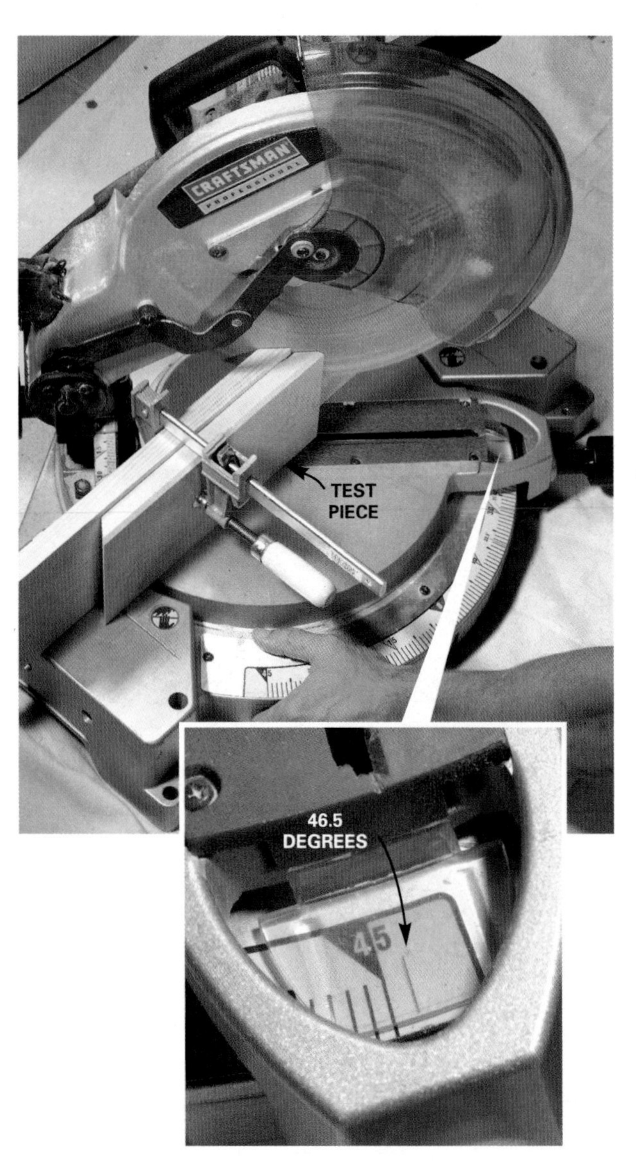

PROBLEM 5: IMPERFECT SPLICES

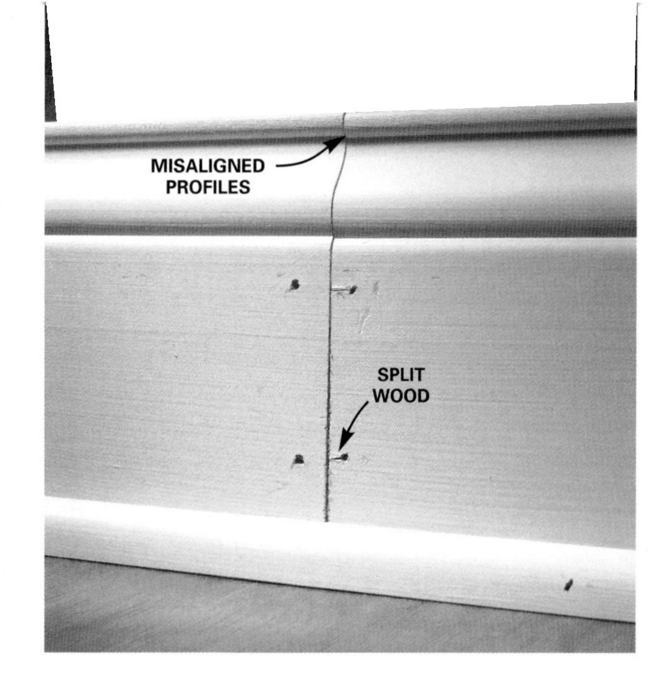

While it's best to run a single length of base on a wall, at some point you'll be faced with splicing two pieces in the middle of a wall. When splicing, make the joint over a stud to keep the ends tight. But a simple butt joint is a poor technique because the glue won't hold the ends together, and it's tricky to line up the profiles perfectly when nailing. And to nail into the stud you have to nail close to the end of the trim, where the wood is prone to split.

SOLUTION: USE SCARF JOINTS WHEN JOINING LENGTHS

The key to a clean splice is a "scarf" joint. Cut the first trim board about 1 in. short of a stud with a 30-degree bevel facing the room. Nail it into all the studs, then cut the second board with the same 30-degree bevel but in the opposite direction. Assemble the joint (no glue) to check the fit and recut a slightly greater or lesser angle as needed for a perfect joint. Smear wood glue on both bevels. Push the joint together, and then nail the overlapping piece into the stud near the joint. The overlapping bevel will clamp the one behind it against the wall. Wipe off the glue squeeze-out with a damp rag right away. If you're installing clear finished baseboards with a prominent grain pattern, select two pieces that match as closely as possible.

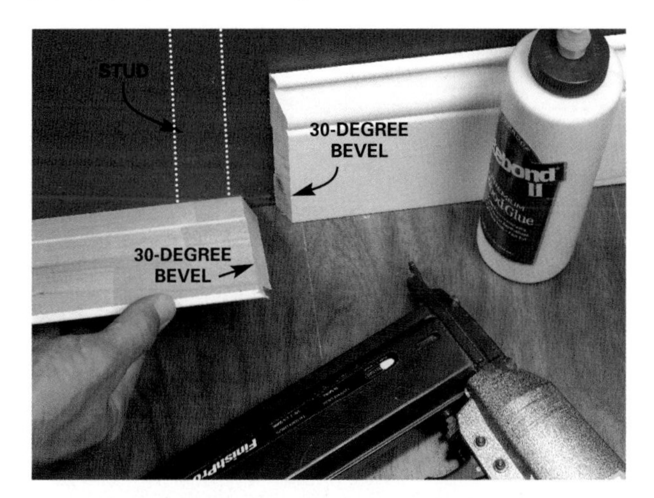

Power nailers really pay off

You can hand-nail trim—carpenters have been doing it for centuries—but there's no reason to anymore. The advantages of using a gun over nailing by hand are numerous. You'll be able to get trim placed exactly where you want it with one hand while you fasten it with the other. Pieces don't move around while you're nailing on them, and of course, no more hammer marks or nail setting. And with some trim gun models selling for under $100, it's worth getting one of your own. Of course you'll need a compressor, too, but kits that have hoses, fittings, a gun and a compressor are available at any home center for about $200. If you're not ready for the investment, we strongly recommend renting the tools (about $50 per day).

Nail guns for trim come in three sizes for shooting 15-, 16- and 18-gauge nails, with 15-gauge nails being the thickest. If you only buy one gun, get an 18-gauge unit that shoots nails ranging between 5/8 in. and 2-1/4 in. long. Although the thin nails won't be hefty enough for anchoring door or window jambs, they'll work fine for most modern trim. When you need extra strength, pull out the old hammer and hand-nail.

8 TIPS FOR A **NEATER PAINT JOB**

How to protect against slop, splatters and spills

by **Gary Wentz**

Strange as it may seem, the most difficult and time-consuming part of painting isn't swinging a brush or roller—it's getting ready to swing a brush or roller. Sure, you can skip laying down dropcloths and masking tape, but the time you save up front will be spent at the end, scraping, retouching and cleaning.

Here are some simple tips for doing the job right:

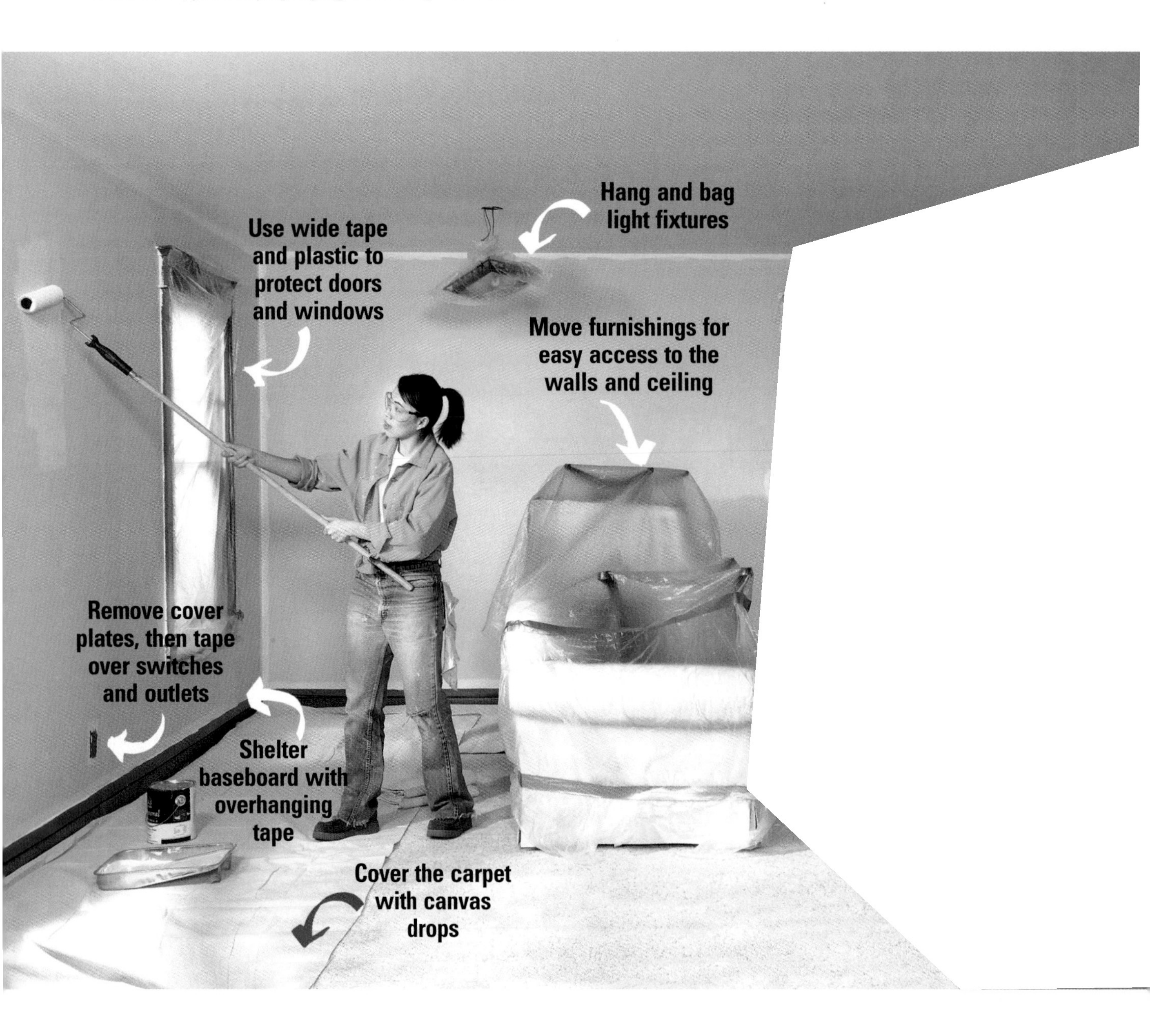

Move furnishings for easy access to the walls and ceiling

Cramped working conditions lead to messy accidents. Every painter has stepped in a paint pan or kicked over a pail while squeezing a ladder past the couch. If you can't move furniture and other big stuff completely out of the room, stack it up. Set upholstered chairs upside down on the sofa. Cover the dining room tabletop with cardboard so you can set chairs on top of it. But don't let your stack become an obstacle. Get out your ladder and roller and make a dry run to be sure you can easily reach all parts of the ceiling. In some cases, two smaller stacks with space for a ladder between them is better than one. Maintain a generous workspace of at least 3 ft. between the stack and the walls. Cover your furniture stack with plastic. Even if you're careful, some drips and splatters are likely. A couple of bands of duct tape will keep the plastic in place and hold the stack together if you bump into it.

Cover the carpet with canvas drops

Canvas dropcloths are absolutely the best coverings for carpet. They're easy to spread out, and unlike plastic, they stay put without tape. And they won't cause your ladder to slip-slide on carpet. Just bunch them up a bit along walls and they'll stay where you want them. Normal drips and splatter won't soak through canvas, but heavy spills will. Pick up the dropcloths and scoop up spills with a broad putty knife or dustpan.

These dropcloths aren't cheap, but you don't have to cover the entire floor. My favorite drop is a long, narrow "runner" that I drag around the room as I go. A runner is also perfect for carpeted stairs; just fasten it to the steps with small nails so you don't trip. A 4 x 15-ft. runner costs about $15.

Protect hard floors with rosin paper

Both canvas and plastic dropcloths are slippery when laid over wood, vinyl and tile. For protection that stays put on hard surfaces, you can't beat rosin paper. Just tape sheets of it together and then tape the perimeter to the floor. Be sure to clean wood floors thoroughly before laying down the paper; grit trapped underneath can lead to scratches. A single layer will protect against paint drips, but wipe up any spills before they can soak through. A 400-sq.-ft. roll of rosin paper costs only about $8 at home centers.

CAUTION: Turn off the power to the room before removing cover plates. With the plates removed, live terminals inside the box are exposed.

Remove cover plates, then tape over switches and outlets

Paint slopped on electrical cover plates, switches and outlets looks tacky. Don't try to paint around them. Removing cover plates takes just a few seconds and makes for a faster, neater job. Grab a small bucket to hold all the odds and ends you'll take off the walls. Unscrew cover plates and then shield each switch or outlet with 2-in. wide masking tape. Also remove curtain hardware, picture hooks, grilles that cover duct openings and anything else that might get in your way. The thermostat is one exception—it's easier to wrap it with masking tape than to remove and reinstall it.

Shelter baseboard with overhanging tape

Don't waste time by completely covering baseboard with several strips of tape. A single overhanging strip of wide tape will catch roller splatters just as the roof overhang on your house keeps rain off the siding. Use 1-1/2 in. tape for narrow baseboard, 2-in. tape for wider baseboard. Tape won't stay stuck to dusty surfaces, so wipe down all your trim before masking. To minimize paint seepage under the tape, press the tape down hard by running a flexible putty knife over it.

Use wide tape and plastic to protect doors and windows

Paint rollers throw off a mist of paint that speckles everything below. Here's the quickest way to protect doors and windows: When you tape around door and window trim to protect the woodwork, use tape that's wide enough to project at least 1/2 in. from the trim. That way, you can stick light plastic to the protruding tape—there's no need to tape the perimeter of the plastic separately. For doors, slit the plastic with a utility knife so you can walk through.

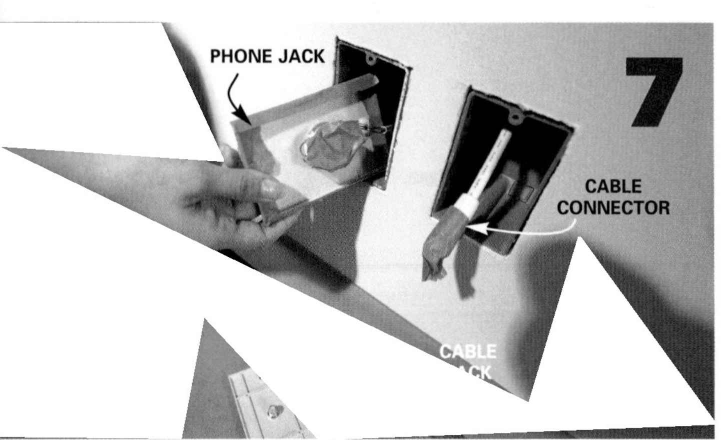

Mask off sensitive wiring and tuck it in the box

A little paint in the wrong place can cripple the connections that serve your phone, TV or computer. To protect phone jacks without disconnecting all those tiny wires, unscrew the faceplate and cover the front with masking tape. Then mask the terminals on the backside of the plate. Slip the plate into the junction box. Disconnect coaxial cable from its plate and tape the cable's connector.

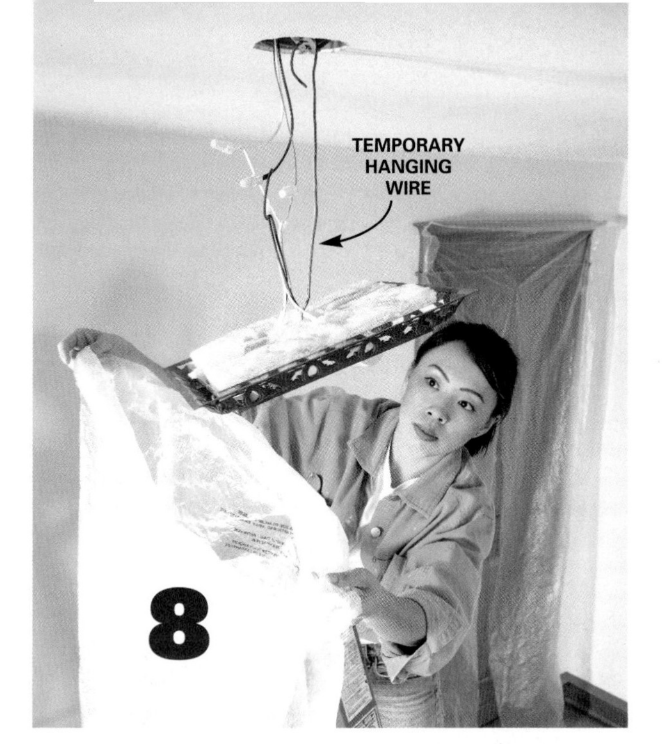

Hang and bag light fixtures

Painting a ceiling is a cinch—except for the light fixture. Here's how to get it out of your way: First remove any glass parts, including the bulbs (make sure the power is off). Unfasten the fixture, usually by removing a couple of screws. Then hook one end of a wire through the fixture and the other to the junction box. Make sure your hanger wire—not the electrical wire—supports the fixture. Then slip a plastic bag over the fixture.

Dealing with chandeliers and pendants is even easier. The decorative plate at the ceiling is usually held up by a ring nut. Just unscrew the nut and the plate will slide down over the chain or tube. There's no need to support the fixture with wire.

FAST BLOTTING WILL SAVE YOUR CARPET

Spilling on carpet may seem like the ultimate painting disaster, but it doesn't have to leave a permanent stain. The keys to complete stain removal are speed and lots of water. Latex paint dries fast and seconds count. Don't go for the water bucket yourself. Shout for someone else to bring it. Immediately scoop up the spill with a wide putty knife, dustpan or whatever is handy. Don't wipe up the spill; you'll just force the paint deeper into the carpet. Then start to blot the paint with a wet (not just damp) rag. Keep the paint wet. Continue blotting, refill the bucket with clean water and blot some more until the paint is no longer visible. When you're done, set up a fan to dry out the soaked carpet.

For small drips or splatters, use the opposite approach. Just let the paint dry. Tiny drops of paint will sit on the carpet's surface. Just be careful not to step on them. After they dry, trim them off with scissors.

Great Goofs™

Stir and stir again

I was hired to paint an interior room in a high-end lake home, and the owners were going to supply the paint. I got the room ready and stirred the paint and started rolling the walls. After about an hour, I noticed the paint was lighter where I'd first cut in. Dismayed, I took a good look at the can and stirred it some more. Apparently it was really old paint and the dark pigment had settled to the bottom. After about 10 minutes of stirring, I repainted the entire room. Luckily, there was just enough paint to finish and the job looked great. Best of all, the homeowner didn't notice that the color was a bit dark!

Using Tools:™ Drywall Sanding

Sanding drywall is tedious, dusty work. But if you do it right, you'll be rewarded with a great-looking paint job that will make all the effort worthwhile. In this article, we'll show you how to avoid a few common sanding mistakes and several tips for getting the best results from your drywall sanding job.

USE A SPECIAL SANDING TOOL

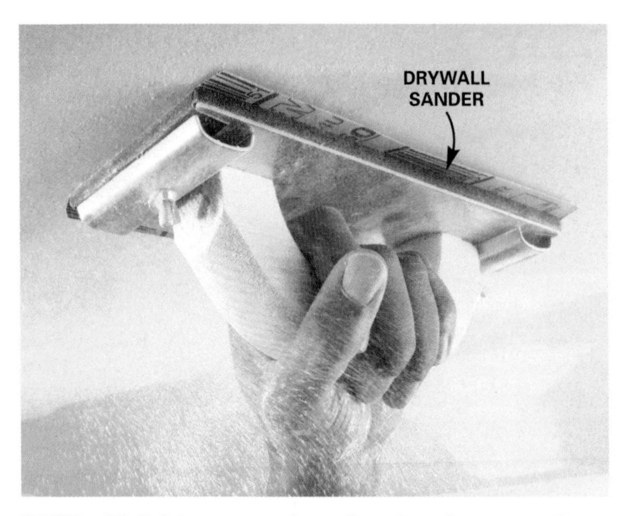

SAND with light pressure along the edge of seams and around screws to avoid "fuzzing" the drywall paper. Sand the center of seams just enough to remove ridges and bumps.

As with most remodeling tasks, having the right tools is the key to a top-notch job. For drywall sanding, you'll need a hand sander ($6), a package of 150-grit drywall sanding paper that's precut to fit your sander, and a sanding sponge for corners and detail sanding. You'll also need a double-strap dust mask rated for nuisance dust and goggles to keep the dust out of your eyes. A hat or scarf to keep the dust out of your hair is a good idea too.

Pole sanders are good for large sanding jobs. We didn't show a pole sander ($15) because it's tricky to learn how to use it. But if you've got more than one room to sand, it may be worth the effort. The trouble with a pole sander is that if you're not careful, the sander can flip over and gouge the surface, causing extra repair work. One tip is to keep the sanding head angled slightly and never let it get at a right angle to the pole. A pole sander works great for sanding the primer coat before painting, a step that requires minimal control and pressure.

CHOOSE FINE SANDPAPER FOR THE BEST RESULTS

It's tempting to buy 80-grit paper to speed up the sanding job. But because modern lightweight joint compound is so soft, you don't need heavy-grit paper to sand it. Coarse-grit paper or sanding screens will leave undesirable sanding marks. We recommend 120-grit or 150-grit paper for the best results. Buy precut sheets made to fit your hand sander. It also fits half sheets of standard size paper.

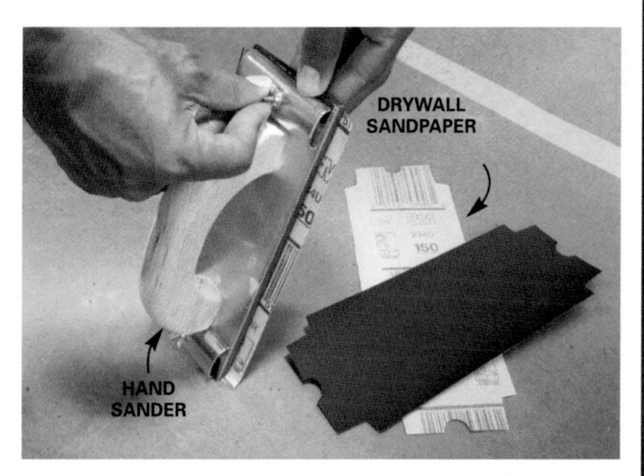

INSTALL 150-grit paper on your hand sander. Make sure it's taut by first anchoring one end under the clamp. Then push the other end under the other clamp with one hand while you tighten the clamp screw with the other.

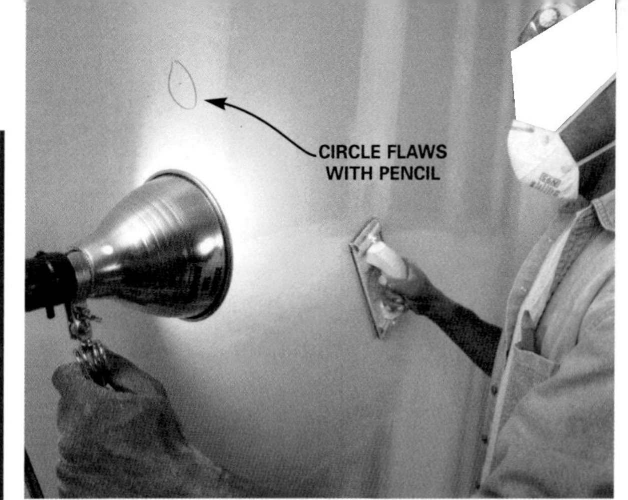

GO BACK over the walls and ceiling with a light and a sander. Circle dings, pits, sanded-through areas and other problems with a pencil. Then go back and touch them up with joint compound. Resand these spots when they dry.

SPOT PROBLEM AREAS WITH A HANDHELD LIGHT

First do a once-over with your hand sander, making sure to hit every surface with joint compound on it. Mark problem areas that need filling or detail sanding. Next get a handheld lamp and go back over the job while shining the light parallel to the wall surface. Use your hand sander and sponge sander to touch up trouble spots. Mark depressions and other spots, then finish the job by filling the marked areas with joint compound and sanding these spots when they dry.

FILL GOUGES—DON'T SAND THEM

Don't try to sand out gouges and big ridges. It's much easier just to trowel on another coat of joint compound. This is especially important at the edge of joints, where too much sanding will damage the paper face on the drywall. It's quick and easy to trowel a thin coat over the edge of the seam to fill a depression. You don't have to cover the entire joint again.

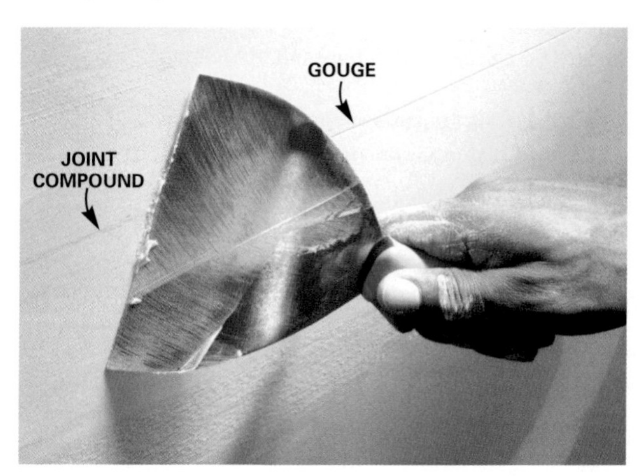

TOUCH UP grooves and large ridges with another coat of joint compound rather than trying to sand them out. It may take a few coats to fill deep grooves.

PRIME THE WALLS, THEN SAND AGAIN

Sanding after priming is a critical step that most beginners skip. But sanding at this stage removes paper fuzz and lumps that will show through your paint job. This is also the time to take care of other imperfections by filling them with joint compound. Don't forget to sand and reprime these touched-up areas or they'll also show up when you paint the walls.

PRIME the walls and sand them lightly after the primer dries to remove paper fuzz and lumps.

Using Tools™: Drywall Sanding

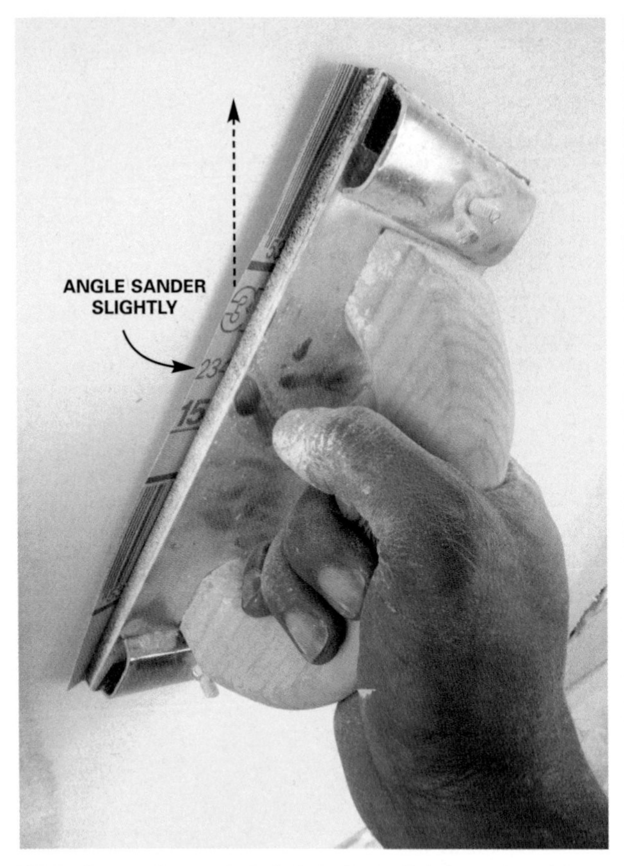

KEEP the sander angled slightly. Press lightly and avoid scrubbing back and forth in one spot.

SAND WITH A LIGHT TOUCH

Even though using a hand sander is straightforward, the drywall pro we talked to offered these helpful tips: Use moderate to light pressure and avoid sanding over the same spot in a straight line. This can leave a groove or depression that will show up when you paint. Instead, move the sander around on the joint as you sand. Don't sand over electrical boxes or other openings. The edges of the box can rip your sandpaper, or a piece of the paper facing on the drywall can roll up under the sander and tear off. Keep a few inches away from electrical box openings and touch up around them later with a sanding sponge.

OOPS! Sanded too much in this spot. Touch it up with joint compound and resand when it dries.

USE A SANDING SPONGE FOR CORNERS

Sanding inside corners with a hand sander is asking for trouble. In the first place, it's difficult to get a crisp corner. But even more troublesome is the tendency to scuff or gouge the opposite side of the corner with the edge of the sander. It's OK to sand within a few inches of the corner with your hand sander. Then go back and touch up with a sanding sponge or folded piece of drywall sanding paper.

SAND corners with a fine sanding sponge rather than the large hand sander.

OOPS! Got too close with a hand sander and gouged the corner. Touch it up and try again, with a sponge this time.

CONTROL THE DUST

If you're not careful, drywall dust can drift through the house, forming a white film on everything in its path. It's hard to get rid of, too. You may have heard about smoothing the joints with a damp sponge rather than sandpaper to avoid the dust. But it's nearly impossible to get a top-notch job with this method. There are dust-catching sanding systems on the market, but they're expensive and tricky to learn. The best option is to suit up with protective gear and follow the advice in "Stop Dust" on p. 114. You'll be glad you did.

2 Kitchen, Bathroom & Laundry Room Projects

IN THIS CHAPTER

10 Simple Cabinet Repairs 48

Fridge Repair for Rookies 52

Great Goofs 56

Handy Hints 57
Quiet loud sinks, jack up a disposer, and add a washer and dryer shelf

Gallery of Ideas .60
Tile backsplash with hood, weekend bathroom makeover

Ask Handyman 62
Painting kitchen cabinets, tiling over linoleum and more...

New Laminate Countertops and Kitchen Sink 64

You Can Fix It 72
Replacing a bathroom fan motor

10 SIMPLE
CABINET REPAIRS

Quick and easy ways to make your cabinets look and work like new again!

by **Tom Gibson**

Doors

1 Adjust hinges on misaligned doors

If your cabinet doors are out of whack and you have European-style hinges, you're in luck. Euro hinges are designed for easy adjustment. Don't let their complex look scare you; all you have to do is turn a few screws, and any mistakes you make are easy to correct. The Euro hinge shown here adjusts in three directions. Others adjust in two directions. Either way, it's a trial-and-error process: You make adjustments, close the door to check the fit, then adjust again until it's right.

first . . .

If the door isn't flush with the doors next to it, adjust the **depth screw**. This screw moves the door in or out. Some depth screws move the door as you turn them. But with most, you have to loosen the screw, nudge the door in or out and then tighten the screw. If your hinges don't have depth screws, start with the side screws.

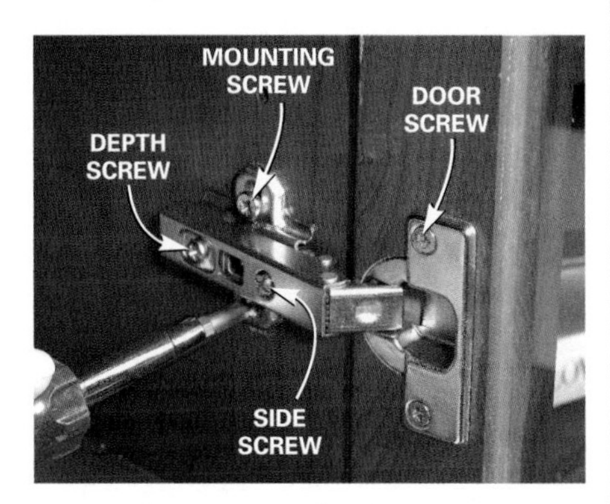

1 TIGHTEN the door screws and the mounting screws before you make any adjustments. Then adjust the depth screw and side screw.

second . . .

If the door is crooked—not standing parallel to adjacent doors or square with the cabinet—adjust the **side screw**. This moves the door from side to side. In some cases, you have to loosen the depth screw slightly to adjust the side screw.

2 CHECK the fit of the door after each adjustment. With double doors like these, perfect the fit of one door first, then align the other door.

third . . .

If the door is flush and parallel with other doors but too high or low, use the **mounting screws** to raise or lower the mounting plates. Loosen the screws at both hinges, slide the door up or down and tighten the screws. Some mounting plates adjust by turning a single screw.

2 Adjust or replace bad latches

Most newer cabinets have self-closing hinges that hold the doors shut. Others have magnetic or roller catches. A catch that no longer keeps a door closed is either broken or out of adjustment. Catches are fastened with two screws, so replacing a damaged catch is simple, and it costs less than $2. Adjustment is just as simple, but you might have to readjust the catch a couple of times before you get it right. Loosen the screws, move the catch in or out, and tighten the screws. If the door doesn't close tightly, try again.

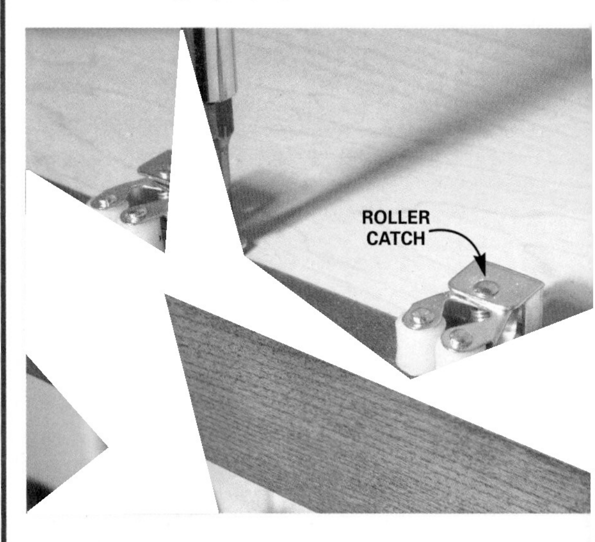

Tip

If you have a door that's slightly warped and won't lie flat against the cabinet, try adding a magnetic catch at the trouble spot. Often the magnet is strong enough to pull the door in tight.

3 Add bumpers to banging doors

Tired of listening to those cabinet doors bang shut? Peel-and-stick door and drawer bumpers are the solution. Get a pack of 20 at a home center for $2. Make sure the back of the door is clean so the bumpers will stick, then place one at the top corner and another at the bottom.

4 Replace worn-out drawer slides

If you find that slides are bent, rollers are broken or rollers won't turn even after lubricating, replacement is the best solution. To keep the project simple, buy new slides that are identical (or almost identical) to the old ones. That way, replacement is an easy matter of unscrewing the old and screwing on the new. Remove a drawer track and a cabinet track and take them with you when you go shopping. Whether you have pairs of side-mounted slides (as shown here) or single, center-mount slides, there's a good chance you'll find very similar slides at a home center for $5 to $15 per drawer. If you can't find them, check with a cabinet materials supplier (in the Yellow Pages under "Cabinets, Equipment and Supplies").

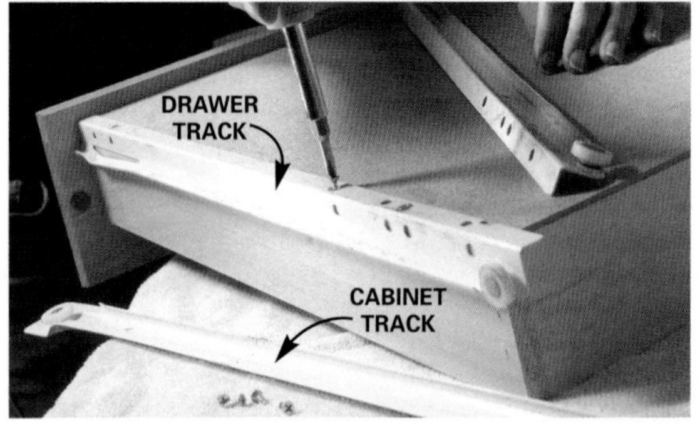

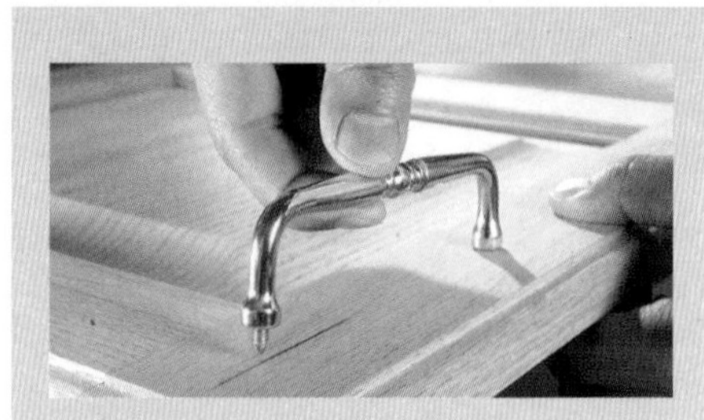

HANDLE MARKER

Here's a surefire way to align the second screw hole for new cabinet handles. Cut the head off one screw and put it in a drill chuck. Run the drill while you grind the threaded post against a file or grinding wheel until it's pencil sharp. Mark the handle center line and drill the first handle hole. Screw the sharpened screw into one end of the handle, and loosely screw the other end of the handle to the cabinet. Align the sharpened point over the handle center line. Push down on the point to mark the exact location of the second handle hole. Remove the handle, unscrew the sharpened point and install the handle—perfectly positioned!

5 Lubricate sticking drawers

A few minutes of cleaning and lubricating can make drawer slides glide almost like new. Start by removing the drawers so you can inspect the slides. You can remove most drawers by pulling them all the way out, then either lifting or lowering the front of the drawer until the wheels come out of the track. Wipe the tracks clean and coat them with a light spray lubricant. Also lubricate the rollers and make sure they spin easily.

6 Repair a broken drawer box

Don't put up with a broken corner joint on a drawer. Fix it before the whole drawer comes apart. Remove the drawer and then remove the drawer front from the drawer box, if possible. Most fronts are fastened by a couple of screws inside the box. Wood glue will make a strong repair if there's wood-to-wood contact at the joint. If the wood at the joint is coated, use epoxy instead of wood glue.

1 REMOVE nails, staples or screws from the loose joint and scrape away old glue with a utility knife.

2 PREDRILL 1/16-in. holes for nails, apply wood glue to the joint and nail it together with 1-1/2-in. finish nails.

Small Stuff

7 Clean a yucky cutting board

If you love the convenience of your pullout wooden cutting board but don't use it because it's stained and grungy, try this chef-approved, two-step process. Simply scour the board with a lemon and a pile of kosher salt, then apply mineral oil. The coarse kosher salt is an excellent abrasive, and the citric acid kills bacteria. When the stains are gone, rinse the board and let it dry. Mineral oil helps prevent the wood from absorbing stains.

1 SCOUR the cutting board with a lemon and kosher salt until the board is clean.

2 APPLY mineral oil to the board and wipe off the excess. After a few hours, apply a second coat.

> **Buyer's Guide**
>
> **All the cabinet hardware and products mentioned in this article are available at home centers and hardware stores. For a larger selection of hinges, catches and drawer slides, check out Woodworker's Hardware at www.wwhardware.com, (800) 383-0130.**

8 Fill stripped screw holes

When cabinet doors, catches or drawer slides aren't working right, step one is to make sure the screws are tight. If a screw turns but doesn't tighten, the screw hole is stripped. Here's a quick remedy:

Remove the screw and hardware. Dip toothpicks in glue, jam as many as you can into the hole and break them off. Either flat or round toothpicks will work. If you don't have toothpicks handy, shave splinters off a wood scrap with a utility knife. Immediately wipe away glue drips with a damp cloth. You don't have to wait for the glue to dry or drill new screw holes; just go ahead and reinstall the hardware by driving screws right into the toothpicks.

9 Glue loose knobs

Any handle or knob that comes loose once is likely to come loose again. Put a permanent stop to this problem with a tiny drop of thread adhesive like Thread Lok (about $3 at home centers). Don't worry; if you want to replace your hardware sometime in the future, the knobs will still come off with a screwdriver.

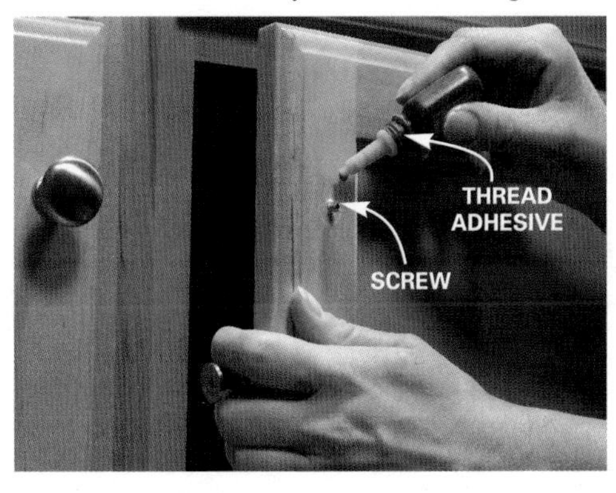

10 Touch up nicks and scratches

If you have shallow scratches or nicks, hide them with a stain-filled touch-up marker. Dab on the stain and wipe off the excess with a rag. But beware: Scratches can absorb lots of stain and turn darker than the surrounding finish. So start with a marker that's lighter than your cabinet finish and then switch to a darker shade if needed. For deeper scratches, use a filler pencil, which fills and colors the scratch. If the cabinet finish is dingy overall and has lots of scratches, consider a wipe-on product like Old English Scratch Coat. These products can darken the finish slightly, so you have to apply them to all your cabinets.

FRIDGE REPAIR
FOR ROOKIES

Fix the most common fridge problems yourself—and save the expense of a service call!

by **Gary Wentz**

If your refrigerator is misbehaving, don't call the repair service yet. The following pages will walk you through the simplest solutions to the most common fridge malfunctions. Chances are, you can solve the problem yourself, save some money and avoid the inconvenience of a service appointment.

PROBLEM:

A NOISY FRIDGE

Refrigerator noise comes from the compressor under the fridge, the condenser fan motor under the fridge, or the evaporator fan motor inside the freezer. Open the freezer door while the fridge is running. If the noise doesn't get louder when you open the freezer, pull out the fridge. Most refrigerators have a condenser fan motor (Photo 3, p. 53). Unscrew the back cover and listen—you'll be able to tell whether the noise is coming from the fan or the compressor. The best cure for a loud compressor is usually a new fridge. To replace the fan motor ($20 to $40), remove its mounting screws, unplug it and install the new one.

EASY SOLUTION: **If the sound gets louder when you open the freezer,** the evaporator fan motor is the noisy culprit. This motor is easy to replace and costs about $25 to $40 (see "Finding Fridge Parts," p. 53). Your fan may not look exactly like the fan we show, but the basic steps are the same (Photos 1 and 2). Start by unplugging the fridge, and then unscrewing the back cover panel in the freezer compartment (Photo 3, p. 55). To install the new fan, reverse your steps.

1 UNSCREW the fan from the rear wall of the freezer and unplug the wires. With some models, you'll need a socket set or nut driver to remove the fan.

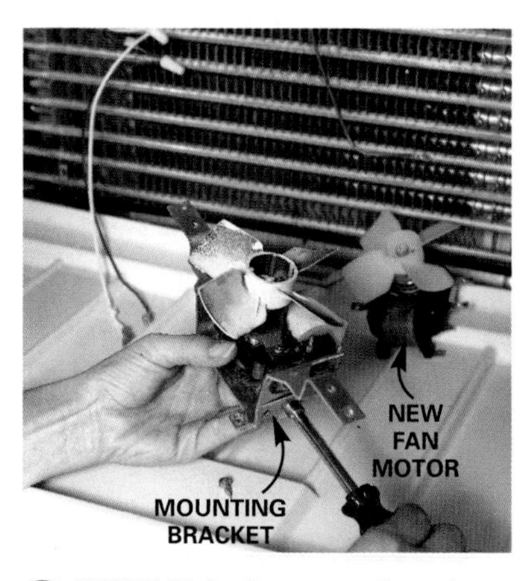

2 REMOVE the fan motor from its mounting bracket. Fasten the new fan to the mounting bracket, reconnect the wires and screw the new fan into place.

FRIDGE OR FREEZER WON'T COOL

There are lots of malfunctions that can take the chill out of your fridge. One common cause of suddenly soft ice cream or warm juice is a simple loss of electricity. If the light doesn't come on when you open the fridge door, make sure the fridge is plugged in and check the breaker panel. If the fridge runs but doesn't get cold enough, chances are one of these fixes will restore the chill:

EASY SOLUTIONS:

FIRST, check the thermostat and vents

The temperature control dial inside the fridge is sometimes irresistible to curious kids. Make sure it hasn't been turned way down. Also make sure the vents in the fridge and freezer compartment aren't blocked by food containers—these vents supply the flow of frigid air.

SECOND, clean the coils.

In order for your fridge to create a chill, air has to flow freely through the condenser coils. On most older refrigerators, these coils are on the backside. Cereal boxes on top of the fridge or grocery bags stuffed behind it can reduce the needed airflow. Most newer refrigerators have coils underneath, where they can get blocked by trash and plugged with dust. Even if your fridge is working fine, you should pull off the front grille and clean the coils every year for efficient operation; do it every six months if you have shedding pets. Long brushes are available at appliance stores for $8.

THIRD, free up the condenser fan.

Coils on the back of a fridge create their own airflow as they heat up. Models with coils underneath have a fan to push air through them. Dust buildup can slow the fan, while wads of paper or other trash can stop it altogether.

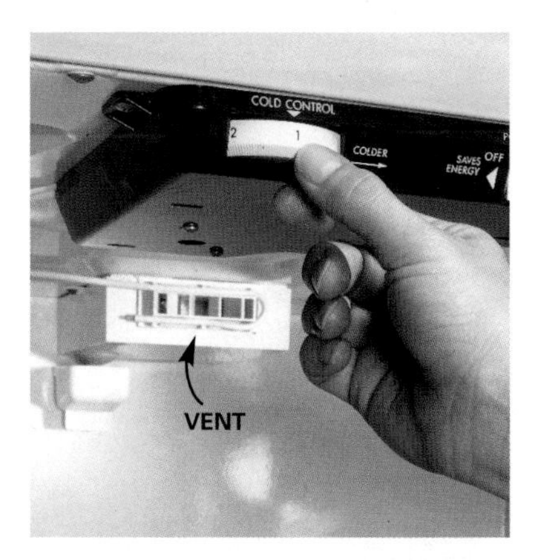

1 ADJUST the temperature control dial. Also make sure the vents inside the fridge or freezer compartment aren't blocked by containers.

2 CLEAN the coils so air can flow through them. Pull dust and fur balls from beneath and between coils with a long brush.

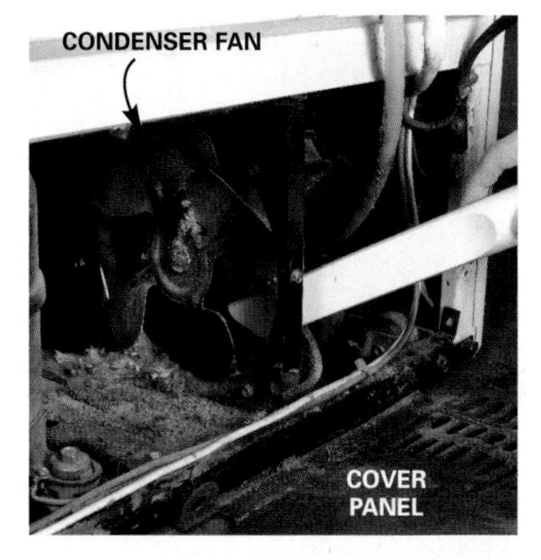

3 PULL OUT the fridge and unscrew the cover panel. Vacuum the fan. Then start the refrigerator to make sure the fan turns freely.

FINDING FRIDGE PARTS

- To get the right part for your refrigerator, you'll need the model number, which is usually stamped on a tag inside the fridge. If you can't find it anywhere on or inside the fridge, check your owner's manual or the manufacturer's Website.
- To locate a parts dealer in your area, look under "Appliances, Major, Parts" in the Yellow Pages.
- To mail-order parts for any major brand, go to www.sears.com or call (800) 4-MY-HOME

PROBLEM:

ICEMAKER ON STRIKE

When an icemaker stops working or produces only tiny cubes, it's usually because the water supply is partially or completely blocked. To find and fix the blockage, check out three common trouble spots:

EASY SOLUTIONS:

FIRST, check the water inlet tube for ice.

The tube that supplies water to your icemaker can get plugged with ice when the water pressure is low. The trickling water freezes and plugs the tube before it reaches the icemaker.

SECOND, unblock the saddle valve.

Most icemakers are connected to the household water supply by a saddle valve. One problem with saddle valves is that the needle hole in the pipe can clog. Fortunately, that blockage is easy to clear once you locate the saddle valve (Photo 3). If you have an unfinished basement, you'll probably find a tube beneath the fridge that leads to the valve. Otherwise, look under your kitchen sink.

THIRD, replace the water inlet valve.

At the back of your fridge, there's a small electric inlet valve that turns the water supply to the icemaker on and off. Before you replace the valve, make sure water is flowing to it: Turn off the water at the saddle valve (Photo 3) and disconnect the supply tube from the inlet valve (see Photo 4). Hold the tube over a bucket and have a helper turn on the saddle valve. If water flows out of the tube, the water supply is fine and chances are the inlet valve is bad. See p. 53 for help finding a new valve ($25 to $35). When the job is done, turn the water back on and check for leaks before you push the fridge back into place.

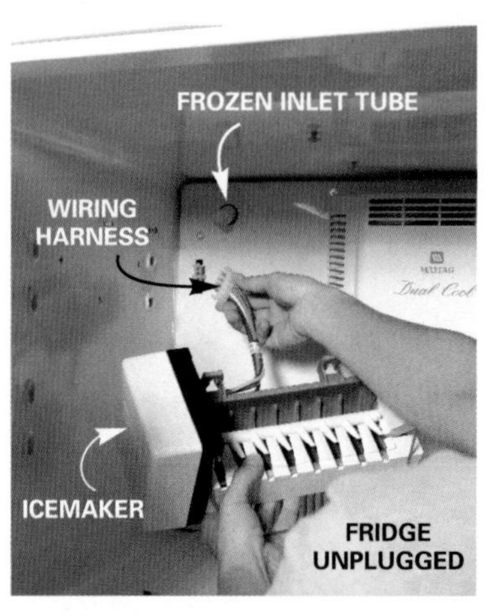

1 REMOVE the screws that hold the icemaker in place. Unplug the wiring harness and remove the ice-maker to expose the water inlet tube.

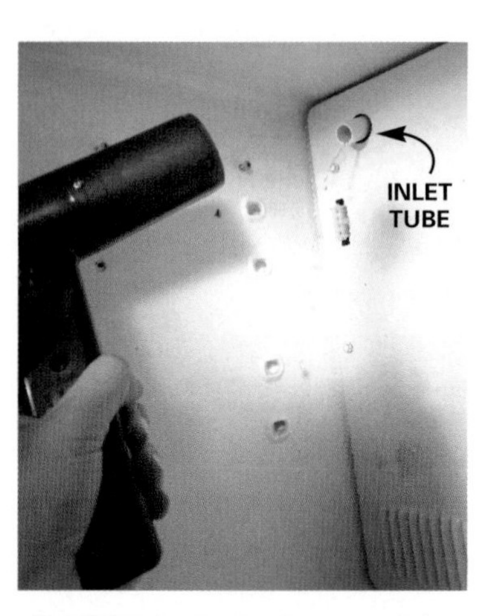

2 MELT the ice in the water inlet tube with a hair dryer. Don't stop until water stops dripping from the tube.

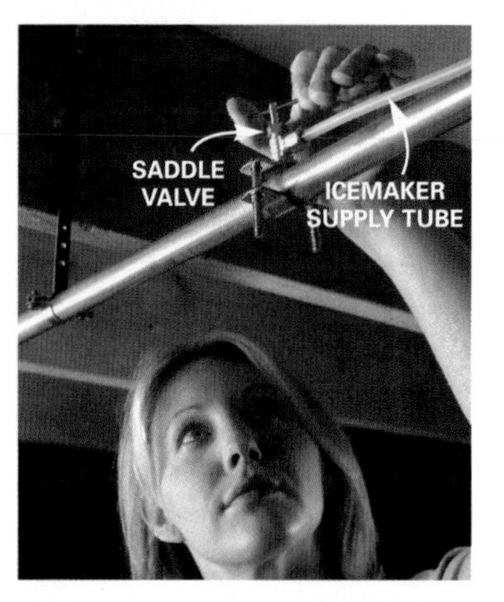

3 TURN the saddle valve clockwise to unblock it. Firmly tighten it to clear mineral deposits from the pinhole. Then reopen the valve.

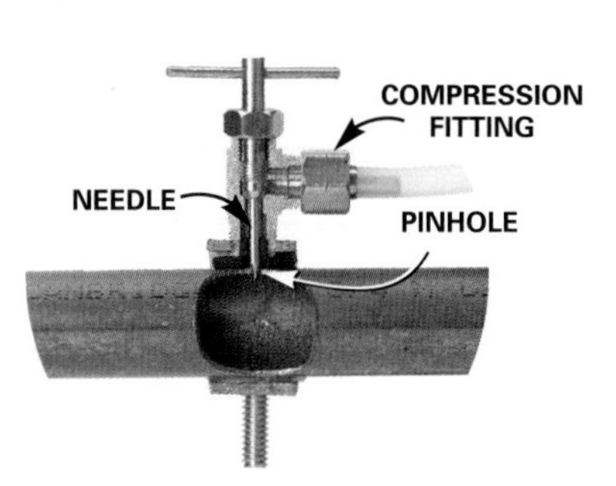

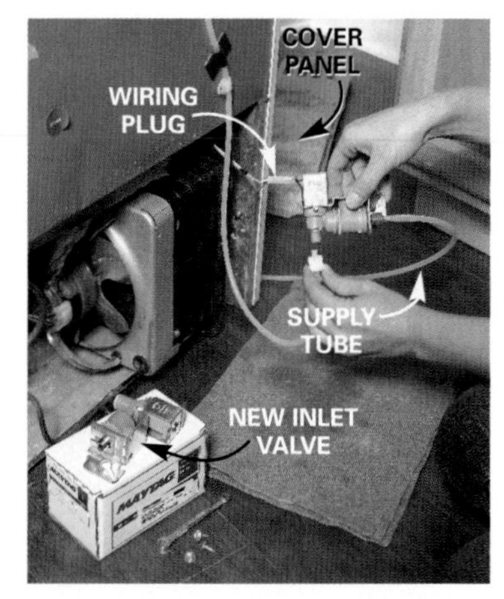

4 REPLACE the inlet valve. Unscrew the cover panel and remove the screws that hold the valve in place. Unplug the wiring and unscrew the nuts that connect the water lines. Reverse these steps to install the new valve.

CAUTION: Always unplug the refrigerator before you make any repairs.

PROBLEM:

THE FRIDGE PRODUCES PUDDLES

The water supply lines that serve icemakers and water dispensers can leak and make pools under the fridge. But a fridge without these features can create water problems too. Every fridge produces water in the form of condensation and melting ice. When the system that deals with this water fails, you can end up with puddles inside and outside the fridge.

EASY SOLUTIONS:

FIRST, check the water supply line.

If your fridge has an icemaker or water dispenser, pull out the fridge and look for a leak. If there's a leak at the inlet valve (Photo 4, p. 54), tighten the compression nuts. If the plastic or copper tube is leaking, replace it. Tubing is usually connected to the saddle valve (Photo 3, p. 54) and inlet valve (Photo 4, p. 54) with screw-on compression fittings.

SECOND, level the fridge.

Water drains into a pan under the fridge where it evaporates. If your fridge is badly tilted, water can spill out of the pan. Leveling the fridge solves this problem (Photos 1 and 2).

THIRD, clear the drain tube.

If the drain tube in the freezer gets plugged, water leaks into the compartment below or onto the floor. To unplug it, first remove the cover panel (Photo 3). In some models, you have to unscrew the floor panel too. Use a hair dryer to melt any ice buildup. Sop away the water with a sponge. Then clean up around the drain hole. Blow air through the tube to clear it. Any tube that fits tightly into the hole will work. You can also use a tire pump or air compressor (turn the pressure down to 30 psi).

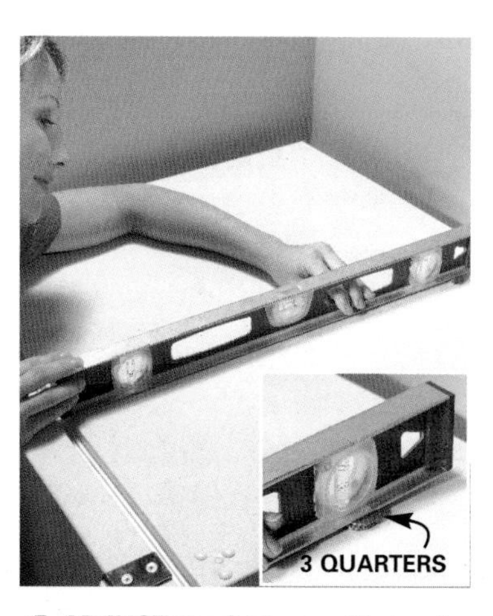

1 ADJUST the fridge so it's level from side to side and tilted backward. Stack quarters near the back and set a 2-ft. level on them. When the bubble shows level, the tilt is correct.

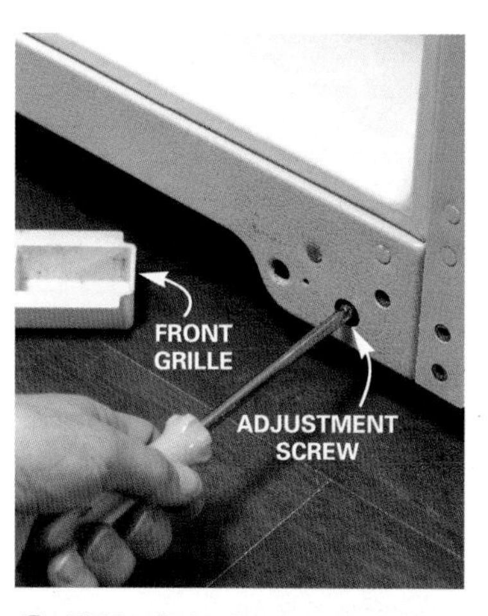

2 PULL off the front cover grille to level or tilt the fridge. Turn adjustment screws to raise or lower the front corners of the fridge.

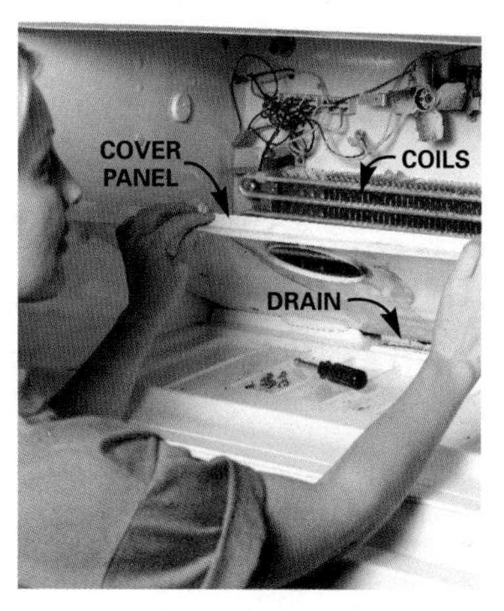

3 REMOVE the screws that hold the cover panel in place. On some models, you have to pry out plastic screw covers with a putty knife to expose the screws.

4 INSERT a tube in the drain hole and blow out any debris. Pour a cup of water into the tube to make sure it drains before you replace the cover panel.

DON'T WRECK THE FLOOR WHEN YOU PULL OUT THE FRIDGE

Nine times out of 10, you can pull out a fridge without any damage to the floor. But a sideways skid or a grain of sand caught under a wheel can scar any floor—I even managed to scratch the ceramic tile in my kitchen.

At the very least, lay down a cardboard runway before dragging out your fridge. For the ultimate floor protection, use 1/8-in. hardboard (about $6 for a 4 x 8-ft. sheet at home centers). A pair of shims create a ramp for easier pulling.

Great Goofs™

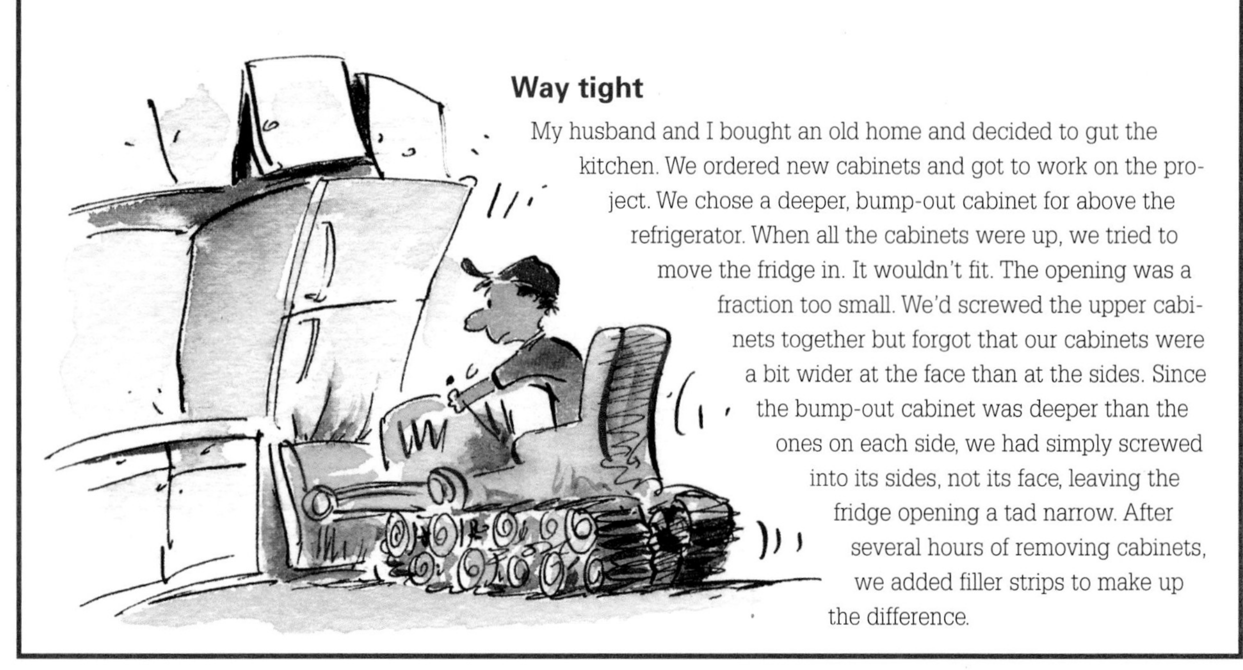

Way tight

My husband and I bought an old home and decided to gut the kitchen. We ordered new cabinets and got to work on the project. We chose a deeper, bump-out cabinet for above the refrigerator. When all the cabinets were up, we tried to move the fridge in. It wouldn't fit. The opening was a fraction too small. We'd screwed the upper cabinets together but forgot that our cabinets were a bit wider at the face than at the sides. Since the bump-out cabinet was deeper than the ones on each side, we had simply screwed into its sides, not its face, leaving the fridge opening a tad narrow. After several hours of removing cabinets, we added filler strips to make up the difference.

Handy Hints® from our readers

SPEEDY REFILL FOR STEAM IRON

Fill a well-rinsed dish soap bottle with distilled water for quick, spill-free refills.

QUIET LOUD SINKS

Fill the space between two stainless steel sink basins with expanding foam. The foam deadens vibrations and lessens the gong effect. It's possible to do this with the sink in place but much neater and easier before installation. Either way, let the foam harden and then trim away the excess with a knife.

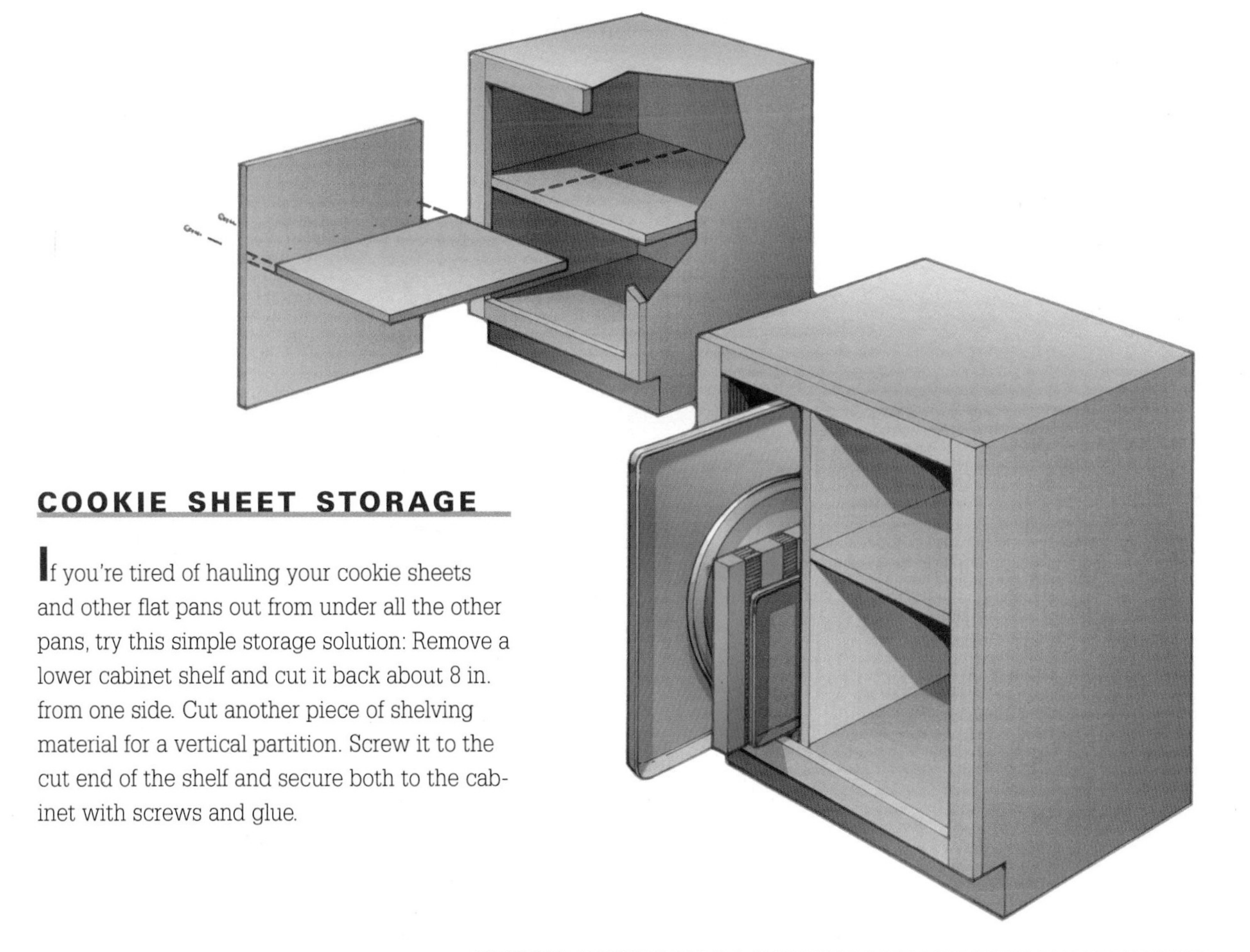

COOKIE SHEET STORAGE

If you're tired of hauling your cookie sheets and other flat pans out from under all the other pans, try this simple storage solution: Remove a lower cabinet shelf and cut it back about 8 in. from one side. Cut another piece of shelving material for a vertical partition. Screw it to the cut end of the shelf and secure both to the cabinet with screws and glue.

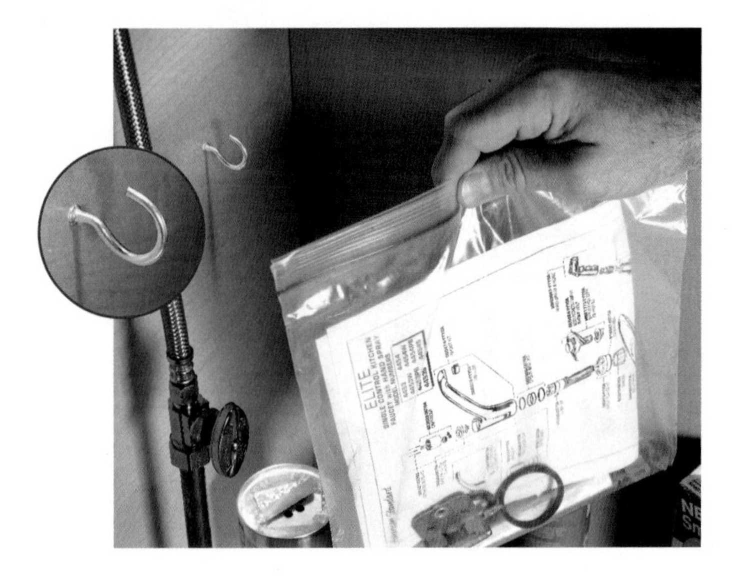

UNDER-SINK ARCHIVES

Don't file away the manuals for your kitchen and bath fixtures. Instead, slip them into a locking plastic bag and hang the bag in the cabinet under the sink. They'll always be right where you need them. Toss in paint samples and spare cabinet hardware too.

JACKING UP A DISPOSER

When you're replacing a garbage disposer, the worst part of the job can be holding up the heavy machine while you tighten the ring nut that attaches it to the sink. The solution: Use the jack from your car to raise the unit into position.

QUICK WASHER AND DRYER SHELF

Clean up the clutter of detergent boxes, bleach bottles and other laundry room stuff. Install a shelf that fits just above the washer and dryer. Screw ordinary shelf brackets to the wall and mount a board that just clears the tops.

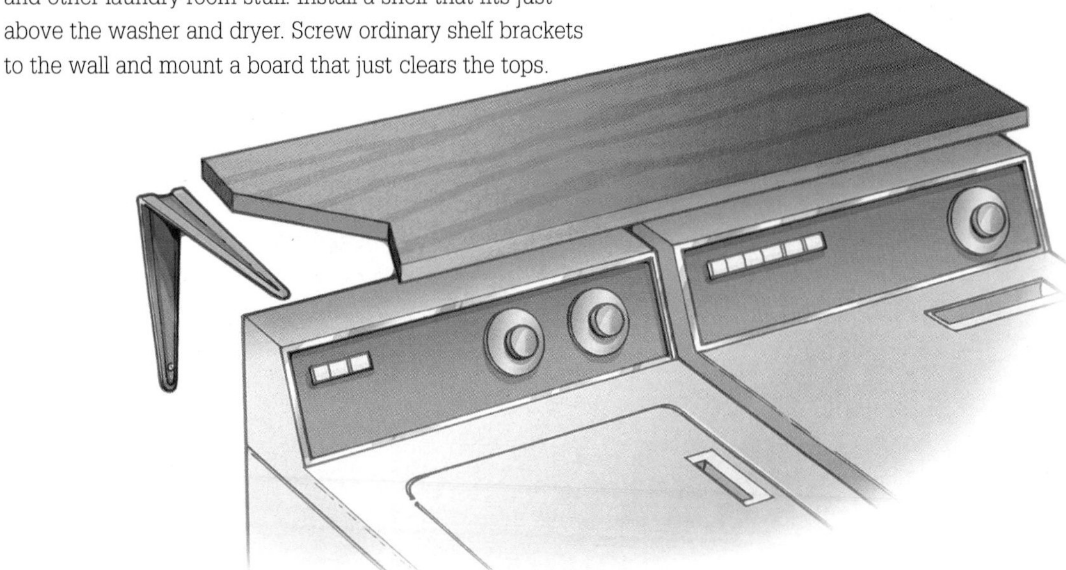

PLUMBER'S GLOVES

Gardening gloves with a rubbery coating ($4) are great for plumbing projects: They grip pipe like a vise and keep that nasty acid flux off your hands. But don't wear them while soldering; some coatings are flammable.

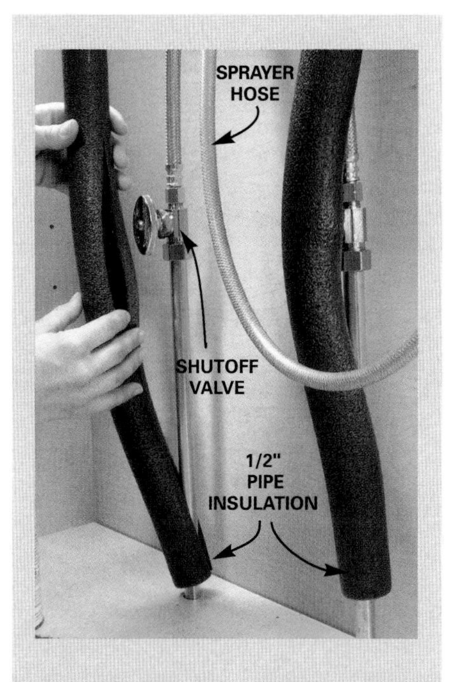

STOP SINK-SPRAYER HANG-UPS

If you have to jiggle the hose as you pull out your kitchen sink sprayer, chances are the hose is catching on the shutoff valves. For smooth operation, slip 1/2-in. foam pipe insulation over the pipes and shutoff handles. Tape it if it won't stay put. Get the insulation at home centers for about $3.

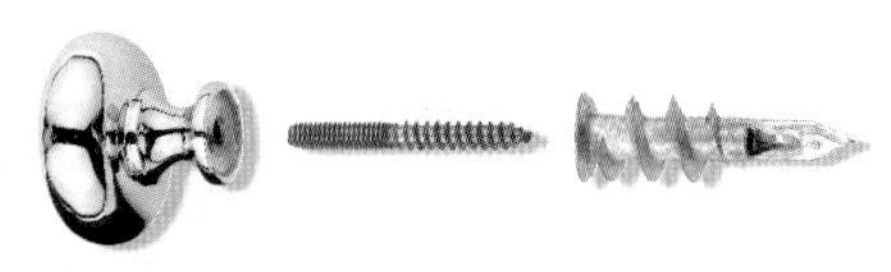

HIS-AND-HERS SHOWER SHELVES

If you need more than shampoo and a bar of soap in the shower, here's how to provide space for all your vital beauty potions: Get a couple of those shelves that are designed to hang from a shower arm and hang them on cabinet knobs. Use No. 8-32 hanger screws ($1) to screw the knobs into studs or drywall anchors.

Gallery of Ideas

TILE BACKSPLASH WITH HOOD

You don't have to do a complete remodel of your kitchen to give it new life. The two projects in this article—a tile backsplash and a new range hood—can quickly and dramatically transform any kitchen. The project doesn't require a lot of skill, just a lot of patience and attention to detail.

Project Facts

Cost: About $7/sq. ft. for tile, plus the cost of the range hood
Skill level: Intermediate carpentry, tile-setting and wiring experience
Time: 1 or 2 weekends

Skill Builders

While completing this project, you'll learn how to:

- **Plan the layout and installation of wall tile and tile borders**
- **Build a self-supporting tile shelf**
- **Use a wet saw to create cutouts in tile**

FROM OCTOBER, 2004, p. 34

WEEKEND BATHROOM MAKEOVER

FROM OCTOBER, 2004, p. 82

Replacing a vanity with a wall-hung sink does more than bring a fresh, welcome look to your old bathroom. It's also one of the best ways to make a small bathroom feel roomier. As the floor space opens up, the room becomes brighter and easier to clean. And it's the perfect time to update the lights, mirror and other features as well.

Project Facts

Cost: Wall-mount sink costs about $400; other costs vary
Skill level: Intermediate plumbing and carpentry experience
Time: 1 weekend for sink installation; other factors vary greatly

Skill Builders

As you work your way through this project, you'll learn how to:

- **Sweat copper pipe and join PVC pipe**
- **Install shutoff valves and supply lines**
- **Install transition fittings to join pipes made of different materials**

To order photocopies of complete articles for the projects shown here, call (715) 246-4521, email familyhandyman@nrmsinc.com or write to: Copies, The Family Handyman, P.O. Box 83695, Stillwater, MN 55083-0695. Many public libraries also carry back issues of *The Family Handyman* magazine.

Ask Handyman™

PAINTING KITCHEN CABINETS

We want to give new life to our old wood kitchen cabinets with a fresh coat of paint. What is the best type of paint to use?

For the best adhesion and a harder, more durable finish, an oil-based (alkyd) paint is tough to beat for kitchen cabinets. But you must be willing to put up with the strong odor and solvent cleanup, along with a longer drying and curing time than you'd get if you used an ordinary water-based paint. Plus, the color may yellow over time.

The best solution to avoid the hassle of oil-based paint is a new-technology waterborne acrylic enamel paint (such as Satin Impervo by Benjamin Moore) that delivers the good flow, leveling and hardening characteristics of an oil-based paint without the odor and long drying time. These new paints dry fast and clean up with soap and water. The main challenge is a smooth finish, but pros say that if the waterborne acrylic enamel is applied heavily enough and worked in small sections, it will flatten out nicely. Avoid a dry brush and going over sections already starting to dry.

Don't forget other keys to success when painting cabinets—surface preparation (degreasing, cleaning and sanding), priming (use a top-quality primer), brushing (use the best-quality brush for the type of paint) and drying (follow label directions).

WHAT TO REMODEL FIRST

We plan to stay in our house for three to five years. When it comes to resale value, is it better to upgrade a kitchen or a bath?

You can't go wrong upgrading either room. You'll usually recoup most of the bathroom and kitchen remodeling dollars you spend. In fact, if you do all the work yourself and do a first-class job, you'll recoup the cost of almost any upgrade. The chart below lists the cost-recovery rate by project in 2003; however, these numbers can be optimistic and misleading. Many other factors influence resale value and the value of improvements, including the location, current real estate market, interest rates, the economy and more.

A simple strategy I've used successfully (with four houses and one hobby farm) is to improve the main areas that look rough or abused, and are less than comfortable for me and my family. For example, if the kitchen is shabby, poorly lit or lacking counter space, make that a priority. Likewise, if a small bathroom has a bulky vanity and a tiny mirror, replace them with a space-saving pedestal sink and a large mirror to add visual space.

Make a priority list, then work your way down it until your home feels comfortable. It may take three to five years or longer, but the results will be gratifying. Your home will look and work better and should be easier to sell with each project completed. Or you just might wind up staying put because you've made your home too wonderful to leave.

Percentage of cost recovered—2003

(National average)

Project	%
Deck addition	104
Siding replacement	98
Bathroom addition	95
Attic bedroom	93
Bathroom remodel	91
Window replacement	86
Family room addition	81
Kitchen remodel	80
Basement remodel	79
Master suite	77

TILING A BATHROOM

We plan to update our bathroom, and the old vinyl floor has got to go—in favor of tile. I'm concerned, though, because a friend told us there might be asbestos in the vinyl. Can we just tile over the top of it?

Yes, chances are you can tile right over it. And you might not have to deal with the asbestos issue at all.

Ceramic tile requires a stiff base to keep it and the grout from cracking. So the first thing you have to do is check the thickness of your floor. You can usually figure the thickness by pulling up a floor register or removing the door threshold. If the ceiling is open below the floor, you can often tell from where plumbing penetrates the floor. As a last resort, remove the toilet and examine the area around the ring; you'll have to pull the toilet anyway at some point.

If your floor framing is spaced 16 in. apart, the combination of subfloor plus underlayment (a second layer of plywood directly under the vinyl) should add up to at least 1-1/8 in. If the floor framing is 24 in. apart, it should add up to 1-1/2 in. If your vinyl floor isn't stiff enough, use tiling Method 1, and add either 1/4- or 1/2-in. cement board to build it up. Keep in mind that in doing so, you'll be raising the floor level 1/2 to 3/4 in. (cement board plus 1/4-in. tile), which means that you'll have to trim the door, raise the vanity, extend the toilet ring, and make a new transition to the hallway.

If your floor is stiff and solid, you can lay the tile directly over the vinyl using Method 2. With this method you only build your floor up 1/4 in. However, if you choose this method, you should be aware of the asbestos issue. Asbestos is a known carcinogen that was used in many products including vinyl tile, asphalt tile, sheet flooring and adhesives made until 1980. So if your floor was laid after 1980, it won't contain asbestos unless the installer used older materials. If you're sure it doesn't contain asbestos, you can clean and sand the vinyl to improve tile adhesion, or even tear it out.

However, if you have an older home, and don't know when the floor was laid, do not sand it or disturb it. Simply strip off the old grime and wax with an ammonia-based cleaner. When it's dry, apply a little tile adhesive and let it dry to test for good adhesion. If thin-set mortar with an acrylic additive doesn't stick well, try a mastic-type adhesive. Both are available at home centers and tile stores.

In any case, before tiling, tighten any loose flooring by screwing down the entire surface with galvanized wood screws spaced every 6 in. Add more screws in especially loose areas.

Method 1: Tile with underlayment

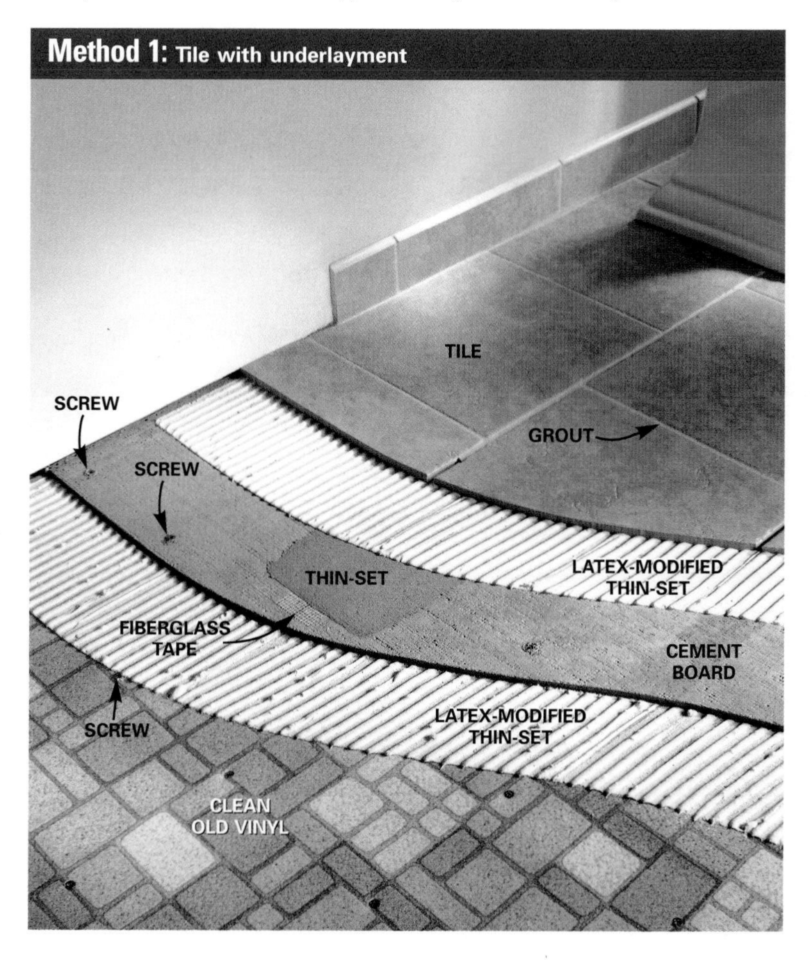

Method 2: Tile without underlayment

SERVE UP STYLE WITH NEW **COUNTERTOPS AND SINK**

Out with the old, in with the new, including a new sink and faucet.

by **Jeff Gorton**

Are your old countertops looking a little worn and outdated? Is the sink showing its age? Installing new countertops is a quick and affordable way to give your kitchen a makeover. And it makes sense to put in a new sink while you're at it. You can update the look and pick a sink-and-faucet combination that works with your style of cooking.

In the first part of this article, we'll show you how to take out your old countertops and install new plastic laminate countertops. Then we'll show you how to complete your kitchen transformation by installing a new stainless steel sink and faucet.

Our countertop installation is a little tricky because the sink section has to fit between two end walls. You have to plan this installation sequence carefully. We'll walk you through the steps. If your countertop sections are open on one or both ends, your job will be considerably easier. On the other hand, if you have a kitchen with a continuous U-shaped countertop that's enclosed by walls, fitting is more difficult. We'd recommend hiring a pro.

If you're handy with power tools and accustomed to precision measuring, you can install your countertops in a weekend. You'll need basic hand tools, a jigsaw, a drill and a belt sander.

We ordered these custom-size post-formed countertops about three weeks before we needed them. You can order countertops from a home center, full-service lumberyard or countertop fabricator. Since countertops are bulky and easily damaged in transit, it's best to have them delivered. Our countertops cost about $30 a linear foot. You'll save about $30 a foot, or about $600 for an average kitchen, by installing the countertops yourself.

PART I: COUNTERTOPS

Draw a sketch and measure carefully

Careful measuring is the most critical step in any countertop installation. Countertop fabricators and retailers may ask for different information, so first ask for measuring instructions from your supplier. The most accurate method is to order the countertops based on cabinet dimensions. Make a sketch of your kitchen. Then measure the width and depth of the cabinets and record these dimensions on the sketch. Include the sink, stove and refrigerator locations. The ends of countertops that don't butt into a wall will have to be finished with matching plastic laminate end caps. Indicate where these end caps are needed.

The salesperson will be able to convert these measure-

1 SHUT OFF the water supply valves and disconnect the tubes to the faucet. Disconnect the sink drain. Pry up the edge of the sink and slide wood blocks under to provide space for a handhold. Lift out the sink.

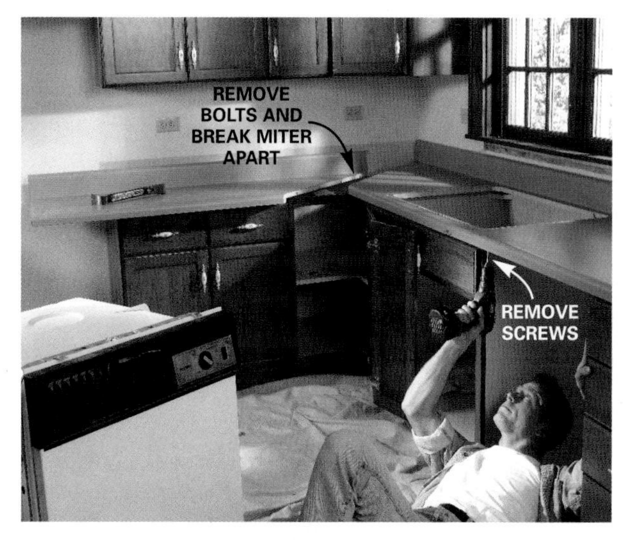

2 INSPECT the underside of the countertop for screws and remove them. Slice the caulk joint along the backsplash/wall joint with a utility knife. Then lift or pry off the countertops.

ments to a countertop order and include allowances for overhangs and extra material for scribing to uneven walls.

In this article, we're showing how to install preformed (also called post-formed) countertops without a backsplash. Use the same techniques for counters with a backsplash. If your countertop has an inside corner like ours, order your tops with precut miters. It's nearly impossible to cut these accurately yourself. Ask for buildup strips with your countertop order (Photo 3). These should match the thickness of the buildup strip under the front edge of the countertop.

Start by removing the old tops

First you'll have to shut off the water supply to the sink and disconnect the plumbing (Photo 1). Keep in mind that old plumbing may need new valves or drain parts. If you have a heavy sink, remove it now and carry it outside. You may have to slice the caulk joint along the edge to get it to release. Otherwise, leave the sink in place and remove it along with the countertop.

Some older countertops may be nailed to the cabinets. You'll have to pry these off. Most newer tops like those shown here are screwed or glued down. Remove the screws (Photo 2). Then pry the tops loose. Cut the countertops with a reciprocating saw if it simplifies removal.

Prepare the cabinets for countertop installation by screwing down the buildup strips (Photo 3). The edges will overhang the cabinet sides. Predrill 3/16-in. clearance holes for the mounting screws (Photo 13); later you'll screw through them to secure the tops. Ends finished with end caps usually don't need buildup strips under them. Check the construction of your tops to be sure. Use metal L-brackets to secure the tops in these areas. Also

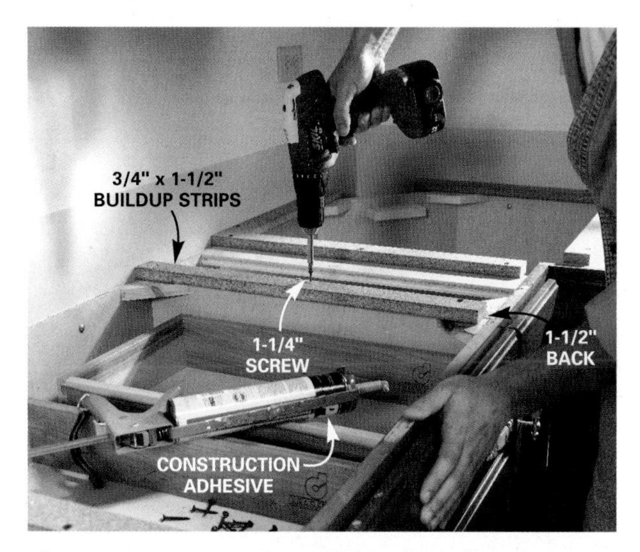

3 GLUE and screw down buildup strips to the top of the cabinet sides. Hold the strips 1-1/2 in. back from the cabinet fronts. Add strips to support corners.

hold the strips back 1-1/2 in. from the front edge of the cabinets.

Scribing is the key to a good fit

Photos 5 and 6 show the scribing process. Scribing allows you to fit the countertop tightly to uneven walls and out-of-square corners. You'll also scribe a counter to remove excess material, as in Photos 9 and 10, where we scribe the entire length of the counter to make the end cap flush with the cabinet side to allow the stove to slip in. Order your tops with an extra 1/4 in. of length and depth to allow for scribing and fitting.

SCRIBING TOOL

4 **SLIDE the point of the miter into a hole in the drywall (inset photo) and lower the counter into place. With the front overhang even with the cabinet fronts, slide the top against the end wall.**

A FEW THINGS TO CHECK BEFORE YOU ORDER NEW TOPS

- Measure the depth of your cabinets. Standard 25-1/4 in. deep countertops are made to fit cabinets that are 24-3/4 in. deep, including the doors and drawers. If your cabinets vary more than 1/4 in. from this, you'll have to order custom-depth counters.
- Compare the height of your existing backsplash with the one you'll be ordering. If the new one is shorter, you'll have to patch or redecorate the walls. If it's taller, watch for conflicts with outlets and window trim.
- Use a straightedge and framing square to check the walls for straightness and to make sure the corners are square. Standard preformed countertops allow you to scribe and cut off up to 1/4 in. to compensate for irregularities. But if your walls deviate by more than 1/4 in. or your corners are way out of square, you may have to order tops extra wide and long to allow for more scribing. Discuss this with a knowledgeable salesperson and order your tops accordingly.

Post-formed counters with backsplashes come standard with a large lip that extends past the backsplash (see "Counters with a Backsplash," p. 68). This is the scribe material that you'll sand to conform to the walls.

Countertops that are sandwiched between two walls are tricky to scribe because initially they're too long to fit in. Photo 4 shows one solution. Study the photos and text until you understand the fitting process. Then you can adapt it to other (usually simpler!) situations. The hole in the drywall allows you to tilt the counter into place and scribe it. Once it's in place, measure the amount of counter that's sticking into the hole and scribe off all but 1/4 in. of this distance from the opposite end (Photo 5). After you sand to the scribe line (Photo 6), you'll still have 1/4 in. extra, allowing you to scribe the adjoining section for a tight fit at the opposite end (Photos 7 and 8).

In our situation, we first scribed the end of the sink counter where it butts the adjoining wall. Then we scribed the

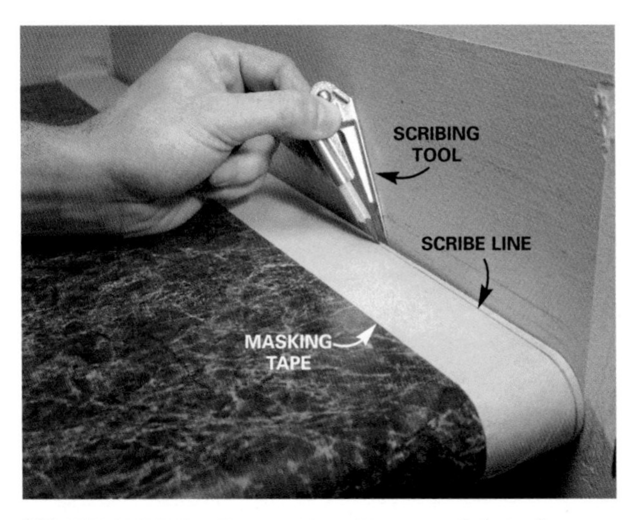

5 **MEASURE** the distance the miter extends into the hole, subtract 1/4 in. and set the scribing tool to this dimension. Scribe a line parallel to the end wall.

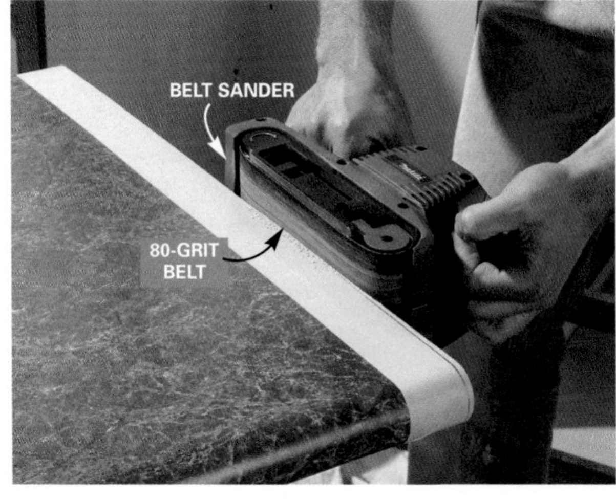

6 **SAND** to the line with a belt sander. Set the top in place to check the fit. Make sure the front edge of the countertop is parallel to the face of the cabinets.

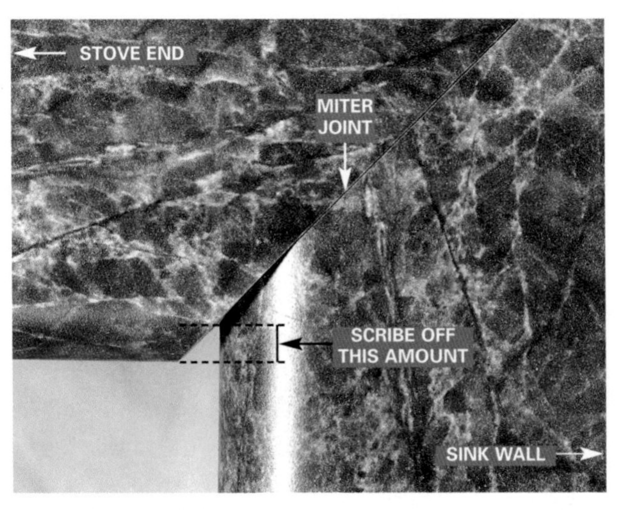

7 **SET** the adjoining countertop section into place, fitting the two miters together tightly. Set the scribe to remove the amount shown.

8 **SCRIBE** a line along the back of the adjoining countertop. Sand to the line and replace the top to check the fit. Connect the tops temporarily with miter bolts (Photo 11).

9 **CHECK** the position of the adjoining countertop end cap in relation to the cabinets. At stove and refrigerator openings where the end cap must be flush to the cabinet end, set the scribe to the amount of overhang.

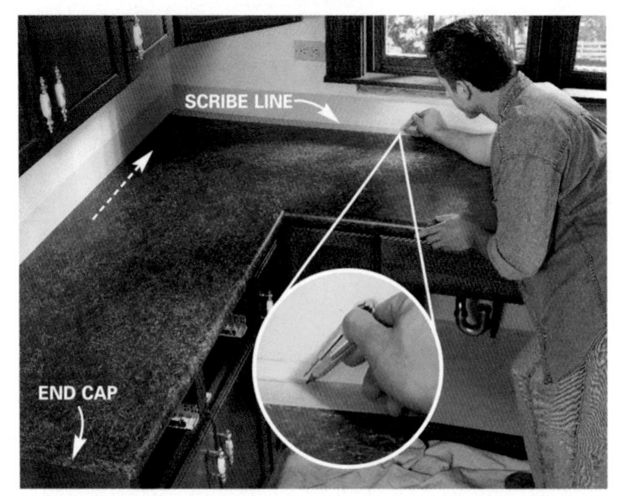

10 **SCRIBE** a line on the backside of the countertop opposite the end cap. Remove the tops and sand to the line with a belt sander. Set the tops back in place and check the fit to the wall and the end cap overhang.

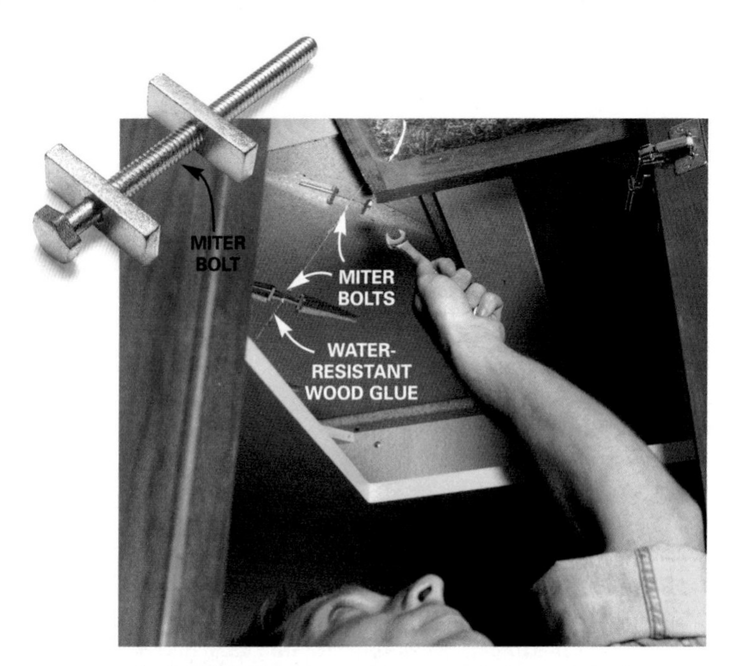

11 **SPREAD water-resistant wood glue onto both miters, slide them together, and snug them together with miter bolts. Don't tighten the bolts yet.**

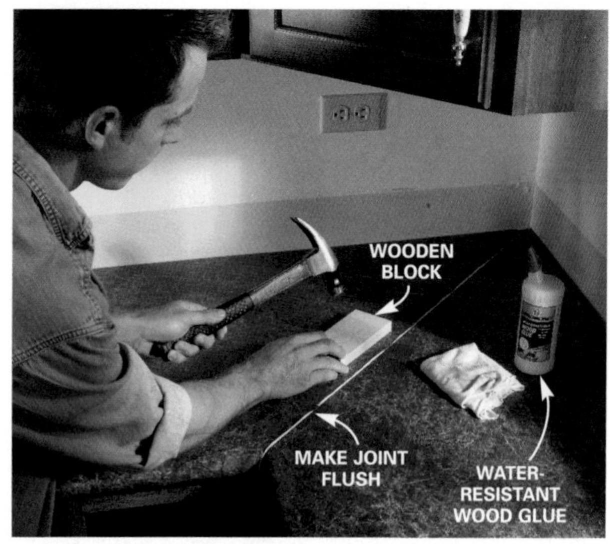

12 **ALIGN the top of the miters by tapping on a wood block placed on the high side. Tighten the bolts when the miters are flush.**

13 **SECURE the tops by screwing through the 3/16-in. predrilled holes in the buildup strips into the countertop (1-1/4 in. drywall screws usually work, but double-check the thickness of the top and buildup strips for your counter). Where there are no buildup strips, use metal L-brackets and shorter screws.**

counter opposite this end and loosely connected the miter. Finally we slid the assembled counter against the wall behind the sink and scribed it both to get a tight fit to the wall and to move the end cap near the stove flush to the cabinet. If your countertop configuration is different, think about the result each scribe will have on the position of the counters and plan a scribing sequence accordingly.

Don't worry; it's normal to have to scribe some counters more than once to get a good fit. It takes time and patience, but the result is a tight-fitting, professional-looking installation with almost invisible caulk joints.

COUNTERS WITH A BACKSPLASH

We ordered countertops without a backsplash because we wanted the wall tile to rest on the countertop. The techniques for installing a countertop with a backsplash are the same. But you'll have to cut a larger hole in the drywall to tilt the countertop in (Photo 4, p. 66). The other difference is in cutting the sink hole (Photo 2, p. 69). With some sinks, the space between the cutout and the backsplash is too small to fit a jigsaw. In that case, either use a handsaw for the back cut or cut out the sink hole from the underside of the countertop before you install it.

SAND the protruding lip (scribe material) on post-formed tops to conform to wavy walls and out-of-square corners.

Finish the job by gluing and bolting the miter (Photos 11 and 12) and screwing down the tops. Be careful to check the length of the screws. They should extend no more than 1/2 in. into the counter. Use matching caulk to seal the joint between the countertops and the walls.

1 **MARK the center of the sink cabinet on the countertop. Center the sink (or sink template) on the mark and set the front edge far enough back to fit inside the cabinet frame. Trace around the sink or template, then add an inner cutting line.**

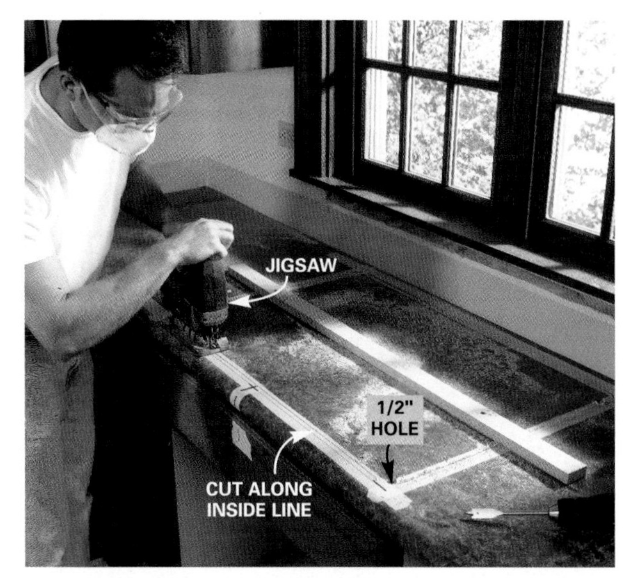

2 **DRILL a 1/2-in. starting hole in each corner and cut out the sink opening with a jigsaw and fine wood-cutting blade. Screw a strip of wood to the cutout to prevent it from falling in when you complete the cut.**

PART II: SINK & FAUCET

Installing a new sink and faucet is one of the easiest things you can do to make a big impact on the way your kitchen looks and functions. With the wide selection of sinks and faucets available from home centers and on-line plumbing suppliers, you can choose features that match your cooking style (such as a deep sink for extra-large pots) and colors that complement your countertop and appliances. And most are designed for easy installation, even for a novice.

We chose a stainless steel sink to coordinate with the new appliances and for its classic looks and durability. The 8-in. deep bowls along with the arching faucet spout make it easily accommodate large pans. Both the sink and faucet were in stock at a local home center. See the Buyer's Guide on p. 71 for details.

The most critical step in the sink installation is cutting an accurate hole in the countertop. Some basic carpentry and plumbing experience would be helpful, but by following our instructions, you'll be able to successfully complete the job in a day.

In addition to basic hand tools, you'll need a drill and jigsaw to cut the hole, and wrenches and a large slip-joint pliers to connect the plumbing. Any fine-tooth saw will work to cut the plastic pipe.

If you have chrome drain parts, we recommend replacing them with new plastic drains. Plastic is much easier to work with, seals better and doesn't corrode like metal. Buy the drain parts you need to fit your situation, including parts for a garbage disposer or dishwasher if you have them.

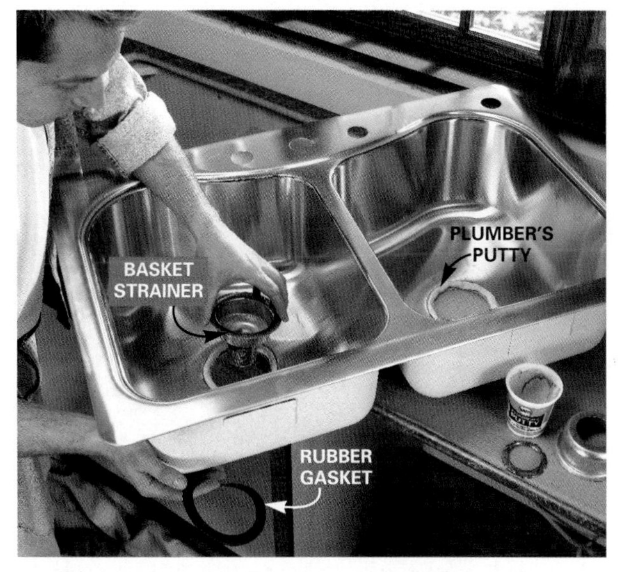

3 **ROLL plumber's putty into a pencil's-width rope and press it around each drain opening. Set the basket strainer into the opening and press it down.**

Use a template or the sink itself to mark the counter for cutting

Some sinks include a paper template that you cut out and use as a pattern. Others, like ours, instruct you to use the sink as a template, and then draw a second cutting line 1/2 in. inside the outline. The key is to locate the sink cutout just far enough back from the front of the countertop to fit inside the cabinet frame (usually about 2 in. back). This will then leave room behind the sink. In Photo 1, we show

4 INSTALL the rubber washer, then the cardboard washer (if included). Assemble the remaining parts. Tighten the nuts with a large slip-joint pliers.

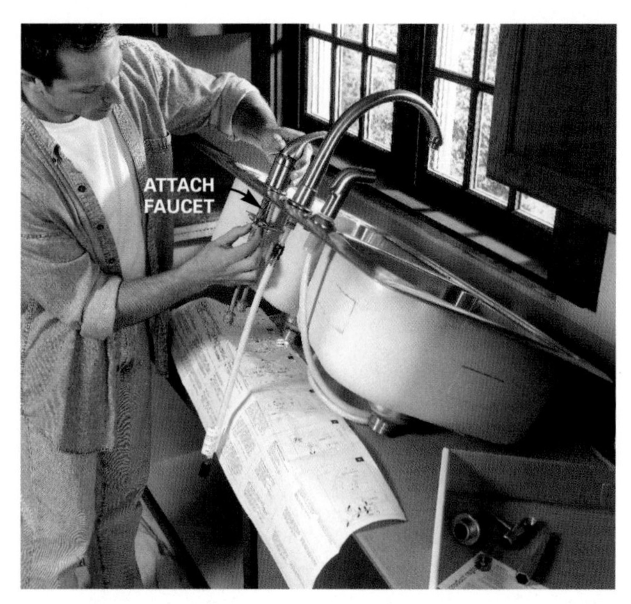

5 INSTALL the faucet handles, spout and spray attachment before you set the sink. Follow the faucet manufacturer's instructions.

6 APPLY a bead of mildew-resistant tub-and-tile caulk to the countertop perimeter and lower the fully assembled sink into the opening.

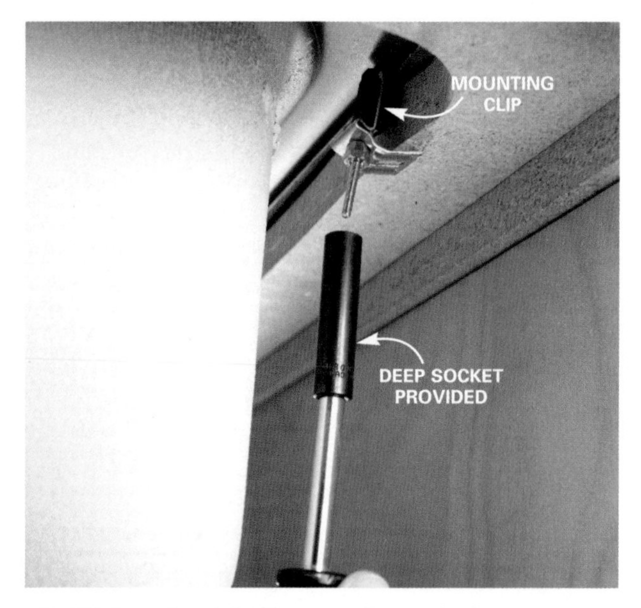

7 SNUG up the sink clips according to the instructions. Be careful. Overtightening can dent the sink. Then wipe off excess caulk around the sink.

how to center the sink on the sink cabinet. We put down masking tape to make the pencil lines more visible on the dark laminate and to protect the top from scratches (Photo 2).

Mark the cutout line according to the instructions and then saw out the hole. Drill 1/2-in. starting holes in each corner to make turning the corner easier. A jigsaw works well for cutting the hole. Just be sure to use a top-quality wood cutting blade and cover the bottom of the saw bed with tape to avoid marring the counter. Screw a scrap of wood to the cutout (Photo 2) to keep it from falling through as you complete the cut. Use a handsaw to cut the back line if your jigsaw doesn't fit.

Install the basket strainers and faucet before setting the sink

The less time you spend on your back under the sink, the better, so install as much of the hardware as possible before setting the sink. Photos 3 – 5 show how. Follow the instructions included with your faucet. If you use the countertop as a workbench, protect the surface with a sheet of cardboard or a dropcloth.

The next step is to caulk around the opening and set the sink (Photo 6). Stainless steel sinks like ours are held in place by clips. These are included with the sink along with instructions on how they work. Tighten the clips from

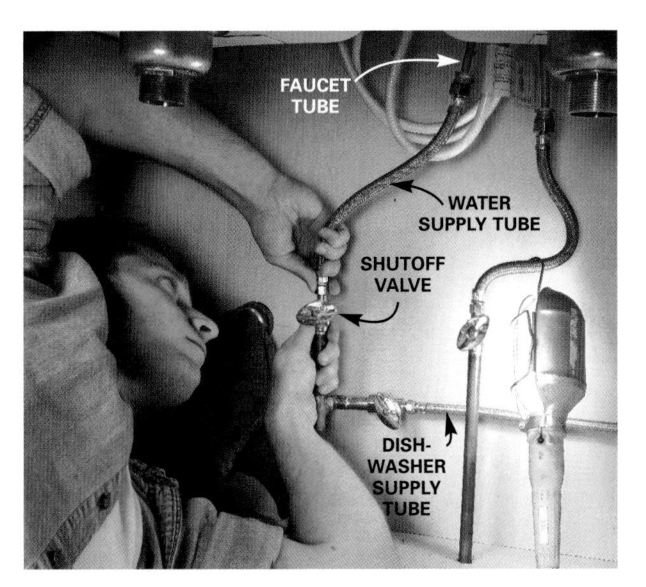

8 CONNECT the faucet to the shutoff valves with braided stainless steel supply tubes. Hold the valve with one wrench while tightening the nut with a second wrench.

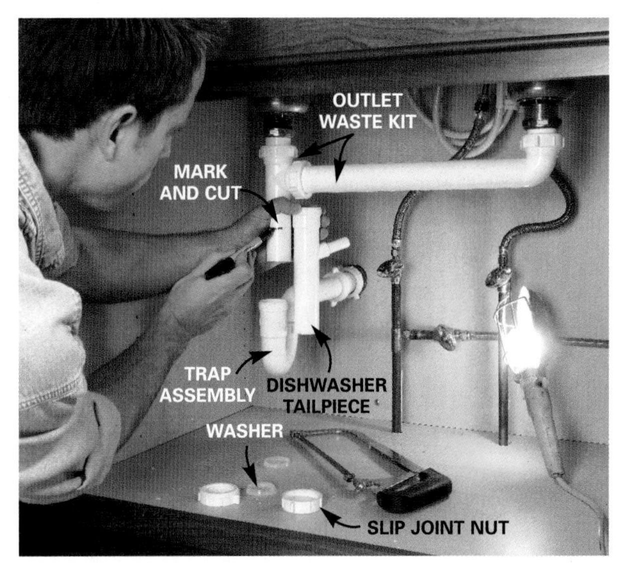

9 MARK and cut the new plastic drain parts and connect them with plastic nuts and washers. Hand-tighten the nuts. Run water in the sink and check for leaks. Tighten the connections if necessary.

underneath (Photo 7). Cast iron sinks usually rest on the counter and are held in place by the caulk. Cast iron is heavy. You'll need a helper to set a cast iron sink in the hole. Clean up the caulk with a wet rag after you tighten the sink clips.

Complete the job by connecting the supply lines and hooking up the drains (Photos 8 and 9). Turn on the water and check for leaks. Most leaks are easy to fix by slightly tightening the supply line connections or slip-joint nut on the drain lines.

Buyer's Guide

We used a Kohler sink (model No. K3369-4-NA; $245) and Delta faucet (model No. 174-SSWF; $269).The following is a partial list of companies that manufacture sinks and faucets.

- **AMERICAN STANDARD: (800) 524-9797. www.americanstandard-us.com**
- **DELTA FAUCET CO.: (800) 345-3358. www.deltafaucet.com**
- **ELJER PLUMBINGWARE INC.: (800) 423-5537. www.eljer.com**
- **ELKAY: (630) 572-3192. www.elkayusa.com**
- **GERBER PLUMBING FIXTURES CORP.: (847) 675-6570. www.gerberonline.com**
- **KOHLER CO.: (800) 456-4537. www.kohler.com**
- **MOEN: (800) 289-6636. www.moen.com**
- **PEERLESS: (800) 438-6673. www.peerlessfaucet.com**

The countertop shown is made by Pionite (www.pionite.com). The color is MV430 Suede, Jade Pavia.

PARTS AND SUPPLIES

- Plumber's putty ($1.50)
- Tub-and-tile caulk ($3)
- Two basket strainer assemblies (only one if you're installing a disposer; $10 each)

You'll need the following 1-1/2 in. plastic drain parts:

- One P-trap assembly ($5)
- One "end" or "center" outlet waste kit ($5)
- Two sink tailpieces ($2 each)—only one if you're installing a disposer. If you have a dishwasher and no disposer, purchase a special "dishwasher" tailpiece that has a tube to connect the dishwasher drain hose.
- One disposer waste arm ($3.50) if you have a disposer.
- Two flexible water supply tubes for kitchen sinks ($4.50 each). Match the nuts on the ends to the threads on your faucet and shutoff valves. Also measure to determine the right lengths.

You Can Fix It™

REPLACE A DEAD BATHROOM FAN MOTOR

If your bathroom fan is dead, here's some good news: You don't have to tear out the entire unit. Even if your fan is decades old, chances are you can get a replacement motor. Although a new motor costs about the same as a new fan, replacement saves time and trouble. You don't have to cut into the ceiling, crawl around your attic or get up on your roof. It usually takes less than an hour.

Your first step is to get the fan's model number. Remove the fan grille (**Photo 1**) and vacuum away the dust to find the number on a label or stamped on the fan's housing. But don't order a new motor until you remove the old one. You might need other parts too.

Bath fans vary in design, but motor replacement requires the same basic steps, no matter which brand or model you have. Turn off the power to the fan at the main breaker panel. Then unplug the fan and remove the motor plate (**Photo 2**). Some motor plates are released by pressing or prying on the side of the fan housing. Others are secured with a screw or two.

Before you can remove the motor from the plate, you have to get the blower off the motor's shaft. This is often the toughest part of the whole project. An older metal blower might be fastened with a screw. Plastic blowers usually aren't fastened at all, but simply slide off the shaft. Either way, removal may require some hard prying and pulling. If you wreck the blower while removing it, don't worry. You can order a replacement for $3 to $10. To install the new motor, simply reverse the process.

CAUTION: Turn power off at the main panel before removing motor.

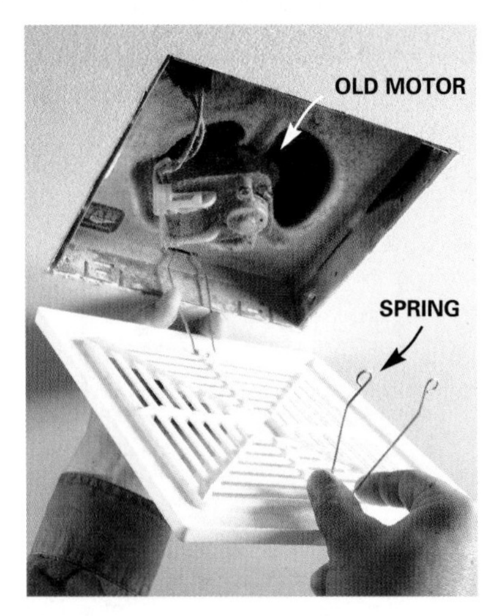

1 PULL the grille down and pinch the springs to release them from the housing. Vacuum out the dust so you can find the model number.

2 UNPLUG the motor and remove the plate that supports it. The plate will tip out of the housing after you release a tab or remove a retaining screw.

3 PULL off the blower wheel and detach the motor by removing screws or nuts. Install the new motor and reattach the blower wheel.

3 Wiring & Electrical

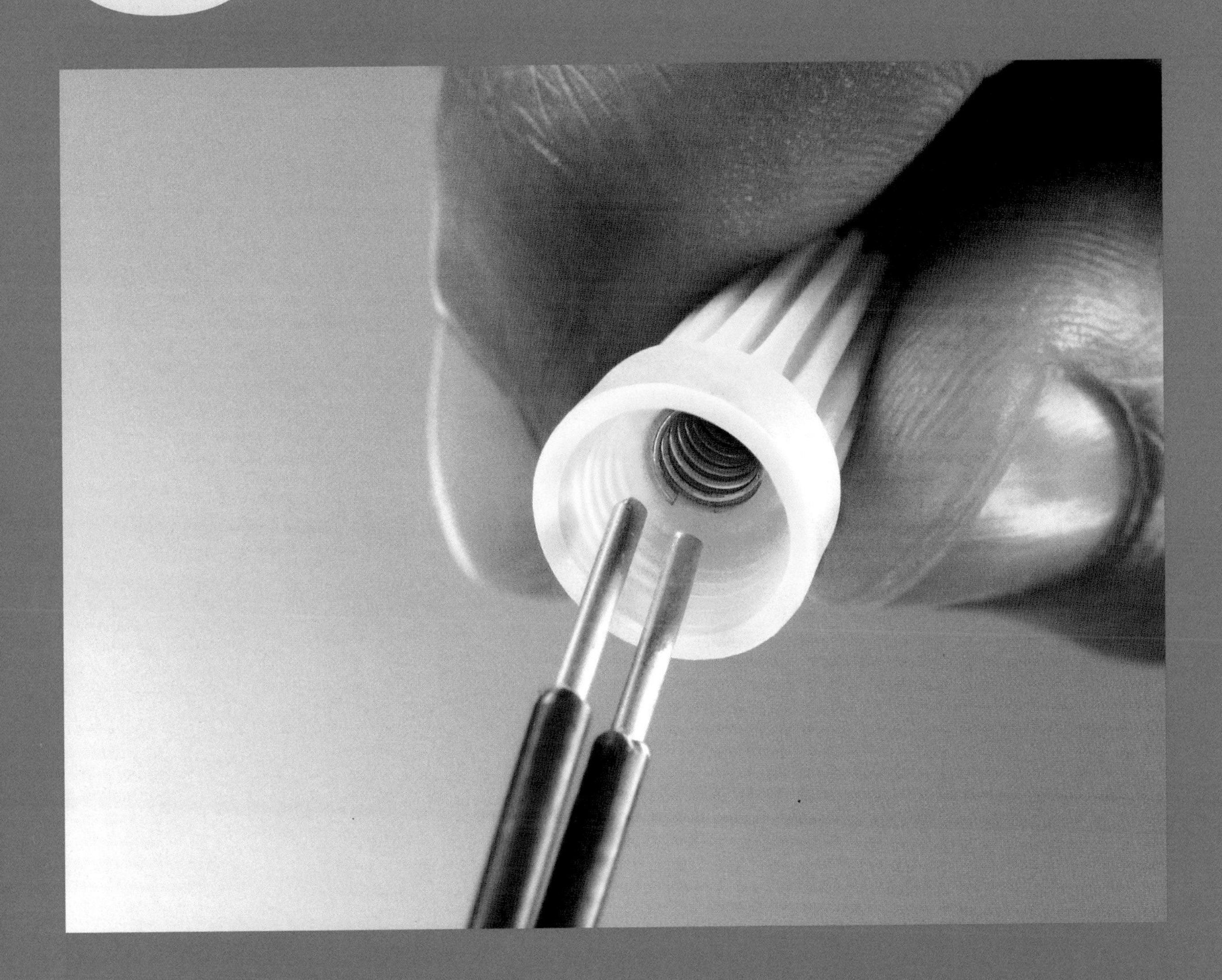

IN THIS CHAPTER

You Can Fix It 74
Fast & easy lamp fixes

Ask Handyman 78
Adjustable electrical boxes, stop GFCI tripping, fluorescent bulbs and more ...

4 Ways to Hide Speaker Wire 80

Troubleshoot a Dead Outlet 82

Surface-mounted Wiring 86

Using Tools: Tips for Safer Wiring 92

Handy Hints 95
No-rattle ceiling fan, wire organizer and more ...

Great Goofs 94, 96

You Can Fix It™

FAST & EASY LAMP FIXES

With a handful of parts and about 30 minutes, you can fix almost any lamp—and make it safe as well.

When a lamp flickers or doesn't light up at all, chances are that one of the parts has gone bad. In the next few pages, we'll show you how to replace all the key parts. But don't overlook the obvious: no power or a bad bulb. Try a new bulb and plug the lamp into a different outlet before taking things apart.

If that doesn't work, operate the switch. It should turn on and off without flickering. Next, unplug the lamp and inspect the cord and plug. If you can't find any obvious problems, replace all the electrical parts. It only takes a few more minutes than replacing just one, and the parts usually cost less than $10.

1. REPLACE A CRACKED CORD

The insulation on cords becomes stiff and brittle as it ages. Eventually, it cracks and might even flake off the wire, creating a shock and fire hazard. *Don't* try to solve this problem with electrical tape. Replace the cord. Cord replacement is also the best fix for a bad cord-mounted switch. You can buy a cord that has a switch attached.

Save yourself some time by buying a cord that's already connected to a plug ($3). Lamp cord sold at home centers and hardware stores is usually 18 gauge. That's large enough to handle 840 watts of lighting. If you have one of those rare lamps that uses bulbs totaling more than 840 watts, have it fixed at a lamp repair shop. Make sure the cord is protected by a screw-on bushing where it enters the threaded tube and by a plastic or rubber grommet through the lamp body (**Photo 1**). Without a bushing or grommet, sharp edges can cut into the cord's insulation. If you can't find a bushing or grommet the right size at a home center or hardware store, see "Lamp Part Sources," p. 77.

To replace the cord, you'll take most of the socket replacement steps shown on pp. 76 and 77. Remove the socket from its base, cut the old cord and pull it out. Feed the cord up through the threaded tube in the lamp's body (**Photo 2**). Then connect the new cord to the socket. Most cords come with the ends already stripped, so you won't even need a wire stripper.

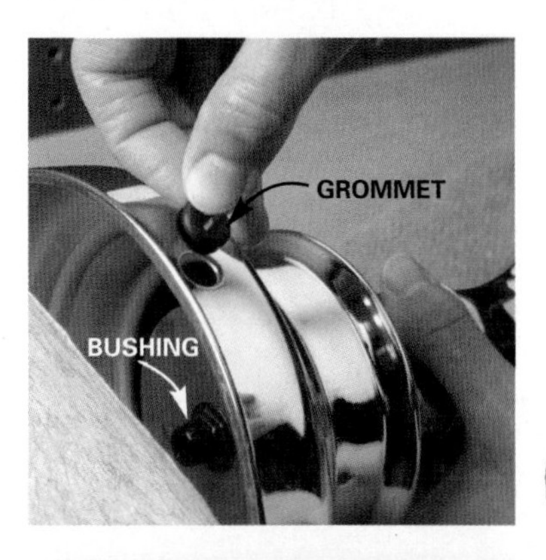

1 CUT the old cord at the socket and pull it out. Push a grommet into the cord hole and screw a bushing onto the tube, if they're missing.

2 FEED the new cord through the threaded tube and socket base. Connect the cord to the socket as shown on p. 76.

2. REPLACE A PROBLEM PLUG

Plugs on lamp cords often have a weak point where the cord enters the plug. Pulling and flexing can break the wires at this point, leaving you with a lamp that flickers when you jiggle the cord. The cure is to replace the plug. To do this safely, choose a polarized plug ($5). A polarized plug has one blade that's wider than the other so it fits into an outlet only one way (**photo**, p. 76). Before you buy a plug, take a close look at the cord. Along with other labeling, you should find "SPT-1" or "SPT-2." This refers to the thickness of the cord's sheathing, and the plug you buy must have the same listing so it will fit over the sheathing. If you can't find the SPT listing, replace the entire cord as shown at left.

The plug you buy may not look exactly like the one shown here, but installing it will be similar. Be sure to read the manufacturer's instructions. When you split the two halves of the cord (**Photo 1**), be careful not to expose any wire. If you do, cut back the cord and start over. Strip the wire ends (see **Photo 3**, p. 76) and make connections (**Photo 2**). The neutral wire must connect to the wider blade. See p. 76 for help in identifying the neutral wire. If you're not able to identify it, replace the entire cord.

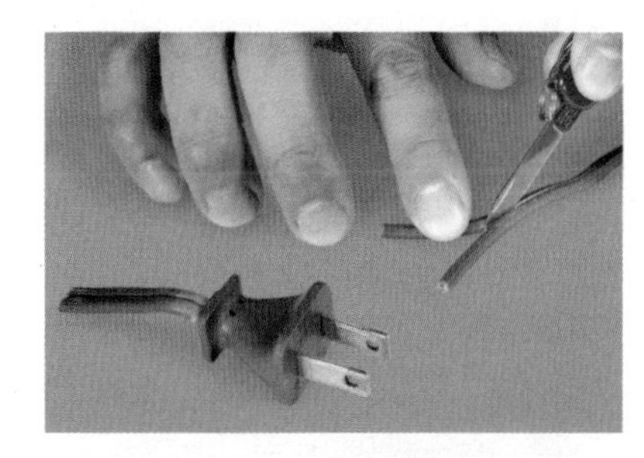

1 CUT the cord a couple of inches from the plug. Then split about an inch of cord with a pocketknife and strip off 3/4 in. of insulation.

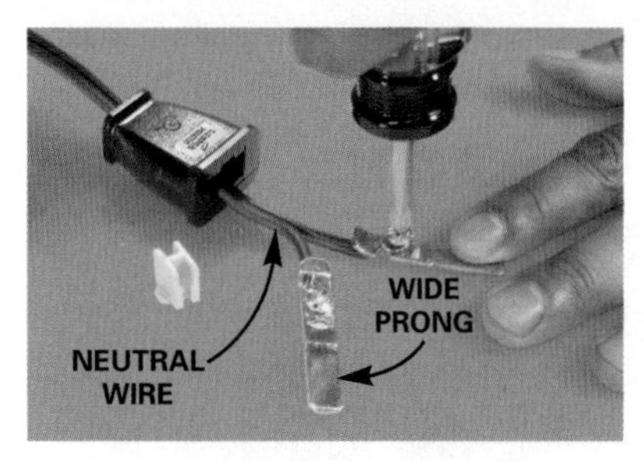

2 WRAP the wires clockwise around the terminal screws of the new plug and tighten. The neutral wire must connect to the wider prong.

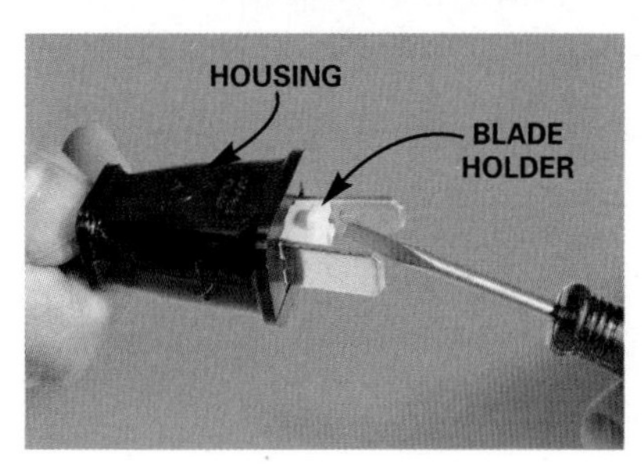

3 SLIP the blades into the housing and push the blade holder into place.

3. REPLACE A FAULTY SOCKET

A lamp socket itself can go bad, but more often it's the switch inside the socket. Either way, the solution is replacement. A new socket costs about $5. Regardless of the existing switch type, you can choose a push-through switch, a pull chain, a turn knob or a three-way turn knob that provides two brightness levels. You can also choose a socket without a switch and install a switched cord instead.

CAUTION: Pull the plug before working on a lamp.

The old socket shell is supposed to pop out of its base with a squeeze and a tug, but you might have to pry it out with a screwdriver (Photo 1). The socket base can be stubborn too. It's screwed onto a threaded tube that runs down through the lamp's body. When you try to unscrew it, you might unscrew the nut at the other end of the tube instead. This will allow the parts of the lamp body to come apart, but that isn't a big problem. Just use a pliers to twist the base off the tube (Photo 2), reassemble the lamp body and screw on the new socket base to hold it all together.

When you connect the new socket, don't reuse the bare ends of the wires. Some of the tiny strands of wire are

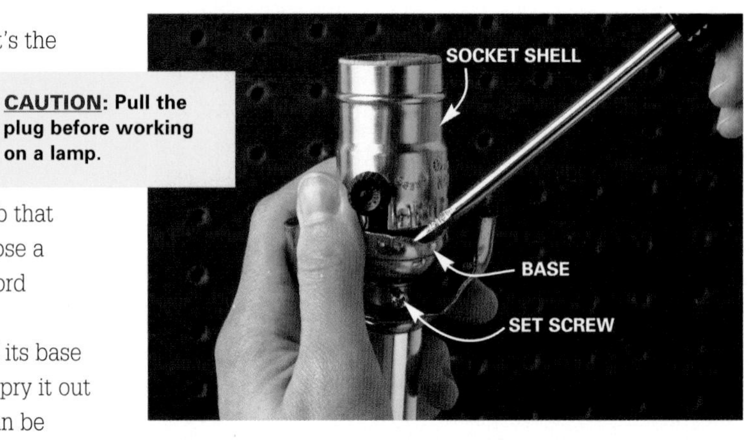

1 PRY the socket shell out of its base. Cut the wires to remove the socket. Then loosen the setscrew so you can unscrew the socket base.

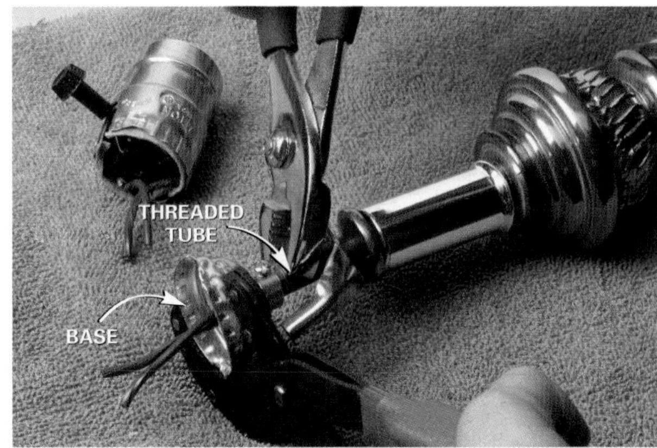

2 UNSCREW the socket base from the threaded tube. If the base won't spin off by hand, grab the tube and the base with a pliers to spin it free. Then screw on the new base and tighten the setscrew.

3 STRIP OFF 1/2 in. of insulation with a wire stripper and twist the wire strands together. If you pull off any wire strands while stripping, cut back the cord and start over.

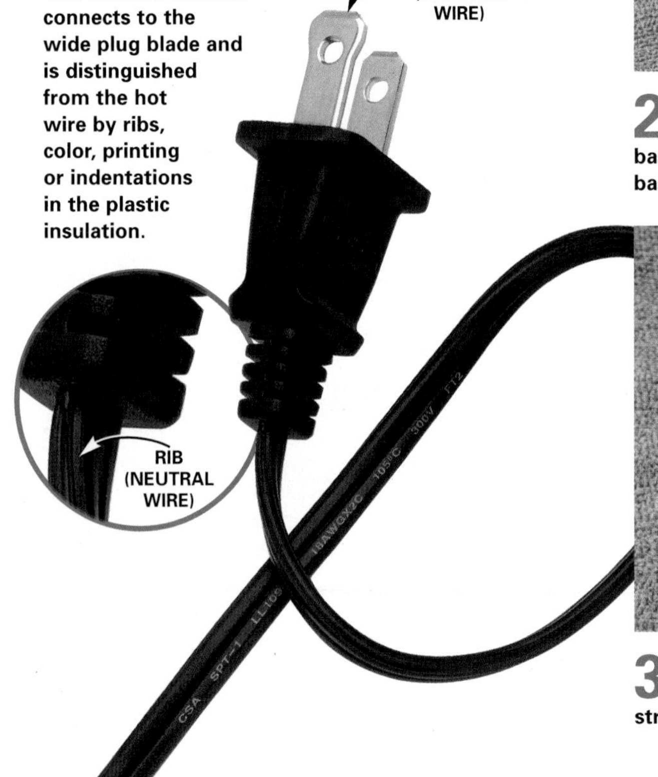

THE NEUTRAL WIRE connects to the wide plug blade and is distinguished from the hot wire by ribs, color, printing or indentations in the plastic insulation.

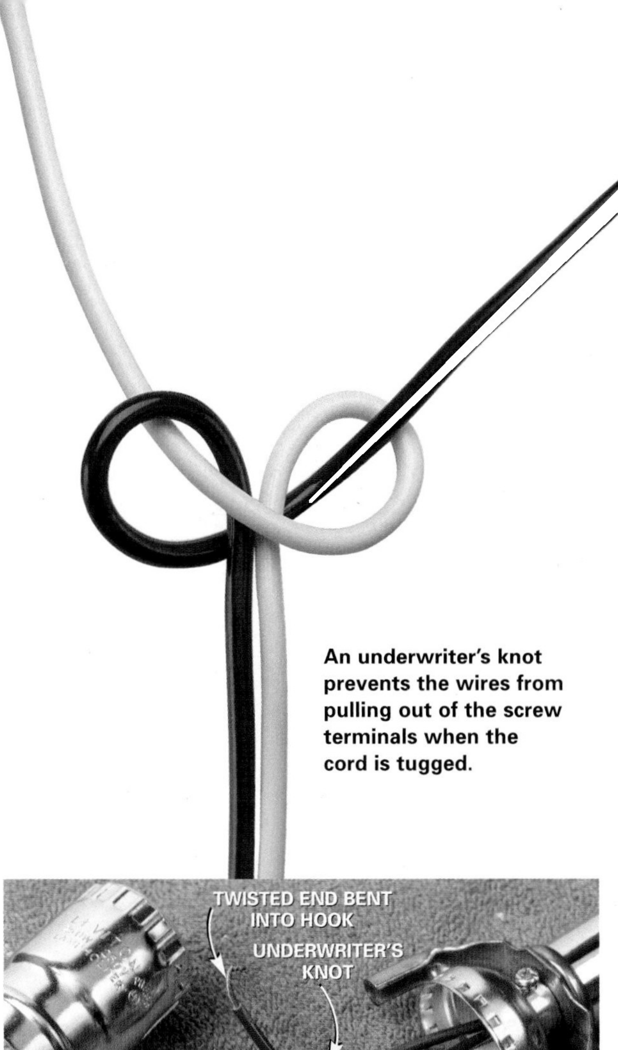

An underwriter's knot prevents the wires from pulling out of the screw terminals when the cord is tugged.

probably broken. Cut them off and strip away 1/2 in. of insulation with a wire stripper (Photo 3). Using a wire stripper is almost foolproof, as long as you choose the correct pair of notches to bite through the wire's insulation. Most wire strippers are sized for solid wire, rather than the slightly larger stranded wire used in lamp cords. You can get around this problem by using the next larger pair of notches. Since most lamp wires are 18 gauge, start with the notches labeled 16. If the stripper won't remove the insulation, use smaller notches. If the stripper removes strands of wire, cut off an inch of cord and start over using larger notches.

When you connect the wires to the new socket, the neutral wire must connect to the silver screw (Photo 4). To identify the neutral wire, start at the plug. The wider plug blade is connected to the neutral wire, and you'll find that the neutral wire is distinguished from the "hot" wire (photo, p. 76). The two wires may be different colors, there may be printing on one or the other, or there may be tiny ribs or indentations in the plastic covering the neutral wire. If your old plug blades are of equal width, replace the plug and cord along with the socket.

4 TIE an underwriter's knot in the cord. Then connect the wires by wrapping them clockwise around the screws and tightening. Connect the neutral wire to the silver screw.

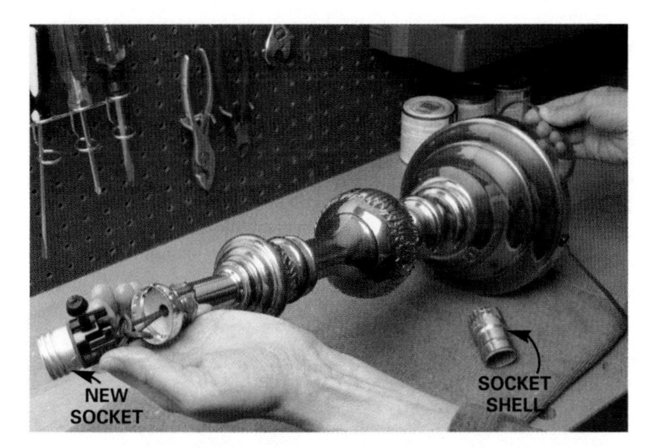

5 PULL the excess cord down through the lamp. Slip the insulation sleeve and socket shell over the socket and snap the shell into the base.

Lamp part sources

Home centers and hardware stores carry basic lamp parts like sockets, cords and plugs. For hard-to-find parts and a wider selection of basic parts, visit a lamp repair shop (in the Yellow Pages under "Lamps & Shades, Repair") or these Web sites:

- **www.grandbrass.com**
  Shop on-line and order on-line or by phone: (212) 226-2567
- **www.paxtonhardware.com**
  Shop on-line and order by phone: (800) 241-9741

Ask Handyman™

ADJUSTABLE ELECTRICAL BOXES

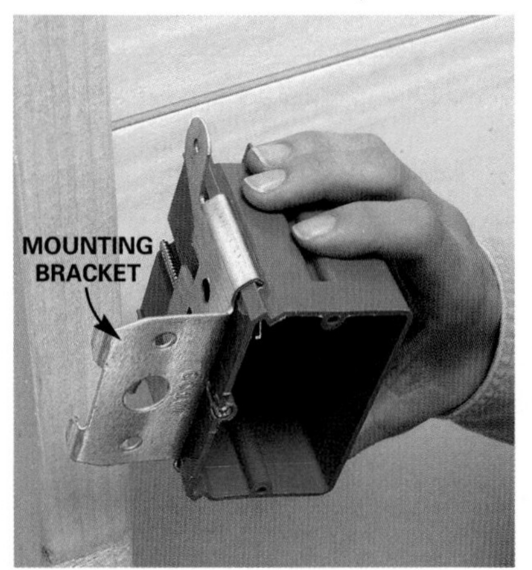

We're wiring a room addition but haven't decided yet on the finished wall surface. It might be 1/2-in. drywall, 3/4-in. wood paneling or something else. How far out should I set the electrical boxes?

According to electrical code, the box face must be flush with combustible surfaces and no more than 1/4 in. from noncombustible surfaces. To keep your options open, install an adjustable box, such as the Adjust-A-Box from Carlon, shown here. They're easier to install and have a stronger mount than conventional nail-on boxes. That's because a built-in steel bracket clips the box to the stud and holds it there while you screw or nail it to the wood. After the wall is finished, you just turn the adjusting screw to move the box in or out until it's perfectly flush with the finished surface. It's really a good idea on walls you plan to tile, panel or face with a cabinet. But at about $2.50 for a single box and $3.50 for a double, they cost much more than standard boxes. So use them judiciously! Adjust-A-Box boxes are available at home centers and hardware stores.

STOP GFCI TRIPPING

Help. Our hair dryer keeps tripping the GFCI outlet in the bathroom. What is causing this, and how can I end this frustration?

The cause is either a problem hair dryer or a worn-out GFCI outlet. To determine the culprit, follow these troubleshooting steps.

Plug the dryer into another GFCI outlet in a different bathroom, the kitchen or the garage and run it. If that GFCI also trips, the dryer is at fault and should be replaced. If the dryer runs normally, the bathroom GFCI outlet is faulty and should be replaced.

It's also possible that the hair dryer is causing the bathroom's circuit breaker to trip. If this occurs, the dryer (along with the other lights, fans and outlets using power on that breaker) exceeds the breaker's rating. This happens more in older homes with bathrooms on 15-amp circuit breakers, because a modern hair dryer—by itself—can use more power than a 15-amp circuit can supply. The bathroom outlets in homes built after the mid-'90s are required to have dedicated 20-amp circuits for this very reason.

To solve this dilemma, have an electrician run a new, 20-amp circuit. Or, get a hair dryer that draws less than 1,441 watts. The label on the box will tell you.

SCREW-ON COVER (750 LUMENS WITH COVER)

15 WATTS (900 LUMENS WITHOUT COVER)

HOW TO CHOOSE COMPACT FLUORESCENT BULBS

I've looked at compact fluorescent bulbs at the home center, but I'm not sure what to buy. How do I know which provides as much light as a regular 60- or 100-watt bulb?

First, look at the lumen rating, not the bulb wattage, to compare "real" light output. Then buy a compact fluorescent lamp (CFL) with 20 percent more lumens than the incandescent bulb you want to replace. For example, if a 60-watt incandescent bulb has 870 lumens, buy a CFL with at least 1,050 lumens.

If you follow wattage guidelines on the package (such as a 13- to 17-watt CFL equals a 60-watt; a 25- to 27-watt CFL equals a 100-watt), you may not be satisfied with the light output. This is especially true if you're over 50, because older eyes take in only half as much light as 20-year-old eyes.

Another reason you need more lumens is that the CFL will dim over time. It will lose 20 to 25 percent lumen power after 4,000 hours (40 percent of a CFL's 10,000-hour-rated life). Incandescent bulbs do not lose lumens, but their life is extremely short compared with that of CFLs.

Finally, while CFLs can last up to 10 times longer than incandescent bulbs, certain circumstances can shorten their life:

- Frequent on-off switching (it's best to use CFLs only in lights that are on more than 1.5 hours per day).
- Excessive vibration or impact (you may not want to install CFLs near doors).
- High humidity levels.

COMPARE the lumen ratings listed on the package and buy a CFL with more lumens than the incandescent bulb you want to replace.

Incandescent 870 lumens

CFL 800 lumens

CFL 800 lumens

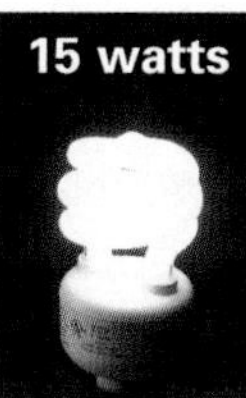

CFL 930 lumens

AIRTIGHT ELECTRICAL BOXES

Our building inspector told me that I need to use airtight electrical boxes. What are these?

Some building codes now require these special boxes to reduce air and moisture movement in exterior walls. Here are two options:

First is a large plastic box (top photo) that you nail to the face of a stud, then install a standard electrical box inside it. It's large enough to handle multi-gang electrical boxes. Cut a slit in the side of the box and push the cable through it and wire the box as you normally would. Caulk around the cable where it penetrates the box to seal it. If you're using a plastic vapor barrier, seal it to the box apron with an acoustic (non-hardening) caulk. If you're applying drywall without the vapor barrier behind it, caulk the drywall directly to the box.

Another option is an airtight electrical box (bottom photo) that uses a soft rubber gasket that seals to the drywall. The box also is wrapped in a rubber skin that seals the cables. Make a small slit in the rubber and push the cable through. Install and wire it as you would a standard box.

You can also order these boxes at electrical supply stores.

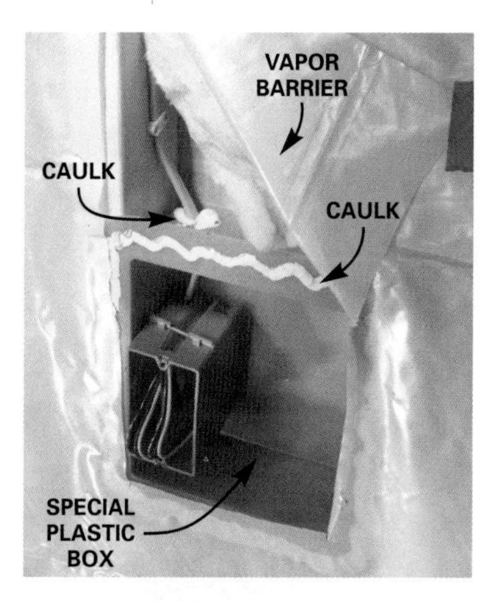

THE LESSCO AIR-VAPOR BARRIER BOX is nailed to the stud and allows use of standard electrical boxes. Slit the top to insert wire, then use caulk to seal as shown. These boxes cost $2.25 to $2.50 each. (Visit www.lessco-airtight.com or call 920-533-8690 to find a local dealer.)

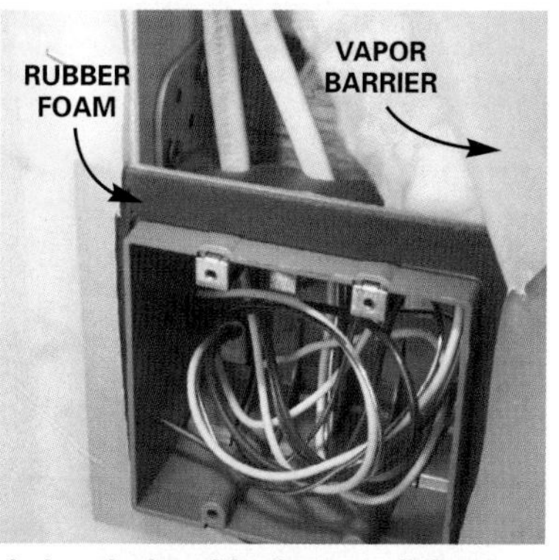

NUTEK'S AIRTIGHT ELECTRICAL BOXES use a foam gasket around the drywall flange and where the cable enters to seal out air. To find a dealer for these single, double and triple boxes (models 1FWSW, 2FWSW and 3FWSW), visit www.tnbelectricalworld.tnb.com; click on "Distributor Locator." Or, call (800) 816-7809. The boxes cost $2.50 to $5.50 each.

4 WAYS TO **HIDE SPEAKER WIRE**

Products and tips for keeping wire undercover

by **Gary Wentz**

Speakers placed around a room sound great, but all that wire can be an eyesore, an annoyance when you vacuum, even a tripping hazard. You may be able to keep low-voltage wires out of sight and out of your path simply by running them under rugs and behind furniture. If not, here are some solutions for hiding speaker wire —or just about any other type of low-voltage wiring (for phones, thermostats, doorbells, low-voltage lighting, etc.).

RUN WIRE INSIDE WALLS

Getting wire inside walls takes more time than other methods, but it lets you run wire anywhere invisibly, even past doorways. And it doesn't have to be a huge project. If there's an unfinished basement below the room, you can run wires through the basement and into walls. First cut holes in the wall to accept junction boxes. Center the holes 8 to 10 in. from the floor, and you'll be able to drill down into the basement with a spade bit and extension. Then push a stiff wire (such as wire from a coat hanger) up from the basement and use it to pull the speaker wire down into the basement. You can also run wire through the attic and feed it down into walls, but that cramped, insulation-filled space makes the job a lot more difficult. Any wire used inside walls must be UL-listed.

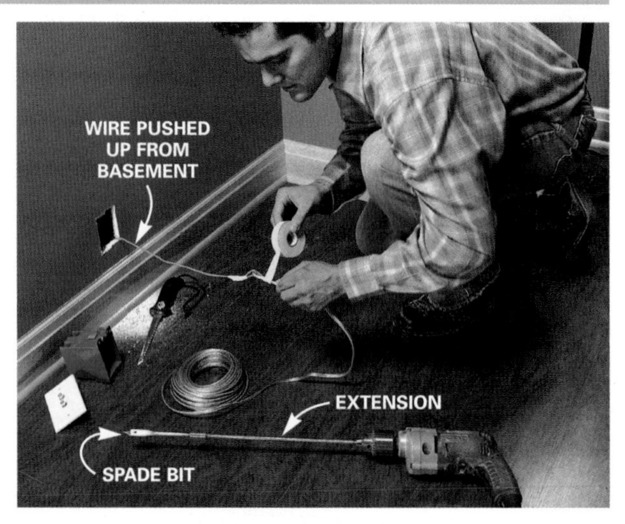

TUCK WIRE BETWEEN CARPET AND BASEBOARD

In rooms with wall-to-wall carpet, you can often force wire between the carpet and the baseboard. This is the fastest, easiest way to hide wire. It's also the least certain, and the only way to know if it will work is to give it a try. There may be enough space for heavy-duty cable, or you may find it tough to push in even the smallest wire. If there's a doorway between the power source and the speaker, run the wire all the way around the other side of the room to avoid it. A ruler or paint stir stick makes a good wire-pushing tool. Don't use anything sharp that might cut into the wire's insulation.

Cord holder

Here's a good way to tidy up lamp cords or speaker wires and keep them up off the floor. Slit short lengths of clear plastic tubing and fasten them to your baseboard with a staple or tack.

INSTALL PLASTIC RACEWAYS

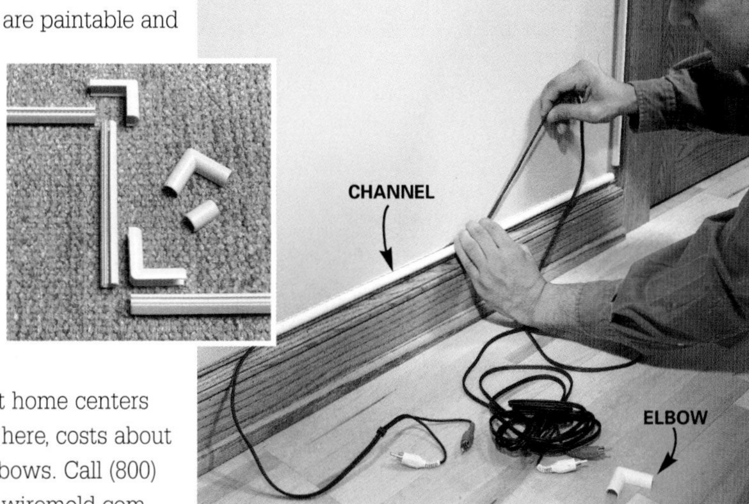

Raceways come in a range of sizes and shapes, are paintable and often have an adhesive backing for quick installation. You'll hardly notice a narrow version like the one shown here if it runs along the top of baseboard. Raceways are a lot more noticeable when they run up walls or around doorways, though. Whether you paint your raceway to match the wall or the trim, avoid fussy brushwork by painting before you install it. Touching up any nicks and scratches after installation is easy.

A variety of raceway systems are available at home centers and hardware stores. Cordmate, the one shown here, costs about $25 for 12 ft. of channel and an assortment of elbows. Call (800) 617-1768 or visit the company's Web site: www.wiremold.com.

STICK SUPER-SLIM WIRE TO WALLS

Flat, adhesive-backed wire comes in versions for just about any low-voltage purpose. The speaker wire shown here is thinner than a credit card. You can paint it, wallpaper over it or even skim a layer of joint compound over it to make it completely invisible. There's one situation where this wire becomes noticeable: If you need to turn a corner (to run wire up and over a doorway, for example), you have to fold the wire back over itself. That folded corner creates a slight lump. At the speaker end, simply leave speaker jacks hanging off the wall. Or for a neater look, install junction boxes. Then run the wire right into them and connect the wire to a faceplate with built-in speaker jacks. Flat wire (called Taperwire) is available at www.21stcenturygoods.com, (866-999-8422). Sixteen feet of the Gekko Flat Wire shown here costs $18.

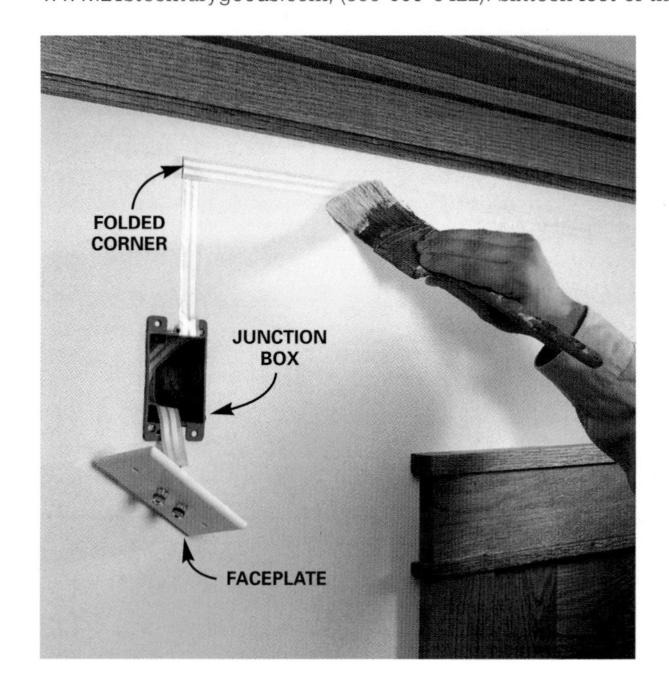

TROUBLESHOOT A **DEAD OUTLET**

Avoid a $100 service call. Try these simple remedies before you call an electrician.

by **Jeff Gorton**

When an outlet goes dead, it's easy to jump to conclusions and assume the worst. But more often than not, the problem is something simple, and you can save the cost of a service call just by taking a few steps to trace the cause. Don't worry if you're not comfortable doing electrical work. Better than half the time you'll solve the problem without even lifting a tool. We'll show you how to start your search for the problem by checking in the most likely places. If that doesn't work, we'll show you where to look for loose connections that may be to blame, and how to fix them. Of course, there will always be problems that are best left to an electrician. But if you take these steps first, there's a good chance you'll find the solution.

STEP 1: See if other outlets are dead

Before you head for the circuit breakers, take a few minutes to check if other outlets, lights or appliances are affected. Switch lights on and off and test nearby outlets for power (use a voltage tester or plug in a lamp to test the outlets). Unplug lamps and appliances from dead outlets to eliminate the possibility that a short or overload from one of them is causing the problem. Note the location of dead outlets or mark them with a piece of masking tape so you'll be able to find them again after you've turned off the power.

Replace burned-out fuses

Look inside the fuse for charred glass or a broken filament—evidence of a blown fuse. Unscrew the suspect fuse and replace it with one of the same type and amperage.

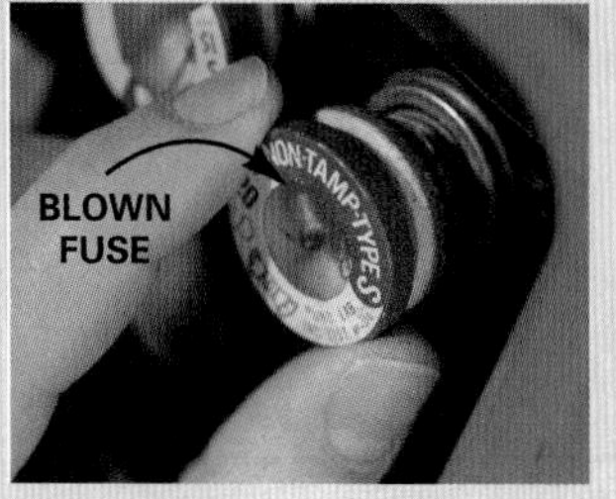

STEP 2: Check the circuit breakers

After you unplug all the devices from the dead outlets, the next step is to check for a tripped circuit breaker or blown fuse. You'll find the circuit breakers or fuses in the main electrical panel, which is usually located near where the electrical wires enter the house. Garages, basements and laundry rooms are common locations. Locate the panel and open the metal door to reveal the fuses or circuit breakers. Photos 1 – 4 show a typical main panel and the process for resetting a tripped circuit breaker. Remember to turn off your computer before you switch the circuit breakers on and off.

Tripped circuit breakers aren't always apparent. If you don't see a tripped breaker, firmly press every breaker to the "off" position (Photo 3).Then switch them back on. If the tripped breaker won't reset without tripping again, there could be a potentially dangerous short circuit or ground fault condition. Switch the circuit breaker off until you've located the problem. In most cases, a tripped circuit breaker is caused by a temporary overload on the circuit or a short circuit in some device plugged into the circuit. But in rare cases, a loose wire in an electrical box could be causing the problem. Follow the photos in Step 4, p. 84, to look for and repair loose connections.

1 LOCATE the circuit breaker box (or fuse box) and open the door to search for tripped circuit breakers.

2 LOCATE tripped breakers by looking for breaker handles not lined up with the rest. Push breaker handles toward "on" position. Tripped breakers "give" a little rather than feel solid.

3 THE FIRST STEP in resetting a tripped breaker is to switch it off. Don't just flick the handle; press the handle firmly to the "off" position. You should hear a click.

4 FINALLY, RESET the breaker by pushing the handle firmly to "on." It should line up with all the rest. If it "pops" back to the tripped position, there's a problem in the wiring or in something that's plugged into the circuit.

STEP 3: Check the GFCIs

GFCI (short for "ground fault circuit interrupter") outlets, are required in areas where shock hazards are greatest. They protect against deadly electrical shocks by sensing leaks in the electrical current and immediately tripping to shut off power. But it's easy to overlook a tripped GFCI as the source of a dead outlet problem. That's because in areas where GFCIs are required, electricians often connect additional standard outlets to one GFCI outlet. A current leak at any of the outlets will trip the GFCI and cause all outlets connected to it to go dead. These GFCI-protected outlets are supposed to be labeled (Photo 1), but the label often falls off.

Look for GFCIs in bathrooms, kitchens, basements, garages and on the home's exterior. Test and reset every GFCI you find (Photo 2). If the GFCI "reset" button doesn't pop out when you press the "test" button, there may be no power to the GFCI or you may have a bad GFCI. If the "reset" button trips again every time you press it, there may be a dangerous current leak on the circuit. In either case, solving the problem requires additional electrical testing that we won't cover here. Refer to electrical repair manuals or call an electrician. If resetting the GFCIs didn't power up your dead outlet, then the last resort is to look for loose connections.

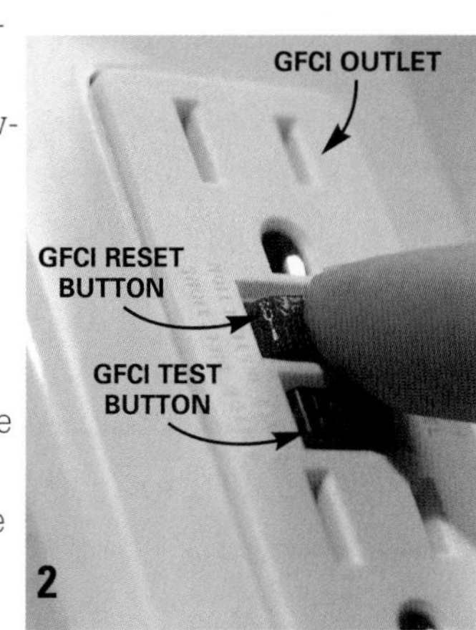

STEP 4: Still no power? Look for a bad connection

If checking the breakers and resetting the GFCIs haven't restored power to the outlet, the next step, without getting into circuit testing, is to remove the outlet from the box and look for loose connections.

We'll show you three common types of loose connections: loose terminal screws, loose stab-in connections, and loose wires at wire connectors. You may find one or more of these when you remove your outlet and look in the electrical box.

CAUTION: If you have aluminum wiring, don't mess with it! Call in a licensed pro who's certified to work with it. This wiring is dull gray, not the dull orange that's characteristic of copper.

Loose or broken wires

The first problem we show is a loose connection under the outlet's terminal screw. In Photo 2, you can see the charred outlet and melted wire insulation that are a result of heat generated by the loose connection. These telltale signs aren't always present, though, which is why you should double-check the connections by gently bending each wire to see if it moves under the screw.

If you do discover a loose connection at an outlet, whether it's at the screw terminal or a stab-in connection, we recommend replacing the outlet with a new one. That's because loose connections almost always create excess heat that could damage the outlet and lead to future problems. Photo 3 shows how to install a new outlet.

If the outlet you're replacing is wired like the one shown in Photo 2, with pairs of hot and neutral wires (wires under all four screws), connect the pairs of like-colored wires along with a third 6-in. length of wire, called a pigtail, under one wire connector (Photo 2, p. 85). Then connect the loose end of each pigtail to the appropriate outlet screw.

This method reduces the chance that a loose connection under a screw will cause a problem with other outlets on the circuit.

1 FIRST make sure all computers are turned off and everyone in the house knows you'll be turning off the power. Then switch off the main circuit breaker. Keep a flashlight handy because all the lights will go out.

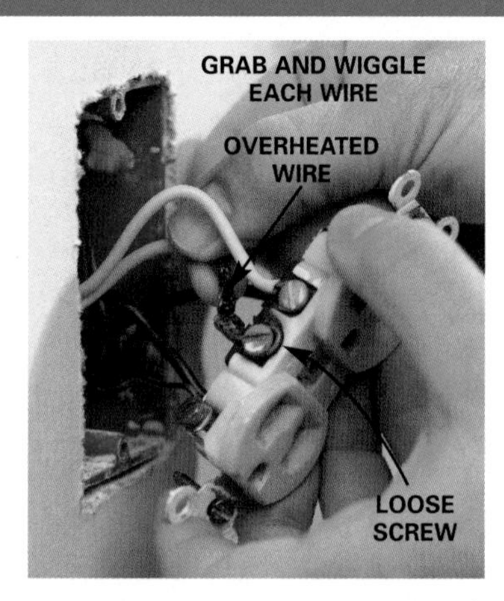

2 INSPECT screw terminals for broken or loose wires. Carefully bend the wire at each terminal to see if it's loose (it will turn under the screw or the screw will move). Also look for broken, burned or corroded wires or screws.

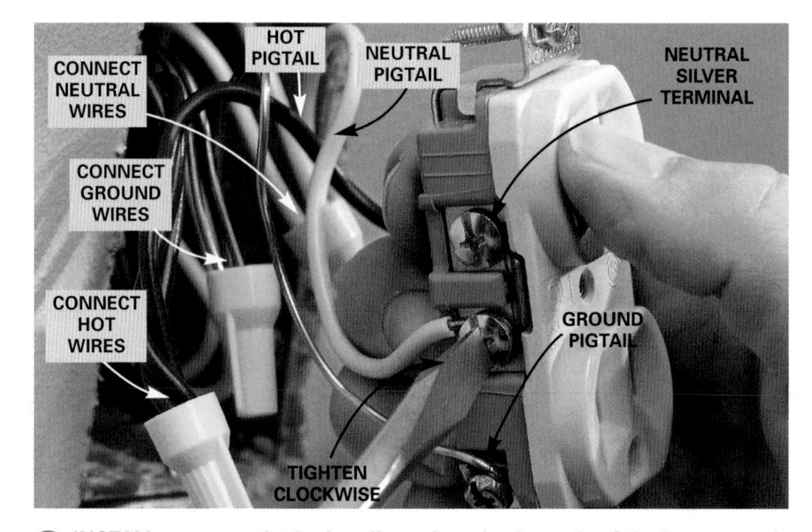

3 INSTALL a new outlet by bending a loop in the ends of the hot, neutral and ground wires. Connect the hot (black) wire to the brass screw, the neutral white wire to the silver screw and the ground wire to the green ground screw. Loop the wires clockwise around the screws and tighten.

Check for simple solutions first

Shortly after moving into our house, we had an electrical problem. The exterior outlets and bathroom lights didn't work. I knew enough to check for tripped circuit breakers and GFCI outlets. But I couldn't find the problem. I was just about to start pulling apart the wiring when I double-checked the main panel and noticed the GFCI circuit breaker up in the corner. Sure enough, the GFCI breaker was protecting the bathroom and exterior outlets and needed to be reset. I was lucky this time—I've been known to remove outlets and start to test circuits and then discover the simpler solution. The moral of the story is, don't jump to conclusions. The fix for a dead outlet is usually simpler than you think.

Loose wires at the stab-in connections

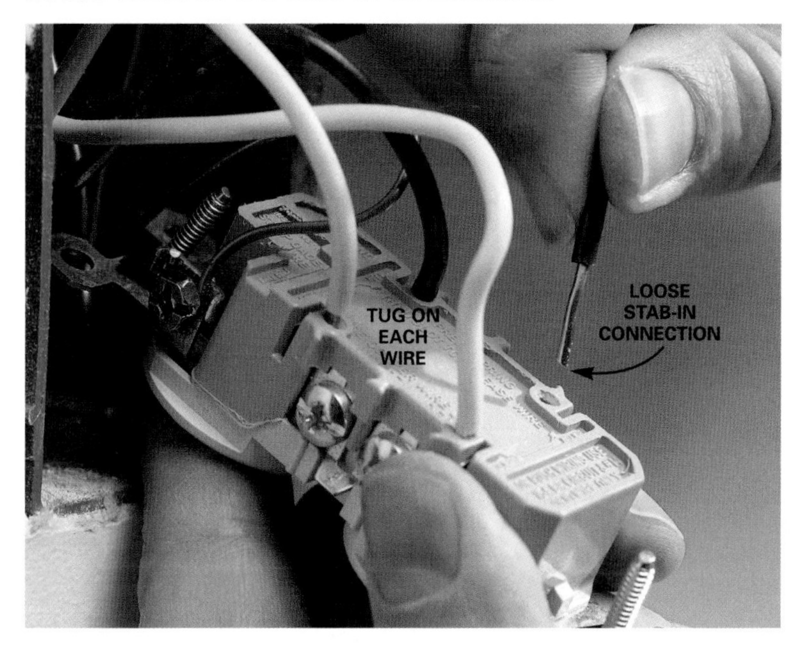

As a timesaver for electricians, some outlets can be wired by pressing stripped wires into holes on the back of the outlet. This wiring method is allowed by the electrical code, but it isn't good practice since these stab-in connections can loosen over time and cause problems. Look for these stab-in connections as you troubleshoot your dead outlet. Tug each wire to check for loose connections. If you find loose stab-in connections, don't just reinsert the wire. Instead, cut and strip the end of the wire and connect it to the screw terminal on the side of the outlet. Or better yet, cut and strip all of the wires and connect them to a new outlet (**Photo 3**, p. 84).

Check wire connectors for loose wires

A wire that's come loose from a wire connector is another problem that can cause a dead outlet. Follow the steps in **Photos 1 and 2** to find and fix this type of loose connection. If you don't find any loose connections in this box and are still anxious to pursue the problem, expand your search to other outlets in the vicinity (start with the ones you marked earlier with masking tape). Make sure to turn off the main circuit breaker (**Photo 1**, p. 84) when you're checking for loose connections.

When you're done looking for loose connections, reinstall the outlets and switch the main circuit breaker back on. Now test the outlets again to see if you've solved the problem. If you still have dead outlets, it's time to call an electrician.

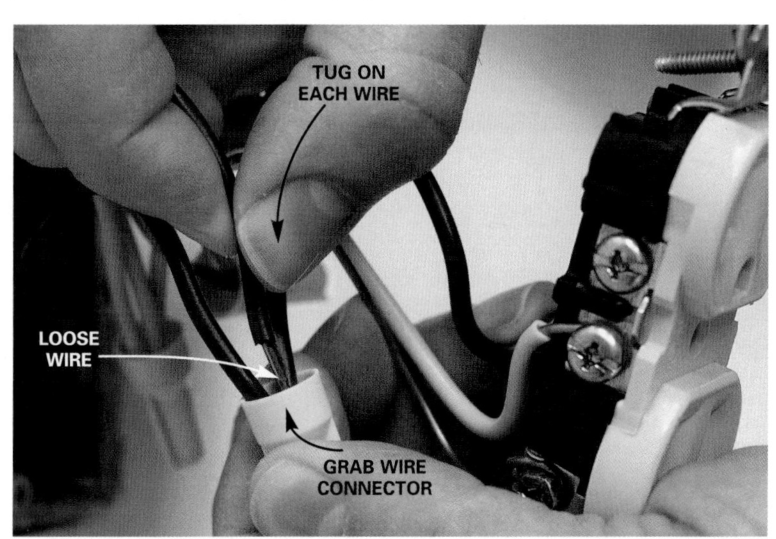

1 GRAB the wire connector. Tug on each wire in the bundle to see if any are loose. If you discover a loose wire, remove the wire connector. Cut and strip all the wires in the bundle to expose 1/2 in. to 3/4 in. of fresh copper wire (check the instructions on the wire connector container for the exact stripping length).

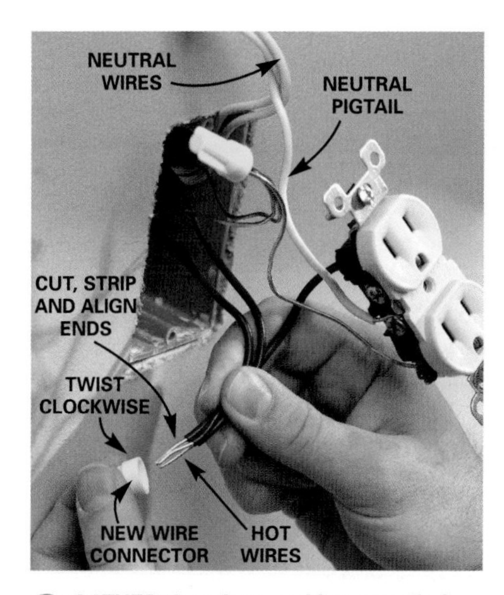

2 GATHER the wires, making sure their ends are lined up, and twist on a new wire connector. Twist clockwise. Match the connector to the number of wires by reading the label on the wire connector packaging.

SURFACE-MOUNTED WIRING

With metal conduit, you can run power almost anywhere. We'll show you how to do it safely and easily.

by **Kurt Lawton**

While it's usually easier and neater to run cables inside walls, sometimes surface wiring is the best way to go. It eliminates the hassle of tearing open finished walls and ceilings, and it solves the problem of running power across masonry surfaces. Plus, it eliminates the risk of running extension cords. The easiest and least expensive surface-mount system is EMT (electrical metallic tubing) conduit with metal boxes for receptacles and switches.

In this article, we'll show you the tools, materials and techniques you'll need to cut, bend and connect a metal conduit system, as well as run wire in it. To illustrate, we chose a garage workbench area that was poorly lit and underpowered. To upgrade it, we added seven receptacles and a switch.

We've kept our conduit route and bends very simple for this job, but you can apply the same techniques to a more complex design with a longer run.

Keep in mind that electrical wiring is not a project for novices. You should have an understanding of basic wiring

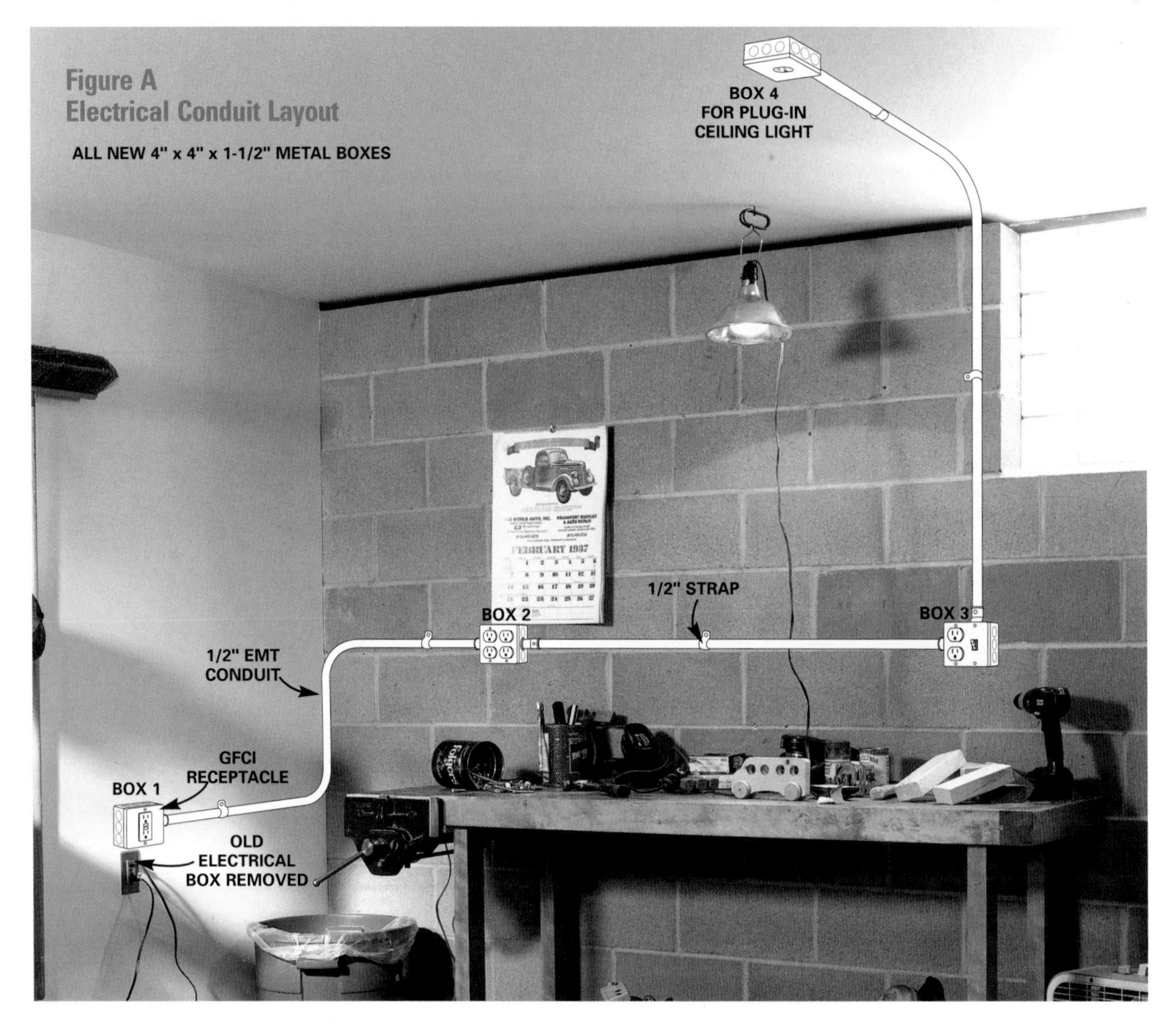

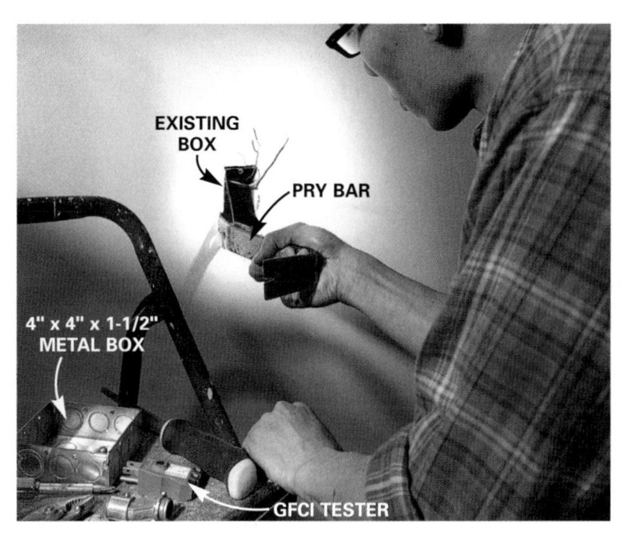

1 TURN OFF the power and remove the old receptacle. Pry the top and bottom box nails away from the stud to remove the box. Pull the wires through the wall opening.

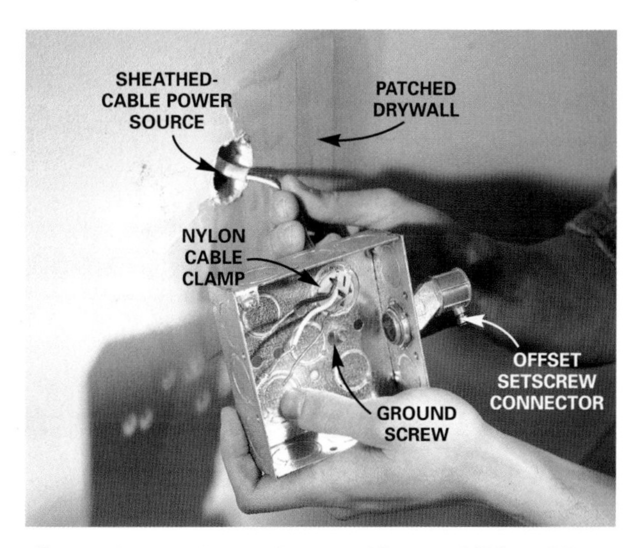

2 REMOVE 1/2-in. knockouts and insert a 3/8-in. cable clamp and an offset setscrew connector. Push the sheathed cable through the clamp and into the box.

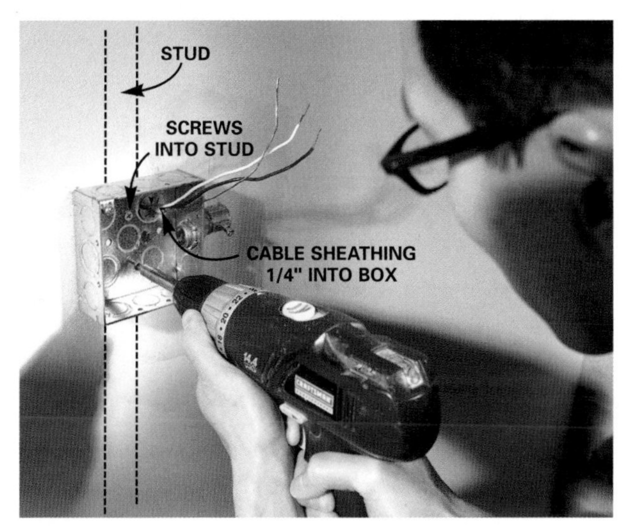

3 MOUNT the box to the wall by driving two 1-5/8 in. drywall screws through the drywall and into the stud. Keep the box level.

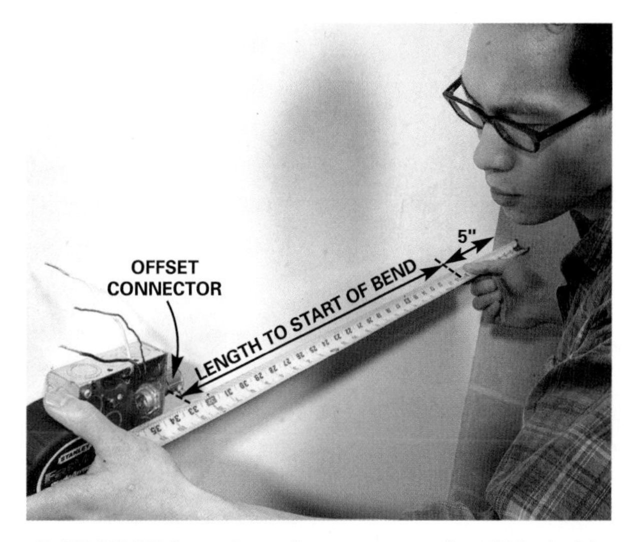

4 MEASURE from the wall corner to a point 3/4 in. inside of the offset connector. Subtract 5 in. for the 90-degree bend, then mark that length on the conduit.

techniques, how to determine circuit size and evaluate loads, and know safety precautions. And always check with your local building department to get a permit and an inspection for all work you do.

For safety, exposed electrical wiring (in the garage, basement and outdoors) must be protected by sturdy tubing. We chose 1/2-in. EMT metal conduit for this project because it's easy to bend and assemble (and take apart if you make a mistake!). PVC conduit is another good option, but it differs in that you glue the joints.

Plan your run

The first step is to find your power source. We tapped in to a 15-amp garage outlet receptacle to power the "light-duty" workbench area. If you copy this project and operate power-hungry tools such as circular or table saws, you may need to tap in to or run a new 20-amp circuit (see "Power-Hungry Tools," p. 89). Check the circuit breaker in the main electrical panel to determine the circuit size. If you're uncertain about circuit sizing, consult a licensed electrician.

Next, sketch the conduit route from your power source to the new electrical box locations and note the length of the run and all the boxes, connectors and wire you need. Our materials included 1/2-in. EMT conduit (10 ft. long, $1.25), 4 x 4 x 1-1/2 in. metal boxes (which hold two receptacles; Photo 2), 4-in. square raised covers, one 1/2-in. offset setscrew connector ($1.25) for each conduit/box connection (Photo 2), plus 1/2-in. couplings (to join two pieces of conduit in longer runs—not shown), conduit straps, a 15-amp switch, receptacles and 14-gauge THHN wiring (the type of wire to run inside the conduit). If

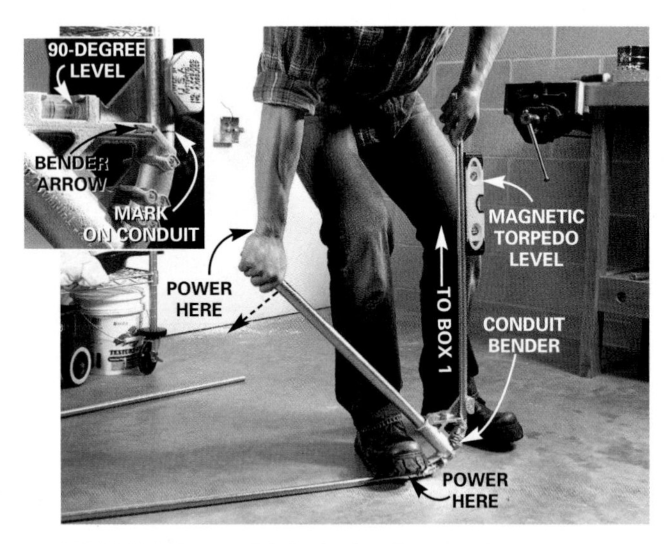

5 PLACE the conduit in the bender with the mark directly in line with the arrow (inset photo). Step on the conduit bender and push down on the handle until the conduit forms a 90-degree angle and is level.

6 MEASURE the difference in height between Box 1 and Box 2 (above the bench; Figure A). Subtract 5 in. from the measurement, then add 3/4 in. to allow for the thickness of the conduit. Mark that distance on the conduit.

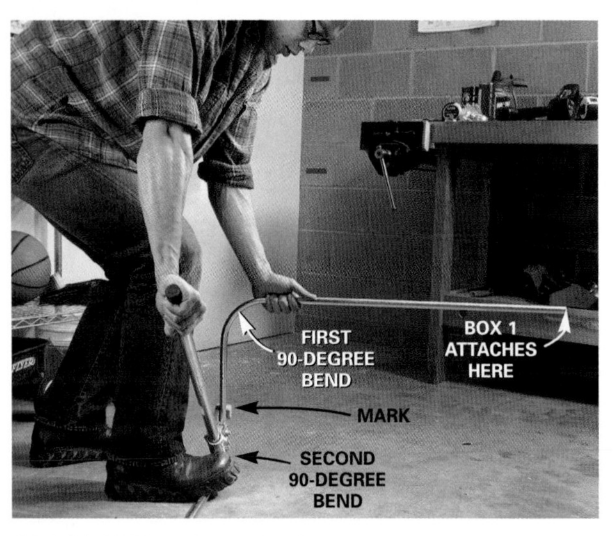

7 REPEAT Step 5 to make the second 90-degree bend. Make sure you bend it 90 degrees in the correct direction.

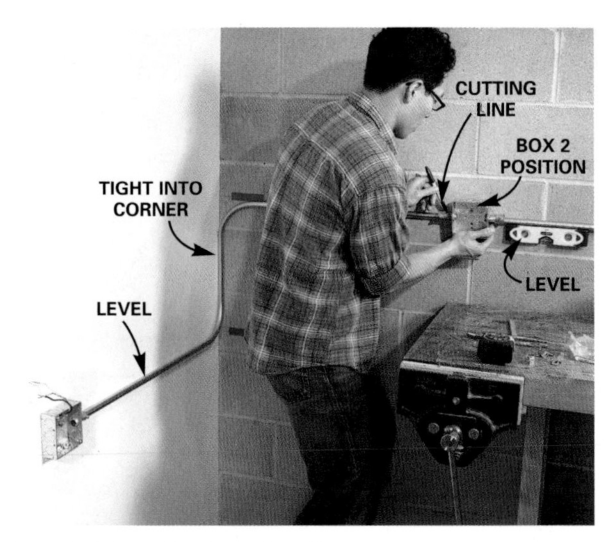

8 ATTACH conduit loosely to Box 1. Level the horizontal sections, then position Box 2 and mark the location of the cut.

you get power from a 20-amp circuit, use only 12-gauge THHN wire. These items are at home centers and full-service hardware stores.

Simple tools

A 1/2-in. conduit bender (Photo 5) is the only specialty tool you need to bend 10-ft. sections of 1/2-in. EMT conduit. You'll spend $9 to $12 for the head and $2 to $3 for a 3/4 x 24-in. water pipe, which serves as the handle and screws into the bender head (Photo 5). Along with that, you need basic hand tools, a hacksaw and a drill with a 1/4-in. masonry bit ($2). And you may need a fish tape ($30, p. 90) to pull wire if you have long conduit runs with multiple bends.

To bend or to buy

We'll only show how to make 90-degree bends, since they're the easiest and most often used. Another common bend is an offset, which is a difficult two-part bend that positions the conduit slightly off the wall to connect straight into electrical boxes. We chose to use offset setscrew connectors (Photo 2) to simplify this task.

Bending conduit isn't difficult (Photo 7). But you may not get perfect bends on the first try, so buy an extra 10-ft. length just in case. If you don't want to bend conduit, you can buy gradual "90-degree sweep bends" or "90-degree square corner elbow fittings." However, your project won't look as professional because of the numerous connectors, and the extra joints make it harder to push or pull wire.

9 CUT the conduit with a hacksaw. Scrape any sharp burrs from both the inside and the outside edges with pliers.

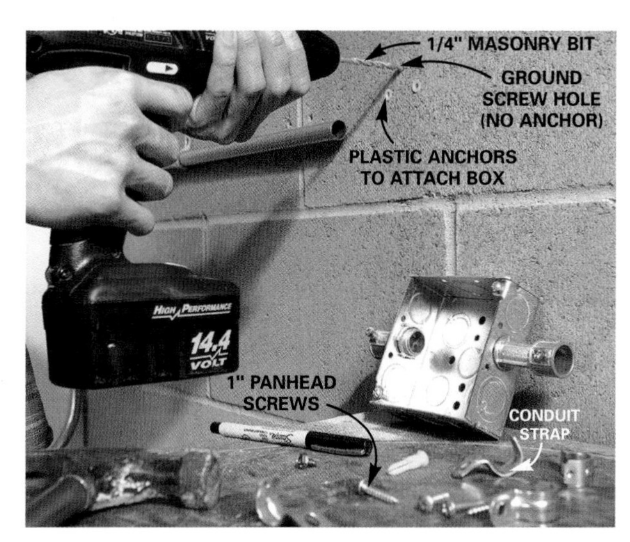

10 REPOSITION the conduit and Box 2 and mark hole locations for plastic anchors. Drill the holes then mount the box and conduit straps with panhead screws.

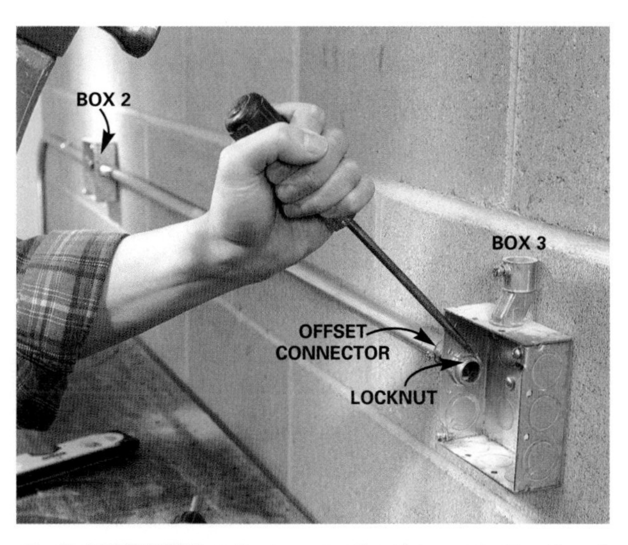

11 POSITION Box 3, measure the distance to Box 2 and cut the conduit to fit. Repeat steps 9 and 10 to mount them. Now tighten all offset connector locknuts with a hammer and screwdriver.

Power-hungry tools

If you plan to power any tools, be aware that a common 15-amp circuit may overload and trip if any of the following tools are run simultaneously (especially if your shop lights are on too):

Miter saw	13 to 15 amps
Circular saw	13 to 15 amps
Router	9 to 11 amps
Belt sander	6 to 12 amps

We recommend a maximum connected load (lights and other permanently plugged-in devices) and operating load (tools and other temporarily running devices) of 1,440 watts (12 amps) for a 15-amp circuit and 1,920 watts (16 amps) for a 20-amp circuit.

Start at the power source

After you've chosen the electrical box to tie in to, turn off the circuit breaker or unscrew the fuse that protects the circuit. Some electrical boxes may contain wires from more than one circuit. Before doing any work, test all the wires with a non-contact voltage sniffer ($12 at hardware stores and home centers) to make sure they're "dead."

Next, remove the existing receptacle and box from the stud (**Photo 1**). Now position (not attach) a 4 x 4 x 1-1/2-in. metal electrical box on the drywall surface, slightly above or below the existing opening so you can pull at least 1/4 in. of the cable sheathing through the back of the box (**Photo 3**). Cut the drywall and shift the box if necessary to get more sheathed cable inside the box. You have to patch the drywall anyway, before you screw the new box to the wall (**Photo 3**). For details on patching drywall, see "You Can Fix It," pp. 10-13.

Bending conduit

For 90-degree bends in 1/2-in. conduit, the rule is to subtract 5 in. from the connector-to-wall measurement. If the total distance is 33 in., mark the conduit at 28 in. Be sure to measure to the inside of the offset connector where the conduit actually seats (**Photos 2 and 4**).

Bend conduit by positioning it in the bender so your distance mark on the conduit lines up with the bender arrow (**Photo 5** and **inset**). Apply pressure with your foot and hand to bend the end of the conduit straight up. Then

12 MEASURE from the Box 3 offset connector to the ceiling, then repeat Steps 4 and 5. Plumb the conduit and attach a strap. Install Box 4.

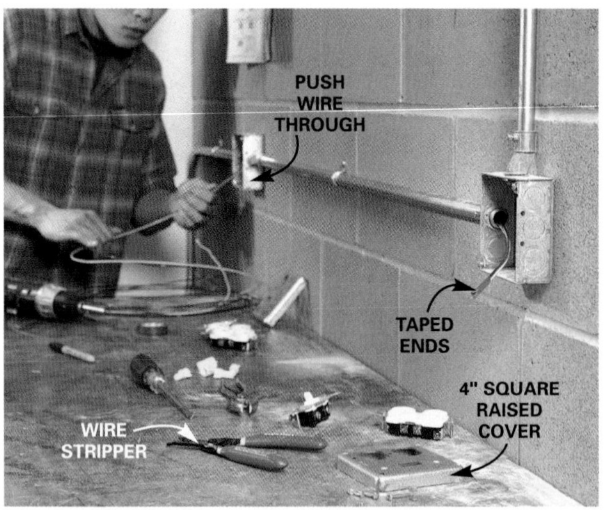

13 TAPE TOGETHER ends of one black and one white 14-gauge wire and push the taped ends through the conduit. Cut the wires, leaving 8 in. extra at each box. Repeat this step from Box 3 to Box 4.

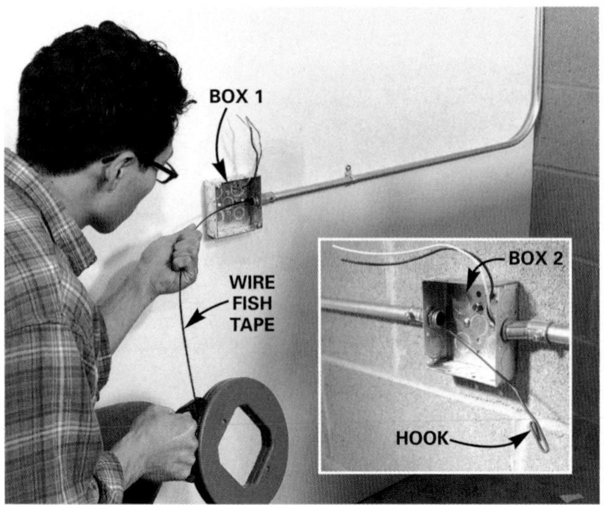

14 PUSH fish tape from Box 1 to Box 2. Bend both wires through the fish tape hook and tape them (photo below), leaving the middle open to flex around corners, then pull wires back from Box 2 to Box 1.

check the angle with a magnetic torpedo level (or with the bubble level built into some bender heads) and adjust the bend until you get 90 degrees.

When measuring for the vertical rise, measure the height difference between the two boxes. Again, take that distance and subtract 5 in. Then add 3/4 in. to account for the thickness of the conduit in the first bend (Photo 6).

Attach boxes to masonry

After leveling the conduit and marking the location for Box 2 (Photo 8), be sure to smooth all cut edges with a pliers (Photo 9). Now drill the two holes for plastic anchors and a clearance hole for the ground screw. Attach the box to the concrete with plastic anchors and panhead screws (Photo 10).

Repeat this process to attach all other boxes, as well as the straps that hold the conduit to the masonry. When using 1/2-in. EMT conduit, position straps within 3 ft. of each box and within 10 ft. thereafter. Once you've installed the conduit and rotated the offsets so the conduit rests against the wall, tighten the offset connector locknuts with a sharp rap of a hammer on a screwdriver (Photo 11).

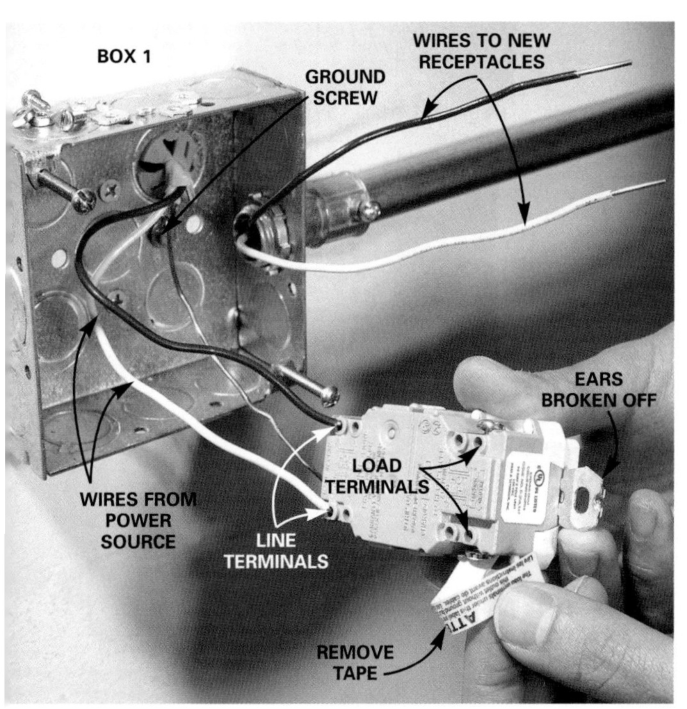

15 CONNECT Box 1 by first breaking the ears off a GFCI receptacle, then connect the wires from the power source to the "line" terminals, the wires to the new receptacles to the "load" terminals, and the ground wire to the ground screw. Then connect the devices in Boxes 2, 3 and 4 (see Figures B, C and D, right).

Running the wire

When running wire short distances with few bends, such as between Boxes 2 and 3, and 3 and 4, you can simply tape the two wire ends together and push them through the conduit (**Photo 13**). For longer distances, or runs that have two or more bends, run a fish tape through the conduit and tape the wires to it (**Photo 14** and the photo below it).

Garage receptacles must be GFCI protected. Before wiring the GFCI receptacle into Box 1, bend or break off the top and bottom ears. Repeat this step with all receptacles so they fit inside the metal box as well as screw to the 4-in. square cover (that is raised 1/2 in.). Now connect the GFCI receptacle as shown (**Photo 15**), followed by the other boxes (**Figures B, C and D**). Then screw all receptacles to the covers and attach the covers to the boxes.

CAUTION: If you have aluminum wiring, leave it alone. Call in a licensed pro who's certified to work with it. This wiring is dull gray, not the dull orange that's characteristic of copper.

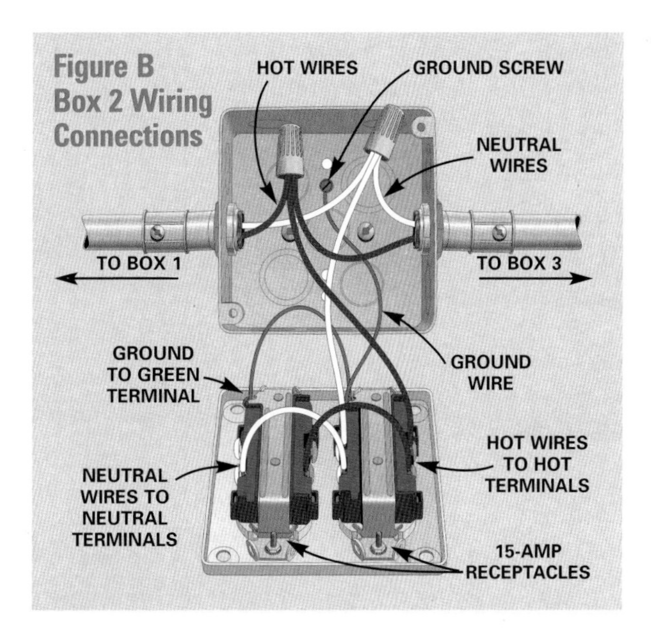

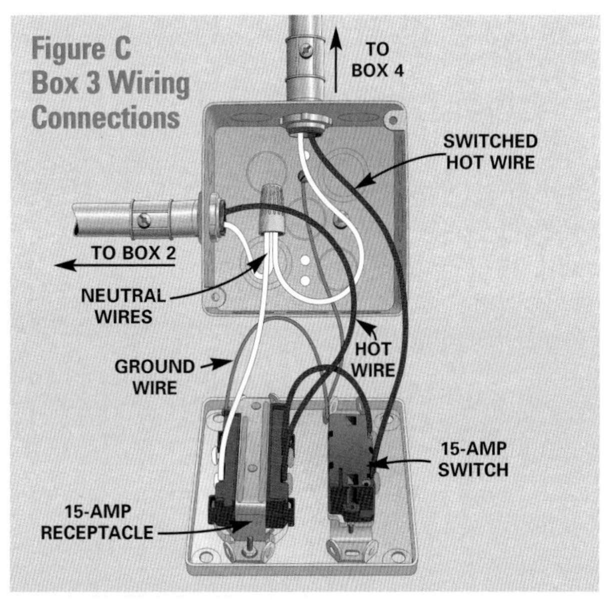

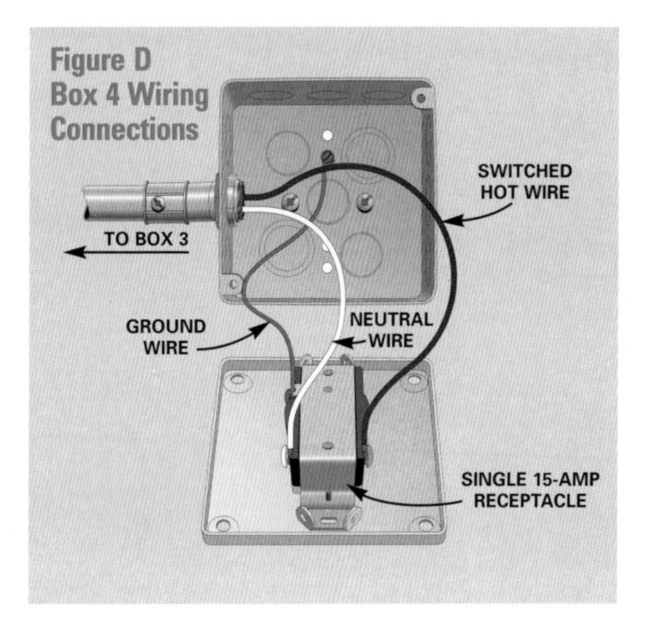

Using
Tips for

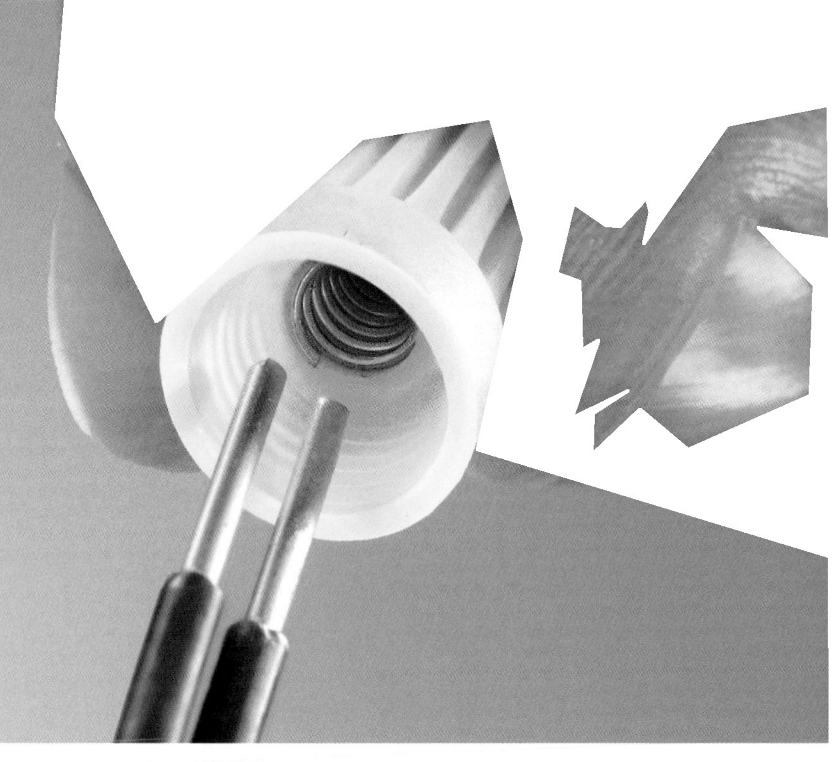

Making tight electrical connections is critical to a safe wiring job. If wires come loose, you could get arcing and overheating, which could lead to a fire. However, thanks to reliable connectors and terminals, it's fairly easy to make safe, strong connections. But there are a few things you have to watch out for. We'll show you how to pick the right connector for the job and how to prepare the wires for the best connection. We'll also show you why you should spend a little extra money when it comes time to buy outlets and other electrical devices. With careful attention to detail, you can rest easy knowing your wiring job is as safe as you could possibly make it.

Line up the wire ends, then tighten

With the exception of stranded wire, which we'll talk about on p. 93, it's important to make sure the ends of all wires are lined up before twisting on the connector. Otherwise the connector won't clamp all wires evenly and one or more could slip out.

Start by stripping the ends of the wires. Check the label on the connector package for the length of bare wire to expose. For all but the smallest and largest connectors, this is usually about 1/2 to 5/8 in. Then arrange the wires parallel to each other with their ends aligned. Keep your eye on the wire ends until the connector covers them to make sure none slips out of position. You don't have to twist the wires together before you screw on the connector. Simply twist the connector until the insulated wires outside the connector begin to twist. Photos 1 and 2 at left show how to install the connector. When you're done, tug on each wire to make sure they're all firmly connected.

1

LINE UP ENDS

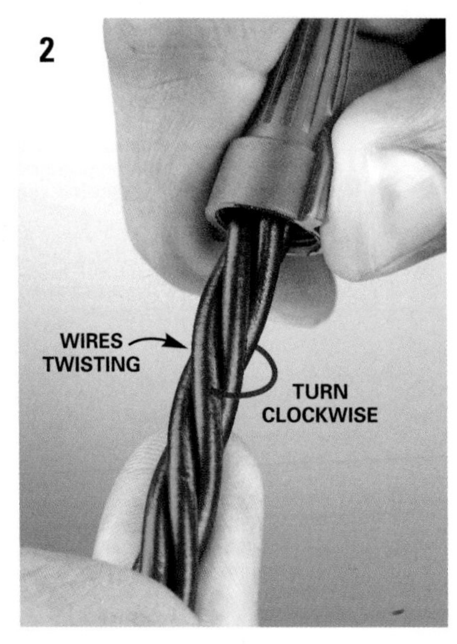

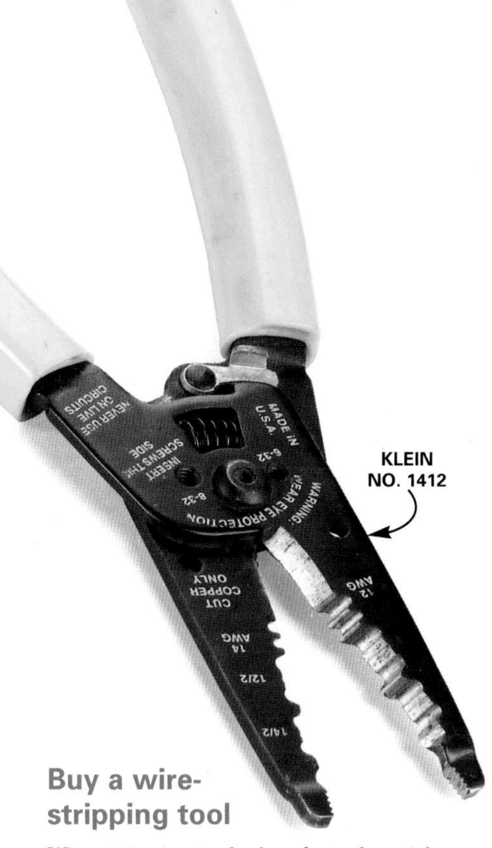

Buy a wire-stripping tool

Wire-stripping tools do a fast, clean job without nicking and weakening the wires. For most standard house wiring requiring 12-gauge and 14-gauge plastic sheathed cable, we like the Klein No. 1412 stripper ($18) shown here. It can cut the plastic sheathing of 12-2 and 14-2 plastic sheathed cable, as well as strip insulation on individual wires.

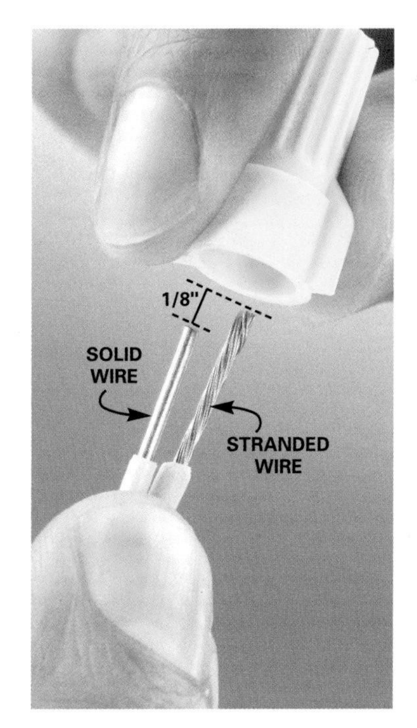

Extend stranded wire 1/8 in. beyond solid wire

If you hold the ends of solid and stranded wire even with each other while you screw on the connector, the stranded wire will often wrap loosely around the solid wires, resulting in a loose connection. This is especially likely when you're joining multiple solid wires to one stranded wire. The problem is easy to prevent by extending the ends of all stranded wires about 1/8 in. beyond the solid wires. Then install the connector as usual.

Tip

Stranded wire is a little larger than the same gauge of solid wire. Use a wire stripper labeled for stranded wire, or use the hole for the next largest gauge of solid wire. Remember to tug on each wire to make sure the connector has a solid grip.

Choose a connector that fits the wires

Every wire connector is made to join a certain minimum and maximum volume of wires: The larger the wire gauge, the fewer it can hold. Always check the approved list on the packaging (**photo right**) to make sure the connector is listed for the wire combination you want to join. Even though the connectors appear to be color coded, you can't rely on this. For example, one style of yellow connector joins up to four 14-gauge wires, while another connects a maximum of three. You have to check the label on the package or go to the manufacturer's Web site to find out. Keep a range of small to large connectors and their packaging on hand so you won't be tempted to make do with the wrong size.

Using Tools™: Tips for Safer Wiring

Loop the wire for a strong screw connection

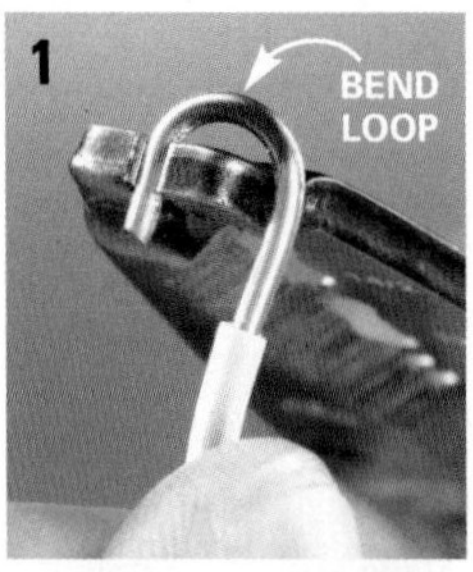

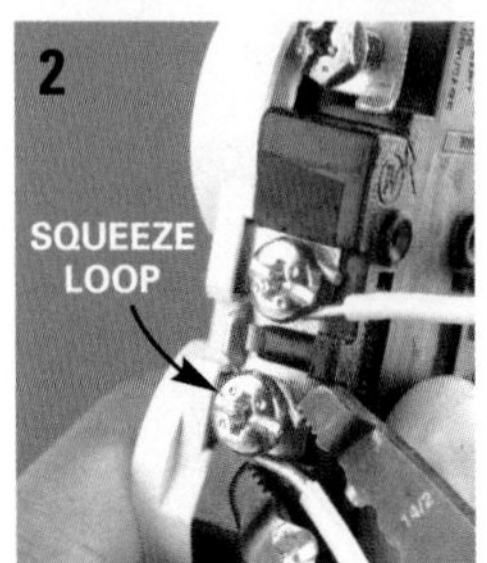

Since switches and outlets vibrate a little when used, it's critical that the connections to them be strong so they don't work loose. For screw connections, start with a 3/4-in. length of bare stripped wire. **Photos 1 and 2** show how to bend the loop and close it around the screw. Wrap the wire clockwise around the screw so that the loop closes as the screw is tightened. Make sure to tighten the screw firmly. Keep in mind that only one wire is allowed under each screw.

Cut off nicked, bent or twisted ends

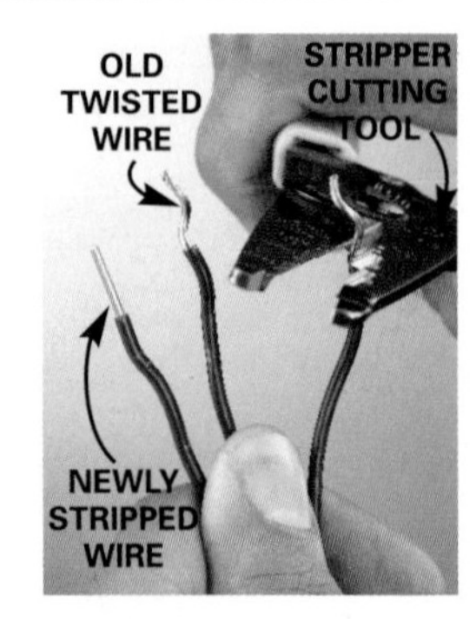

Wires that are bent, twisted or nicked are weaker and won't nest together as easily in the connector. Before you reconnect wires to an outlet or switch, or rejoin several wires with a connector, cut off the old bare wire ends and strip the insulation to expose clean, straight wire. It takes a few extra seconds but ensures a better connection.

If cutting a wire leaves it too short to work with easily, splice on an additional 6-in. length with a wire connector.

Buy top-quality outlets for the best connections

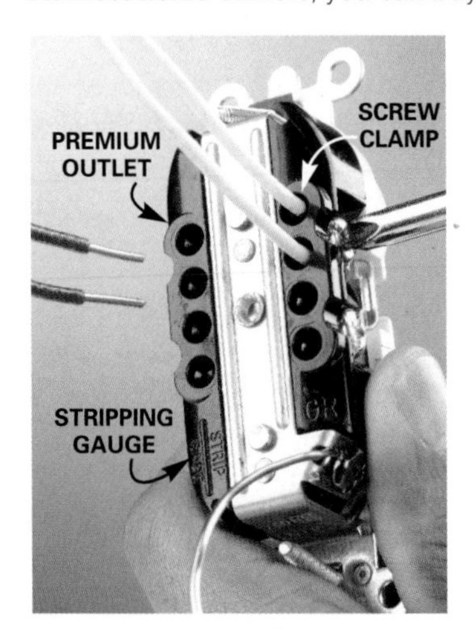

At most home centers, you can buy an economy outlet for about 50¢ or you can spend about $1.75 for a better one. Premium outlets are stronger, make better contact with plugs and work more smoothly. Cheap outlets can literally wear out if you use them frequently. If you decide to buy premium outlets, look for the kind with clamp screw terminals (photo at right). They resemble the "stab-in" holes you'll find on economy outlets but actually clamp down firmly when you tighten the screw. If you don't want to spend the extra money to install premium outlets everywhere, at least put them in heavy-use areas like kitchens, garages, workshops and laundry rooms. Some of these areas may require GFCI protection. Always check with your electrical inspector before replacing outlets.

Strip the wires to the length shown on the stripping gauge (photo, far left). Loosen the terminal screw by turning it counterclockwise to open the clamp. Then hold the wire or wires, one in each hole, while you tighten the screw. Tug on the wires when you're done to make sure they're securely connected.

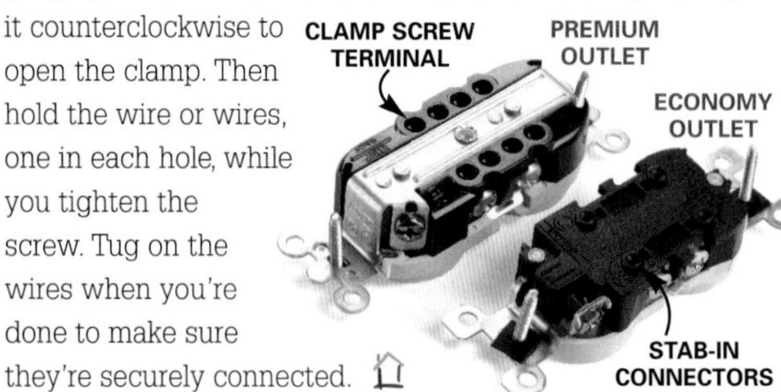

Great Goofs™ Dim and dimmer

One day as I was cleaning the house, the vacuum lost power. Thinking there was something wrong with it, I asked my husband (a licensed electrician) to help me figure it out. He unplugged it, took it apart, cleaned it and put it back together, but it still didn't work properly. As he examined the problem, I turned up the wall dimmer switch that controlled the floor lamp and all of a sudden the vacuum worked perfectly. Turns out I had plugged the vacuum into the same receptacle that powered the lamp—the one controlled by the dimmer switch. We both laughed it off, feeling a bit foolish that our own "light bulbs" seemed to be on a dimmer switch that day.

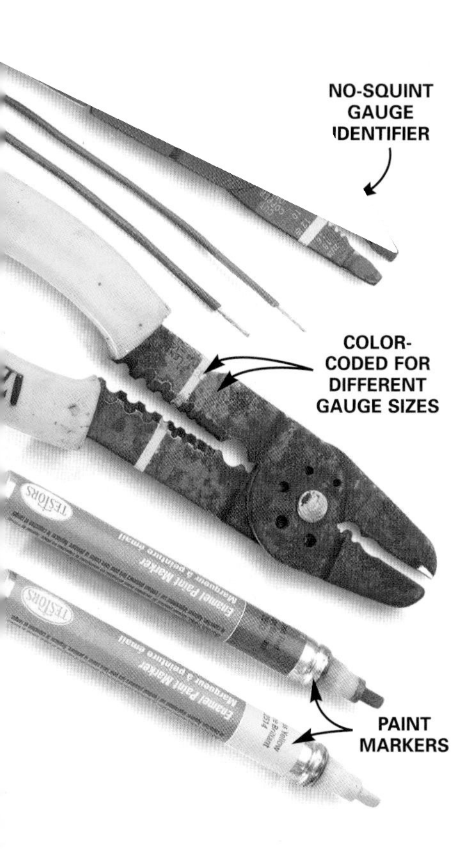

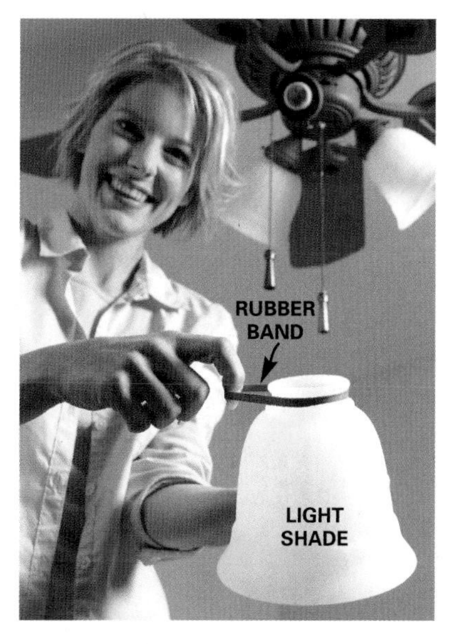

No-rattle ceiling fan

If the screws that hold the light globe to your ceiling fan tend to work loose and then hum or rattle, slip a wide rubber band around the neck of the globe where the screws grip it. The rubber band prevents the screws from loosening, dampens any noise and protects the globe from overzealous screw tighteners.

Squint-free wire stripper

Ninety percent of the time, you use your wire stripper to strip the same gauge wire. Now, the days of searching your wire stripper for the right size hole are over, thanks to this electrifying tip from Scott Silverman. Use a Testor's Enamel Paint Marker ($3 at a home center) to mark a line across the hole. After a couple of minutes of drying time, you'll be able to stick the wire in the marked hole with zero eyestrain and work a heck of a lot faster on your latest wiring project. If you're stripping more than one wire gauge size, mark the holes in different colors.

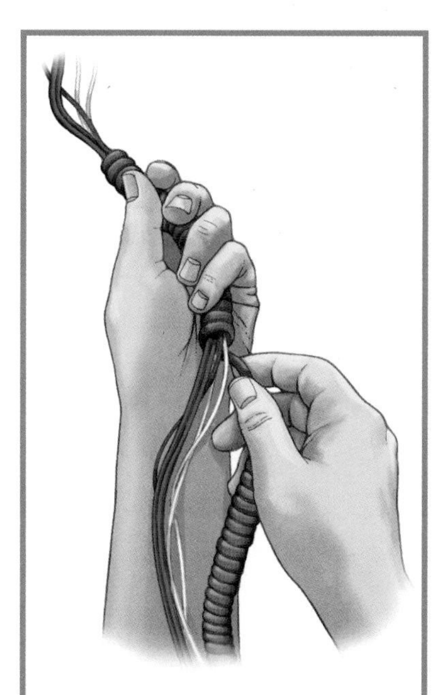

Wire organizer

Clean up that jungle of computer, TV, DVD, receiver and other wires by wrapping them in an old-style coiled telephone cord. Just clip the snap-in plugs off the ends and wrap the coils around the wires.

Protect brass from cement

Cement-based materials like mortar and stucco contain chemicals that corrode brass. Keep brass light fixtures out of contact with masonry using 1/4-in. clear tubing. Just slit the tubing with a utility knife and slip it over the edge of the fixture's base. The tubing is inexpensive and available at most home centers and hardware stores.

Great Goofs™

Honey, someone's at the furnace!

We needed a new doorbell, so my handy brother-in-law helped us install one. A few days later, very early in the morning, the doorbell rang. We got up to check the door and nobody was there. About a half hour later, the doorbell rang and again nobody was there. Convinced it was a practical joke, we camped out by the door. It rang again, and this time we could see there was definitely nobody there. We knew that a doorbell uses low voltage supplied by a transformer. We traced the wires and noticed that my brother-in-law had wired the doorbell into an existing transformer that was also hooked to the furnace thermostat. As a result, whenever the furnace turned on, the doorbell rang. We purchased a dedicated transformer for the new doorbell and are now sleeping in on weekends.

Power to spare

Last year I wanted to install a new remote exterior light and had to find the circuit breaker that controlled the outlet that I needed to tap in to. I plugged the portable radio into that outlet, then had my daughter listen and tell me when the radio went off while I flipped the breaker switches one at a time. I went through the entire breaker panel twice. She told me the radio just kept on playing. Impossible! I yelled in frustration. My wife then asked me if I thought it made a difference if the radio was also battery powered. Sure enough, I unplugged the radio and it kept right on playing! Sheepishly, I decided to use a lamp instead of the radio.

Light my fire

Many years ago, my wife and I lived in a very small house with only one electrical circuit. We decided to add a receptacle in the ceiling so she could iron in the laundry room. I turned off the power, lit a candle for light and got right to work. Soon my wife and boys were complaining about the smell of something burning. But I assured them the power was off and there was nothing to worry about. As I spoke, they all said in unison, "Your pants are on fire." I'd backed into the candle and the seat of my corduroys started smoldering. For my next project, my wife volunteered to hold a flashlight!

4 Plumbing, Heating & Appliances

IN THIS CHAPTER

Stop Faucet Drips .98

Ask Handyman .102
Ailing septic systems, chipped sinks, replacement parts on-line and more ...

Handy Hints 106
Neater caulking, quieter pipes and a better way to cut pipe

Great Goofs 109

Using Tools: Leakproof Solder Joints . .110

STOP FAUCET DRIPS

You can fix almost any drippy single-lever kitchen faucet in about an hour

by **Jeff Gorton**

Doing your own faucet repair may seem daunting, but once you learn the basics, modern faucets are pretty easy to fix. In fact, the hardest step is usually finding the right replacement parts. In this article, we'll tell you how to find replacement parts and show you how to stop spout drips on the three main types of single-lever faucets: rotary ball, cartridge and ceramic disc. We're showing kitchen faucets, but you can fix most single-lever bath faucets using the same procedures. We'll also show you how to stop leaks around the base of the spout.

The tools you'll need vary a little depending on the faucet you're repairing. You'll probably need an Allen wrench to remove the handle. Buy a set of small Allen wrenches ($6 to $12), and you'll be prepared for any faucet. Most repairs also require screwdrivers and a large slip-joint pliers.

Rotary-ball faucets

Water flow and temperature in a rotary-ball faucet are controlled by a hollow ball that rotates in a socket (**Figure A**). Delta and Peerless are two of the major brands. Your faucet may have a brass or plastic ball. Both work well, although the long-lasting stainless steel ball comes with most repair kits. We recommend that you buy a repair kit that includes the ball, springs, seats and O-rings for the spout, as well as a small repair tool, for about $15. With this kit, you'll be prepared for almost any repair.

If water is leaking out around the base of the handle, you may be able to fix the leak by removing the handle (**Photo 1**) and simply tightening the adjusting ring slightly (**Figure A**). Turn it clockwise with the spanner tool included in the repair kit. If the faucet drips from the end of the

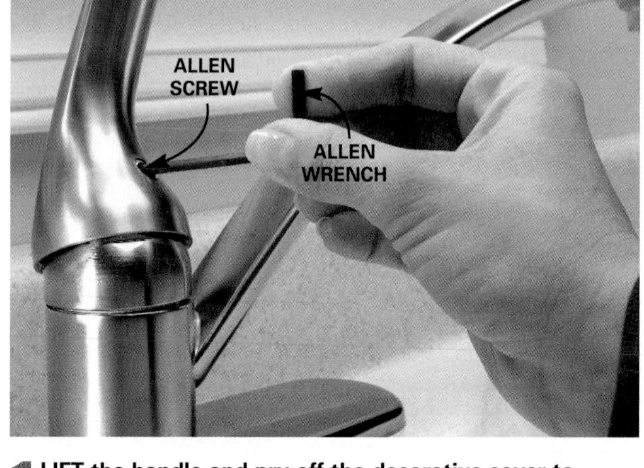

1 **LIFT the handle and pry off the decorative cover to expose the Allen screw. Turn the screw counterclockwise until it's loose enough to lift the handle up from the stem.**

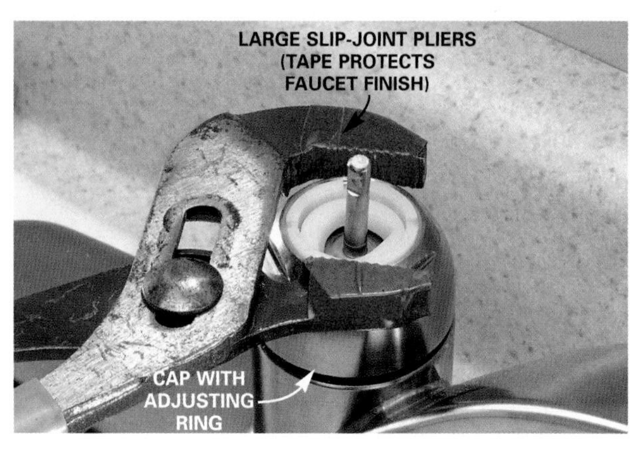

2 **UNSCREW the cap by turning it counterclockwise with a slip-joint pliers.**

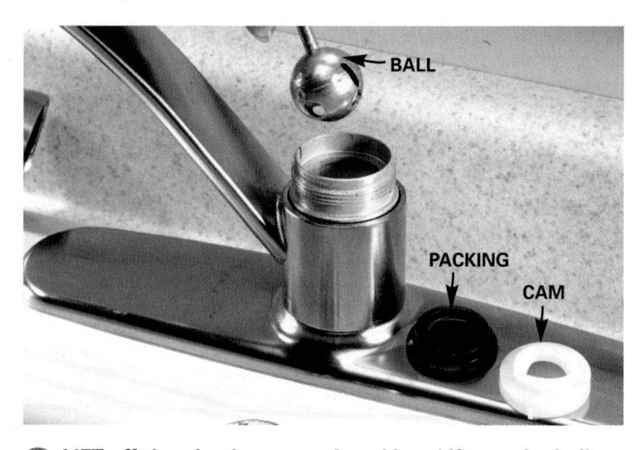

3 **LIFT off the plastic cam and packing. Lift out the ball and inspect it. Replace the ball if it's scratched, cracked or visibly worn.**

spout, replace the seats and springs (**Photo 4**).

Reassembly is straightforward. Drop the springs in the recesses and press the rubber seats over the top with your fingertip. Then align the groove in the ball with the pin in the socket and drop the ball in. Align the lug on the plastic cam with the notch in the valve body and set it over the ball. Thread on the cap with the adjusting ring and tighten it with the slip-joint pliers. Now you can turn on the water to check for leaks. If water leaks from around the ball stem, use the spanner tool to tighten the adjusting ring until the leak stops. Replace the handle and you're done.

4 LIFT out the two rubber seats and springs with a screwdriver. Make note of the orientation of the tapered spring and install the new springs and seats the same way. Reassemble the faucet.

Follow these basics for all faucet repairs

Before you start, examine the faucet closely to determine where the water is coming from. Leaks around the base of the spout require a different repair than a drip from the end of the spout. Then turn off the water supply to the faucet. You'll probably find shutoff valves under the sink. If those valves don't work or if you don't have any, you'll have to close the main water valve to your entire home. After you turn off the water, open the faucet in the center position to relieve water pressure and make sure the water is shut off. Finally, cover the sink drain holes with strainer baskets or rags to avoid losing small parts down the drain.

Pay close attention to the order and orientation of parts as you remove them. A digital camera or video camera is handy for recording each step in case you forget. For easier reassembly, set the parts aside in the order they were removed. When all the parts are out, inspect the interior of the valve for bits of deteriorated gaskets or mineral deposits. Use a cloth or fine nylon abrasive pad to clean the surface. Loosen mineral deposits by soaking them in vinegar. Slow water flow can be caused by plugged holes in the faucet body. Use a small screwdriver or penknife to clean them out. Before you replace worn parts and reassemble the faucet, hold a rag over the faucet and open the water shutoff valve slightly to flush out debris that may have been loosened during the cleaning and inspection.

After the faucet is reassembled, open the faucet to the middle position and gradually open the shutoff valves to turn on the water. Leave the faucet open until water flows freely and all the air is out of the pipes. If the water flow through the faucet is slow, the aerator (**Figure A**) may be plugged. Unscrew the aerator and clean it out.

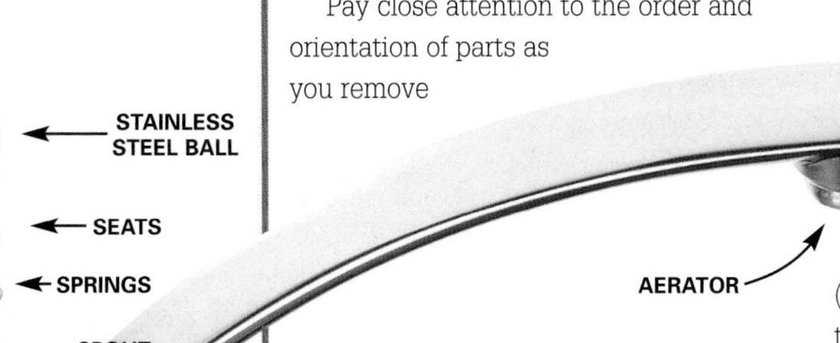

Figure A: Ball Faucet Parts

Cartridge-style faucets

Many faucet brands use a cartridge of some type (**Figure B**). We show how to replace a Moen cartridge, but the process is similar for other brands. To stop drips at the spout or correct problems with hot and cold mixing, remove the cartridge and either replace the O-rings on the cartridge if they're worn or replace the entire cartridge. Take the cartridge to the home center or hardware store to find a replacement ($10 to $15).

Photos 1 – 6 show how to remove the cartridge.

Replacement cartridges for Moen faucets include a plastic spanner cap that allows you to twist and loosen the cartridge to make it easier to pull out (**Photo 5**). Don't be surprised if the cartridge seems stuck. It may take considerable force to pull it out. Really stubborn cartridges may require the use of a special cartridge-pulling tool. Moen's version costs about $15 and is available at most home centers.

Reassemble the faucet in the reverse order. Pull the stem up before inserting the cartridge. You may have to twist the cartridge slightly to line it up for the brass retainer clip.

1 PRY OFF the handle cap (gently) with a knife. Turn the Allen screw counterclockwise to remove it and lift off the handle.

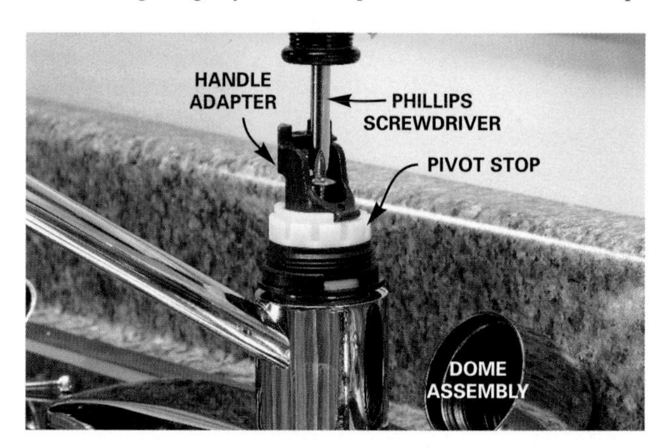

2 UNSCREW the dome assembly under the handle. Then unscrew the metal handle adapter and lift it off. Lift off the plastic pivot stop.

3 REMOVE the retainer nut by turning it counterclockwise with a large slip-joint pliers.

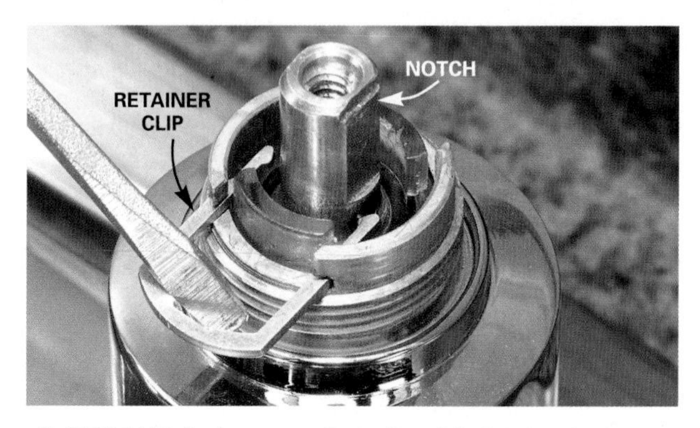

4 PRY OUT the brass retainer clip with the tip of a screwdriver. Grab the clip with a pliers and pull it the rest of the way out to avoid losing it.

5 LOOSEN the cartridge by slipping the plastic spanner cap (included with the new cartridge) over the cartridge and twisting it back and forth.

6 GRAB the cartridge stem with a pliers and pull it straight up and out. Replace worn parts and reassemble the faucet in the reverse order.

Use the plastic spanner cap or the tips of a needle-nose pliers to rotate the cartridge. Slide the brass clip into the slots in the valve body to hold the cartridge in place. Look for the small notch on top of the stem and rotate the stem until the notch faces you (**Photo 4**). Install the remaining parts and reattach the handle. The directions that come with the stem will help orient you here. Then test the faucet. If the hot and cold water are reversed, simply remove the handle, dome assembly and handle adapter and rotate the stem 180 degrees.

Take the old parts to the store to find replacements

You'll often find the brand name stamped on the faucet. And this information will help when it comes time to find repair parts. But in most cases, the safest bet is to take the worn parts to the store with you.

If you have a Delta or other rotary ball faucet (**Figure A**), you're in luck because you'll find repair kits in most hardware stores and home centers. Cartridges and repair kits for Moen "cartridge-type" (**Figure B**) faucets are also readily available. But if you have another brand or a disc-type faucet, you may have to order parts, since there are too many variations for most stores to keep in stock. It helps to know the faucet's model name or number when searching for a replacement cartridge. Otherwise, take the cartridge with you to the store so you can match it to a photo in the parts catalog. Plumbing supply specialists are also a good source of repair parts. If you're having trouble finding parts, call the manufacturer.

Great Goofs™

Glue goof

My brother-in-law and I decided to help his father remodel his bathroom. Being pretty handy, we thought it would be a snap. When it came time to set the tub, we hooked up the water supply and the PVC waste lines, then took a break for dinner to let the glue dry. When we finished eating, we turned on the water to try it out. After a few seconds, my brother-in-law said he could hear water dripping. Then it turned into a gusher. After investigating the problem, we found we'd used rubber cement instead of PVC glue. The containers were similar and were right next to each other on the shelf. After a couple of hours of fixing our mistake, we were ready for a hot shower!

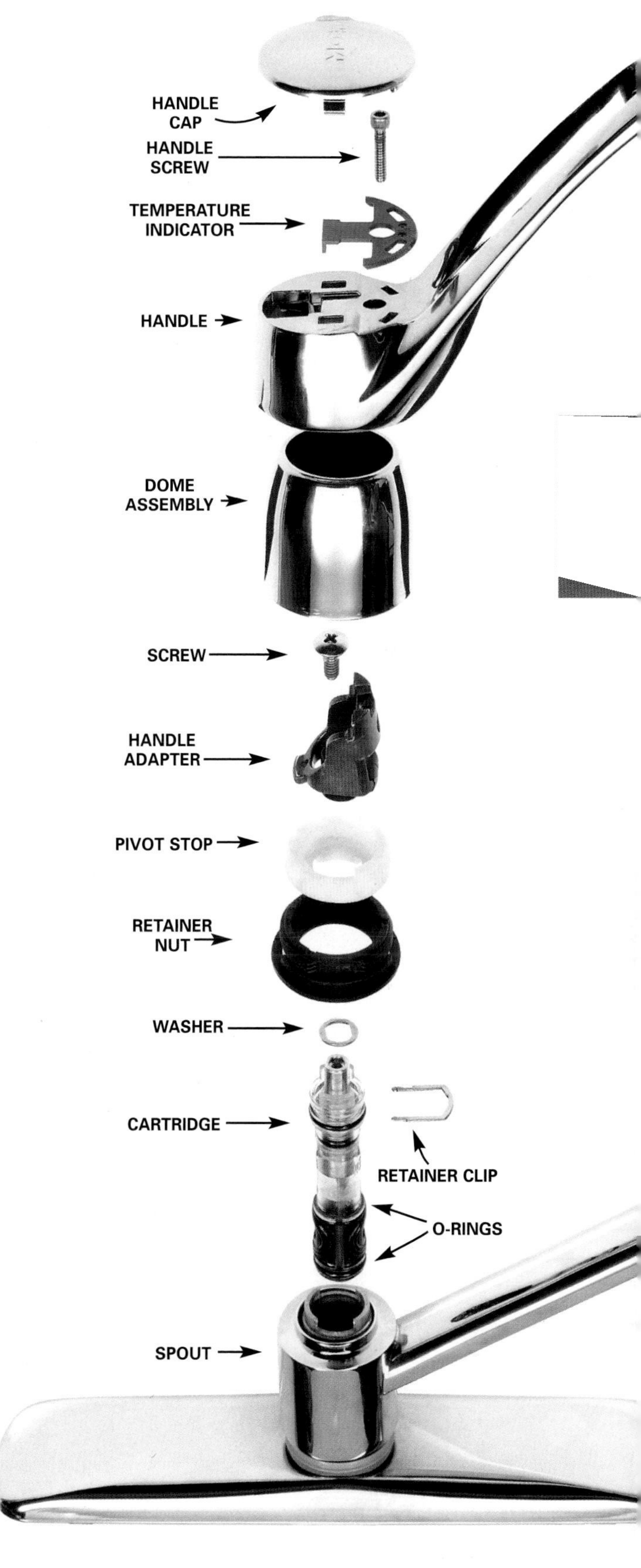

Figure B: Cartridge Faucet Parts

Ask Handyman™

WHY DO SEPTIC SYSTEMS FAIL?

I want to know what causes septic systems to fail. Do you have to do anything to encourage bacteria? Every guy at the coffee shop has an opinion on this subject. I want to hear from the experts.

The main cause of failure is neglecting to pump out the tank every one to three years. Excessive scum and sludge leak from a full tank of solid waste into the drain field and plug the sand, gravel and soil. This prevents the normal filtering of wastewater that enters the drain field—and the whole system backs up.

Two other main causes of failure are excessive water use over short time periods (many laundry loads or showers in one day) and adding harmful chemicals. As a high volume of wastewater enters the septic tank, an equal volume must exit into the drain field. This high volume churns the tank and the suspended sludge, scum and nonbiodegradable products (see "Clog-causing materials" below) travel with the wastewater to clog the drain field.

Other septic stoppers

- Improper design or installation
- Clogged or broken pump (mound system only)
- Frozen pipes
- Saturated drain field soils

Regarding your bacteria question, no, you do not need starters, feeders or other additives to keep your septic system's millions of naturally occurring bacteria in good health. Those hungry bacteria will continue to break down solids if you limit disposal of harmful products and harsh chemicals into your septic system (see list).

For more advice, the University of Minnesota offers good troubleshooting articles at www.extension.umn.edu. Click on "Environment," then "Waste Management."

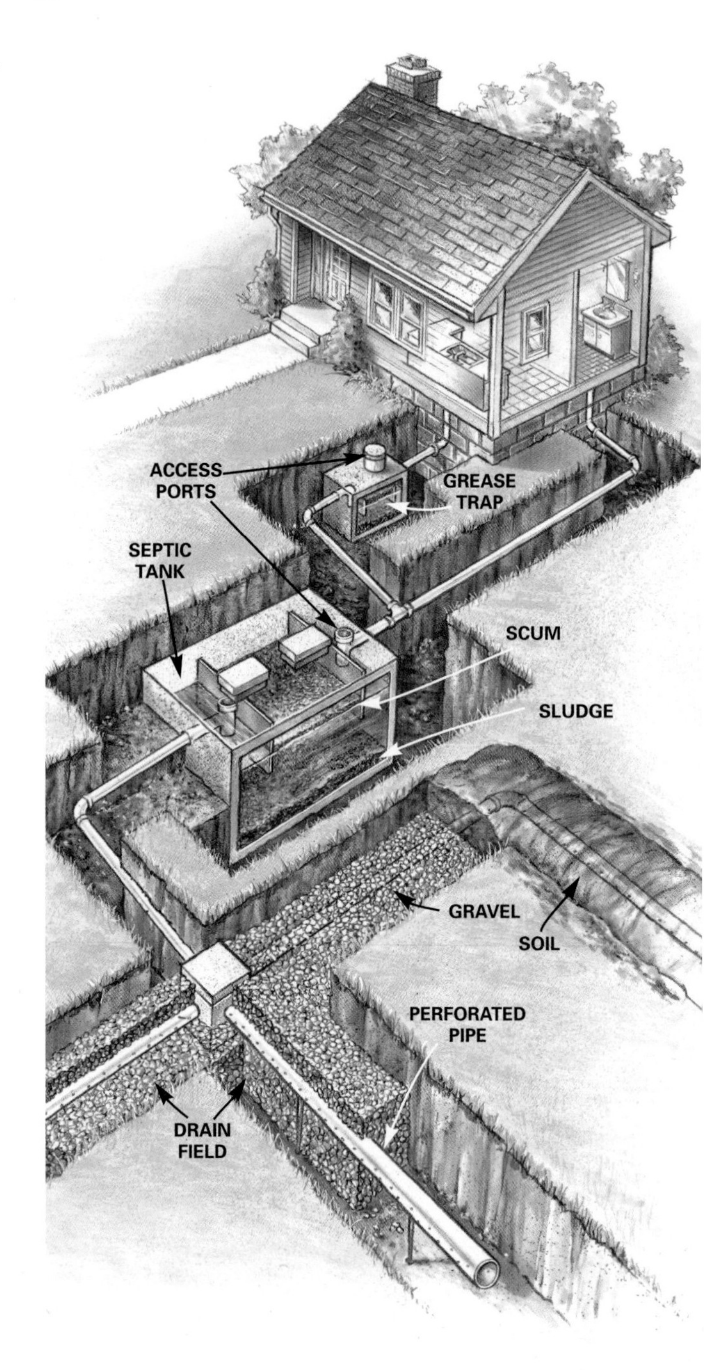

Clog-causing materials

- Tissues (only flush toilet paper)
- Feminine hygiene products
- Cigarette butts
- Food particles (from disposer)
- Grease and oils
- Lint (from clothes washer)
- Anything that won't break down

Bacteria-harming chemicals

- Paints and solvents
- Pesticides and fertilizers
- Bleach, disinfectants and antibacterial soaps
- Drain cleaners and acids
- Prescription antibiotics and other medications

CLEAN A WINDOW AIR CONDITIONER

We bought a new window air conditioner several years ago, and aside from installing and removing it every year, we haven't touched it. What should we be doing to keep it running efficiently and extend its life?

When you remove the unit this fall, take a half-hour or so to clean the filter, wipe out the unit and flush dirt from the condenser coil. If you keep the coils clean, that's 90 percent of keeping an air conditioner in shape to last long and run efficiently. In fact, if you have an air conditioner that just won't blow cold air, clean the coils before you call a pro to add coolant. Dirty coils are usually the culprit.

First, remove the filter and clean it with soap and water according to your owner's guide. Then vacuum the fins of the evaporator coil (which is directly behind the filter) to remove dust and dirt.

Now move to the rear of the air conditioner to clean the condenser coil, which is usually the dirtier of the two. Cover the electric motor with a plastic bag to keep it and the wiring dry. Then take a hose-end nozzle and spray water from the outside inward (see photo). Wipe off the entire unit until it's dry, then let it air dry for a couple of days before storing it. If you have an air compressor, it's a good idea to blow air through the fins to speed drying and reduce the risk of rust setting in during storage.

REPLACEMENT PARTS ON-LINE

Are you one of those people who could fix just about anything, if only you had the parts? OK, big shot, no more excuses. Sears now offers access to more than 4.5 million parts for most major brands of appliances, small engines, power tools and electronics. Still stuck because the parts diagram is long gone? Sorry, Sears has 90,000 diagrams on-line or accessible at its Parts and Repair Centers. There are three ways to get the parts:

- On-line: Click on the Parts Page at www.sears.com.
- By phone: Call (800) 4-MY-HOME and have one of the parts specialists help.
- In person: Visit one of the 500 Sears Parts and Repair centers to view diagrams and have the specialists help you find the part.

Now park the remote and get that dishwasher back on-line!

FIX A CHIPPED SINK

Unfortunately I dropped a kettle and chipped our white enamel and cast iron kitchen sink. I'd like to repair it so it's fairly invisible. Can you help me?

I know the sinking feeling, having chipped one myself hardly a year after installation. Puns aside, it's fairly easy and inexpensive to repair chips so they're almost invisible. You can find two-component epoxy (catalyst and hardener) in the adhesive section of most hardware stores and home centers. It's usually available in a variety of colors. If necessary, two colors can be mixed for a more precise match.

First, scrub the chipped area thoroughly with a sponge and soapy water. Then rub 400- to 600-grit "wet-and-dry" sandpaper over the damaged area to remove dirt and rust, as well as rough up the chip so epoxy will stick to it. Next, mix the two epoxy ingredients according to label directions.

Use a wooden matchstick or small brush to fill the chip. If the chip is deep, apply the material in several coats, and don't forget to allow for the drying time specified on the label. Once the repair is complete, wait 24 hours before you use the sink, and don't scrub that area for seven days.

Ask Handyman™

HEAT FOR AN ADDITION

We want to add a family room to our home. Can we just tap into the adjacent room's ductwork to heat it?

Sometimes. If a main rectangular (trunk) line is adjacent, you can tap into the top of it. If it's a round 6-in. branch duct, you should not. However, keep in mind that air distribution within a home is very complex. It's based on the performance characteristics of your furnace, the local climate, structural features, and the heating and cooling loads of individual rooms.

First, you need to know if your furnace has enough heat output as measured in Btu (British thermal units) and enough blower capacity in cfm (cubic feet per minute) to handle the added square footage.

Next, you must determine the duct size that will deliver the needed cfm and how accessible your basement/crawlspace/attic will be for running new branch ducts from the supply-air part of the furnace. Plus, you may need a return-air duct to make a steady, balanced airflow.

Assuming your head isn't spinning yet, you may need to increase the size of the existing supply-trunk line, then step it down to increase the air velocity so properly heated air enters the new room. Then you must decide how many supply lines the room will need, based on variables such as the number of windows and outside walls, the climate, whether your home was built on a slab or basement (heated or not?) and more.

Because the job is complex, you're likely to make a mistake and be disappointed by drafts or a cool room. The two biggest DIYer mistakes are (1) tapping a new duct into a 6-in. round branch duct and (2) not adding return-air ducts.

You also have to test the system to avoid a heating system imbalance. (The job is even more complex if you run air conditioning in the same ductwork.)

Best advice? Call in a heating pro. First, pros determine the heat loss/gain for the entire house and for the room addition. That tells them whether the furnace is big enough and how much heat (and cooling) the room needs.

Next, pros size up the existing furnace and duct system, then map and calculate whether a system can handle the added load.

Older furnaces can usually supply the extra heat needed, but the return-air ductwork often needs improvement. Newer high-efficiency, forced-air furnaces often don't have spare capacity, so you may have to replace the furnace with a higher capacity one.

If capacity exists, pros size up the new ductwork to make sure heated air reaches the new space at the proper velocity to keep the room at a comfortable temperature and avoid drafts, while maintaining the comfort of other rooms in the house.

Rather than have you replace a furnace that's too small, a pro may recommend other, less expensive options, such as an independent system or electric baseboard heating.

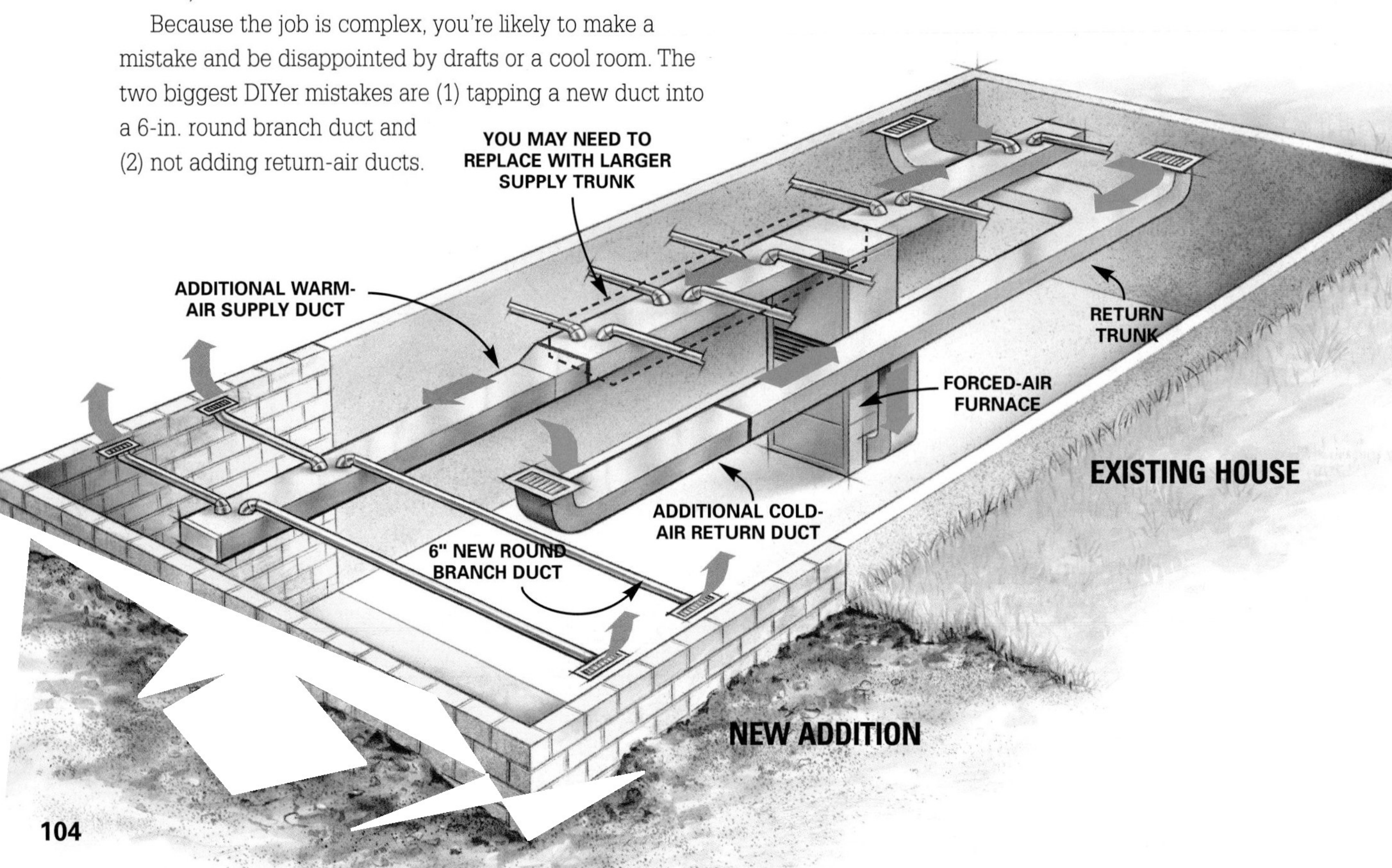

PLUMBING A REFRIGERATOR

Our fridge is dying, so we're going to splurge and get one with the ice and water dispenser in the door. Is it difficult to run a water line to it, and can I do it myself?

You can do this yourself if you have some plumbing experience. The biggest challenge is tapping into the cold-water pipe and running the 1/4-in. O.D. (outside diameter) flexible copper tubing. You can buy icemaker installation kits at home centers and some hardware stores, but we don't recommend them. Most contain a saddle valve (which doesn't meet plumbing code in some regions) and some contain plastic tubing (which can dry, split and leak over time). We recommend more permanent valves and copper tubing for better water flow and reduced risk of leaks, which can cause extensive damage.

Plumbers recommend removing a section of the cold-water pipe to solder in a regular 1/2-in. copper tee (below). If you have CPVC (plastic) or steel pipes, add tee fittings made of the same material. If you don't want to solder, you can cut the copper water pipe and install a 5/8-in. O.D. compression tee (right, top) instead; just don't use this type of tee inside walls because it's not safe and plumbing code won't allow it. Add pipe compound to the threads to make it easier to tighten compression joints.

The least dependable option is a saddle valve (right, bottom) designed for 1/2-in. copper pipe. It has a tiny shutoff valve that uses a sharp pointed metal rod to pierce the outer wall of the pipe when screwed inward. Then you back out the rod and water flows through a tiny hole into the tubing. Some appliance installers say saddle valves work, but most refrigerator makers recommend that you drill a hole in the pipe for better flow instead of using the valve to pierce the hole, then attach the saddle valve (check your owner's manual).

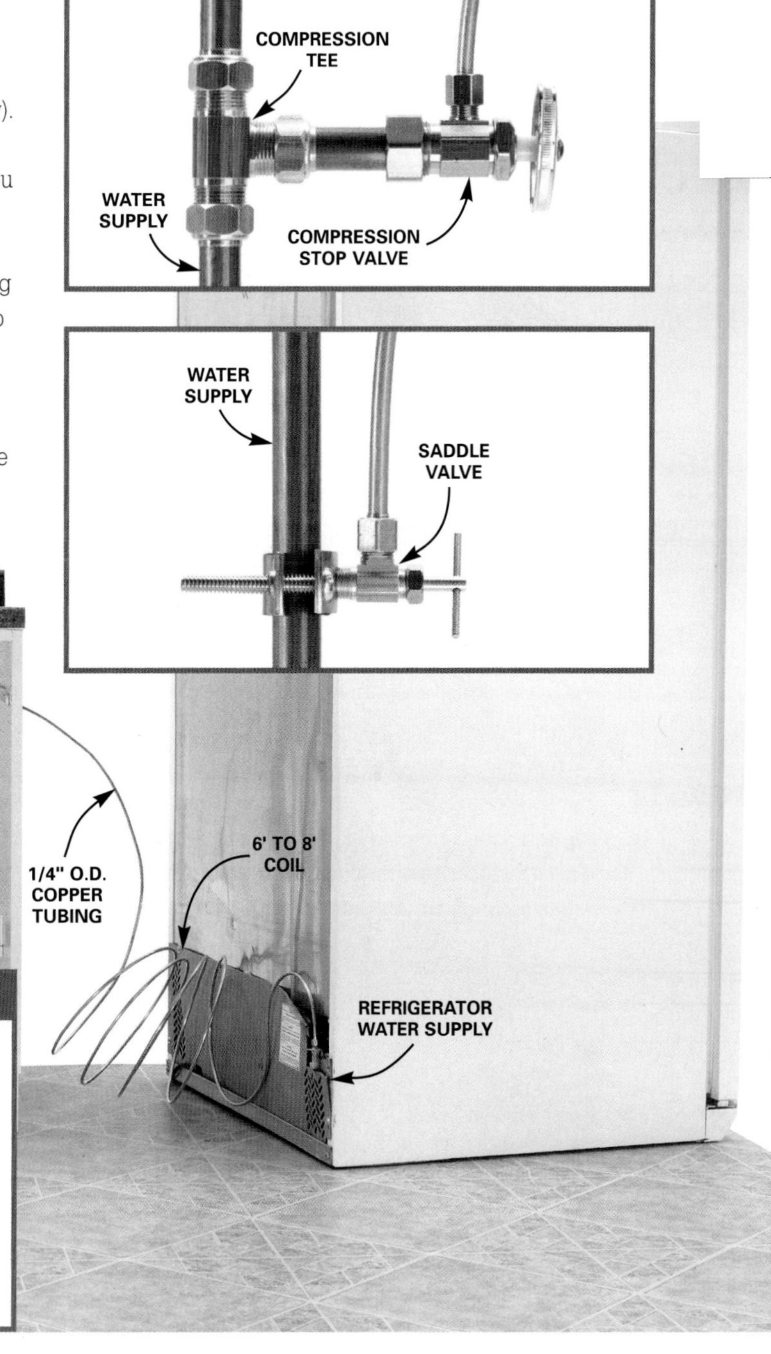

Handy Hints® from our readers

STUCK WATER SHUTOFF

When you have to turn off an old water shutoff valve that hasn't been used for a long time, put a few drops of oil on the valve stem around the packing nut. Loosen and tighten the handle about one turn to let the packing absorb the oil. This should moisten the packing and keep it from cracking. After a few minutes, you should be able to turn the valve handle without leaks. If seepage appears, tighten the packing nut slightly.

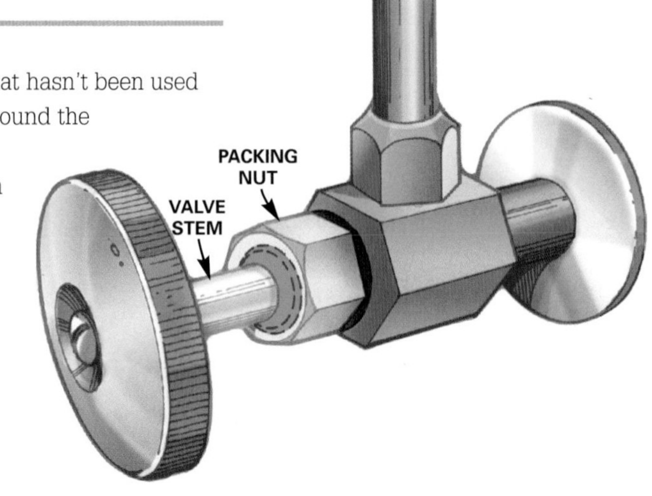

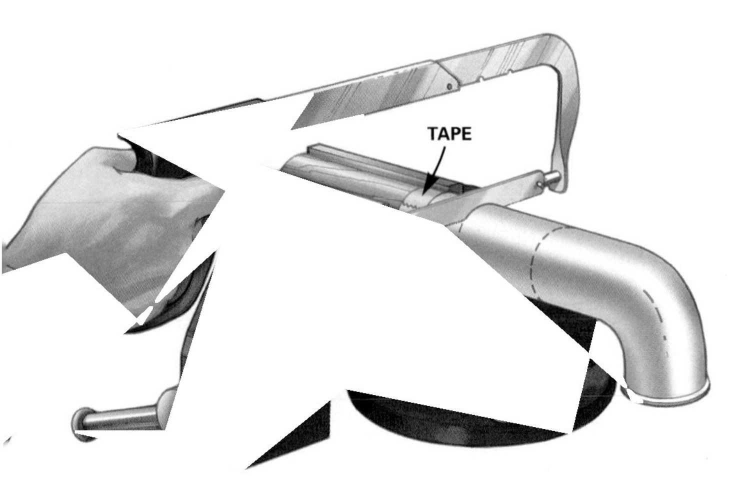

BETTER PIPE CUTTING

It's difficult to cut a thin metal pipe, such as a P-trap, with a hacksaw without squashing the pipe or mangling the cut. To make a nice cut, insert a section of wood closet rod or handrail into the end of the pipe to be cut. Wrap one end of the rod with tape to fill out the rod to the pipe's inner size. Clamp the wood in a vise and cut through both the pipe and the wood.

SILENCE CREAKING PIPES

The groaning in my basement made me think I had ghosts. Then I realized that running the hot water made my copper pipes expand and grind against pipe hangers and joists. So I picked up some adhesive-backed felt at the hardware store and cut it into strips. Then I removed each hanger and wrapped the pipe before refastening the hanger.

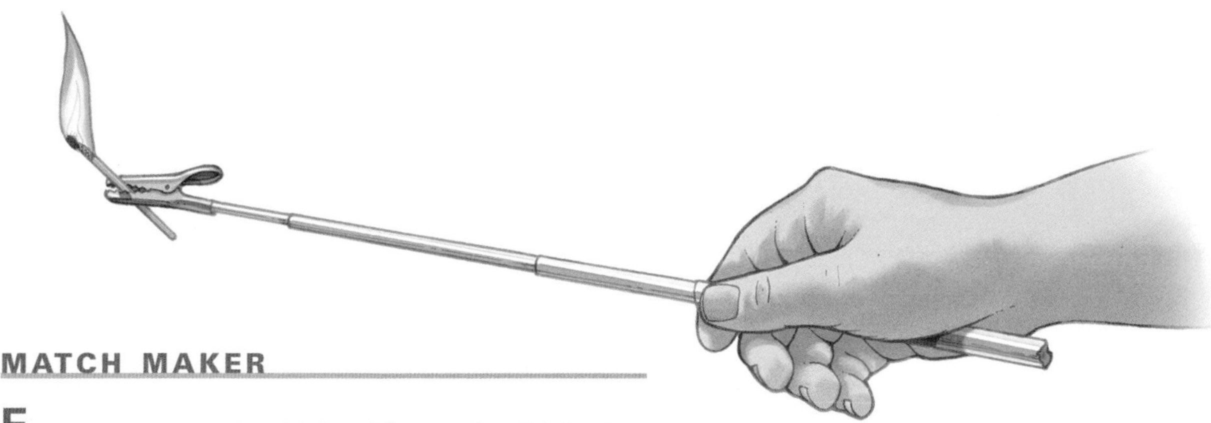

MATCH MAKER

Extend your reach and avoid singed fingers when lighting the pilot light on a stove, water heater or furnace. Crimp or tape an alligator clip to the end of an old telescopic radio or TV antenna. Then clamp in your match.

DISHWASHER BASKET TOUCH-UP

When the plastic coating on dishwasher baskets wears away, the dishes will get scratched. Before paying the high price of a new basket, try covering the worn spots with hot-melt glue. It works great.

SMALL-PARTS KEEPER

When you're disassembling something that has small screws or parts that you want to keep in order, lay out a strip of duct tape on your workbench, sticky side up. As you remove the parts, lay them out in order on the tape so they're ready when it's time to reassemble.

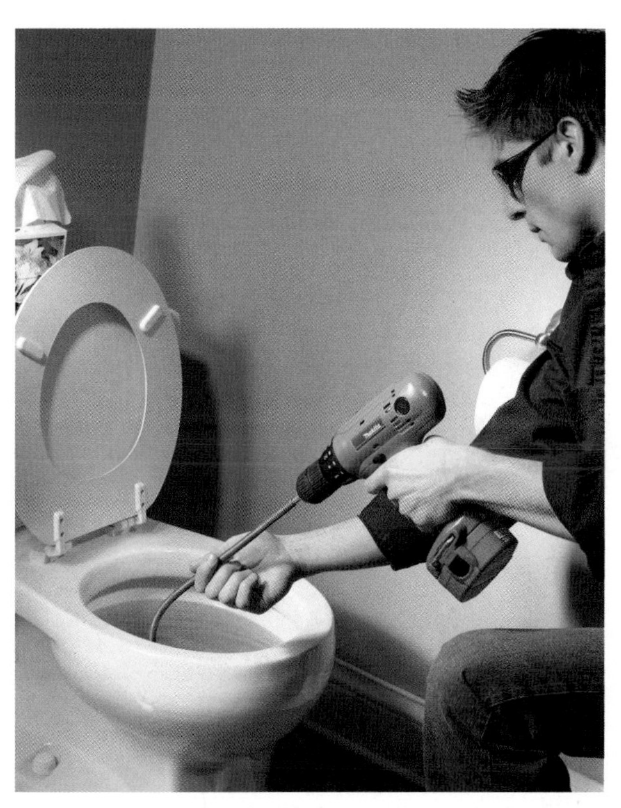

POWER SNAKE

I never had much luck augering toilets with those crooked, S-shaped handles that come with plumbing snakes. Instead, I cut my snake down to 6 ft. and made an adapter I can hook up to a cordless drill. Cut the head off a long lag bolt that'll thread inside the snake. Chuck the bolt into a cordless drill, and on the "slow" setting screw the lag bolt into the snake. The power auger will bust through the worst clogs. Go easy on the trigger; it doesn't have to spin fast.

SOFT JAWS FOR SLIP-JOINT PLIERS

Here's a classic hint worth repeating: When you're working on pipes, prevent scratches and get a better grip by covering the jaws of your slip-joint pliers with short pieces of garden hose. When you're done, store the "soft jaws" on the handles.

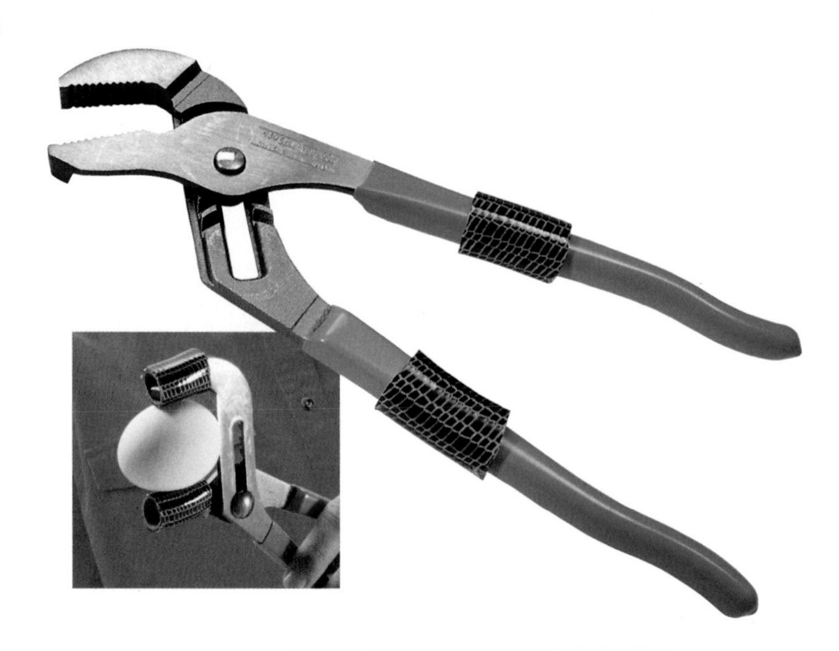

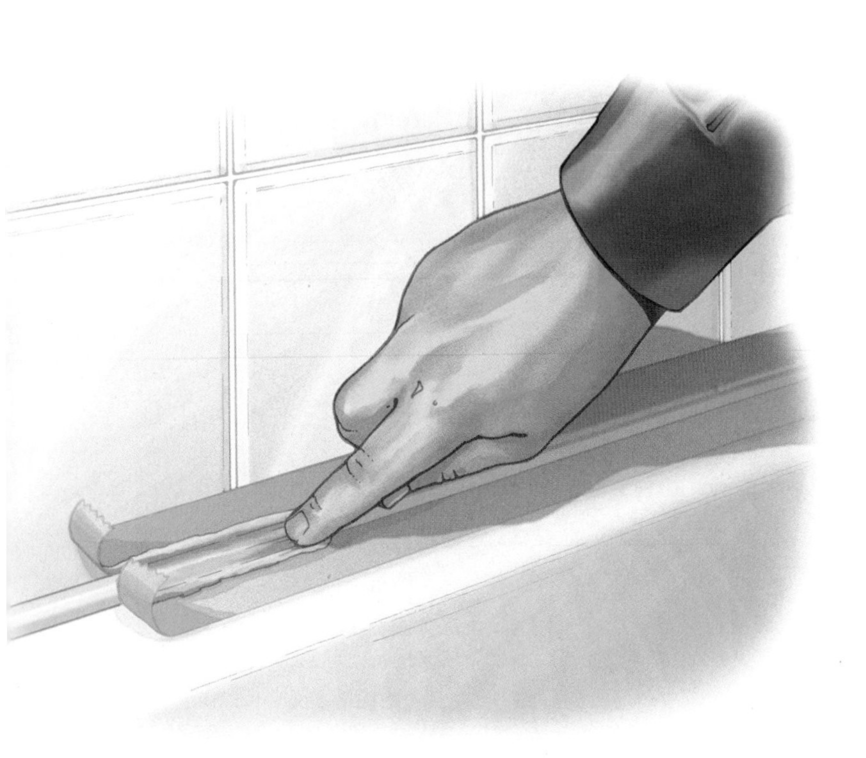

NEAT CAULKING

When you want a neat, uniform bead of caulking in a highly visible area, use masking tape to keep the surrounding area clean. That way you won't mess up the bead when you clean up. Position the masking tape so that your finger will plow all the excess caulk onto the tape when you form the bead.

EASIER TOILET MOUNTING

Toilets are heavy and awkward to get over the flange bolts, especially by yourself. Make the job easier by putting straws over the bolts to lengthen them and guide them into the bolt holes.

Great Goofs™

Snake on the loose

One Sunday morning, I woke to a clogged sewer drain. Frustrated, I went to my local rental shop and picked up a 150-ft. power plumber's snake to clean the line once and for all. I inserted the snake into the cleanout, and everything seemed to be fine until I got to the end of the snake and still didn't seem to have reached the clog. I went outside and discovered that the snake had traveled out the roof vent and down the side of the house and had become tangled in my neighbor's perfectly pruned rosebushes. I carefully removed the snake, pulled it back through and tried again—this time successfully.

Catastrophe

While I was rolling the fridge in and out to clean behind it, the copper tubing to the icemaker got crunched. I decided to replace it with plastic tubing. I removed the old copper, pushed the new tubing through the floor and into the old saddle valve, and then gave it a try. Wow! Everything worked just fine (and on the first try). Suddenly I heard our cat dashing across the floor. I rushed into the kitchen and saw water spraying everywhere. After shutting off the water, I examined the tubing and saw that it was covered with tiny cat tooth marks. I immediately decided that I like copper better!

Just a trickle

I was helping my brother remodel a kitchen, and when it came time to install the sink cabinet, I saw that one of the water-supply pipes coming out of the wall was dripping. I stuffed a small piece of cloth into the pipe as a plug to keep the bottom of the sink cabinet dry. After a few weeks, we installed the sink and hooked up the faucet but only got a trickle of cold water. We called the faucet company and tried several remedies but nothing worked. Finally, I removed the shutoff valve and there it was: the little piece of cloth still stuffed into the pipe and blocking the flow!

Using Tools:™ Leakproof Solder Joints

I hold my breath every time I finish a soldering job and turn the water back on. Even a pinhole leak creates a bunch more work. But luckily, if you take a methodical approach and a little extra care in cleaning and fluxing the joints, leaks in newly soldered copper pipes are rare. Soldering copper plumbing is a skill anyone can learn with a little practice. And it doesn't require a large investment in tools. In this article, we'll show you how to do a leakproof soldering job the first time—and a few cool tools to make the job quicker and easier.

Buy a self-lighting torch for safety and convenience

After years of using a regular $10 torch, I finally splurged on a fancy model with a built-in lighter. They cost more, between $20 and $35, but boy, what a difference. Just pull the trigger to light the flame. No more fumbling with a striker or match. And it's safer, too. I used to leave the torch burning just to avoid relighting it. Now I turn it off when I set it down to avoid accidentally igniting my blue jeans. In addition to the self-lighting feature, look for one that burns MAPP gas. MAPP gas produces a hotter flame, which is better for soldering larger diameter pipes (1-in. and larger) and brass valves. Once you're comfortable with how much heat to apply for a good solder joint, you can switch to MAPP gas to speed up all of your soldering jobs.

BUILT-IN LIGHTER

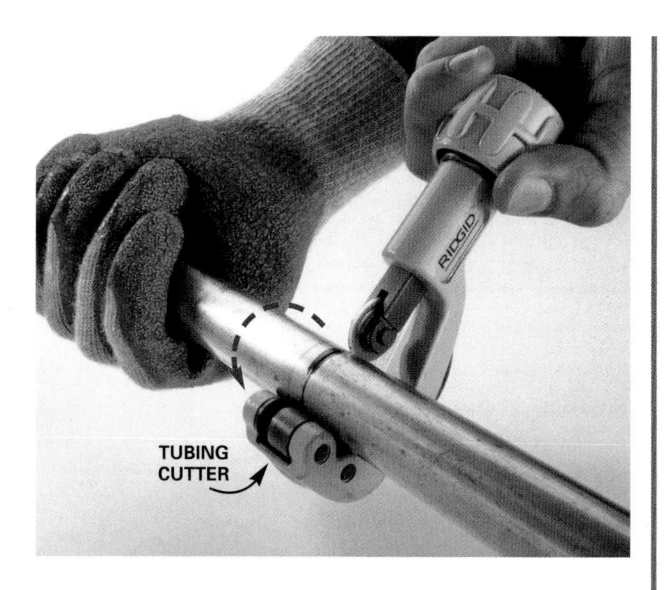

Use a tubing cutter to cleanly cut copper pipes

Use a good-quality tubing cutter ($15 to $25) rather than a hacksaw. You'll be assured clean cuts with square ends that fit neatly into the fittings. The cutting process leaves a small burr inside the pipe. To avoid creating undesirable turbulence inside the pipe, remove the burr with the flip-out burr remover on the cutter or with a special pencil-shaped, burr-removing tool.

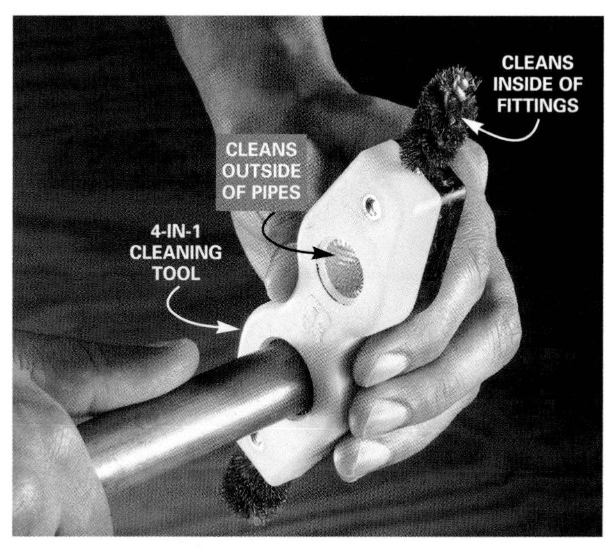

Use a steel brush for complete cleaning of pipes and fittings

Oils, oxidation and other impurities on the outside of pipes and inside of fittings prevent solder from sticking. To clean them, you can use just about anything that's abrasive, including sandpaper and emery cloth. But for the quickest, cleanest results, buy a 4-in-1 cleaning tool like the one shown ($9). Use it to clean the outside of pipes and the inside of fittings for 1/2-in. and 3/4-in. copper.

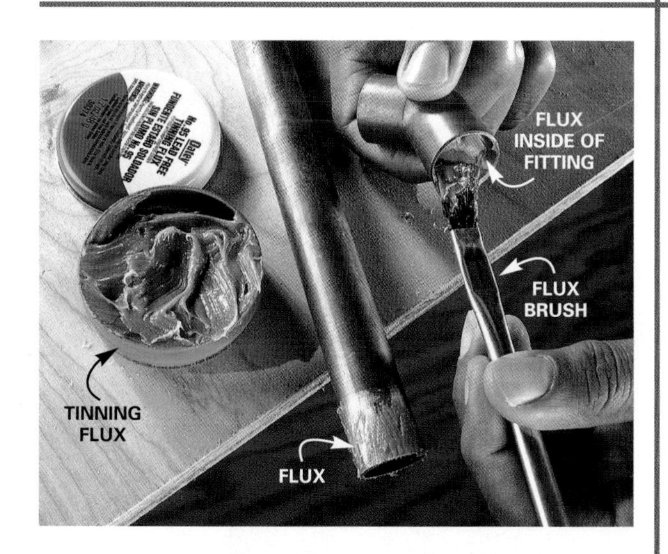

Apply tinning flux rather than regular flux

After a thorough cleaning, coat the pipe and fitting with flux before heating the joint. This helps solder flow into the joint. You may find two or three kinds of flux on the shelf. We recommend tinning flux. It contains a bit of powdered metal alloy that is similar to solder. The alloy melts and coats the inside of the joint and helps ensure a solder joint that's completely filled and leakproof.

Assemble the pipes, then solder the joints all at once

We don't recommend trying to assemble the entire plumbing run before starting to solder, but cutting, sanding and fluxing a grouping of pipes is a good practice. It allows you to accurately cut and fit the pipes before soldering. With this done, it's an easy matter to solder the joints one after the other. Since the pipes are held firmly in position, you don't have to worry about accidentally disturbing a joint before it's cooled.

Using Tools™: Leakproof Solder Joints

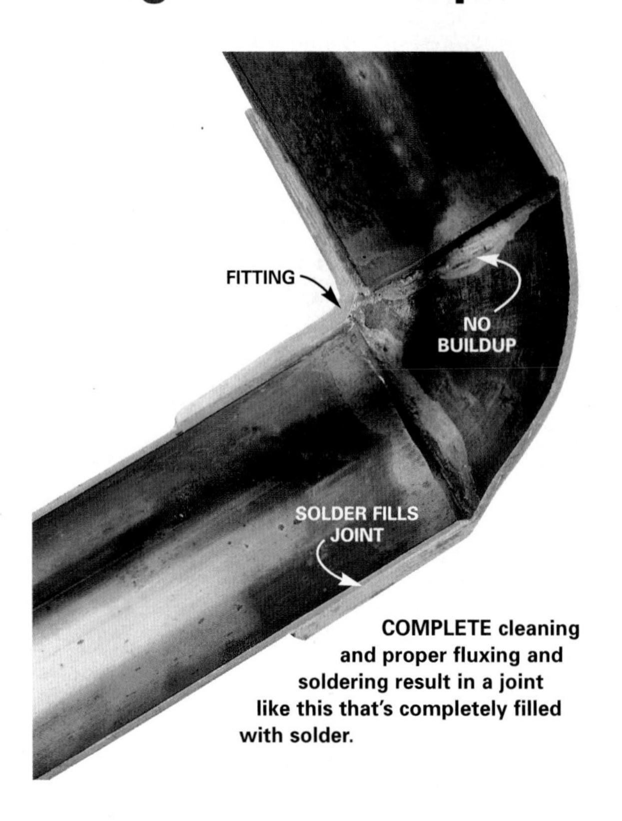

COMPLETE cleaning and proper fluxing and soldering result in a joint like this that's completely filled with solder.

Check to make sure the joint is filled

With practice, you'll know by feel when you've successfully soldered a joint. The solder will flow easily and completely around and into the fitting. But when you're just starting out, it's a good idea to inspect the joints for voids. A good solder joint should have an even band of solder showing all the way around. If you see an area that looks as if it needs more solder, brush a little flux onto the joint. If the joint is still warm, the flux will melt and flow into the void. Then reheat the joint and resolder it.

Heat the joint just enough to melt the solder

If you don't heat the joint enough, the solder won't flow into it. If you heat the joint too long, you'll burn the flux (it'll smoke and turn black) and make it difficult to get the solder to flow into the joint. Applying just the right amount of heat comes with practice, but it's not hard to learn. Here's how: Light the torch and, if possible, adjust the torch until the blue part of the flame is about 1 to 2 in. long (this depends somewhat on the type of torch and tip you use). Then position the tip of the blue part of the flame on the fitting and heat the joint about five seconds or until the flux starts to bubble and sizzle.

Test the joint by touching the solder to the seam on the side opposite the flame. When the copper is hot enough, the solder will melt like butter. Move the flame away from the joint and feed about 1/2 in. to 3/4 in. of solder into the joint. The solder will flow into all areas of a properly cleaned and fluxed joint. Then to make sure the joint is completely filled, run the tip of the solder quickly around the seam. It's easier to reach around the backside of the joint if you bend a hook on the end of the solder first.

If the solder beads up and rolls off rather than flowing into the joint, you've probably burned the flux or the copper isn't clean enough. You'll have to take the joint apart to clean and reflux it before trying again.

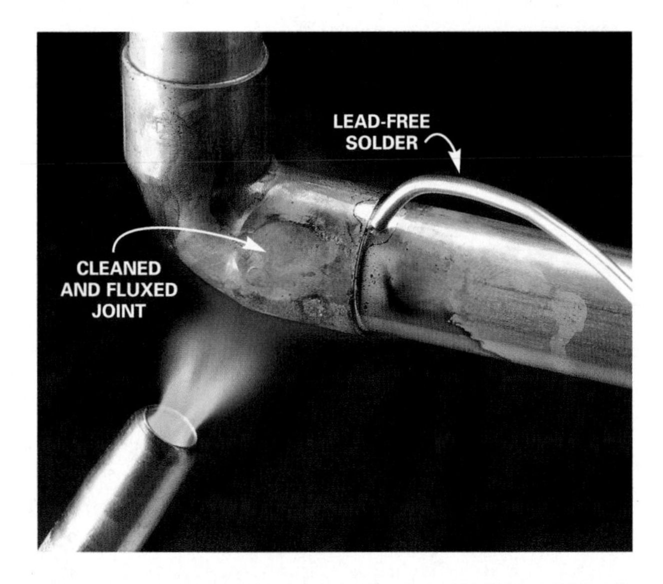

Don't burn down the house!

I'm always a little nervous when working so close to wood with a flaming torch, especially when the water is turned off. That's why I make a point of filling a bucket with water first. I also keep a fire extinguisher handy and protect flammable materials with a flame protector (about $15).

5 Interior Projects, Repairs & Remodeling

IN THIS CHAPTER

Stop Dust! 114

You Can Fix It 118
Stubborn bifold doors

Ask Handyman 121
Cracked walls and frozen doors

Using Tools: Leveling Tips 122

Home Theater 126

Gallery of Ideas 128
Crown molding, stair rails and finished basements

Handy Hints 131
Tips on hanging pictures, cutting insulation, touching up woodwork and more ...

Burglar-Proof Your Door 134

Great Goofs 139

STOP **DUST!**

Protect your home from dust and damage during remodeling

by **Gary Wentz**

DRIVE DUST OUTSIDE WITH A FAN

A fan blowing out the window helps to keep dust levels down, and it creates a slight vacuum in the work area. That way, any gaps in your dust barrier will let air flow into the work zone, but dust-laden air can't sneak into surrounding rooms. This works so well, in fact, that you may not even need a dust barrier for light-dust projects. Just be sure to close large gaps around the fan with cardboard or plastic so wind gusts don't blow the dust right back inside. For good airflow, you may have to crack open a door or window on the opposite side of the room.

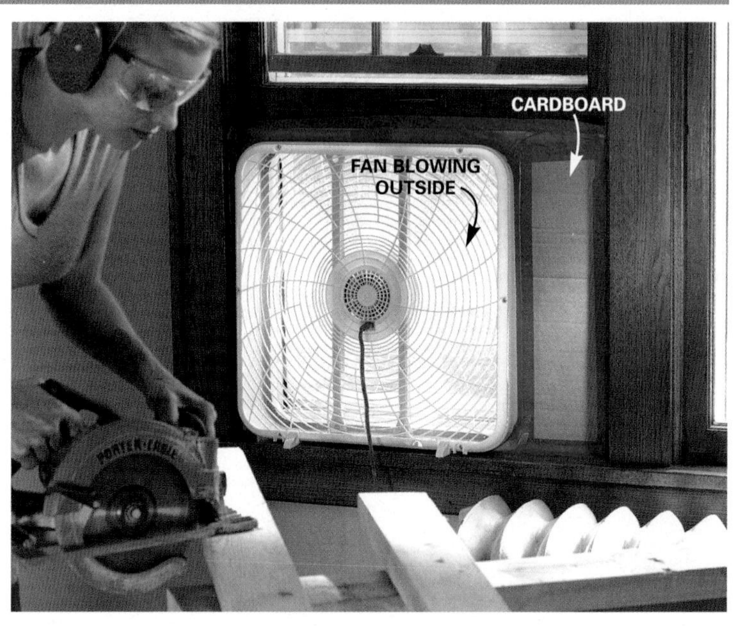

VACUUM WITHOUT RAISING MORE DUST

The exhaust stream from a shop vacuum can raise more dust than the vacuum sucks up. And small particles (like drywall dust) can sail right through the vacuum filter to form a fine dust cloud. You can solve both problems with some extra vacuum hose: Connect a hose to the exhaust port and run it outside, or set the vacuum outside and run the hose inside. If you want a filter that traps even the tiniest dust particles, try a high-efficiency version such as the CleanStream filter. These filters are pricey ($25 to $35), but they're easy to clean and last for years.

Ten feet of 2-1/2 in. vacuum hose costs about $20 at home centers. CleanStream filters are available at Sears, Lowe's and Menards. For other dealers, see www.cleanstream.com or call (800) 758-6755.

SEAL OFF WITH PLASTIC

Dust goes everywhere air flows, so the key to stopping dust is stopping airflow. A loose curtain of plastic hung with a few strips of tape won't do the job. Instead, make your dust barrier as airtight as possible. Completely seal the top and sides with tape. Taping to walls is usually easier than taping to woodwork. If you can't seal the bottom edge with tape, lay a board across it. Light plastic (1 mil or so) is fine for most jobs. But if you need to pass through the dust barrier, use heavier 4- or 6-mil plastic and add an adhesive-backed zipper.

A variety of tarp zippers is available at home centers and hardware stores. One product, the "Tarp Zip-Up" by Tarpline Products, is available at The Home Depot for about $8.50.

COVER UP AIR DUCTS

Construction dust sucked into return air ducts can plug your furnace filter. Even worse, small particles can pass through the filter and coat every room in the house with a blanket of fine dust when the blower turns on. Air supply ducts can be a problem too—dust that settles inside will come blasting out when your heating/cooling system starts up. You can close the damper on a supply register, but it won't seal out dust as effectively as plastic and tape. Note: Turn off the heating/cooling system while the ducts are covered. Operating the system with restricted airflow can damage it.

AVOID MASKING TAPE HASSLES

Painters go through miles of masking tape, and every pro has a horror story: the flimsy tape that tore into a million pieces during removal; the cheap stuff that left a trail of adhesive behind; or worst of all, the too-sticky tape that took the finish right off the woodwork. Follow three rules to avoid the hassle.

- Use a medium-adhesion tape for most jobs. These tapes have names like "Safe Release" or "Clean Release." There are also low-adhesion tapes for delicate surfaces like wallpaper, and high-adhesion tapes for hard-to-mask surfaces like brick. A painting store often has the best tape selection.
- Remove the tape as soon as possible. The adhesive bond strengthens over time. Depending on the type of adhesive, masking tapes are meant to stay in place from one to 14 days. Check and heed the label.
- Forget about price. Cheap tape won't seem like a bargain if it takes hours to remove or pulls the paint off the wall. And no tape will perform well if it has sat on your shelf for a year or more; buy a fresh roll.

WRAP DOORWAYS FOR BUMP PROTECTION

Remodeling means lugging tons of big, clumsy stuff through doorways and tight spaces and around corners. Even if an object isn't heavy, it's best to have a helper to steer big stuff through tough spots. With or without a helper, cardboard is a good defense against accidents. You can wrap door jambs with it, cover up wall corners, or even shield large sections of wall along main pathways. To make sure the cardboard stays in place, crease it thoroughly to fit corners and don't be stingy with the masking tape. Doors can take a beating during remodeling too. The best protection is to remove them from the work zone. If removing a door isn't practical, clad it with cardboard.

COVER BASEBOARD WITH CARDBOARD

Whether you're moving a ladder or stacking 2x4s, it's all too easy to bang up baseboards. But protecting them is simple: Just cut strips of cardboard about an inch wider than your baseboard, set them against the wall and tape them top and bottom (also see the bottom photo on p. 114). If nearby walls are at risk, don't hesitate to tape cardboard over them as well. It'll save you from having to spend a weekend repainting.

SHIELD FLOORS FROM SCRATCHES AND DENTS

Carpeted floors are easily protected from snags and stains with a heavy canvas dropcloth. Safeguarding hard flooring isn't so simple. A hammer knocked off a ladder can dent wood flooring, chip ceramic tile or even puncture vinyl, and heavy foot traffic will grind grit into the floor. For protection against falling tools (and just about everything else), cut sheets of 1/8-in. hardboard to fit the room and duct-tape them together at the seams. Also tape around the perimeter with masking tape so grit can't get underneath the hardboard and scratch the floor. For quicker protection of hard flooring, use strips of rosin paper taped at the seams and around the perimeter. While rosin paper can't match the impact and puncture protection of hardboard, two or three layers of it provide good defense against scratches and spills.

A 4 x 8-ft. sheet of 1/8-in. thick hardboard costs about $7 at home centers. A roll of rosin paper costs about $8 and covers about 400 sq. ft.

PROTECT STAIRS SAFELY

Protecting stairs is tricky because you don't want to use anything that will cause a slip or trip. Rosin paper is a good choice for wood stairs because you can crease it over the edge of the tread and tape it securely around the entire perimeter. You can also tape separate sheets to the risers. For carpeted stairs, use a long, narrow dropcloth (called a runner). Secure the runner by driving small nails right through the carpet and into the treads. A 4 x 12-ft. runner costs about $18 at home centers.

You Can Fix It™

STUBBORN BIFOLD DOORS

ADJUST A DOOR THAT STICKS

Are you frustrated with a bifold door that doesn't close smoothly, or never opens without sticking, scraping or binding? Chances are it's out of alignment in the door frame. The fix is usually simple and often takes less than 10 minutes.

First close the door and look along the edge of the door as it lines up with the frame (**opening photo**). The door edge and frame should line up nice and parallel. Even if it's off by only 1/4 in., the door will probably bind. Most often the problem is a loosened top pivot and bracket, which allowed the door to slip sideways out of alignment (**Photo 1**). Open the door and then loosen the setscrew for the top bracket slightly with a screwdriver. Then close it again. Push or pull the top of the closed door to align its edge parallel to the frame. Close the door to check for smooth operation and to see how the doors meet. Open the door gently so the pivot doesn't slip, then tighten the setscrew. You may have to repeat these steps a few times with both doors to get the "perfect" result.

If the door binds against the lower part of the frame, check the bottom pivot and bracket next. (Look for a worn edge on the door and scrape marks on the door frame.) The bottom pivot often loosens and slips. Either raise the door slightly to shift the pivot in or out, or loosen the setscrew and shift the bracket seat (**Photo 2**), depending on the type of hardware you have. (See "Replacement Parts," p. 120, for types.) Sometimes the entire bracket comes loose because the mounting screws are stripped, broken or missing (**Photo 2**). You'll need to remove the door to fix these. Test the door for smooth, non-binding operation by opening and closing it several times. You may have to readjust the top pivot bracket to make the door parallel to the frame again.

The top roller guide rarely needs attention, but make sure that it runs smoothly in the track. Apply a light coating of wax or silicone spray to eliminate any sticking.

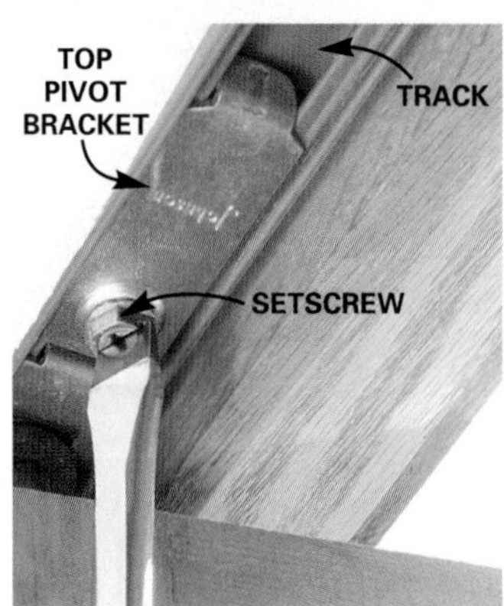

1 LOOSEN the top pivot bracket setscrew with a screwdriver. Slide the bracket in the track until the door is parallel to the jamb. Tighten the setscrew firmly.

2 TIGHTEN a loose bottom bracket with 1-1/2 in. screws driven through the drywall into the framing. Avoid screwing through the carpeting, if possible.

TRIM A DOOR THAT BINDS ON CARPET

1 MEASURE up 1/2 in. from the highest point on the new carpeting and mark the door.

2 OPEN the door completely and lift it to compress the top pivot spring (1). Swing the door bottom out from the bottom bracket (2). Pull the door down and out of the top pivot bracket.

Adding carpet or changing to a thicker pile may cause the bottom of a bifold door to scrape and bind along the floor. First try to raise the door to clear the carpet using the bottom pivot adjustment (see the height adjustments in the "Replacement parts" photo on p. 120). But usually you have to trim off the door bottom.

The easiest way to measure a bifold door for cutting is with the door slightly opened. A half inch of clearance is adequate (**Photo 1**).

Removing a bifold door doesn't always go as smoothly as **Photo 2** shows. Sometimes the top pivot doesn't compress enough to free the bottom pivot. Turn the bottom pivot height adjustment to lower it, if possible. Or gently lift the door off the lower bracket with a flat pry bar. As a last resort, loosen the top pivot bracket setscrew and slide the top away from the door frame.

To replace the door, follow the steps in **Photo 2** in reverse order. Check for proper alignment.

Lay the door face down on a worktable. Cut from the backside of the door to leave a clean cut on the front. You can reduce splintering by first scoring the cutting line (**Photo 3**) and, using a guide, sawing slightly to the outside of it (**Photo 4**). Bevel the cut edges with 100-grit sandpaper (**Photo 5**).

Cutting the door will shorten the bottom pivot hole. You may have to redrill to deepen it.

Extend the bottom pivot the same amount as the door was shortened, using the height adjustment screw. (See "Replacement Parts" on p. 120.)

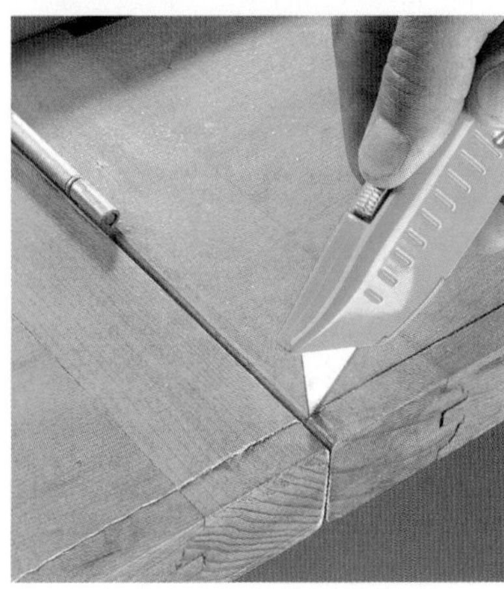

3 MARK the cutting line on the back side of the door and then score the line with a utility knife to reduce splintering.

4 CLAMP a cutting guide to the door, mount a crosscut-type blade in your saw and cut slightly to the outside of the line.

5 KNOCK the sharp edges off the fresh cut with sandpaper. Add a coat of sealer to the raw edge to prevent swelling. Remount the door.

TIGHTEN A LOOSE KNOB

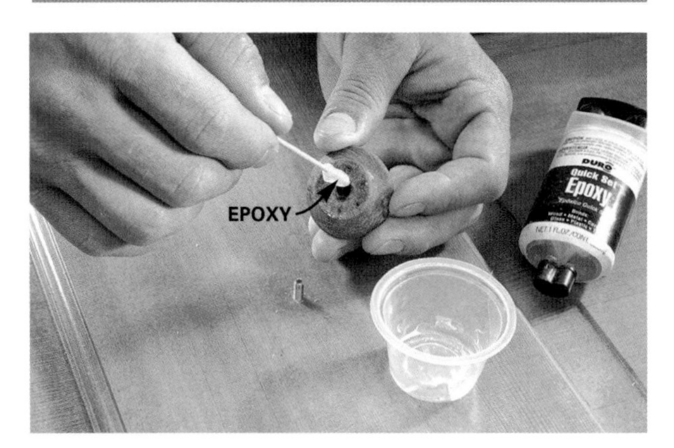

ADD a drop of epoxy to repair a loose door pull. Screw it on and allow it to set for 24 hours before use.

You can fix that wiggly knob so it won't come loose again! Simply put a drop of epoxy into the knob hole before reattaching the knob. And add a washer under the screwhead inside, if the screwhead is pulling into the door. Allow the epoxy to set up for 24 hours before use.

Buyer's Guide

One good source of bifold replacement parts is Blaine Window Hardware, (800) 678-1919, www.blainewindow.com.

Replacement parts

If you need to replace worn, broken or missing parts, look for exact replacements at home centers or hardware stores. If you can't find what you need, be creative. If the parts are basically the same size and shape, they should work fine. You may need to redrill the pivot holes to fit a larger pivot, or plug and redrill to fit a smaller one.

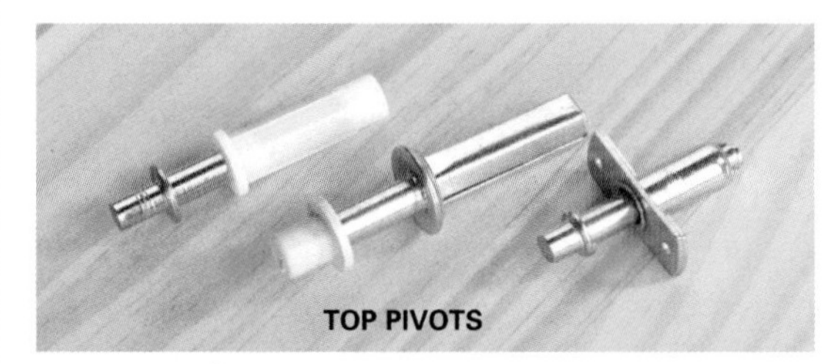

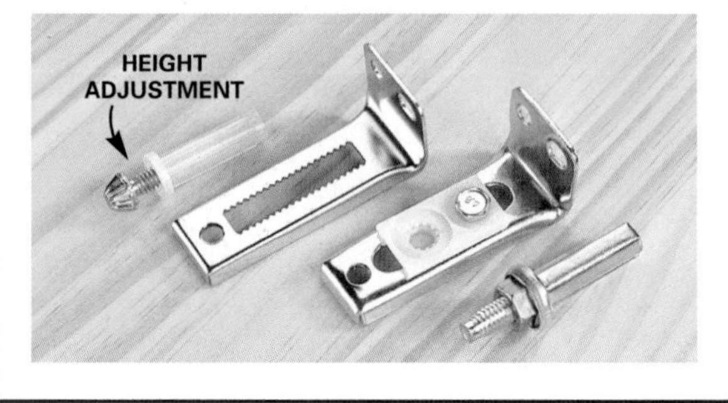

New Product

FIX YOUR BIFOLD DOOR

Often, heavily used bifold doors wobble and don't work because the top pivot has broken loose. We stumbled upon a neat repair gizmo called "The Bracket" (800-343-3275) that reinforces the pivot. It costs about $3 at hardware stores. To install it, grab the closed bifold door with both hands and lift up while you pull the bottom pivot free of the floor bracket. (To make re-installation easier, first mark where the bottom pin sits in the floor bracket.) Set the door on a workbench or on sawhorses and remove the pivot. After you secure "The Bracket", rehang the door by aligning the top pivot with its bracket, lifting the door and setting the bottom pivot back into the floor bracket.

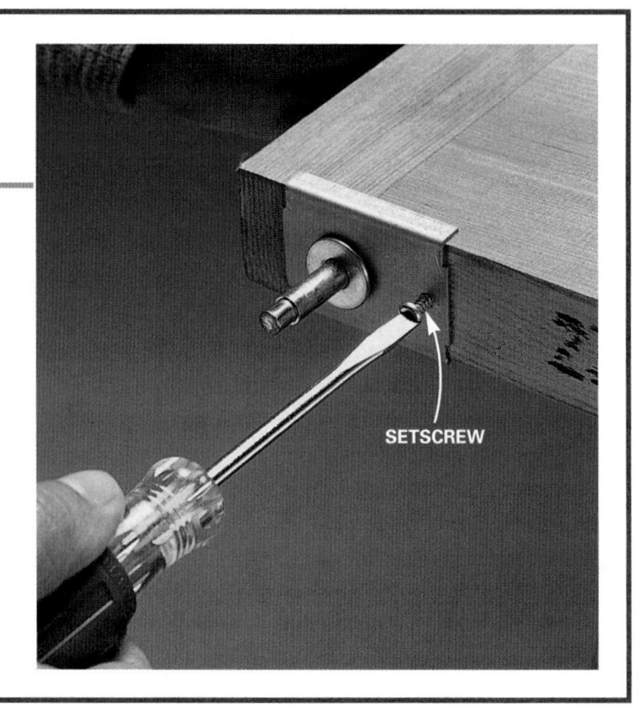

Ask Handyman™

CRACKED BASEMENT WALL

I have a crack running horizontally along my basement concrete block wall. There's a stair-step crack on each end of this main 1/4-in. crack, and the wall has bowed in about 1 in. Is this wall stable? Can I just fill the crack and finish the basement?

NO. Don't handle this cracked wall by simply filling the crack and finishing off the basement. If you only had the stair-step cracks, you could go ahead with your basement finish work, because that type of crack is a normal sign of settling. Stair-step cracks may cause cracks in other walls above or a door to rub, but they don't compromise the strength of the foundation.

However, the horizontal crack that has bowed the wall inward is the sign of a severely weakened wall that can fail. Even if it has been stable for awhile, it can no longer reliably support the load it's supposed to carry.

Our advice is to ask a local general contractor or building official to direct you to a structural engineer who can examine the wall and surroundings and suggest the correct method to reinforce the wall. Then you can proceed with your project.

To view more details about basement wall repair and types of bracing, check out www.structuraldynamics.com.

FROZEN DOOR

I have a metal sliding glass door that freezes shut in the winter. Any advice on how to prevent this?

There's no inexpensive solution to this problem except to lower the humidity level inside your house. Metal is a good heat conductor, so it cools rapidly in cold weather and provides an ideal surface for moisture to condense on. The colder it gets, the more condensation builds up and the more likely it'll freeze your door shut.

Condensation commonly occurs when warm humid indoor air strikes cold windows, leaving moisture on the glass (and metal frame in your case). When thermostats are lowered at night and the temperature drops, condensation increases. Ideally, as the day warms up, the door should warm up and dry within a few hours with the curtains open.

To reduce your indoor humidity level, run bath fans while showering, kitchen fans while cooking, and reduce the number of houseplants. If that strategy doesn't work, or your indoor humidity is already low, increase air circulation by leaving curtains open. Set a forced-air furnace so the fan runs continuously until the condensation problem stops.

If nothing works, consider replacing the metal door and frame with a more energy-efficient one.

Using Tools:™ Leveling Tips

Whether you're hanging a picture or building a wall, getting things level or plumb is essential for first-class results. Here are several of my favorite techniques for performing common leveling and plumbing tasks quickly and accurately.

Check the accuracy of your level

I've never understood how it happens, but it seems like every level eventually gets a little "off." In some cases, this small inaccuracy won't matter. But if you're doing finicky work like setting kitchen cabinets or installing doors and windows, you'll want an accurate level. The photos show how to check your level. Expensive levels may be worth repairing. Call the manufacturer to find out if yours is repairable. When you're buying a new level, use the same technique to check it for accuracy before leaving the store with it.

Follow the same procedure to check the level's accuracy in the "plumb," or vertical, position. You'll have to hold the playing cards in place while you check the level.

SHIM the end of your level with playing cards until the bubble is centered. (If the bubble is already centered, you won't need any cards.) We've marked one end of the level with blue tape to distinguish it from the opposite end.

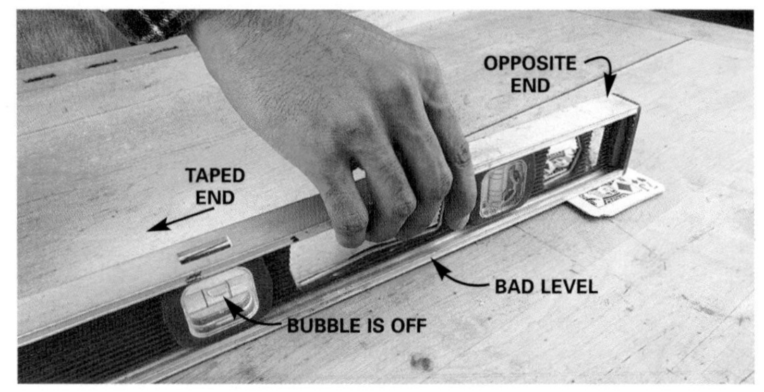

ROTATE the level 180 degrees (end for end) and rest it on the same stack of cards. If the bubble is in the center, your level is accurate. If not, have it repaired or get a new level.

MARK the wall at both ends of the level.

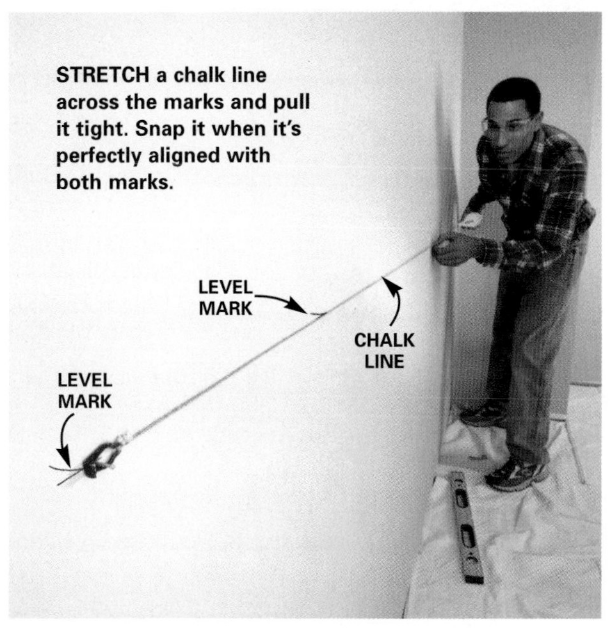

STRETCH a chalk line across the marks and pull it tight. Snap it when it's perfectly aligned with both marks.

Make long, level lines with a short level

Wainscoting, wallpaper borders and suspended ceilings all require a level line before you can start installing them. Here's a tip I learned from a suspended-ceiling installer (before low-priced laser levels became available). It's simple. Carefully adjust your level at the correct height until the bubble is perfectly centered and mark the wall at both ends of the level. You must have an accurate level, because any error will be multiplied by the length of the line. Then stretch a chalk line across the marks to extend the line. Use the longest level you own. It's best to have a helper who can hold the other end of the line and stretch it tight while you align it with both marks. Then snap the chalk line and double-check to make sure it's exactly aligned with the marks. If you're careful, you can expect the line to be accurate within 1/4 in. over 12 ft.

Lasers work great for long-distance leveling

There are many types of laser levels that simplify long-distance leveling. The $50 version we're showing is a small "torpedo" level with a built-in laser light (RoboToolz RT-3210-1 from www.robotoolz.com, 800-984-0404). Turn on the laser light and adjust the level until the bubble is centered between the lines. The point of visible laser light will be level with a reference mark on the body of the level. More expensive laser levels have self-leveling mechanisms that eliminate the need to adjust the bubble.

You can mount laser levels on a tripod, but if you don't own a tripod, thread a 1/4-in. No. 20 machine screw into the hole on the bottom of the level, letting it protrude about 1/4 in. to serve as a pivot point. Set the level onto the pivot and use shims to center the bubble (**photo below**). Mark the wall at the dot of light and measure up or down to the desired height. Then swivel the laser on the pivot, level it, mark the wall again, and measure up or down the same distance. Snap a line between the points.

SCREW NOT INCLUDED

LASER

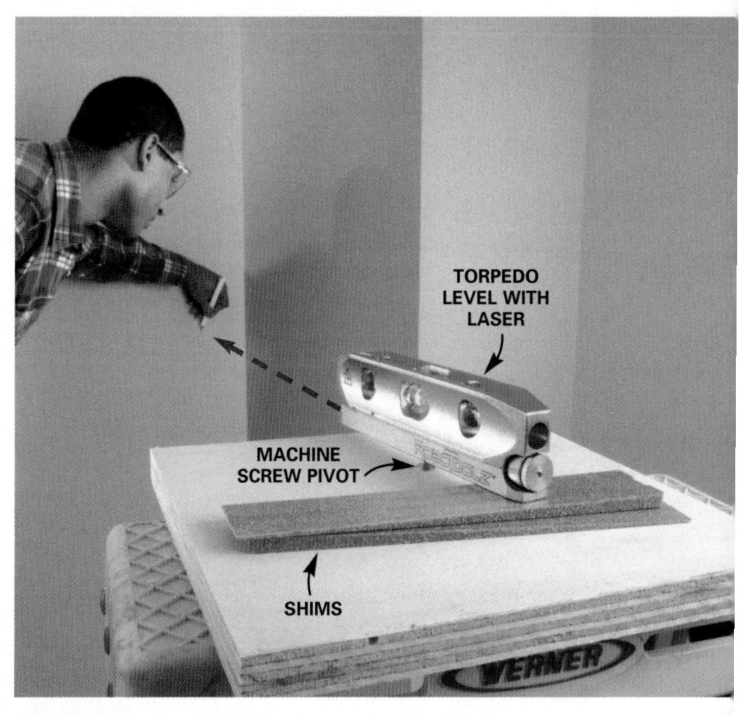

ADJUST the torpedo with shims to level it. Mark the wall at the point of light. Swivel the level on the pivot and adjust it with shims again. Mark the wall at the new location.

Using Tools™: Leveling Tips

DROP the plumb bob from the ceiling and suspend it about 1/2 in. above your floor.

Build walls plumb with a plumb bob

One of the quickest and easiest ways to plumb up or down from any given point is with a plumb bob. The brass plumb bob shown costs about $12, but less expensive versions will work just as well. We're using the plumb bob to transfer wall layout marks from the ceiling to the floor. Suspend the plumb bob about 1/2 in. above the floor and center the point exactly over the intersecting lines. Then mark the location on the ceiling. The key to accuracy is to wait for the bob to stop swinging. To speed things up, ask a helper to steady the plumb bob while you adjust the position of the string. Plumb bobs have one major drawback: They don't work in windy conditions.

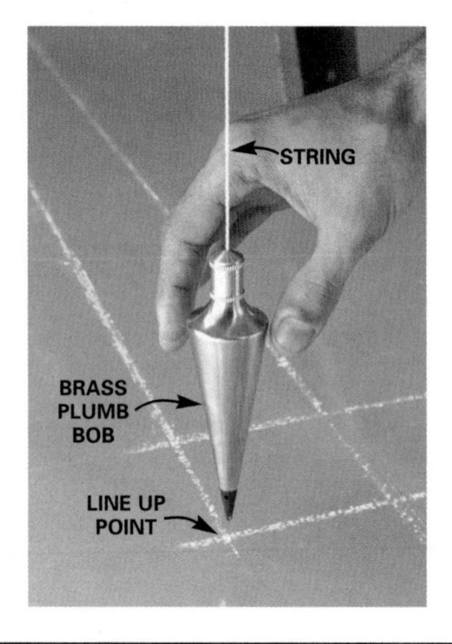

ASK a helper to steady the plumb bob and tell you which way to move the string to center it over the point on the floor.

Slope pipes with a shim

The next time you need to put a consistent slope on pipes, concrete formwork or landscaping projects, try this hint. Tape a shim to one end of your level to establish the desired slope—say, 1/4 in. per foot for a drain. Center the bubble and your project will be perfectly sloped. Calculate the thickness of the shim by multiplying the length of your level in feet by the desired slope (inches per foot). We wanted 1/4-in. per foot slope on this drainpipe, so for our 2-ft. level we needed a 1/2-in. thick shim. If it's more convenient to set the level on top of your project, tape the shim to the bottom instead.

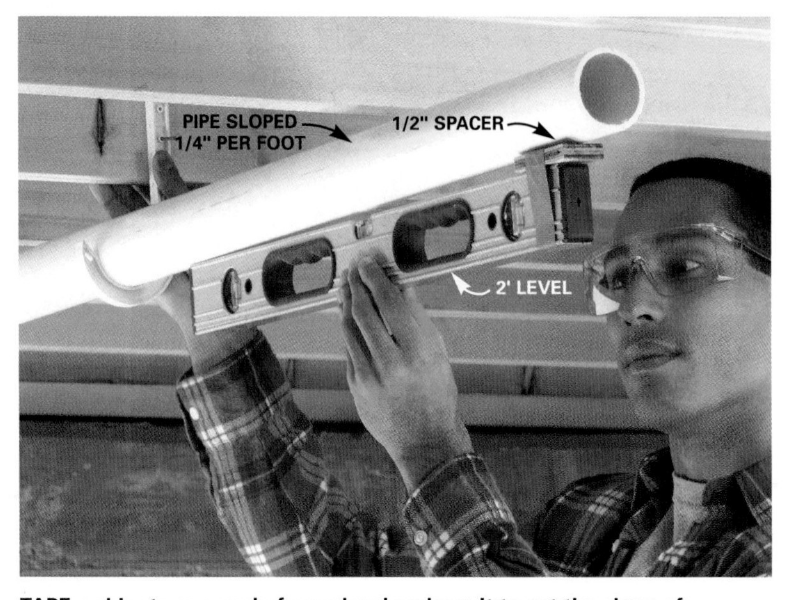

TAPE a shim to one end of your level and use it to set the slope of plumbing pipes.

Block a straightedge for crooked walls

You could plumb a wall by simply setting your level against the stud, but it wouldn't give you an accurate reading unless the stud was perfectly straight and smooth. The method shown spans irregularities in the stud and allows you to align the top and bottom plates exactly plumb with each other. Make sure the spacer blocks are the same thickness and that the board they're attached to is perfectly straight. Check to make sure your setup is accurate by flipping it end for end. You should get the same reading on the level. If not, the straightedge may be crooked.

PLUMB walls using a straight board with spacer blocks of equal thickness nailed to each end.

Great Goofs™

Just plumb wrong

My father-in-law asked me to convert his newly acquired Greyhound bus into a camper. Being pretty handy, I got right on the project, working every weekend for several months. I took great pains to get every new partition plumb and level. Finally the project was complete and my father-in-law drove the bus from my place over to his. Upon entering the bus at his house, I was horrified to see that all the partitions were a few degrees out of plumb! It hadn't occurred to me that the bus wasn't level when it was parked at my house.

THE BEST **HOME THEATER**

Convert an extra room into a home theater ... and it won't cost you thousands

by **Gary Wentz**

The very best home theaters are in rooms designed and built just for that purpose. But bringing home theater to your house doesn't have to call for major remodeling or a huge expense. You can adapt a family room, an extra bedroom or just about any other room for a perfectly fine home theater system that your family will love. The key is to know the factors that make a room more or less suitable. This article will help you choose a room and furnish it for optimal sound and viewing. We won't, however, cover home theater technology or equipment. Visit an electronics store for a review of the many choices that will best fit your room.

What's so great about home theater?

A bigger screen is nice, but it's the sound that really makes home theater shine. Unlike a standard TV, which provides sound through a built-in speaker or two, a home theater system has several speakers (usually six) placed around the room. The system divides the soundtrack and sends different sounds to different speakers. So when James Bond is flirting with his latest girlfriend, the voices seem to come straight from the screen. When the bad guys open fire from the right, you hear it from the right. When a helicopter zooms over, you might duck as the roar seems to pass right over you and the subwoofer shakes the room. And this isn't just for 007 wannabes. A simple conversation in a restaurant is more realistic as you hear the clink of silverware and the sound of waiters rushing all around you.

Choose a room for optimal sound

Don't dismiss home theater if you don't have a perfect room. Simple alterations help make up for shortcomings, and almost any room can become a good home theater. For the best sound and viewing, however, choose a room with these characteristics:

■ **An enclosed room.** Four walls and a door form the best home theater room. An enclosed room lets you nudge up the volume without disturbing others and limits the area that has to be filled with sound, so you'll get a more powerful effect from your system. Blocking out light and getting speakers in the right place is easier too (**Figure A**, p. 127).

■ **A rectangular room shape.** Shape influences how sound bounces around the room. Perfectly square rooms or rooms that are twice as long as they are wide can create

Figure A: Home Theater Room Layout

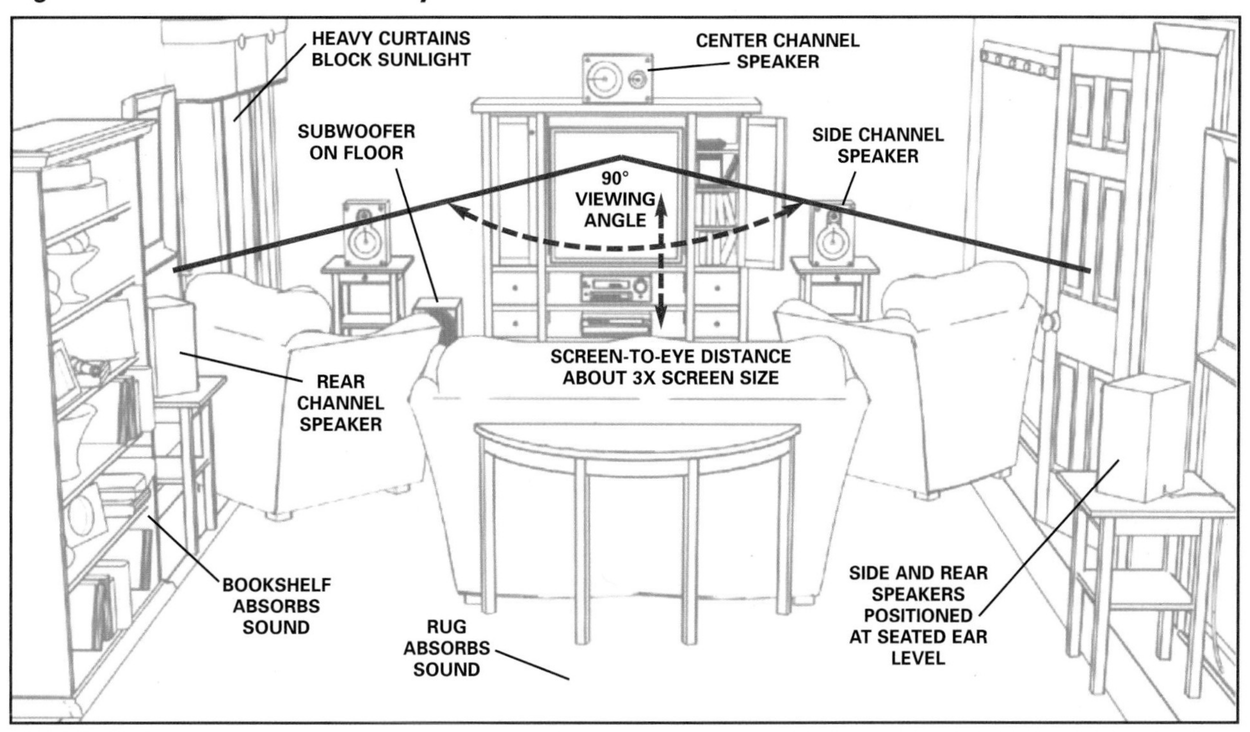

FURNISH a home theater room with sound-absorbing materials. Locate seating so the screen-to-eye distance is about three times the screen size. Side and rear speakers sound best when positioned at ear level when you're seated.

muddy sound patterns. The perfect room is about 1-1/2 times as long as it is wide, with the screen and front speakers placed against one of the short walls.

■ **Large enough for the audience and the screen.** If your home theater only has to accommodate a few people, you can use a very small room—I've seen them as small as 8 x 10 ft. But you don't want a large screen in a small room. Sit too close to a large screen and you'll see the individual dots that make up the picture. Ideally, the eye-to-screen distance is about three times the screen size (measured diagonally). So a 36-in. screen looks just right from about 9 ft. away. When shopping for a TV, bring a tape measure so you can judge picture quality from the seating distance in your home.

■ **Centered seating space.** You don't just need seating space; you need it in front of the screen. An onscreen image appears sharpest when viewed straight on. The farther you move off center, the dimmer it gets. Most screens present a good picture within an arc of 60 to 90 degrees.

Furnish the room for sound and screen

As with any other room, style and comfort will drive your furnishing decisions. But also keep light and sound in mind. For a vibrant picture, you want very little light in the room. For better acoustics, choose soft furnishings that absorb sound, not hard surfaces that reflect it (**Figure A**).

■ **Cover hard floors.** Wall-to-wall carpeting is ideal, but a large rug over wood or tile flooring is almost as good.

■ **Decorate walls with sound absorbers.** Heavy fabric wallpaper is an acoustical improvement over bare walls, and cloth wall hangings—such as decorative quilts—are even better. Pictures or paintings help, but not if they're covered with glass or plastic. A bookshelf against a wall is also an effective sound absorber.

■ **Block out light.** Heavy curtains that completely cover windows are best (for both light and sound). Window coverings that fit inside window openings, such as blinds or shutters, block light pretty well but sometimes allow shafts of light to pass around them. Whatever light does enter the room will be less distracting if you choose darker colors for walls, carpet and other furnishings.

■ **Reduce light reflections.** You already know how annoying strong reflections off a TV screen are. But you've probably learned to ignore the subtle reflections that cloud your TV screen. For picture clarity (and less eyestrain), avoid reflective surfaces, especially glass: mirrors, picture glass, table tops or cabinet doors. Even paint sheen has a noticeable effect. Choose flat or eggshell instead of satin or gloss.

Gallery of Ideas

FROM NOVEMBER, 2004, p. 40

CROWNING TOUCH

Substantial crown molding can change the look and feel of a living room, dining room, even bedroom. It can be a substantial task to install, too. To simplify the project, you can create the molding by "building up" with three smaller pieces. This article uses 22 step-by-step photos to show you how.

Skill Builders

Sure you'll wind up with a gorgeous room! But you'll also be able to tuck a few more carpentry skills into your bag of tricks. You'll learn how to:

- **Make customized cuts on a power miter saw**
- **Cope joints for perfect inside corners**
- **Create large crown moldings using three or more individual moldings**

Project Facts

Cost: About $3.50/lin. ft. for the 3-part, pine crown molding
Skill level: Intermediate to advanced carpentry skills
Time: 1 day for a simple square room; longer for more complex rooms

FROM OCTOBER, 2004, p. 94

ROCK-SOLID STAIR RAIL

More accidents happen on the stairway than anywhere else in the house. A strong stair rail goes a long way toward making stairs safer and easier to use. And, if it's attractive as well, you'll be that much further ahead in the game.

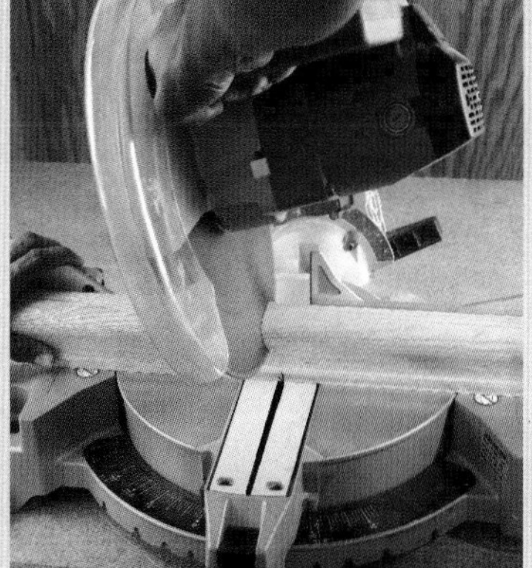

Project Facts

Cost: About $5/ lin. ft. for the oak railing shown
Skill level: Basic carpentry skills
Time: 4 to 6 hours

RESTRETCH A CARPET

Whether you need to tighten up carpet after installing a built-in bookcase or simply restretch a roomful of carpet that's wrinkled, but in good shape, this article will show you how. It's not a big money saver, but it allows you to get the job done on your own time schedule—and get the job done right.

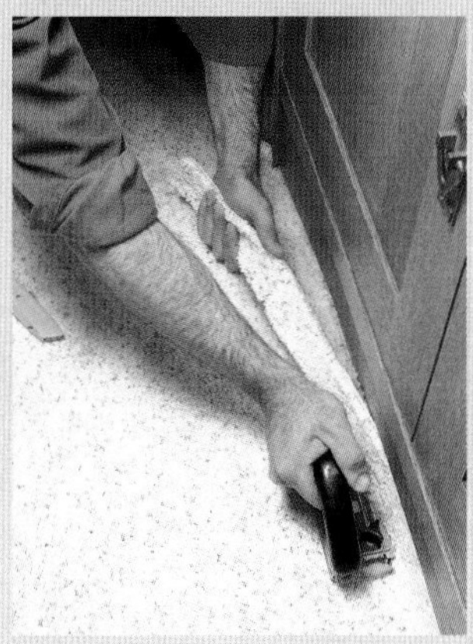

Project Facts

Cost: About $50 for carpet stretching tools
Skill level: Most beginners can tackle this job successfully
Time: 4 to 6 hours

FROM JUNE, 2004, p. 92

To order photocopies of complete articles for the projects shown here, call (715) 246-4521, email familyhandyman@nrmsinc.com or write to: Copies, The Family Handyman, P.O. Box 83695, Stillwater, MN 55083-0695. Many public libraries also carry back issues of *The Family Handyman* magazine.

FROM MAY, 2004, p. 82

FRAMING A BASEMENT

Your basement can be more than a utility and storage area. With some forethought and good techniques, you can make it as warm, comfortable and inviting as any other room in your house. This article shows you how to do the job using only basic carpentry skills and one special tool—a hammer drill for concrete fasteners.

Project Facts

Cost, skill level, and time: All vary greatly depending on project

Skill Builders

In the course of finishing off your basement, you'll learn how to:

- **Properly insulate below-grade walls with both rigid and fiberglass insulation—without creating interior moisture problems**
- **Frame and install both full-height walls and half-height kneewalls**
- **Build soffits for enclosing ductwork, pipes and other obstructions**

To order photocopies of complete articles for the projects shown here, call (715) 246-4521, email familyhandyman@nrmsinc.com or write to: Copies, The Family Handyman, P.O. Box 83695, Stillwater, MN 55083-0695. Many public libraries also carry back issues of *The Family Handyman* magazine.

Handy Hints® from our readers
for hanging pictures

PICTURE-HANGING POINTER

Tired of straightening pictures on the wall every few days? Try this: Use a pliers to push a regular sewing needle about 1/4 in. into the lower back of the wood picture frame. Clip the needle off with a wire cutters so that about 1/4 in. sticks out of the frame. (Remember to wear safety glasses while clipping the needle.) Rehang the picture, straighten it and then push the protruding needle into the wall. No more shifting pictures!

PINPOINT PICTURE HANGING

Here's a nifty way to mark nail hole positions on walls when you're hanging that new picture. Glue two pushpins top to top with a cyanoacrylate glue (such as Super Glue). Find the center of the picture along the upper back edge of the frame and press in one of the pins. Now just hold the picture up, maneuver it to the best spot, and press in to mark for the nail. This tip works best when you're hanging pictures with hardware screwed on the back of the frame, but if you're putting up wire-hung pictures, just measure the distance from the top of the wire to the pushpin hole and move the nail down that distance.

POSITION AND PUSH

GLUE TOP TO TOP

SODA TAB PICTURE HANGERS

The photo says it all! These hangers work great for pictures and even small shelves, and you can't beat the price.

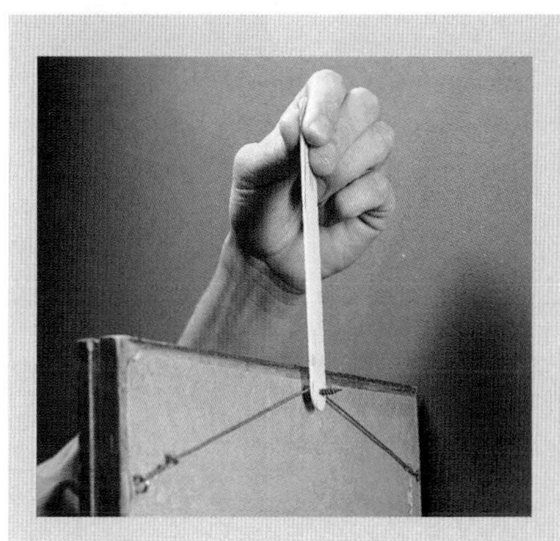

ON-THE-MARK PICTURE HANGER

Drive a 1-1/4 in. drywall screw halfway through one end of a thin wood strip. Hang the picture wire on the screwhead and hold the picture in the desired position. Gently press the upper edge of the picture against the wall to leave a mark for a nail or hanger.

Handy Hints® from our readers

WELL-ARMED TAPE DISPENSER

Use your wrist as a masking tape dispenser during your next painting project. Cut a 4-in. piece from the ankle section of a gym sock, slip it on your wrist, then slide the tape over your hand. The sock protects your arm so the tape won't scratch it. The tape is always close at hand, leaving both hands free for your work.

MAKE YOUR OWN PAINT BRUSH

Instead of buying disposable foam brushes, make your own from 3/4-in. thick foam carpet padding (uncoated). Most carpet stores have scraps of foam padding they'll give you for free. Use a razor blade to cut the padding to the width you need and to form the angled tip. Clip on a clothespin for a handle.

THREE-RING TOOL AND APPLIANCE FILE

Store your appliance and tool manuals in three-ring binders so you can find them when you need them. Insert labeled dividers to organize them for quick reference.

DOOR STAND

Keeping doors upright and stable when you're planing or sanding them just got a whole lot easier with this classic tip. This simple door stand made from shop scraps actually has upright arms to pinch the door and hold it rock-solid while you tune up your door. The secret to the pinching action is the 3/8-in. plywood base that bends from the weight of the door, forcing the tops of the 2x4s together. Here are the key measurements you'll need to make your own:

- 1-1/2 in. x 3-1/2 in. x 24-in. upright arms
- 3/8-in. x 3-1/2 in. x 24-in. plywood base
- 1-1/2 in. x 1-1/2 in. x 4-in. feet
- 1-1/2 in. x 3-1/2 in. x 12-in. 45-degree diagonal braces
- Two strips of carpeting hot-glued to the inside of the uprights

Cut these pieces and assemble them with screws. Be sure to position the uprights 3 in. apart excluding the carpet (a bit closer for thin carpet).

WOODWORK TOUCH-UP

When you're painting a room that has natural finished woodwork, it's pretty hard to avoid getting paint on the trim. Use a wedge-tip permanent marker that's similar to the color of the trim to cover the paint marks. It saves a lot of extra touch-up work.

NO-HOLES CURTAIN ROD

Don't drill holes in your steel entry door to hang a curtain rod. Instead, place self-adhesive plastic hooks on each side of the window. Then hang your curtain from a cafe pocket rod, which rests on the hooks.

STEPLADDER TOOL BUCKET

Bolt a 5-qt. plastic bucket to the shelf on your stepladder to hold paint cans and tools. Use two 1-in. x 1/4-in. machine screws, washers and nuts. You can fold the ladder for storage without removing the bucket.

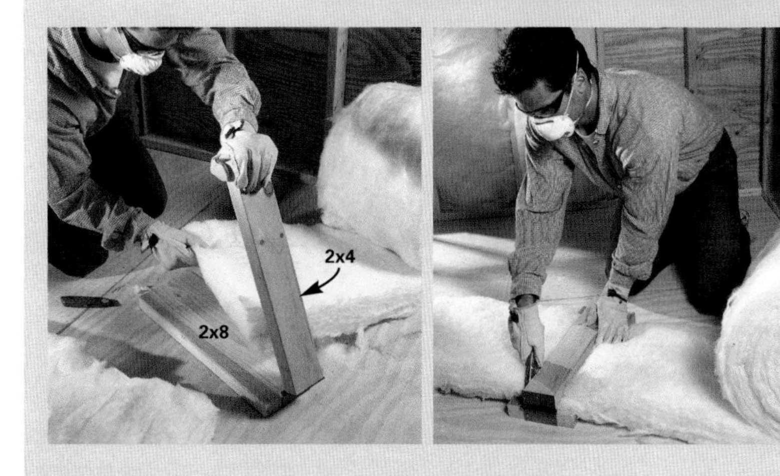

INSULATION CUTTING JIG

Cut wall insulation clean and fast with this jig made from two boards and an old door hinge. Cut a 2x4 and a 2x8 4 in. longer than the width of the insulation. Connect them with the hinge. Then open the jig and slide in the insulation. Press down on the 2x4 to compress the fiberglass and slice along the 2x4 with a utility knife. Clean cuts every time.

BURGLAR-PROOF YOUR DOOR

Three simple upgrades to improve door security

by **Kurt Lawton**

I never realized how easy it is to kick in a solid door that has old hardware until I tried it on our demonstration door. With two kicks in only five seconds, I destroyed the doorjamb and was in the house.

You need to upgrade the deadbolt and lockset plates of your exterior doors if you haven't already done so. FBI burglary statistics show that 65 percent of break-ins occur by forcing in the front, back or garage service door (not to mention the 12 percent of entries where burglars find your "hidden" key or simply walk in through an unlocked door).

In this story, we'll show you how to strengthen your exterior doors in three ways. We'll replace an old deadbolt with a quality Grade 1 deadbolt. Then, we'll replace the deadbolt strike plate with a four-screw strike box and faceplate—attached with 3-in. wood screws that reach the wall frame. Finally, we'll replace the lip strike plate and its wimpy 3/4-in. screws with 3-in. wood screws. We'll also show you a handy method to turn a small deadbolt hole into a larger hole.

The techniques we show in this article will work on any type of exterior door. But keep in mind that these techniques may not be as effective if you have glass sidelight windows or large glass panels in your doors.

For this project, you need only basic carpentry tools, as well as a 2-1/8 in. hole saw bit and a 1-in. spade bit (check the deadbolt packaging for the exact bit size required). Home centers usually carry deadbolt installation kits with the right size bits.

1. Upgrade the deadbolt

2. Strengthen the deadbolt strike plate

3. Strengthen the lockset strike plate

Check all exterior doors

A secure entry starts with a solid door and a Grade 1 or Grade 2 deadbolt with a solid 1-in. long throw bolt (see "Buying a Deadbolt," p. 138). Any exterior door that only has a lock in the doorknob isn't secure. A sturdy screwdriver or small pry bar can quickly bow the doorjamb enough to release the latch.

Check your existing deadbolt. First, make sure the screws are tight. Open the door and extend the throw bolt. If it extends less than 1 in., or is wobbly, install a new deadbolt.

Next, check the doorjamb and both strike plates. Remove the screws from the deadbolt and lockset strike plates on the door frame. If the screws aren't 3 in. long, replace them, and also upgrade both plates (pp. 136-137). (**Note**: Use shorter screws if sidelight windows are less than 3 in. from the doorjamb.) These longer screws will reinforce the doorjamb, which is a vulnerable spot, as you can see by the damaged doorjamb that was kicked in (**photo at left**).

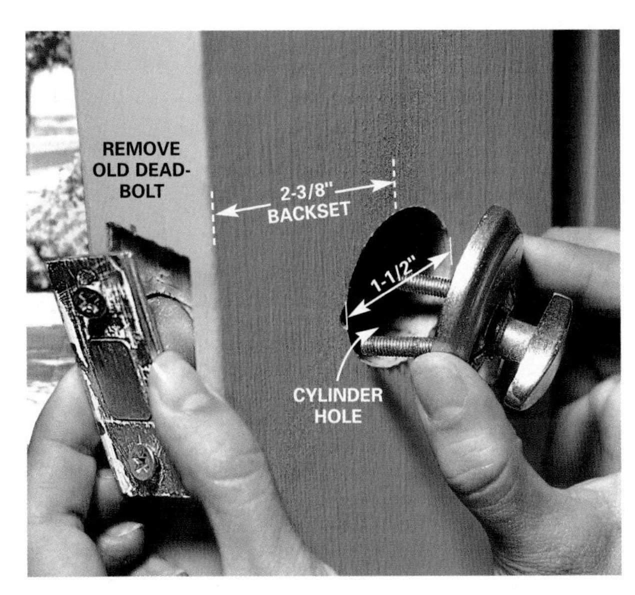

1 UNSCREW and remove the old deadbolt. Measure the hole size and backset distance before buying a new deadbolt.

1. REPLACE THE DEADBOLT

Begin by removing the old deadbolt. Almost all types are held by two screws on the interior side of the door and two screws on the faceplate (**Photo 1**). Measure the cylinder hole size and the "backset" distance, that is, the distance from the center of the hole to the door edge (**Photo 1**). You'll need these dimensions when you purchase a new deadbolt (see "Buying a Deadbolt," p. 138).

Photo 2 shows how to enlarge a deadbolt hole using scrap lumber, a task that is only necessary if your new deadbolt is too big to fit the existing hole (the normal size for a cylinder hole is 2-1/8 in.). The scrap board engages the center guide bit of the hole saw and keeps the new hole centered. Otherwise, you can't get a clean and accurate cut.

To find the starting point for the hole saw bit, clamp the scrap board to the door and mark both the vertical and the horizontal center of the new cylinder hole. Make sure to hold the drill level and straight so the hole saw bit doesn't bind and jerk your wrist and arm. If you don't have a full-depth hole saw bit, chip the wood away from a partially drilled hole, then continue drilling. Go slow so you don't splinter the opposite side when the bit goes all the way through the door.

Now clean up the hole and test-fit the deadbolt. If the throwbolt hole (which runs from the cylinder hole to the door edge) is too small, clean it out with a file. Make sure the attached throwbolt strike plate fits flush (**Photo 3**), then attach the bolt followed by the deadbolt cylinder. Hand-drive the screws; a power drill may strip the threads.

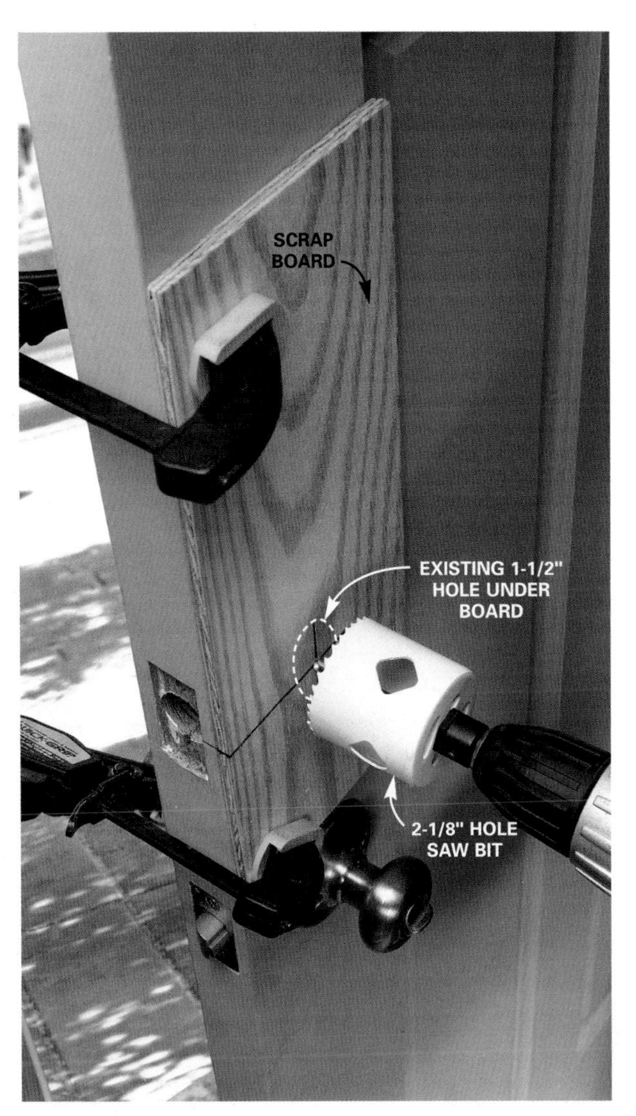

2 CLAMP 1/4-in. plywood over the hole location. Mark the new, larger hole centered over the existing hole, then bore it with a hole saw.

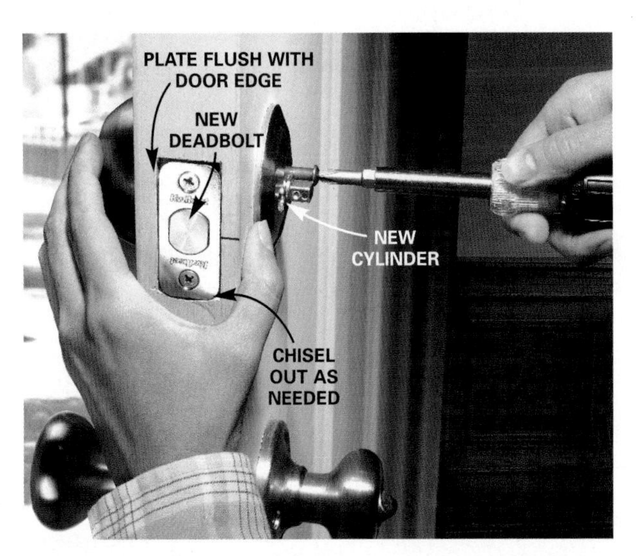

3 SCREW in the new deadbolt, chiseling out additional wood if necessary to get a flush fit. Then insert and screw in the new cylinder.

2. REPLACE THE DEADBOLT STRIKE PLATE

Install a heavy-duty strike plate to strengthen the doorjamb. We didn't use the strike plate that came with the deadbolt. We opted for a more secure strike box plate (made by Mag Security; $5.50 at Home Depot; see Buyer's Guide, p. 138) that features four screws instead of two. (Two screws are installed inside the strike box to add strength; see Photo 6.) Mark the center of the old deadbolt strike plate (Photo 1), then temporarily install the new faceplate and deeply score around it to mark its position (Photo 2).

Next, remove the plate, then chisel and drill out space for both the new plate and the strike box. If the strike box is larger than the existing hole, use a 1-in. spade bit to bore two holes, spaced apart the width and the depth of the box (Photo 3).

Now remove the wood with a wood chisel to fit both the strike box plate and the faceplate (Photo 4). Be sure to use the wood chisel with the bevel side against the wood to keep from gouging too deep.

Finally, mount the plate and box and attach them with four 3-in. screws (Photo 5). Predrill pilot holes into the wall studs to make the screws easier to drive. Set the screws snug to the plate; overdriving might bow the jamb.

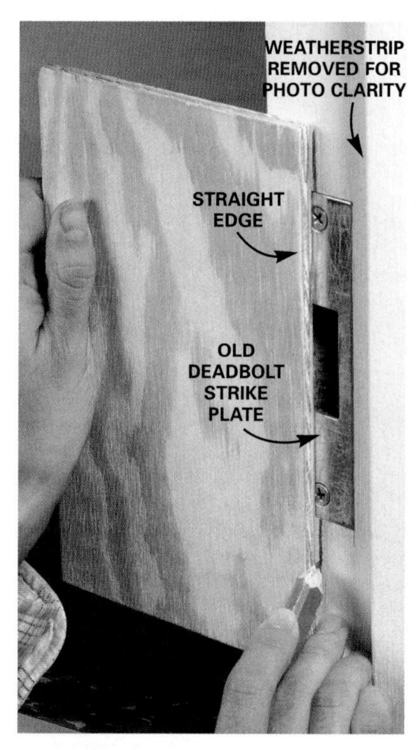

1 MARK the center of the existing deadbolt hole. Then remove the old strike plate.

2 ALIGN new strike faceplate on the jamb, predrill screw holes and attach it. Score around the inner and outer edges with a utility knife. Remove the faceplate.

3 DRILL two holes that span the strike box dimensions, using a 1-in. spade bit.

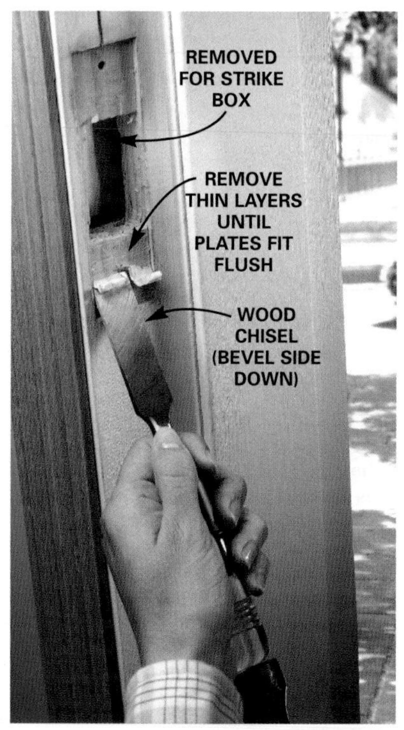

4 CHISEL OUT the strike box and strike plate areas so the strike plate will fit flush with the doorjamb surface.

5 DRILL pilot holes for all four No. 10 x 3-in. wood screws. Install the top and bottom screws.

6 DRIVE the final two screws so they're flush inside the box.

Figure A Doorjamb Cutaway

3-in. screws will go through the frame and penetrate the wall studs 1-1/2 to 2 in. Angle the screws back slightly into the wall to make sure they hit the studs. The studs become the primary door reinforcement, not the jamb.

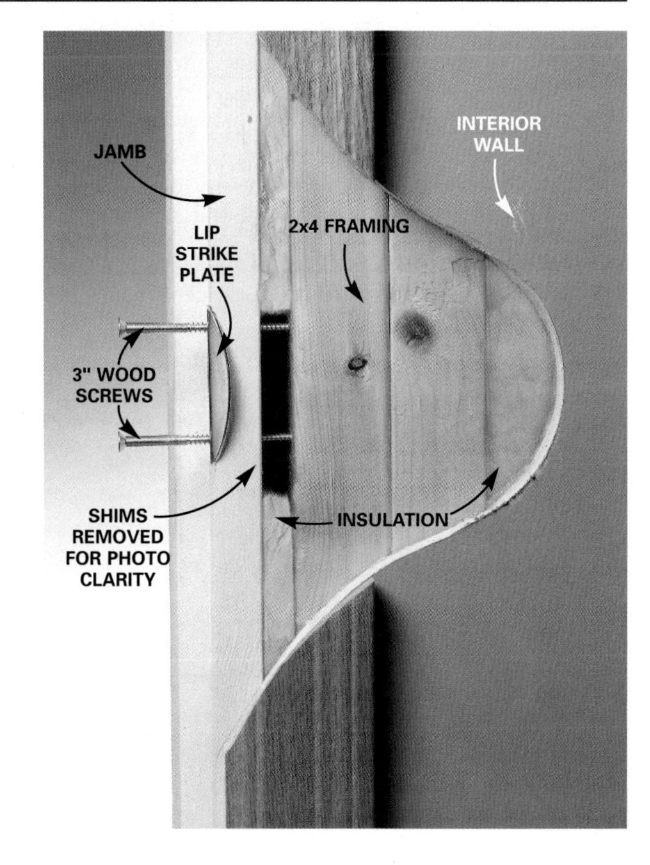

Odds of home burglary*

Your house is at greater risk if:

- It sits on a corner lot (more visible to a browsing burglar and a natural place to stop and ask for directions)
- It is located close to a major highway exit (less than 1 mile)
- It is located on a through street, which gives a burglar a quicker escape (dead-end streets and cul-de-sacs are safer)
- It borders a wooded area or playground (provides concealed access for burglars)
- It is in a wealthier neighborhood ($150,000 value and up)
- It features no signs of young children living there (burglars avoid as someone may be home)
- It was recently purchased (burglars know you haven't yet developed close familiarity with neighbors)

Effective burglary deterrents*

- Burglar alarm installed
- Deadbolt locks on all doors
- House is occupied
- Newspaper and mail picked up
- Lights and noise (TV, radio) inside house (set on timer when gone)
- Car in the driveway
- Motion-activated exterior lights
- Dog in the house

(*Taken from research study, "Knowing Your Odds: Home Burglary and the Odds Ratio," by S. Hakim, G. Rengert and Y. Shachamurove, City College of New York and University of Pennsylvania, Sept. 2000.)

REMOVE the lockset's lip strike plate and 3/4-in. screws. Predrill and attach a new plate with No. 8 x 3-in. screws that are angled in slightly to catch the stud. Predrill with a 1/8-in. bit.

3. REPLACE THE LOCKSET STRIKE PLATE

To further reinforce the doorjamb, install a new plate in place of the old lip strike plate that serves the doorknob lockset. Attach it with 3-in. screws (**photo left**). Make sure the screwheads seat flush with the face of the strike plate. We used No. 8 x 3-in. screws. No. 10 x 3-in. screws (used for the deadbolt plate) were too large. Remember to angle the screws back slightly to be sure to catch the framing (**Figure A**, p. 137). Again, you may have to chisel a slightly larger mortise and predrill to drive the screws.

Now, kick back and rest a little easier, knowing you've made your home more secure.

BUYING A DEADBOLT

Most people choose a deadbolt for its color or finish, but when entry security is paramount, the critical deadbolt feature is its grade. The American National Standards Institute (ANSI) subjects all locks and components to attacks by hammers, saws, wrenches and other tools. Then it grades the lock: Grade 1 (best and toughest), Grade 2 or Grade 3.

Most locks you find in home centers and hardware stores are Grade 2 or 3. Some Grade 2 locks may list Grade 1 components on the package, but that doesn't give the lock a Grade 1 rating. However, Grade 2 is still a good-quality lock for residential use. We only found one fully compliant Grade 1 deadbolt in local home centers and hardware stores (see Buyer's Guide, below).

Professional locksmiths also are a good resource to find Grade 1 deadbolts, but you'll pay $80 to $200 for the top-quality products they carry.

And before you shop for a deadbolt, measure the hole size where the current cylinder fits, as well as the "backset" distance from the center of the cylinder hole to the edge of the door (Photo 1, p. 135). Most new deadbolts require a 2-1/8 in. cylinder hole, but some of them have inserts to fit the smaller 1-1/2 in. hole, so you don't have to drill to enlarge the hole (Photo 2, p. 135). The backset distance is usually either 2-3/8 or 2-3/4 in., so make sure the new deadbolt has the identical backset. Most new locks are adjustable to fit either backset dimension. Just read the box carefully (you may have to open it and read the directions to find the information).

Also decide whether to buy a single cylinder (keyed on exterior side of lock only) or a double cylinder deadbolt (keyed on both sides). Check local building codes too, as they may prohibit double cylinder locks for fire safety reasons (it's more difficult to escape because you must have the key).

Buyer's Guide

- KWIKSET: (800) 327-5625. www.kwikset.com. (We used a Grade 1 UltraMax Security deadbolt, Model 980, $30.)
- MAG SECURITY: (800) 624-9942. www.magsecurity.com
- SCHLAGE: (800) 847-1864. www.schlagelock.com

Great Goofs™

Insulation frustration

My wife and I rented an insulation blower to add insulation in our attic. When I got the unit home, I noticed it had remnants of tape on the hose connection. I checked it out and it seemed to work fine. With my wife feeding bags into the hopper and me up in the attic with the hose, we proceeded to get the nasty job done. Working my way around the attic, I noticed that the hose seemed to be caught, so I gave it a tug. Then nothing was coming out, and finally I heard the machine stop. I squeezed back downstairs to discover the downstairs covered in insulation. After a whole day of cleaning, I figured out what all the tape was for!

This side UP?

After we'd finished painting several rooms in the house, it was time to repaint the wood window sashes. I thought they'd be much easier to paint if I removed them and took them out to the garage. I set up a workspace and got right to work. Once they were dry, I installed them. Then I discovered my goof! I'd painted about half the windows on the wrong side. The exterior on some of the windows was now the interior trim color. The next weekend I found myself painting both sides of the window sashes I'd mixed up.

Clueless cordless owner

Not long ago, I installed a new medicine cabinet in our bathroom. I removed the old recessed cabinet, leaving a large hole between the studs. The new medicine cabinet was a flush-mount style and a bit smaller than the old one, so I cut a piece of drywall to cover the old hole. Just then, my cell phone rang. I told the caller I'd talk after I was done. I set the phone down and remeasured the opening and cut the drywall and screwed it into place, then taped and mudded the seams. As soon as I finished, my cell phone rang again. I looked everywhere but the phone was nowhere in sight. I placed my ear close to the newly patched wall and I could hear it plainly inside the wall! I was careful to look inside before I installed the second drywall patch.

Great Goofs™

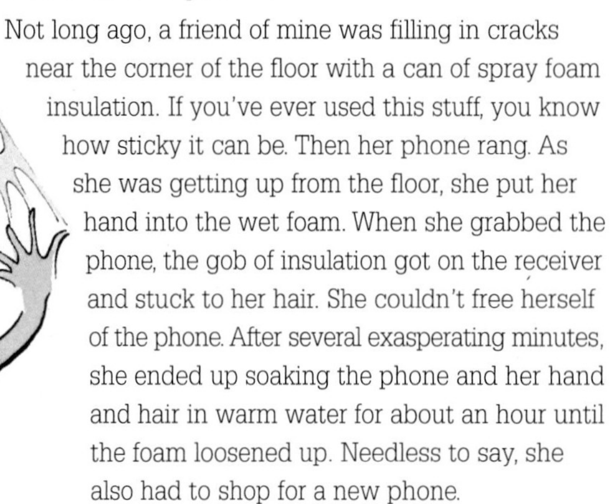

Stuck on the phone

Not long ago, a friend of mine was filling in cracks near the corner of the floor with a can of spray foam insulation. If you've ever used this stuff, you know how sticky it can be. Then her phone rang. As she was getting up from the floor, she put her hand into the wet foam. When she grabbed the phone, the gob of insulation got on the receiver and stuck to her hair. She couldn't free herself of the phone. After several exasperating minutes, she ended up soaking the phone and her hand and hair in warm water for about an hour until the foam loosened up. Needless to say, she also had to shop for a new phone.

Raindrops keep falling . . .

After I left for college, my father decided to empty my waterbed. Unable to get a good siphon going, he gave up and dropped the hose on the floor and left the room to take care of other chores. Hours later he noticed water dripping through the ceiling below. The siphoning had started after all. When I went home that weekend, he had several garbage cans in the living room and had drilled holes all over the ceiling to let the water out. Poor Dad. I'd never seen him more frustrated and forlorn. I don't think we'll be shopping for another waterbed anytime soon!

Insulation inflation

My husband and I bought a big bundle of insulation to insulate our shop. The huge bundle was actually five bundles wrapped together. I could barely lift it into the truck, so we decided to cut the bundle and load the individual bundles one at a time onto the truck bed. As soon as we cut it, it expanded to about four times its original size, much too large to fit into the truck. We had to buy some rope and spend a half hour wrestling the stuff into a manageable size.

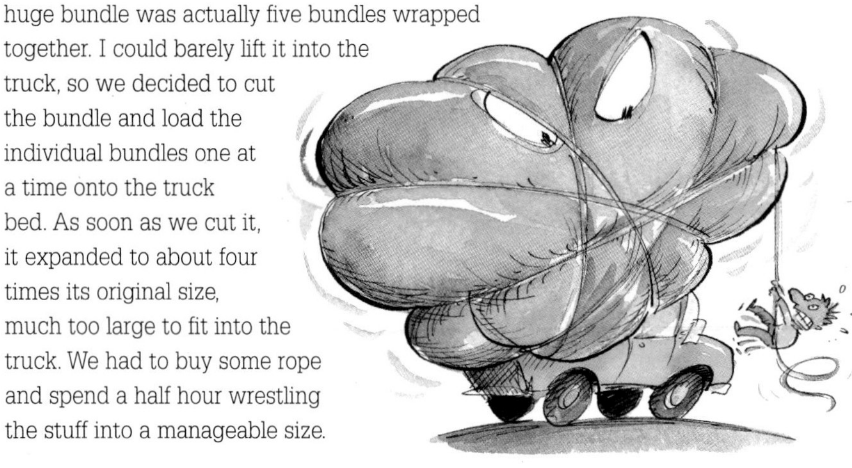

Chirp, chirp

One evening last summer, just after going to bed, my wife and I heard a chirping sound coming from the hallway. In the morning I promptly changed the battery in the smoke alarm, thinking that would fix it. The next night we heard it again. The next morning I changed the batteries in the remaining smoke alarms. That night we heard it again. I assumed that the smoke alarms must be faulty, as they were several years old. I went to the home center the next day and bought three new alarms and installed them. Eager for a good night's rest, we went to bed. That night the periodic chirping continued. I called the home center and asked what the problem might be. After an extensive search, we found it—a lonely cricket. I coaxed it into a jar and put it outside. Now I'm sleeping better than ever. No crickets, and all that peace of mind from the new smoke alarms.

6 Woodworking Projects & Built-Ins

IN THIS CHAPTER

Adirondack Chair & Love Seat 142

Workshop Tips 148
Gentle-grip pipe clamps, decorative wood plugs, circular-saw cutting guide and more ...

Leaning Tower of Shelves 150

Gallery of Ideas .155
Cherry bookcases, stylish shelves, garden hutch and closet organizer

Super-Strong Glue Joints 158

THE COMFORTABLE ADIRONDACK **CHAIR & LOVE SEAT**

Finally, outdoor furniture that's easy to get in and get out of

by **David Radtke**

This chair and love seat combo is just perfect for outdoor lounging. The seat has a nice curved recess to conform to your body, and wide arms to hold your favorite snack and drink. And because the seat doesn't slope steeply downward like on a traditional Adirondack chair, even your grandfather will be able to help himself out without a boost.

You won't need an arsenal of power tools to build this furniture. In fact, you'll only need a circular saw, a drill and simple hand tools. I've designed this project for simplicity as well: With a bit of patience, even a novice can do a great job.

The wood is pressure-treated pine, chosen for its low cost, high strength and longevity. And don't worry about the drab green look of treated wood. You can brush on an exterior oil or latex stain and give it a beautiful warm glow that makes it look more like mahogany or teak than treated pine. Figure on spending about $45 for the materials for the chair and about $65 for the love seat.

Select straight, knot-free, pressure-treated pine

Most outdoor wood furniture is made from cedar or expensive teak, but regular treated boards from your home center or lumberyard are perfect for this project. The trick is to select boards that are as straight and free of knots as you can find. A few tight knots are OK, and if you spot a board that looks great except for a huge loose knot, just cut it out and use the knot-free sections. It's a good idea to buy a couple of extra boards, just in case you end up cutting out more sections than you'd planned. Also avoid boards that are still wet from the treatment process (they'll feel cool and damp) because they might warp or crack as they dry.

Don't assume that the treated boards are dimensionally consistent. When I got my lumber home, the boards varied by as much as 3/16 in. in width. These variations can screw up the assembly process, especially for the back slats, which require spacers to get an exact back width. Once you get the boards home and begin to cut the pieces, use the rip guide on your circular saw (or borrow a neighbor's table saw) to trim them to the exact widths in the Cutting List.

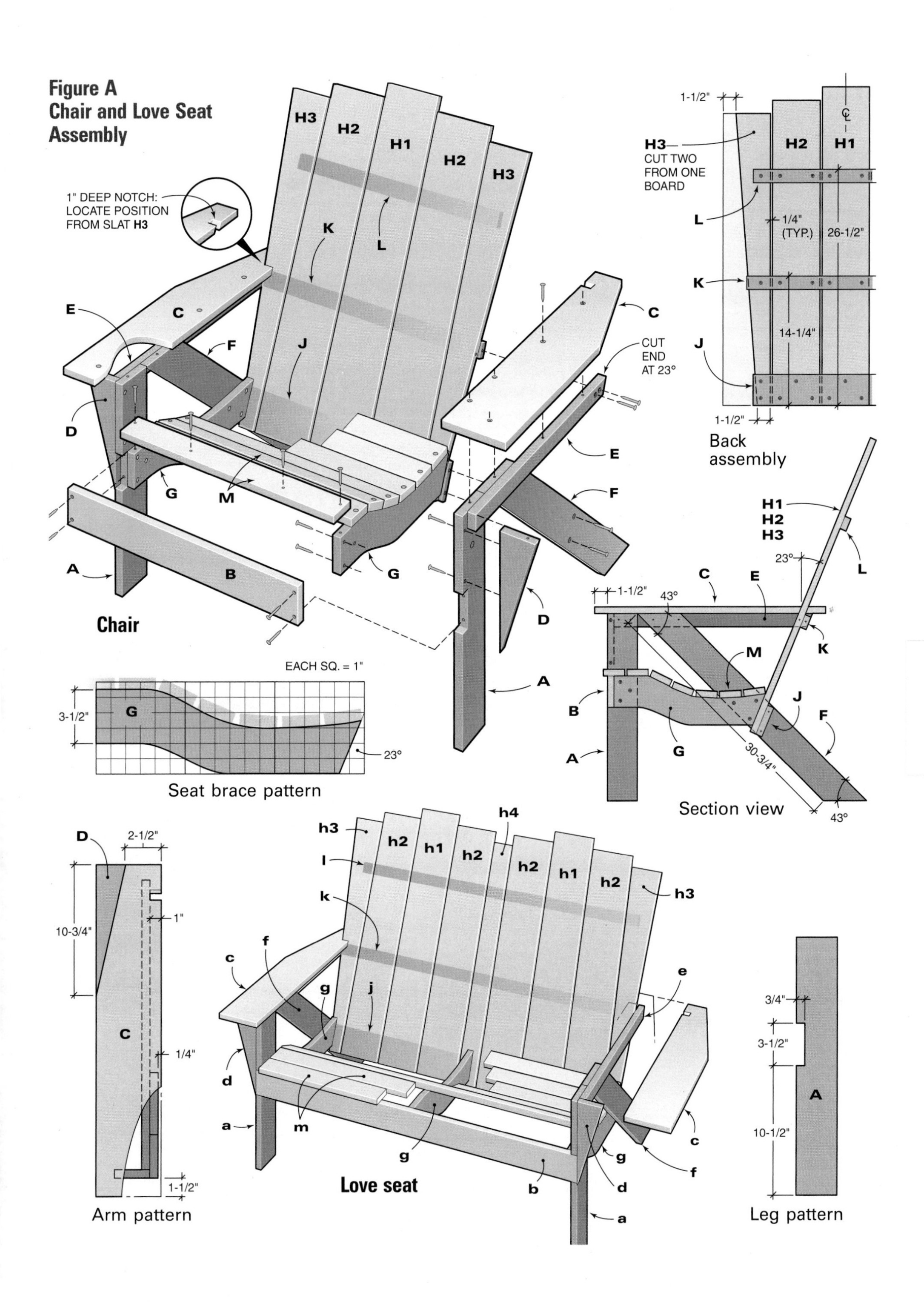
Figure A
Chair and Love Seat Assembly
1" DEEP NOTCH: LOCATE POSITION FROM SLAT H3
H3
H2
H1
K
L
J
C
E
F
D
G
M
A
B
CUT END AT 23°
Chair
EACH SQ. = 1"
3-1/2"
23°
Seat brace pattern
H3— CUT TWO FROM ONE BOARD
1-1/2"
1/4" (TYP.)
26-1/2"
14-1/4"
Back assembly
43°
30-3/4"
Section view
2-1/2"
10-3/4"
1"
1/4"
Arm pattern
h1
h2
h3
h4
l
k
j
f
c
g
d
a
m
b
e
Love seat
3/4"
10-1/2"
Leg pattern

Assemble the main frame

Cut the notches in the front legs to accept the front stringer as shown in Photo 1. As you chisel out the waste wood in the notch, shave the bottom carefully and fine-tune it with a rasp to keep the notch from getting too deep.

As you assemble the basic frame (Photos 2 – 6), make sure your work surface is flat so each piece aligns with the adjoining pieces at the correct angle. Be sure to use a dab of construction adhesive in every joint and predrill a pilot and countersink hole for each screw. You can buy a bit at your local hardware store that drills a pilot and countersink in one operation for the No. 6 screws.

Spacers make the back assembly a snap

To achieve the gentle taper of the back assembly, you'll need to taper the outer seat slat and cut it as shown in Photo 7. First, place a mark 1-1/2 in. from the edge on opposite ends as shown. Connect the marks with a line and then saw right down the middle of the line with your

CUTTING LIST FOR CHAIR

KEY	QTY.	SIZE & DESCRIPTION
A	2	3/4" x 3-1/2" x 21" front legs
B	1	3/4" x 3-1/2" x 23" front stretcher
C	2	3/4" x 5-1/2" x 27" arms
D	2	3/4" x 3" x 10-3/4" triangular arm supports
E	2	3/4" x 1-1/2" x 23-1/4" horizontal arm supports
F	2	3/4" x 3-1/2" x 34-1/2" rear legs
G	2	3/4" x 5-1/2" x 17-3/4" seat braces
H1	1	3/4" x 5-1/2" x 35-3/4" center back slat
H2	2	3/4" x 5-1/2" x 34-1/4" inner back slats
H3	1	3/4" x 5-1/2" x 32-3/4" outer back slats (taper cut into two pieces)
J	1	3/4" x 3-1/2" x 21-1/2" bottom back brace
K	1	3/4" x 1-1/2" x 23" center back brace
L	1	3/4" x 1-1/2" x 21-1/2" top back brace
M	7	3/4" x 2-1/2" x 21-1/2" seat slats

CUTTING LIST FOR LOVE SEAT

KEY	QTY.	SIZE & DESCRIPTION
a	2	3/4" x 3-1/2" x 21" front legs
b	1	3/4" x 3-1/2" x 43" front stretcher
c	2	3/4" x 5-1/2" x 27" arms
d	2	3/4" x 3" x 10-3/4" triangular arm supports
e	2	3/4" x 1-1/2" x 23-1/4" horizontal arm supports
f	2	3/4" x 3-1/2" x 34-1/2" rear legs
g	3	3/4" x 5-1/2" x 17-3/4" seat braces
h1	2	3/4" x 5-1/2" x 35-3/4" back slats
h2	4	3/4" x 5-1/2" x 34-1/4" back slats
h3	1	3/4" x 5-1/2" x 32-3/4" outer back slat (taper cut into two pieces)
h4	1	3/4" x 2-1/2" x 32-3/4" center back slat (trim to fit)
j	1	3/4" x 3-1/2" x 41-1/2" bottom back brace
k	1	3/4" x 1-1/2" x 43" center back brace
l	1	3/4" x 1-1/2" x 41-1/2" top back brace
m	7	3/4" x 2-1/2" x 41-1/2" seat slats

Add a personal touch to your outdoor furniture

You can build our step-back version of the chair and love seat or experiment with other shapes to suit your sense of style. Feel free to try the gable or round back shown below or draw a different shape on paper, tape it to the chair and step back to see how you like it.

Create a round back by measuring down 15 in. from the top and draw a 14-in. radius with a homemade compass.

circular saw. Sand or plane the cut edge to smooth away any saw marks.

Before you assemble the back of the chair or love seat, cut 1/4-in. thick spacers from scrap wood. The spacers (Photo 8) will ensure that the back assembly is the right width. Lay each slat on the floor and make sure the best-looking side of each board is facing down. As you screw the three back braces to the back slats, use a framing square to make sure they're perpendicular. You'll find it easier to get the proper alignment if you match the center point of each brace with the center line drawn down the middle back slat. Drill pilot holes and drive 1-1/4 in. deck screws through the braces into the slats as shown in Figure A and Photo 8.

Once you've assembled the back, it's time to fasten it to the chair frame. Flip the frame assembly upside down and insert the back assembly into it (Photo 9). This can be a bit challenging, so make it easier by laying two nonskid rugs or mats on the floor under the chair frame and the top of the back assembly. These will help keep everything in

1 CLAMP the two front legs together, measure for the 3/4-in. deep notch and make repeated cuts with your circular saw set to 3/4-in. depth of cut. Chisel the pieces between the cuts and then file smooth.

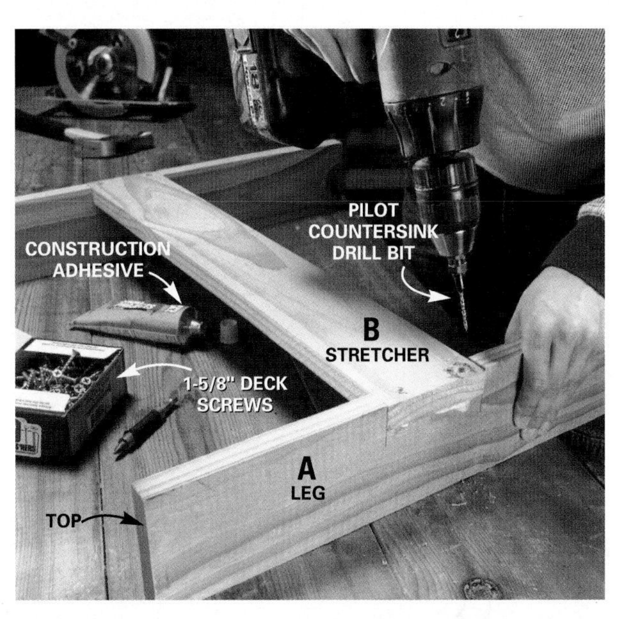

2 SPREAD a light bead of construction adhesive into each notch and align the front stretcher (B) with the edge of the legs. Drill and screw the stretcher to the legs.

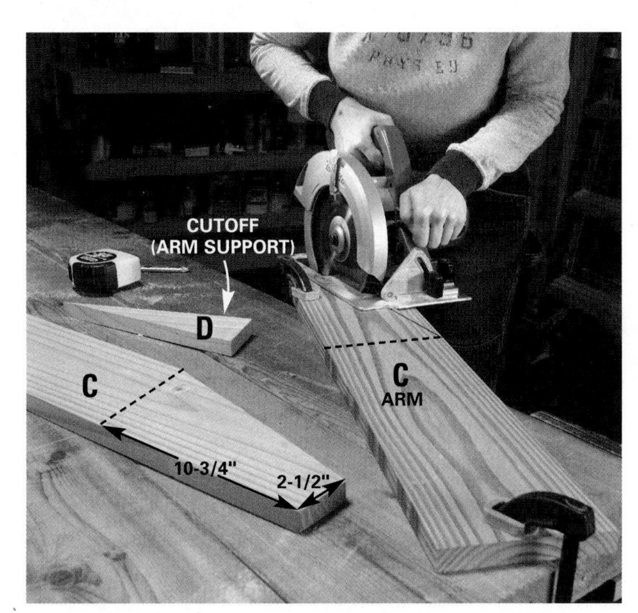

3 MARK the angle on the back side of each arm and cut the arms (C) and arm supports (D) with your circular saw.

4 ALIGN the arm supports with the top and front edges of the legs, then drill and screw each front leg to the arm support with two 1-5/8 in. deck screws.

place. As you align these assemblies, it's critical to get the back of the seat braces flush with the outer back slats (H3) and then screw through the rear legs into the bottom back brace (J) as shown in Photo 9 and Figure A. Next, glue and screw the horizontal arm supports (E) into the center back brace (K) and then into the side of the outer back slat as well.

With the completion of this phase, you'll start to see a chair emerging. Flip the chair onto its legs and cut and predrill the seat slats. Glue and screw them to the seat braces with 1-5/8 in. deck screws (Photo 10). Don't overdrive the screws—the heads should be just flush with the seat slats. The last step of the assembly is to fasten the arms to the arm supports and the legs as shown in Photos 11 and 12. The notches you cut near the back of the arms hold the back assembly firmly in place and reduce the stress on the screws at other joints. These compound notches slice through the arm at an angle. Cut the depth carefully with a handsaw and then chisel out the notch.

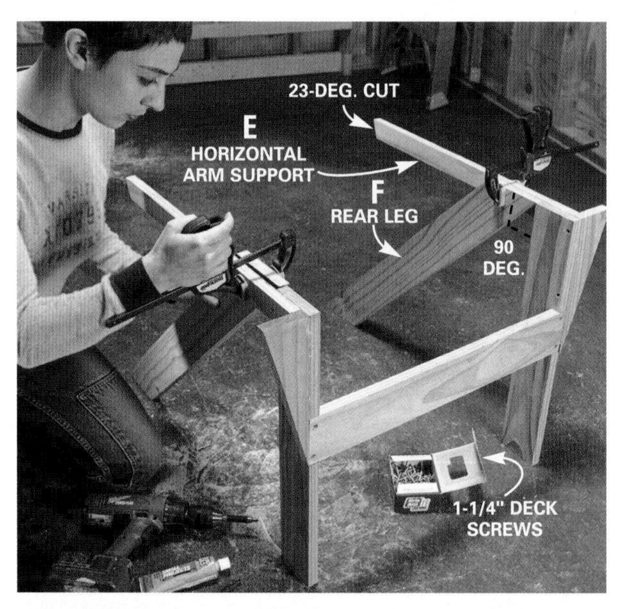

5 FASTEN the horizontal arm supports (E) at 90 degrees to the front legs. Then glue, drill and screw the rear legs to the arm supports, making sure the arm supports are parallel to the floor.

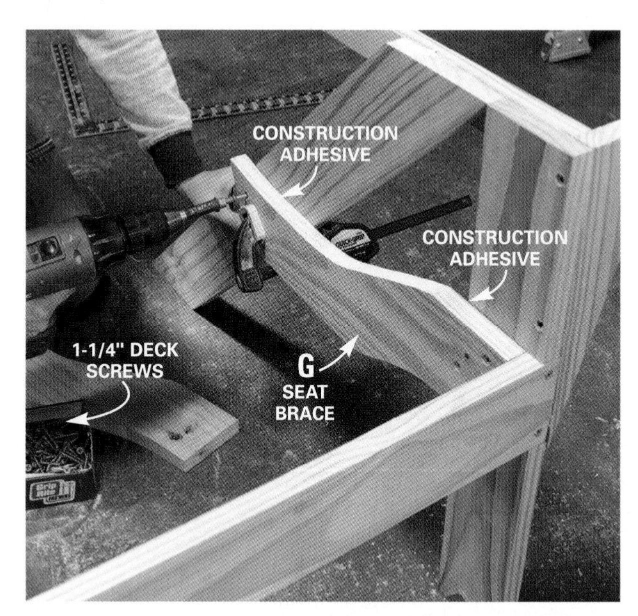

6 CUT the seat supports (G) from 1x6 boards. Align the square front edge of the seat brace with the back of the front stretcher (B) and glue and screw them to the front and back legs.

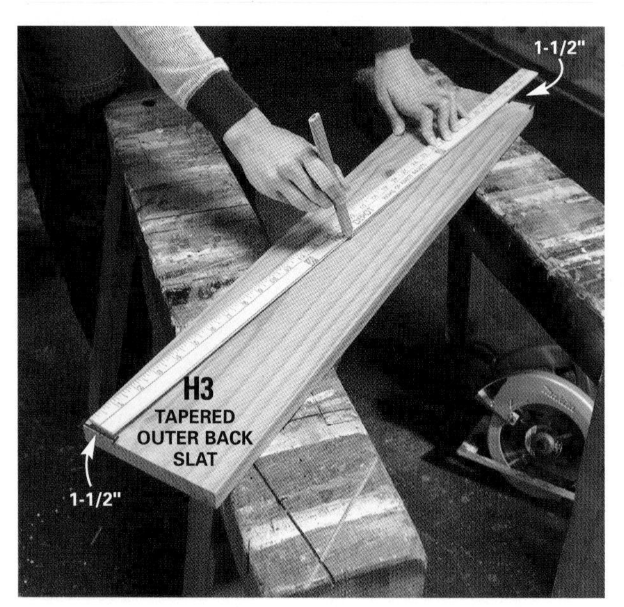

7 MARK a diagonal line on H3, then clamp the board to your sawhorses and cut along the line to make a pair of outer back slats.

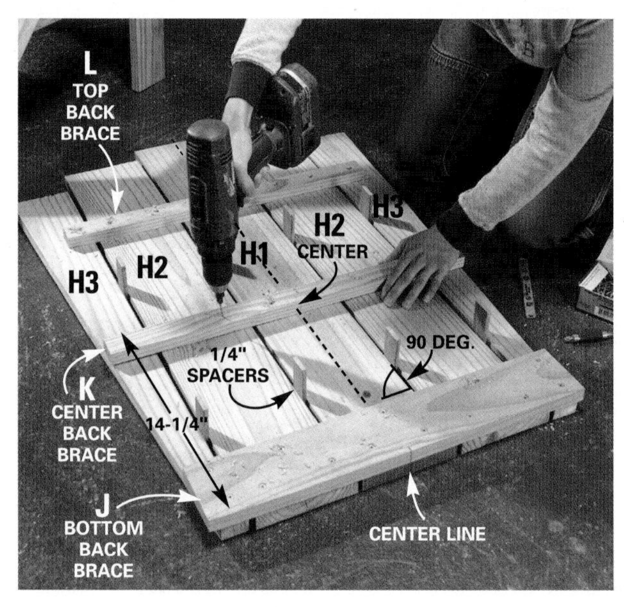

8 SET the back slats on a flat surface with 1/4-in. wide spacers. Center the back braces on the slats. Glue, drill and screw them with 1-1/4 in. deck screws.

Brush on an exterior stain

Once the chair is assembled, ease all the edges with 100-grit sandpaper, paying particular attention to the seat and arms. If the wood feels damp or cold to the touch, you may need to let the chair dry in a shaded area for a few days before you sand or stain it.

We used an Olympic oil-based cedar natural tone stain that lets the grain show through. Several options are available, including custom semi-transparent stains that a paint supplier can mix for you. A quart will easily do a pair of chairs or a chair and love seat. This finish will last at least several years and can be cleaned and recoated as it shows signs of wear.

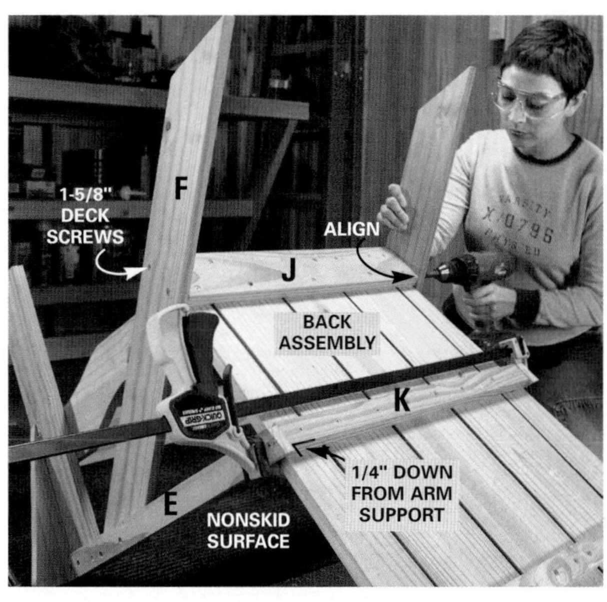

9 **ALIGN the bottom of the back assembly with the seat braces and the tops of the rear legs. Screw the legs to the back brace and screw the horizontal arm supports to the center back brace.**

10 **SPACE the seat slats (M), evenly starting at the back. Drill one pilot hole on each end of the slats and screw them to the seat brace. Screw the front seat slat to the seat brace as well as the front stretcher (B).**

11 **SET the arm flush with the edge of the arm support (E), overhanging the front leg 1-1/2 in. Mark the arm where it meets the back slat.**

12 **NOTCH the arm with a handsaw and fasten it to the horizontal support, the top edge of the back legs and to the front leg and arm support with 1-5/8 in. screws and glue.**

Workshop Tips™

GENTLE-GRIP PIPE CLAMPS

Attach short pieces of 1/2-in. plywood to pipe clamp jaws to protect board edges from dings and dents while gluing. First, drill holes on the upper ends of the jaws so you can screw on the plywood pieces with No. 8 x 5/8-in. sheet metal screws. Then drill holes in the plywood 1/8 in. larger than the pipe diameter, slide the pieces on the pipes and screw the jaws to the plywood pieces with the sheet metal screws. Now you won't be fumbling around with pieces of wood to stick between the boards and clamps—they're permanently in place.

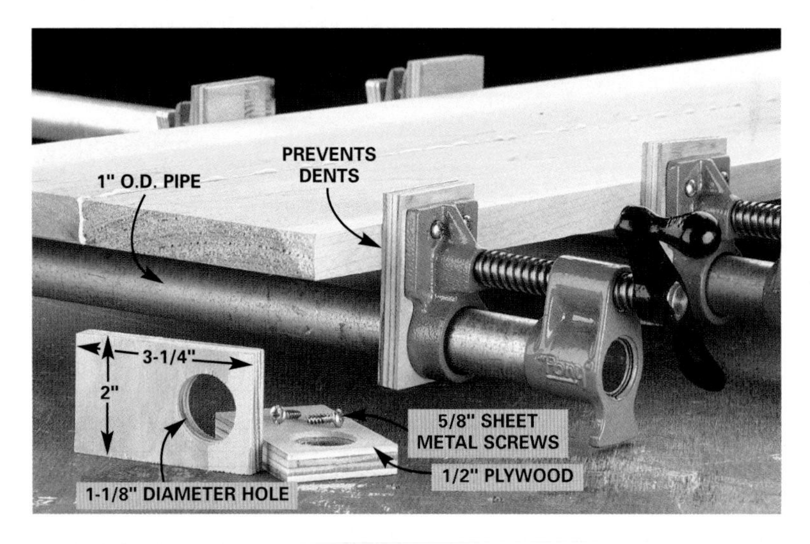

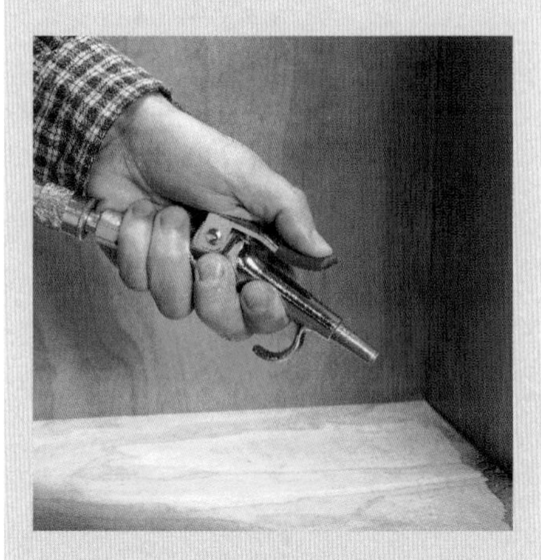

A BLAST OF AIR

A great tip is to use your air nozzle to blow excess stain from tight corners and intricate moldings. A quick blast of the air nozzle cleans out the recesses, and then you can wipe up the stain with a cloth. You can also use the air hose before finishing to get rid of sawdust buildup in corners.

SHOP-MADE DECORATIVE WOOD PLUGS

Here's a swift way to churn out wood plugs for furniture projects. Buy a plug cutter from a woodworking supplier. (One source is Woodcraft Supply, 800-225-1153, www.woodcraft.com.) Using a drill press and a fence for stability, cut plugs along your board of choice. Saw off the plugs with a band saw or handsaw, then return to the drill press and cut another set. Advantage over store-bought plugs? You can cut them to match your project or from your favorite woods not available in plug form.

PIPE CLAMP EXTENDER

Gluing and clamping larger items like tabletops or entertainment centers can require 6-ft. or 8-ft. long clamps. These clamps are expensive and difficult to use on smaller projects. Here's the solution for pipe clamps. When longer clamps are needed, simply connect additional sections of pipe with pipe couplings. Slide cardboard scraps under the couplings to prevent dents in the wood. The couplings and additional pipe sections are a lot cheaper than a new set of clamps.

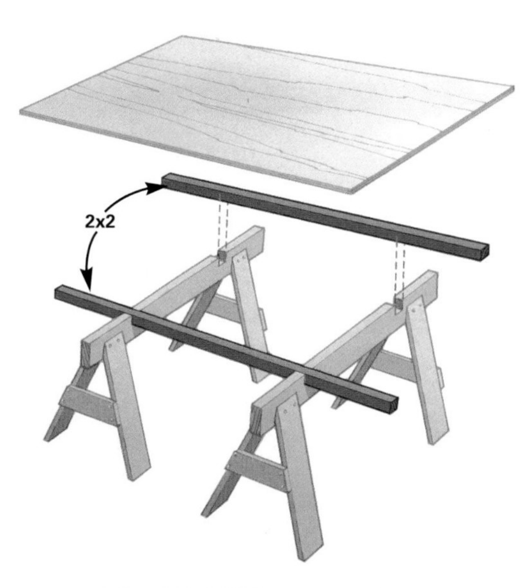

BIG-SHEET STABILIZER

Keeping a 4 x 8-ft. sheet of plywood stationary while cutting can be a hassle. Solve this problem by cutting two 1-1/2 in. x 1-1/2 in. notches in your sawhorses and then inserting 8-ft. 2x2s into the notches. This makes a sturdy work base that can also be used as a portable workbench.

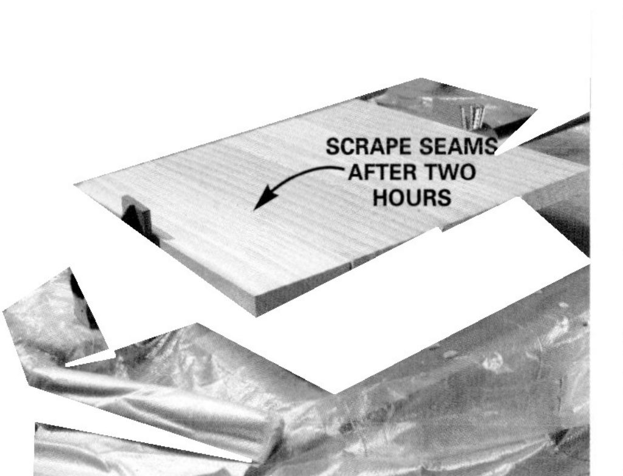

GLUE BEGONE

No more scraping hardened glue off your workbench. Before you set up for gluing, lay a sheet of inexpensive, thin painter's plastic underneath. Another nifty tip to avoid rock-hard glue on your workpiece is to glue it, then wait two hours and scrape off the excess. The glue is still pliable at this stage, so the job is quick and easy.

CIRCULAR-SAW CUTTING GUIDE

We've used this great tip in our shop for years because you can cut plywood as accurately with a circular saw as you can with a table saw—and no helper necessary! To make it:

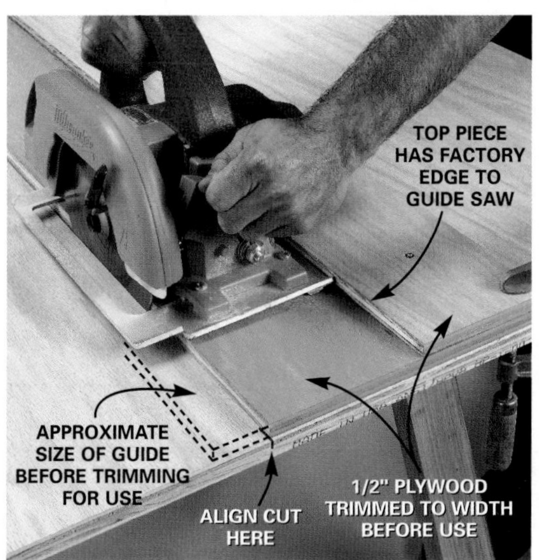

- Cut a 5-in. wide strip from one factory side of an 8-ft. x 1/2-in. sheet of plywood.
- Cut a 12-in. strip and screw the 5-in. strip on top of it with 3/4-in. drywall screws. Be sure the factory edge on the 5-in. piece runs toward the saw side on top of the 12-in. piece.
- Run the circular saw down the jig using the factory edge as your guide. This cuts off the waste.

To use the guide, mark both ends of the plywood you're cutting to the width you need, then align the edge of the jig with your marks. Clamp it. Now run the saw along the guide to cut the plywood. You'll cut straight and accurately every time as the factory edge holds the saw on line.

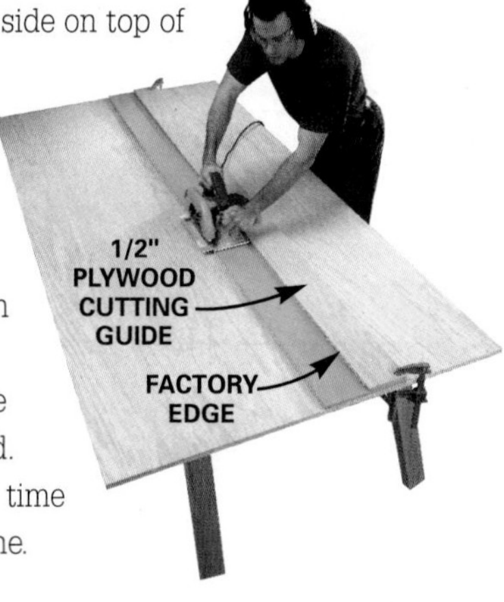

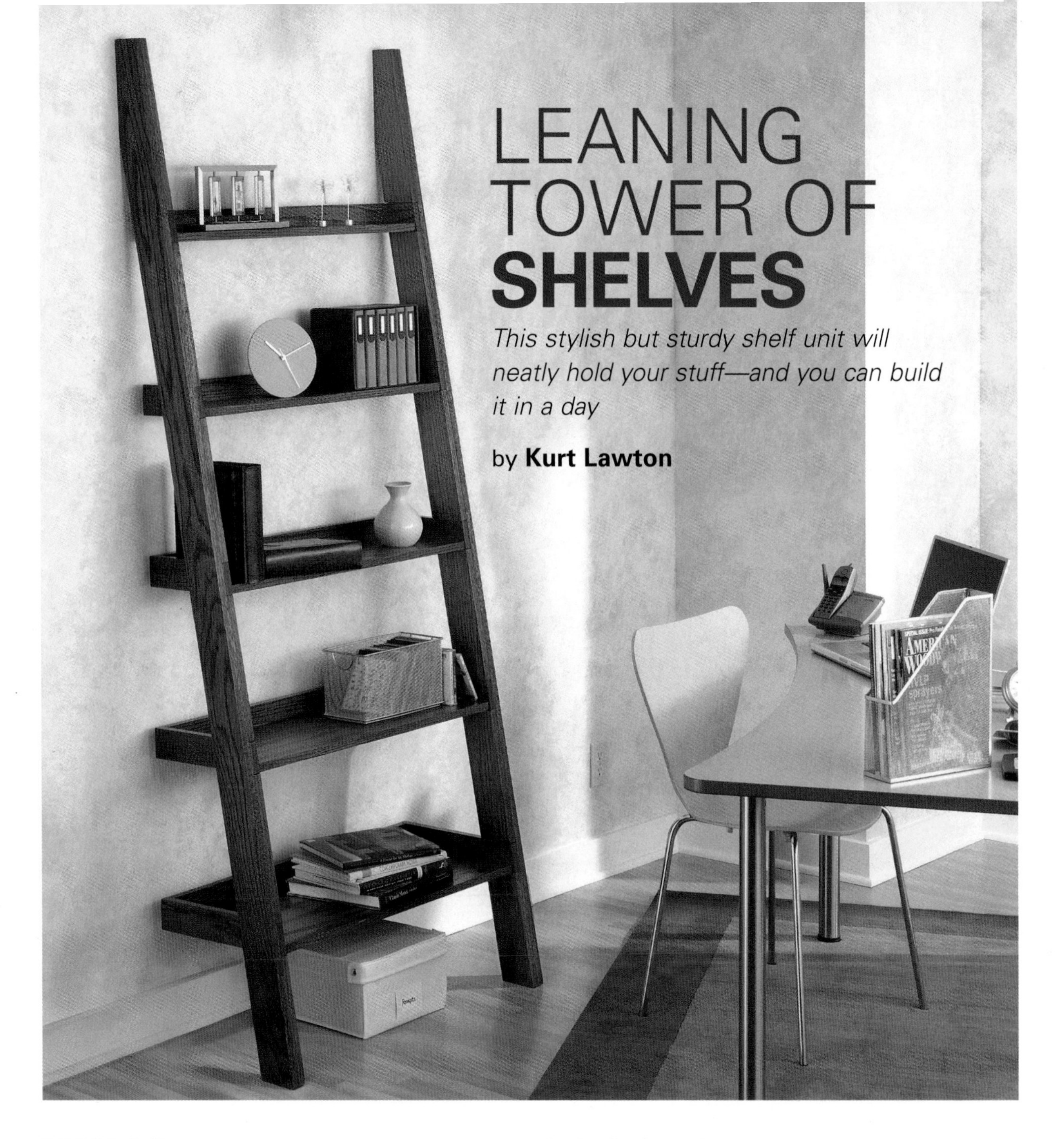

LEANING TOWER OF **SHELVES**

This stylish but sturdy shelf unit will neatly hold your stuff—and you can build it in a day

by **Kurt Lawton**

This shelf unit may look lightweight and easy to topple. But don't be fooled. It's a real workhorse. The 33-1/2 in. x 82-3/4 in. tower features five unique, tray-like shelves of different depths to hold a wide variety of items up to 13-1/4 in. tall. Despite its 10-degree lean, the unit is surprisingly sturdy (as our office woodworker pros will attest), and its open design won't overpower a room.

Whether you choose to make this piece more functional, as in this office setting, or place it in a family room to showcase treasures, the basic construction is the same. You select the type of wood and stain or paint to dress it up or down to fit the look of any room.

All the materials can be purchased in home centers or lumberyards. The only special tools you'll need are a power miter box for crisp angle cuts and an air-powered brad nailer for quick assembly and almost invisible joints. And you'll have to rustle up an old clothes iron for applying oak edge-banding material. Once you've gathered all the material, you can build the shelf unit in one afternoon.

Buying the wood

We built our unit with red oak and oak veneer plywood and finished it with two coats of red oak stain. The beauty of this project is that any wood species will work. If you plan to paint it, select alder or aspen for the solid parts and birch for the plywood.

One note when buying boards: Use a tape measure to check the "standard" dimensions of 1x3s and 1x4s. They sometimes vary in width and thickness. Also check the

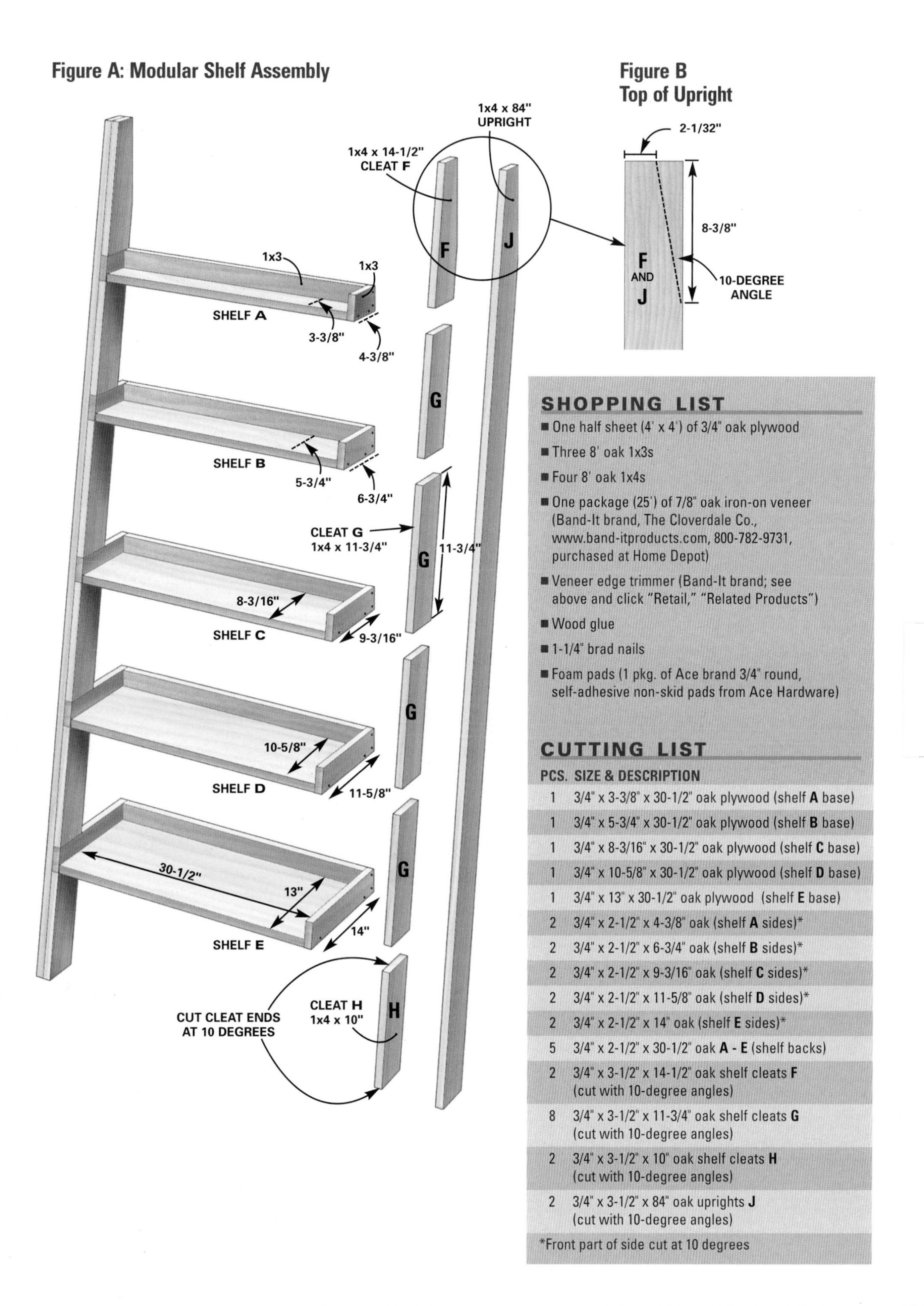

SHOPPING LIST

- One half sheet (4' x 4') of 3/4" oak plywood
- Three 8' oak 1x3s
- Four 8' oak 1x4s
- One package (25') of 7/8" oak iron-on veneer (Band-It brand, The Cloverdale Co., www.band-itproducts.com, 800-782-9731, purchased at Home Depot)
- Veneer edge trimmer (Band-It brand; see above and click "Retail," "Related Products")
- Wood glue
- 1-1/4" brad nails
- Foam pads (1 pkg. of Ace brand 3/4" round, self-adhesive non-skid pads from Ace Hardware)

CUTTING LIST

PCS.	SIZE & DESCRIPTION
1	3/4" x 3-3/8" x 30-1/2" oak plywood (shelf **A** base)
1	3/4" x 5-3/4" x 30-1/2" oak plywood (shelf **B** base)
1	3/4" x 8-3/16" x 30-1/2" oak plywood (shelf **C** base)
1	3/4" x 10-5/8" x 30-1/2" oak plywood (shelf **D** base)
1	3/4" x 13" x 30-1/2" oak plywood (shelf **E** base)
2	3/4" x 2-1/2" x 4-3/8" oak (shelf **A** sides)*
2	3/4" x 2-1/2" x 6-3/4" oak (shelf **B** sides)*
2	3/4" x 2-1/2" x 9-3/16" oak (shelf **C** sides)*
2	3/4" x 2-1/2" x 11-5/8" oak (shelf **D** sides)*
2	3/4" x 2-1/2" x 14" oak (shelf **E** sides)*
5	3/4" x 2-1/2" x 30-1/2" oak **A** - **E** (shelf backs)
2	3/4" x 3-1/2" x 14-1/2" oak shelf cleats **F** (cut with 10-degree angles)
8	3/4" x 3-1/2" x 11-3/4" oak shelf cleats **G** (cut with 10-degree angles)
2	3/4" x 3-1/2" x 10" oak shelf cleats **H** (cut with 10-degree angles)
2	3/4" x 3-1/2" x 84" oak uprights **J** (cut with 10-degree angles)

*Front part of side cut at 10 degrees

1 CUT 3/4-in. shelf plywood to width first, using a circular saw and a homemade jig (see p. 149) for exact cuts. Use a sharp plywood blade and cut with the best side of the wood facing down to minimize splintering.

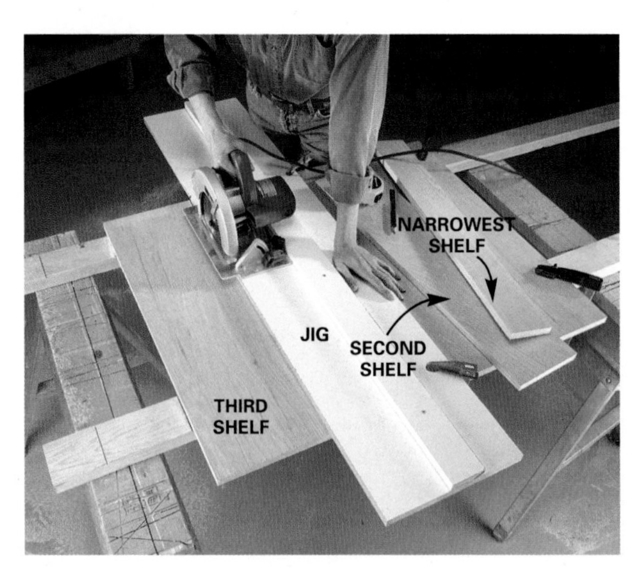

2 CUT the individual shelves, beginning with the narrowest, using the jig for perfectly straight cuts.

3 CUT both shelf uprights to length with a miter saw. Clamp to sawhorses. Mark the 10-degree angle at the top (dimensions in Figure B), then cut with a circular saw.

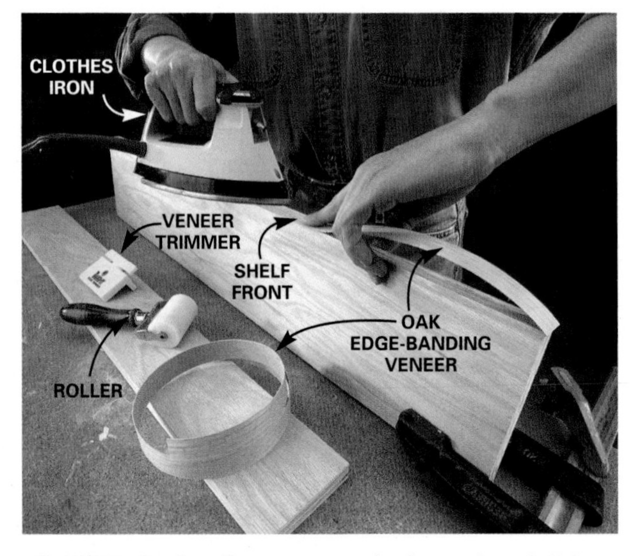

4 IRON edge-banding veneer to the front edge of all five shelves. Roll the entire surface to ensure a solid bond, and trim the edges.

two full-length 1x4s you plan to use as the uprights to be sure they're straight, without warps or twists. And always examine the ends, edges and surface for blemishes or rough areas that won't easily sand out.

Cut plywood shelves first

Lay a couple of 2x4s across sawhorses (Photo 1) to cut the half sheet of 3/4-in. plywood cleanly and without pinching the saw blade. Since all five shelves are 30-1/2 in. wide, cut this width first, making sure the grain will run the long way across the shelves. Remember to wear safety glasses, earplugs and a dust mask. Make a homemade jig to fit your circular saw and clamp it to the plywood. (See "Circular-Saw Cutting Guide," p. 149 to learn how to construct a jig.)

Next, cut all five shelf depths, starting with the smallest shelf (3-3/8 in.) first. Cut smallest to largest so you'll have enough wood to clamp the jig. **Important:** Make sure you account for the width of your saw blade when you cut each shelf.

Now mark and cut the top of all four 1x4 uprights (the end that rests against the wall), according to Photo 3 and the two dimensions provided in Figure B. Use a sharp blade in your circular saw to prevent splintering. Then stow the sawhorses and move to the workbench.

Select the best front of each plywood shelf, clamp it to the bench on edge and sand it smooth with 150-grit paper

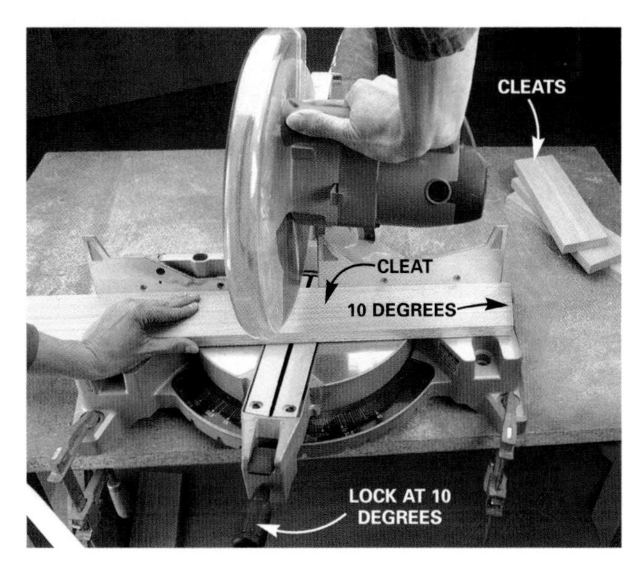

5 **TO MAINTAIN accuracy, lock the miter box at 10 degrees, then cut all angled pieces—uprights, cleats and one end of shelf sides—without changing the table.**

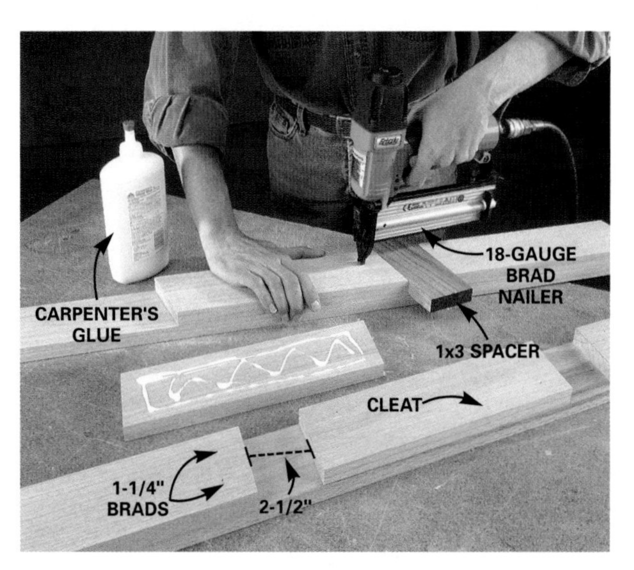

6 **GLUE AND NAIL the shelf cleats to the uprights using a 1x3 spacer. Hold each cleat tight to the spacer.**

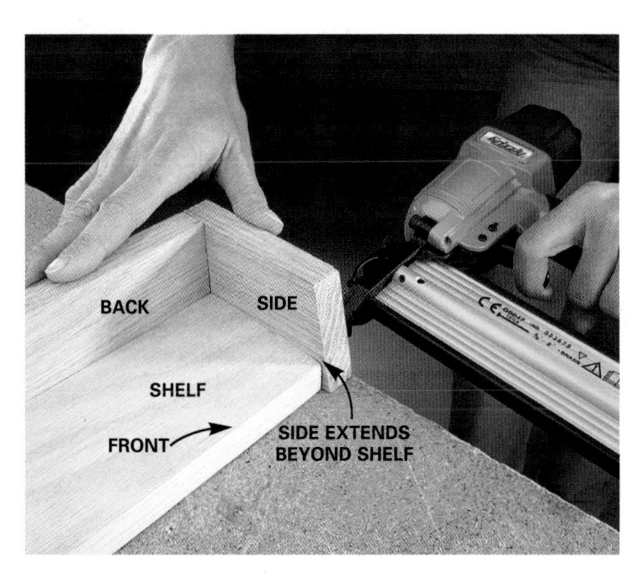

7 **GLUE AND NAIL the shelf backs, then attach the sides to the plywood shelves. Position the sides to overlap the shelf base as shown.**

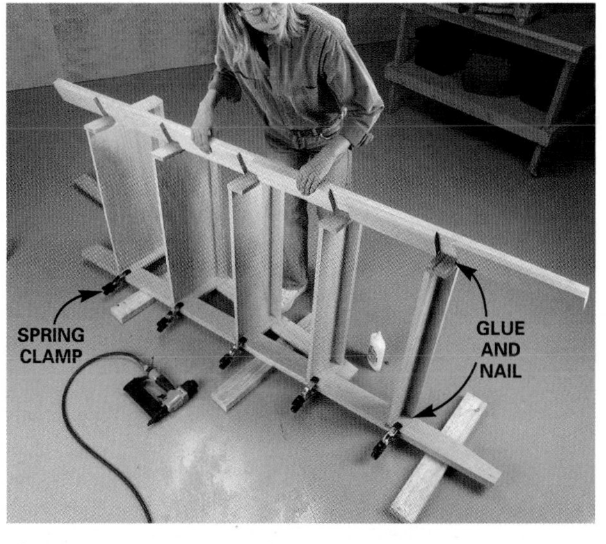

8 **CLAMP the shelves into one upright. Spread glue in the shelf notches of the other upright, position it flush with the front of the shelves and nail. Flip the unit over and attach the other upright.**

on a sanding block. Then preheat a clothes iron to the "cotton" setting and run it over the top of the edge-banding veneer, making sure the veneer extends beyond all edges (**Photo 4**). Roll it smooth immediately after heating. Let each shelf edge cool for a couple of minutes before trimming and sanding the edges.

Cut the uprights and shelf frame next

Now enter the miter saw, which you use to make all the 90-degree straight cuts first (five shelf backs and 10 shelf sides; see Cutting List). **Important:** Remember that one end of each shelf side has a 10-degree cut, so we recommend first cutting them square at their exact length, then cutting the angle carefully so the long edge of each piece remains the same.

Next, rotate the miter saw table to the 10-degree mark and cut all the angle pieces. First cut the bottom of both uprights so each upright rests flat against the floor and wall (see **Figure A**). Then trim the top of the upright to match the bottom, being careful to maintain the 84-in. total length. Next, cut the cleats based on the Cutting List dimensions, which are measured edge to edge (**Photo 5** and **Figure A**). Leave the top cleats long and cut them to exact fit during assembly. Then, to speed finishing, use an orbital sander with 150-grit sandpaper to smooth all pieces before assembly.

9 **SET the shelf unit against a straight wall, check for squareness and apply three bar clamps until the glue dries.**

Assemble uprights first, then the shelves

To begin assembly, lay out both uprights and all cleats to ensure that the angles are correct so the shelves will be level when the unit is against the wall. Then glue and nail the first cleat flush with the base of each upright (using five or six 1-1/4 in. brads) on each cleat. Work your way upward using 1x3 spacers (Photo 6). Make sure the spacer is the exact same width as the shelf sides! Set these aside to dry.

For shelf assembly, first glue and nail on the shelf backs. Next, apply the sides with glue and nails (Photo 7).

For final assembly, lay one upright on 2x4s, then clamp on the shelves as shown in Photo 8. Apply the glue, position the second upright on top flush with the front edge of the shelves, then sink four 1-1/4 in. brads into each shelf from the upright side. Carefully turn the unit over and repeat the process to attach the second upright. Work quickly so the glue doesn't set. Lift the ladder shelf and place it upright against a straight wall. Check it with a framing square and flex it if necessary to square it up and to make sure that the uprights rest flat against the floor and wall (assuming your floor is level). Attach three bar clamps as shown in Photo 9 while the glue dries.

The shelf is highly stable as designed, but once you've stained or painted it, you can add self-adhesive foam gripping pads to the bottom of the uprights. And if you don't feel secure having it on a slippery floor, the unit's width is perfect for screwing the top of the uprights into wall studs.

STEPLADDER OUTBOARD SUPPORT

Hey, our ladders just got a lot more useful, thanks to this stand-up tip. When sawing longer boards with a miter saw, set a folding ladder beside the saw and clamp a narrow board to the ladder with a pair of C-clamps so the board lies level on the saw table. Now you can saw sharp, accurate miters safely on those long railings without employing a second pair of hands.

Gallery of Ideas

CHERRY BOOKCASE

Some bookcases have plenty of charm but are shy on actual shelf space. Others will house stacks of books but are short on looks. This elegant design does it all, featuring more than 43 ft. of shelf space. This multi-component system has two 7-ft.-tall end bookcases plus a shorter center cabinet with glass doors to create dust-free storage for electronics or your favorite collectibles. You can build narrower or wider individual components to custom-size it to fit nearly any room. And you have the option of building it into a corner, centering it along a wall or building it in wall-to-wall.

FROM DECEMBER/JANUARY, 2004, p. 34

Project Facts

Cost: About $1,500
Skill level: Intermediate to advanced carpentry skills
Time: 2 to 3 weekends

Skill Builders

You'll not only get a showpiece and great place to store all your stuff, you'll also learn how to:

- **Build and use a jig for drilling uniform holes for shelf supports**
- **Use a pocket-hole jig for building face frames and other components quickly and accurately**
- **Make and install attractive dentil molding**
- **Construct glass inset doors with decorative muntins**

To order photocopies of complete articles for the projects shown here, call (715) 246-4521, email familyhandyman@nrmsinc.com or write to: Copies, The Family Handyman, P.O. Box 83695, Stillwater, MN 55083-0695. Many public libraries also carry back issues of *The Family Handyman* magazine.

FROM SEPTEMBER, 2004, p. 44

STYLISH SHELVES

If you think building this wall-to-wall shelving system is beyond your skill level, take another look. This project is designed around the use of standard cabinets, which eliminates most of the difficult work. The rest is just plywood and boards—no tricky joints or fancy curves. This project will fit gracefully into just about any room; stylish enough for a living room, yet casual enough for a bedroom. Its open shelves will display collectibles and the closed cabinets add practical storage space.

Project Facts

Cost: About $1,000 for the project as shown
Skill: Intermediate to advanced carpentry skills required
Time: 3 weekends

Skill Builders

In addition to a fabulous built-in book-case you can crow about, you'll learn how to:

- **Use a pneumatic brad nailer for speed and better results**
- **Modify off-the-shelf cabinets to create a custom look**
- **Create your own custom moldings using a router and table saw**

FROM APRIL, 2004, p. 92

PINE GARDEN HUTCH

Ever dream of having all your garden tools and supplies in one handy location? This attractive pine hutch holds long-handled tools like shovels, rakes and hoes on one side, and smaller tools and supplies on shelves on the other side. The structure is built from readily available materials and the copper roof not only looks great, but also keeps the contents dry.

Project Facts

Cost: About $250 for lumber; $50 for copper roof material.
Skill level: Intermediate carpentry skills
Time: 3-4 days

MAXIMIZE YOUR CLOSET

Is your closet too small and over-stuffed? Do your cluttered shelves, packed and sagging clothes rods and jumbled shoes all cry out for more space? If you can't expand your existing closet, you can organize your space to make every cubic inch count. This article shows you how to remodel a basic 8-ft.-wide, 30-in.-deep closet to maximize storage.

Project Facts

Cost: About $300
Skill level: Intermediate carpentry skills
Time: 1 or 2 weekends

FROM FEBRUARY, 2004, p. 34

To order photocopies of complete articles for the projects shown here, call (715) 246-4521, email familyhandyman@nrmsinc.com or write to: Copies, The Family Handyman, P.O. Box 83695, Stillwater, MN 55083-0695. Many public libraries also carry back issues of *The Family Handyman* magazine.

SUPER-STRONG **GLUE JOINTS**

How to glue wood joints that are stronger than the wood itself

by **Art Rooze**

Insert glue biscuits to double joint strength

They may not be good to eat, but glue biscuits are the do-it-yourself cabinetmaker's best friend. A biscuit joiner (Photo 1) costs $100 to $200, and is very user friendly and simple to operate. It cuts precise oval slots in the ends and the surfaces of wood parts that enable you to position the parts for clamping and gluing quickly and accurately. The glued-in-place biscuits provide broad gluing surfaces that make for a strong joint. A special glue bottle (Photo 2), available from the supplier noted in the Buyer's Guide, p. 162, speeds up the application of glue and distributes it evenly in the slots. Don't delay during glue-up! Biscuits swell after gluing (which adds to their strength), so you don't have much time for assembly. Preassemble with dry biscuits to check fits—you won't get a second chance.

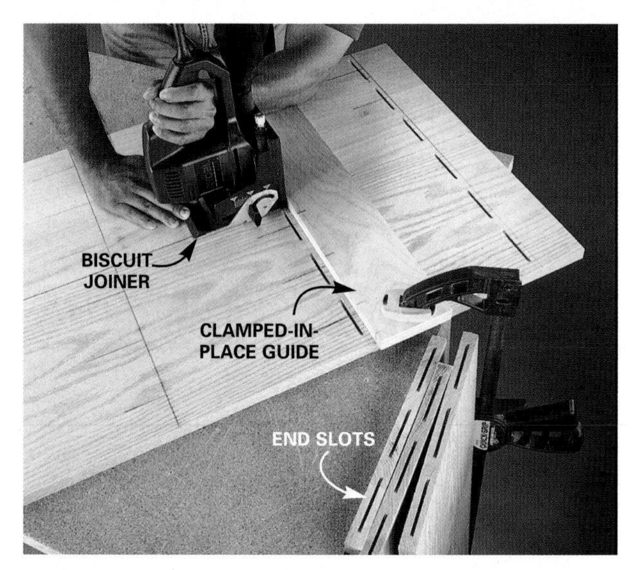

1 CUT oval slots with a biscuit joiner. Use a guide to carefully align the slots to match the slots in the pieces to be joined.

2 APPLY glue to all surfaces of the slots on both pieces. Insert the special biscuits in one side.

3 SLIDE the joining pieces over the biscuits, square up your project and clamp all joints firmly.

REMINDERS FOR STRONG GLUE JOINTS

■ Make sure your gluing surfaces are clean and smooth but not too glossy. Rough surfaces don't allow enough glue contact. Glossy surfaces prevent the glue from penetrating the fibers and getting a good grip. You can sand lightly to smooth roughness or remove gloss, but don't try to actually shape a joint by sanding; it's impossible to get a good mating fit that way. If you're sanding, use a block and be careful not to round over sharp edges.

■ Clamp all glued joints. Pressure is necessary to form a tight, gap-free bond, and to help force glue into the wood fibers. Clamping also prevents movement while the glue is hardening. In situations where you can't use clamps, use screws, elastic cords or weights.

■ Do a dry run with clamps before you apply any glue. This not only allows you to check for a good fit but also ensures that you will have your clamps adjusted to proper length, and all other necessary tools at the ready. It's important to complete a glue-up fairly quickly; even though it takes about an hour for most wood glues to set and 24 hours to cure, the initial "grab" takes place in two or three minutes, and clamping should be completed by then.

■ Get a good fit between the two glued surfaces. Wood glues (except for epoxy) won't bridge gaps, so any joint with gaps will be weak. The parts should fit together snugly. If you can't reshape the part with a router or table saw, try gluing thin wood curls in place to fill the gaps. (You can cut curls from a scrap board using a wood plane.)

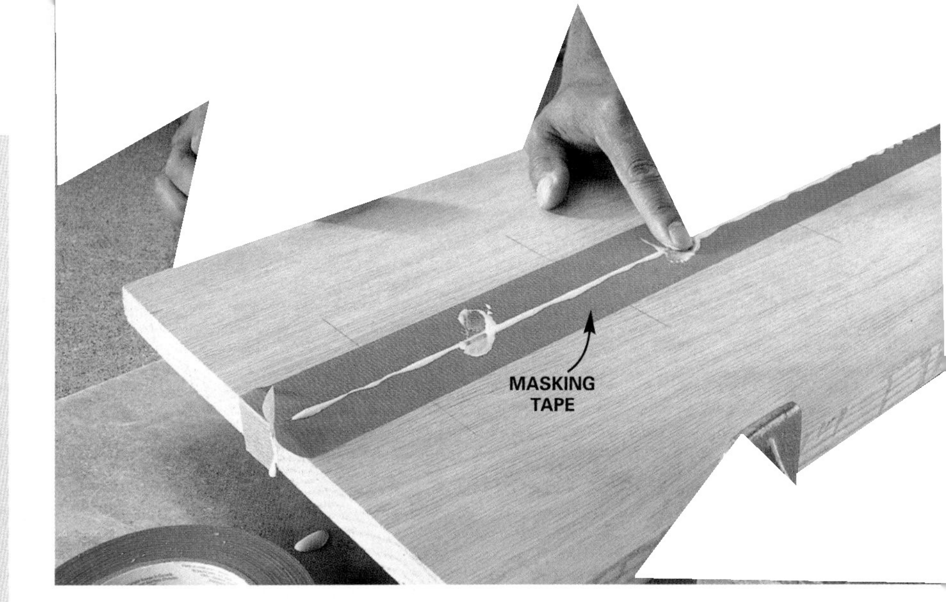

Apply tape to control glue squeeze-out

Glue squeeze-out soaks into the fibers of raw wood, leaving blemishes when you later apply the finish. The usual solution for this is to clean it off with a wet rag or sponge. But too much water around the joint can weaken the bond. It's better to stick down masking tape along both edges of the joint before gluing. The excess glue will then squeeze out onto the tape instead of the wood, and you can just peel the glue away when it's dry.

Use tape to clamp cracked wood

It's often tough to repair cracked cabinets and furniture with regular clamps. But transparent tape makes a great substitute. If the wood is just cracked, flatten the end of a drinking straw and blow the glue into the crack. Then tape it.

If a piece has broken off, follow **Photos 1 and 2**. One drawback: Super-sticky tape can pull off finishes and paint when you remove it. Use light-duty tape or adhere regular tape lightly. And remove it as soon as the glue dries.

1 CHECK the fit first, then stick the ends of transparent sealing tape to the underside of the larger piece being repaired.

2 APPLY glue to the smaller piece and fit it into place. Then wrap the free ends of the tape tightly around the piece. Transparent tape allows you to see the joint so you can get it perfectly aligned.

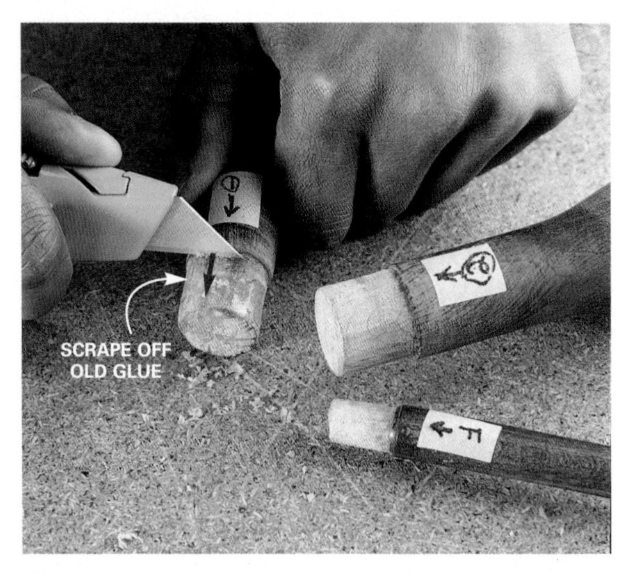

1 **CLEAN all the old glue off the dowel ends by scraping with a utility knife. Don't remove any of the wood or your reglued joint will have gaps and be less strong.**

2 **REMOVE old hardened glue from sockets with a round wire brush. Scrape old glue from the socket bottom with a narrow chisel.**

Clean and clamp when regluing a chair

Regluing a chair is challenging because you usually have to at least partially disassemble the chair and glue the same joints all over again. One critical step is to clean off every bit of the old glue. There will be quite a bit of it, since you'll probably have several loose joints and may have to knock others apart to disassemble the loose ones. You have to clean both the dowel end (Photo 1) and the socket (Photo 2). The trick is to do it without digging into the wood. The more wood you shave away, the larger the gaps that the new glue will have to fill. Use sandpaper only as a last resort, because it tends to sand away wood as well as glue.

You'll find the steel brushes for cleaning the sockets (Photo 2) in the plumbing section of a home center or hardware store. They're designed to clean the insides of copper pipe and fittings and are available in several sizes.

Clamping may call for creativity (Photo 3). The trick is to first dry-fit all the parts you intend to glue at one time. If possible, glue the chair in two stages: the seat and legs first, and then when they're dry, the backrest section. Test-fit the clamps to make sure where every clamp will go. Then you can work swiftly when applying the glue. Even so, use liquid hide glue rather than yellow glue; hide glue gives a much longer open time before "grabbing," so you can get all the parts and clamps in place.

3 **CLAMP the joints to ensure a tight bond. Improvise using a combination of elastic cords, clamps, wood scraps and other devices to clamp the entire seat/leg assembly first.**

Add glue blocks

When the backside of a joint is out of sight, glue blocks make great reinforcement. Cut 1/4-in. x 1/4-in. strips of wood, then cut the strips into shorter lengths. Use plenty of glue on each contact surface, and press the blocks firmly in place where they won't interfere with a drawer's movement. This is one of the few times you won't need clamps when gluing, since there's very little stress on the joint.

Glue and screw whenever possible

Screws are ideal for joints that call for extra strength, or where accurate positioning of a glued piece would be difficult.

1 CLAMP the part in place, then drill a clearance/countersink hole in the top piece, and a pilot hole in the bottom piece. With a combination drill/countersink bit, this drilling can be done in one operation.

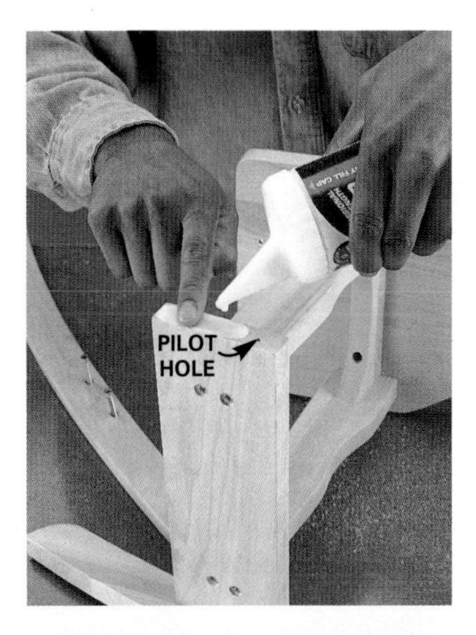

2 APPLY the glue to the bottom piece. Let the glue sit for a minute before you join the parts, since the glue soaks more deeply into end-grain fibers.

3 PLACE the screws in the holes of the top piece so their points project slightly through the bottom. Align the points with the pilot holes for proper positioning, then drive the screws tight. Wipe off glue that squeezes out.

Spread glue evenly on large areas

While a notched glue spreader is the most effective and neatest tool for spreading glue on a flat surface, you can use an old credit card in a pinch. Draw it lightly over the glue to leave a thin film. For spreading glue on smaller or curved surfaces, you can buy stiff-bristled 1/4-in. throw-away brushes in the home center plumbing department. Or use the time-honored finger; just make sure you wipe your finger clean before you mess up that masterpiece you're building.

Choose the best type of glue

Yellow exterior glue (sometimes gray): Use it for outdoor projects, but not continuous submersion. Will be labeled "water resistant" or "exterior." About $6 for 8 ozs.

White and yellow interior glue: The most common "workhorse" wood glue. Not for outdoor use. About $6 for 12 ozs.

Liquid hide glue: Use it for furniture repair; very long open time for assembly—up to 30 minutes. Requires a long curing time. About $6 for 8 ozs.

Polyurethane glue: Use it when you need a completely waterproof glue. Also glues metal and some plastics. Long open time for assembly—up to 15 minutes; curing time: up to five hours. About $13 for 8 ozs.

Epoxy: Use it when you need to fill gaps and for great strength. Comes in two parts that must be mixed just before using. Epoxy will glue most materials, and it's waterproof. Won't wash off your skin—or anything else. $16 for 12 ozs.

Buyer's Guide

Biscuit slot glue tips, glue spreaders, polyurethane glue, hide glue and epoxy are available at some hardware stores and home centers. Or find them at specialty woodworking stores (check the Yellow Pages under "Woodworking"). These items can also be purchased from the following mail order sources:

- **CONSTANTINE'S: (800) 443-9667. www.constantines.com**
- **ROCKLER WOODWORKING: (800) 279-4441.www.rockler.com**
- **WOODCRAFT: (800) 225-1153. www.woodcraft.com. Biscuit glue bottle, part No. 128927.**

FAST AND CHEAP GLUE ROLLER

Here's a smooth tip for spreading carpenter's glue: Slide a piece of 1-in. diameter pipe insulation onto a 4-in. paint roller frame and use it to evenly roll on the glue. When the job's done, just throw away the insulation. No more wasting store-bought rollers on a one-time job.

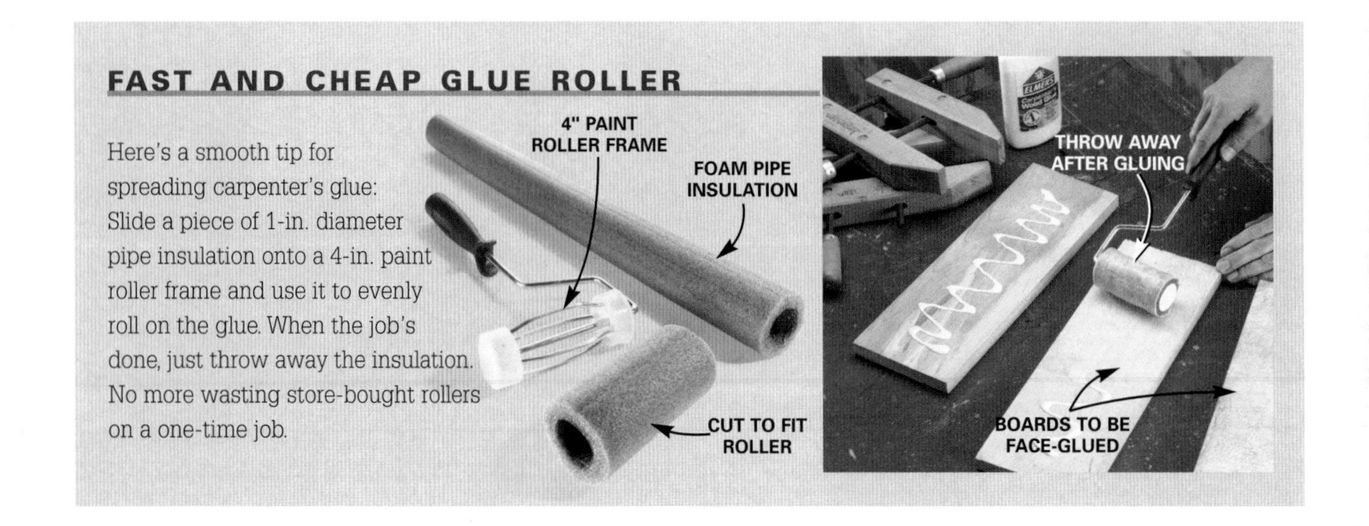

7 Workshop Tools, Tips & Storage

IN THIS CHAPTER

Using Tools:
Driving Concrete Screws 164

10-Minute Workshop Storage Projects 168

Tips for Tough Cuts 172

Budget Workbench 177

Control Shop Dust 178

Workshop Tips 184
Hinged sawhorses, rolling hardware and lots more...

Using Tools™ Driving Concrete Screws

Concrete screws are the perfect fastener for speedily anchoring light- to medium-weight objects to concrete. Just as with any concrete anchor, you still have to drill a hole in the concrete. But with a concrete screw, the hole can be smaller and you don't need a separate anchor. You drive the screw right through the material you're attaching and into the concrete.

While you can't use concrete screws to mount things that vibrate, like motors and door frames, or to attach a heavy load like a deck ledger board, they're plenty strong for most household uses. In this article, we'll tell you how to choose the best concrete screw for the job, and how to drill pilot holes and drive screws quickly and easily.

Choose 3/16-in. screws for most light- to medium-duty tasks

Home centers and hardware stores stock concrete screws in two diameters, 3/16 in. and 1/4 in. The 3/16-in. diameter screws are plenty strong for most home tasks like installing furring strips, screwing down walls to concrete floors, and attaching hardware to block or brick. And since they're a little cheaper and the smaller hole is easier to drill, the 3/16-in. size is usually the better choice. If you're having trouble with the 3/16-in. screws snapping off because the concrete is too hard, switch to stronger 1/4-in. diameter screws instead. You could also keep some 1/4-in. screws handy in case you strip out the hole for a 3/16-in. screw. Switch to 1/4-in. screws for heavy-duty work like securing a wall cabinet to a concrete or block wall, or supporting shelving that will hold a lot of weight.

Use hex head screws where appearance isn't an issue

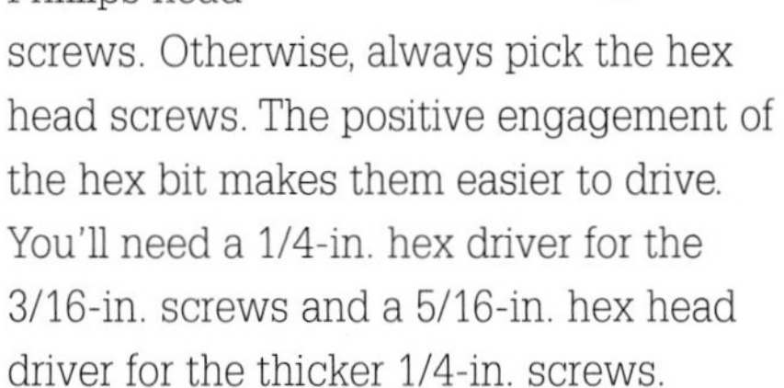

Concrete screws are available with either flat head Phillips or hex heads. In situations where the screwhead must be flush to the surface (furring strips under drywall), or where a Phillips head would look nicer, use the Phillips head screws. Otherwise, always pick the hex head screws. The positive engagement of the hex bit makes them easier to drive. You'll need a 1/4-in. hex driver for the 3/16-in. screws and a 5/16-in. hex head driver for the thicker 1/4-in. screws.

When you're using Phillips head screws, keep extra No. 2 (No. 3 for 1/4-in. screws) Phillips head bits on hand. The hardened screws wear out bits quickly.

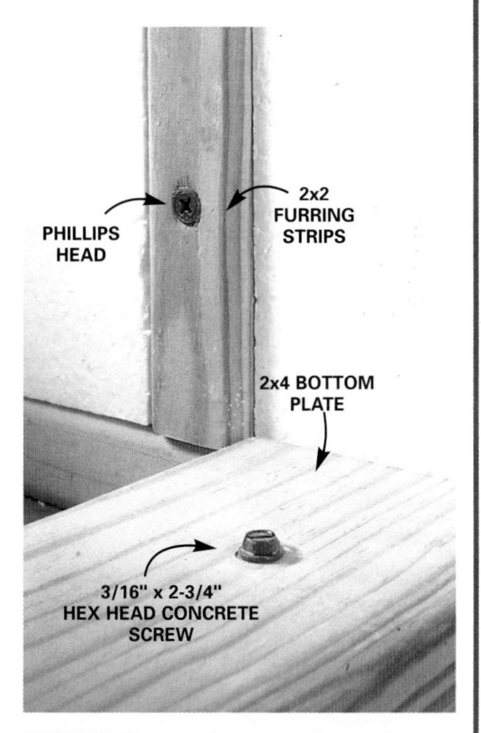

DRIVE Phillips head screws where a flush surface is required and where a Phillips head would look better. Otherwise use hex head screws.

Use a hammer drill

In some less dense materials like soft brick, you can drill pilot holes using a carbide-tipped bit in a regular drill. But in most cases, you'll need a hammer drill. Corded hammer drills cost $65 to $400, or you can buy a cordless model starting at $230. You can also rent hammer drills for about $35 per day.

Precisely sized carbide-tipped bits are often included with packs of screws, or you can purchase one separately ($4.50). Match the bit to the size screw you're using: 5/32-in. bit for 3/16-in. screws and 3/16-in. diameter bit for 1/4-in. Keep a spare bit on hand, since the tip can wear out rapidly in some hard materials, resulting in a hole that's too small. One indication of a worn bit is screws that are difficult or impossible to drive completely.

CARBIDE-TIPPED DRILL BIT

INSTALL the correct bit in your drill. Set the drill to hammer mode and drill the hole using moderate pressure. Blow or brush the dust from around the hole before you withdraw the bit.

Using Tools™ Driving Concrete Screws

Make sure the hole is deep enough

Holes for concrete screws should be at least 1/4 in. deeper than the screw will penetrate to allow a little extra space for dust accumulation from the drilling process. See the illustration below, right. But it's not always easy to judge how deep you're drilling. Too shallow and the screw won't go in. And drilling deeper than necessary is a waste of time and effort. That's why most hammer drills come equipped with an adjustable depth stop.

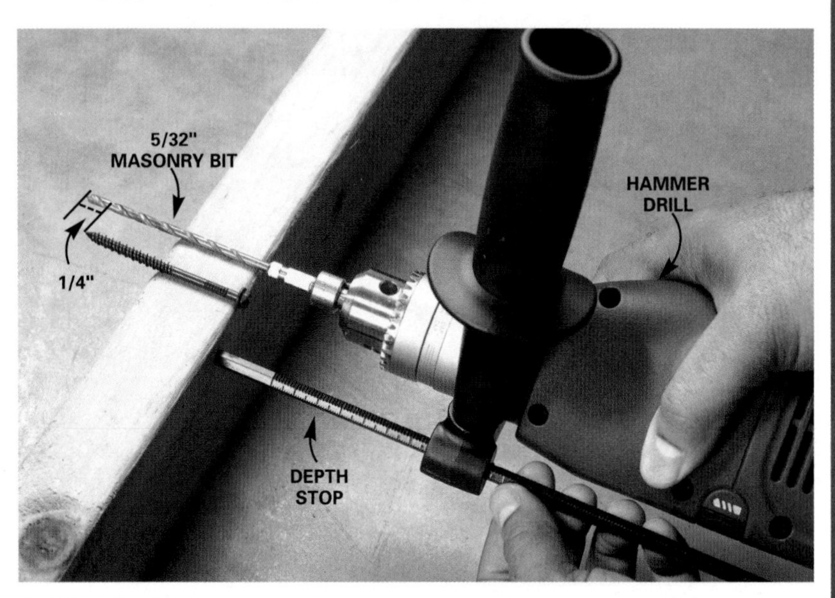

ADJUST the depth stop to drill a hole 1/4 in. deeper than the screw will penetrate.

Troubleshooting

If you're having trouble driving the screw all the way, first make sure the hole is deep enough. If it is, there's probably too much grit in the hole. Remove the screw and clean out the hole by running the bit in and out a few times. Try driving the screw again. If it's still stubborn, back it out and redrive it a few times. If all else fails, install another screw a few inches away. Consider a shorter screw for the rest of the holes.

Sometimes you'll have the opposite problem. The screw will spin without gripping. If this happens, the material you're fastening to is probably too soft or crumbly. Try a longer screw, or if you're using a 3/16-in. screw, try a 1/4-in. diameter. You may have to use a concrete anchor that expands as you tighten the fastener (p. 167).

Buy a variety of lengths so you have the correct screw size on hand

Select a screw length to penetrate the concrete at least 1 in. Add 1 in. to the thickness of the material you're attaching to get the minimum length of screw needed. In hard, dense materials like concrete or stone, this minimum 1-in. screw embedment will work fine. But for maximum strength, use longer screws, up to 1-3/4 in. embedment, in soft brick or other less dense materials. You may have to experiment with a few different lengths to find a screw that you can drive fully and that holds securely.

You'll find concrete screws at home centers, hardware stores and lumberyards, or you can order them by phone or on-line. Depending on the size, screws cost about $6 for eight screws, $15 for 25 screws or $24 for boxes of 100. A drill bit is usually included in boxes of 25 or more. It's worth having a couple of screw sizes on hand if you do a lot of projects. See the Buyer's Guide below for sources.

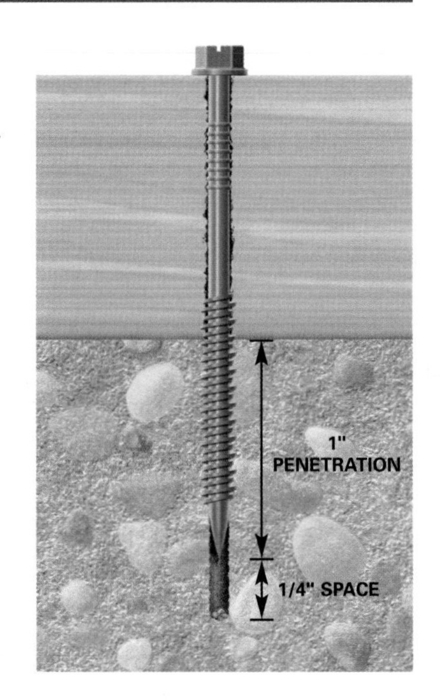

Buyer's Guide

- **CONCRETE FASTENING SYSTEMS: (888) 498-5747. www.confast.com. Order discount concrete screws and the installation tool by phone or on-line.**
- **SEVEN CORNERS HARDWARE: (651) 224-4859. Order concrete screws by phone. www.7corners.com.**

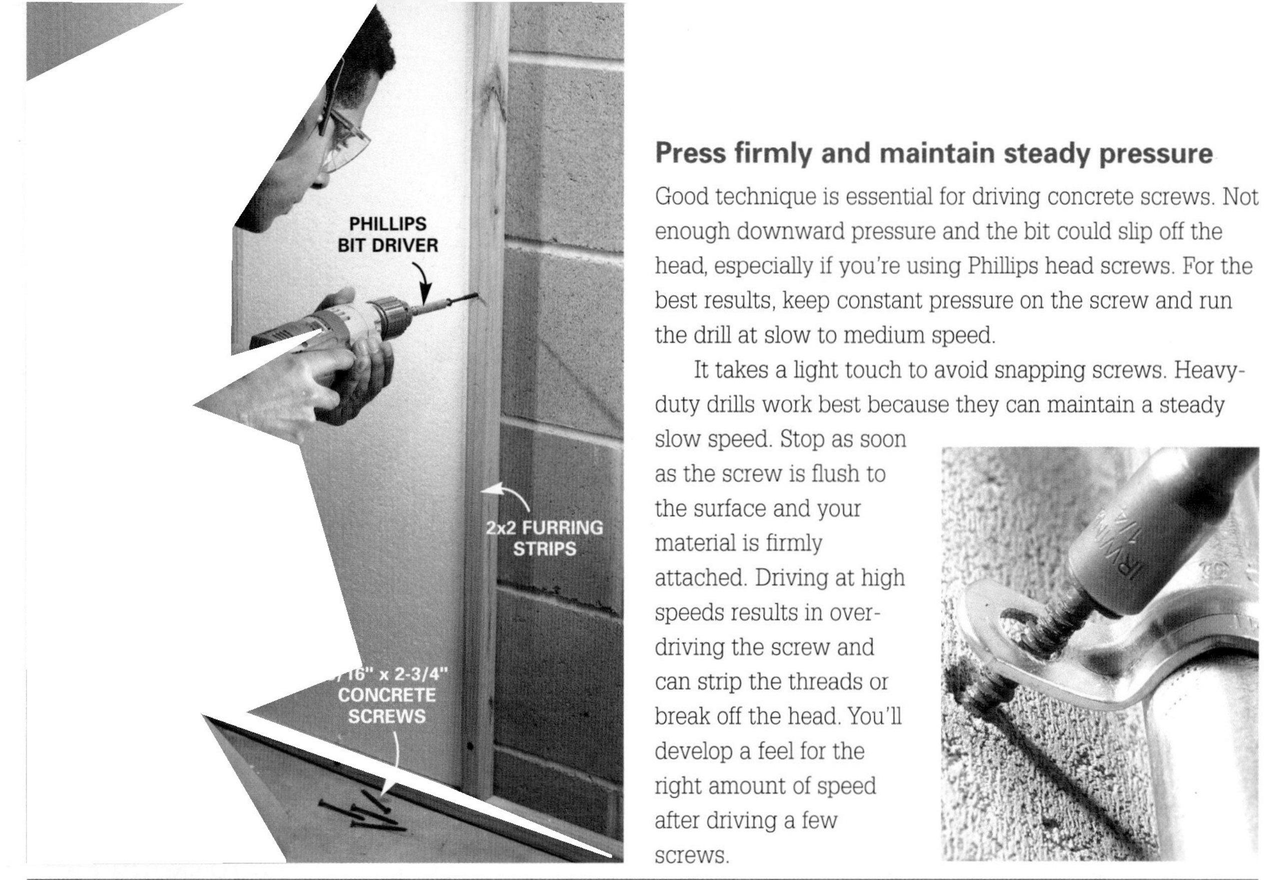

Press firmly and maintain steady pressure

Good technique is essential for driving concrete screws. Not enough downward pressure and the bit could slip off the head, especially if you're using Phillips head screws. For the best results, keep constant pressure on the screw and run the drill at slow to medium speed.

It takes a light touch to avoid snapping screws. Heavy-duty drills work best because they can maintain a steady slow speed. Stop as soon as the screw is flush to the surface and your material is firmly attached. Driving at high speeds results in over-driving the screw and can strip the threads or break off the head. You'll develop a feel for the right amount of speed after driving a few screws.

Use two drills or buy an installation kit to speed up the job

Install the masonry bit in your hammer drill and a driver bit in a variable speed drill. Then you won't have to switch bits constantly. Another option is to buy an installation tool. It allows you to switch quickly from drilling to driving mode and back again, and includes Phillips and hex head bits to drive both 3/16-in. and 1/4-in. screws. We found an installation kit ($24) alongside the concrete screws at the home center. See the Buyer's Guide (p. 166) to locate a local retailer or buy on-line.

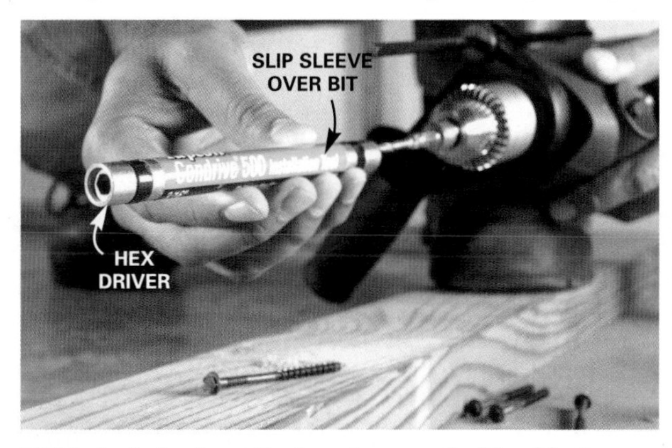

DRILL the hole, then slip the tube over the bit with the correct-sized hex driver facing out.

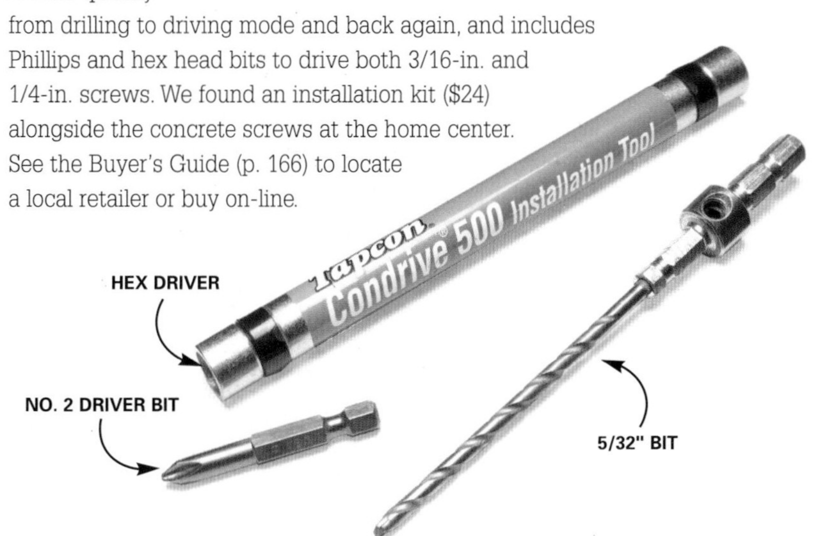

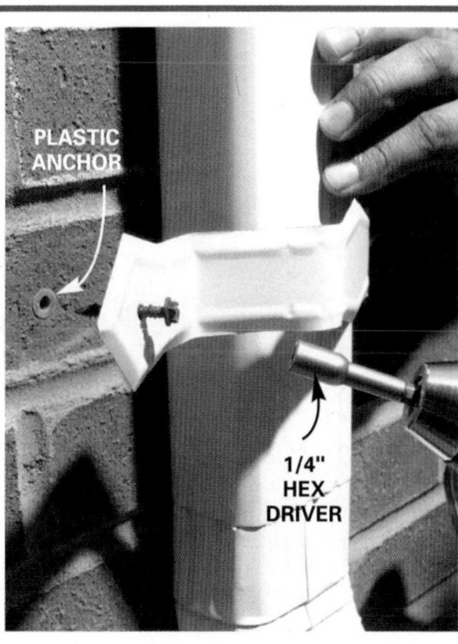

Keep a handful of plastic anchors in case of strip-out

Occasionally the threads of a screw won't grip and the screw will spin in the hole. Usually you can just abandon this hole and drive another screw a short distance away. But if relocating the screw isn't a good option, simply enlarge the hole and slip in a plastic anchor. Then drive the concrete screw into the anchor.

10-MINUTE WORKSHOP
STORAGE PROJECTS

ROTARY-BIT ORGANIZER

This rotary-bit organizer may just inspire a renaissance of rotary tool use in your shop. Friction-fit a piece of 3/4-in. plastic foam in a snap-lid plastic food container. Then poke holes in the plastic foam with an awl to hold shafted bits, and slice crevices with a utility knife to hold cutoff discs. Using a spade bit at high speed, drill sockets for larger bits and tube-shape containers.

I'm no rotary-bit fanatic, but once I stored my bits in this case, I found myself wanting to use them. And when my son asked me to fix his sunglasses, I soldered the broken frame and grabbed a fine-tip burr to shape the mend like a pro. Once your bits are in order, you can rediscover how useful they can be.

TOILET PAPER HOLDER FOR TAPE

An old toilet paper holder makes a handy tape dispenser for the shop. You can use a surface-mounted holder or impress the neighbors with a recessed version.

RECYCLED PEANUT BUTTER JARS

Plastic peanut butter jars work better for storage than glass baby food jars because they hold a lot more hardware and won't smash into slivers if you drop one. Attach the lids of 28-oz. jars under a shelf with two screws (so the lid can't spin when you loosen the jar) and screw on the loaded jar. For quick access, cut away half of a 64-oz. peanut butter jar with a sharp utility knife, leaving the neck intact, then attach the lid and jar to the side of a cabinet. If you load it with lemon drops, we won't tell.

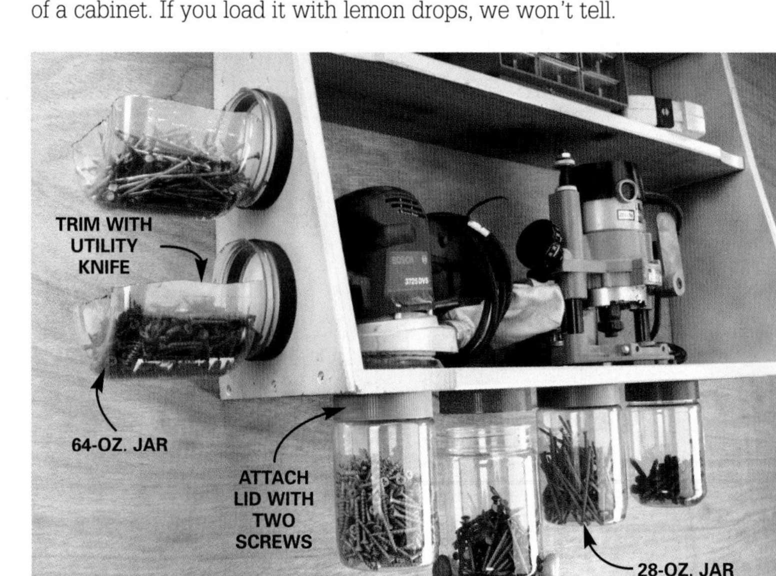

CORNER-ON PEGBOARD HOOKS

Ever had a plane, level or square get dinged up after falling off the pegboard? Never again. Bend an 8-in. long pegboard holder into a corner shape by holding it in a vise and pounding it with a hammer to make the series of right angles. Make one corner to hold the left side of the tool and another to hold the right. Now just hold the tool up to the pegboard and insert the corner peg so it clasps the tool's corner.

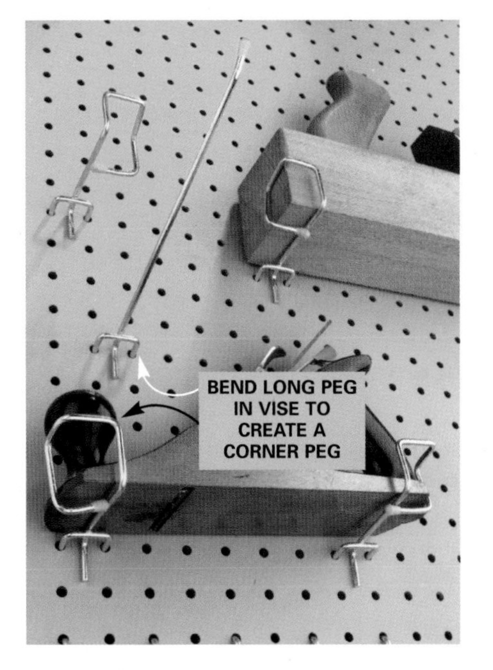

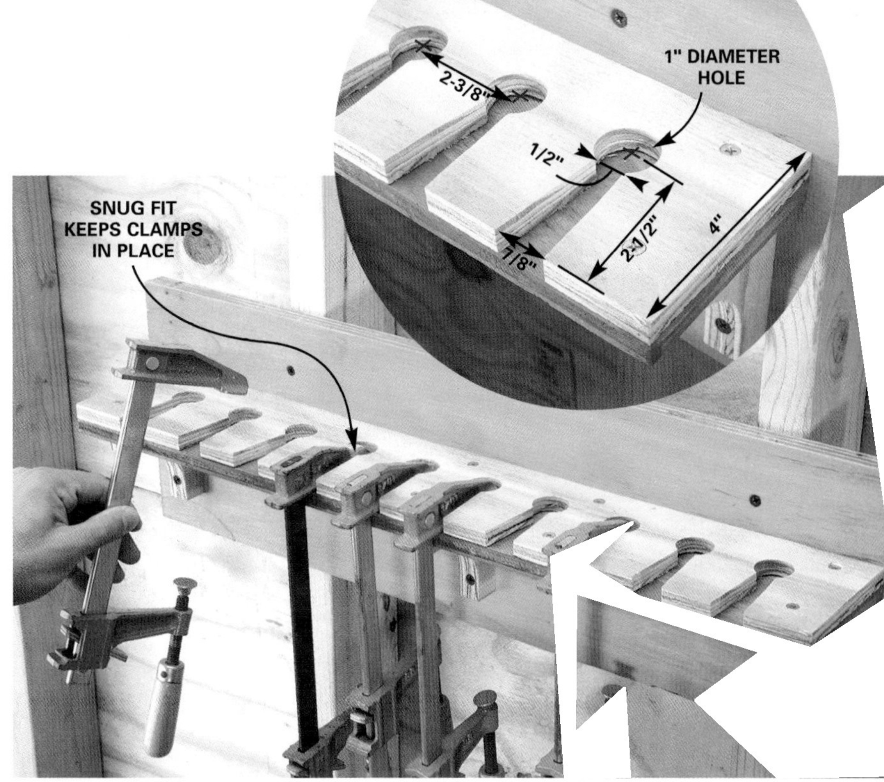

KEYHOLE BAR CLAMP ROOST

You'll love this bar clamp rack because you can holster the clamps securely without tightening the lower jaw against the rack. Just drop in the clamp and pull it out when needed. Notch the top piece of 1/2-in. plywood with the keyhole-shaped cutouts as shown, then screw it to the bottom piece of plywood. Make brackets from scrap wood and screw the rack to the wall. Our notch dimensions fit the most commonly used bar clamps.

INSTANT TOOL HOLDER

Store chisels, files, large drill bits, screwdrivers and other long tools so they're both visible and close at hand. Simply cut off the top from a clear 2-liter plastic soft drink bottle, leaving a flap for hanging. Use smaller bottles for smaller tools.

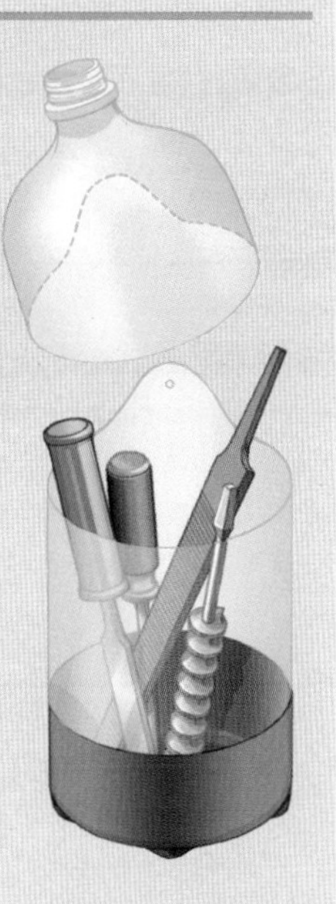

CAULK TUBE NEST

Make this caulk nest for your shop and the tubes will no longer roll all over the shelves like slippery logs. To build one, cut 10-in. long pieces of 2-in. PVC pipe and glue them side to side with PVC cement. To get straight glue lines, use the print along the side of the pipe as a guide. As you glue, hold the pieces together for 60 seconds with hand pressure or a clamp until the glue sets. Be sure to apply the glue only in a well-ventilated area. Glue on one tube at a time to fit the available space.

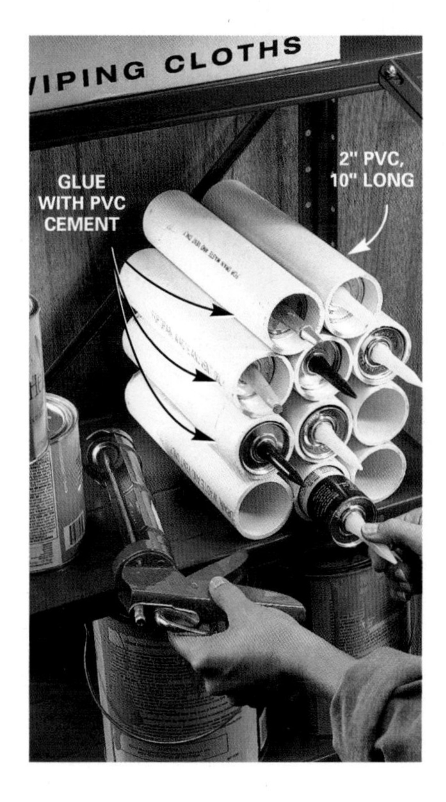

NEW ANGLE ON SMALL TOOL STORAGE

Find a bare spot on a wall or workbench and screw on a 2-ft. piece of 2-in. wide, slotted angle iron available at home centers. It's the perfect hang-out for screwdrivers, bits, safety glasses and sanding drums.

PIPE CLAMP HOLDER

Store bar and pipe clamps right under your workbench where they'll always be close at hand. Just screw sections of 4-in. dia. PVC pipe under your workbench and slide the clamps into the pipe.

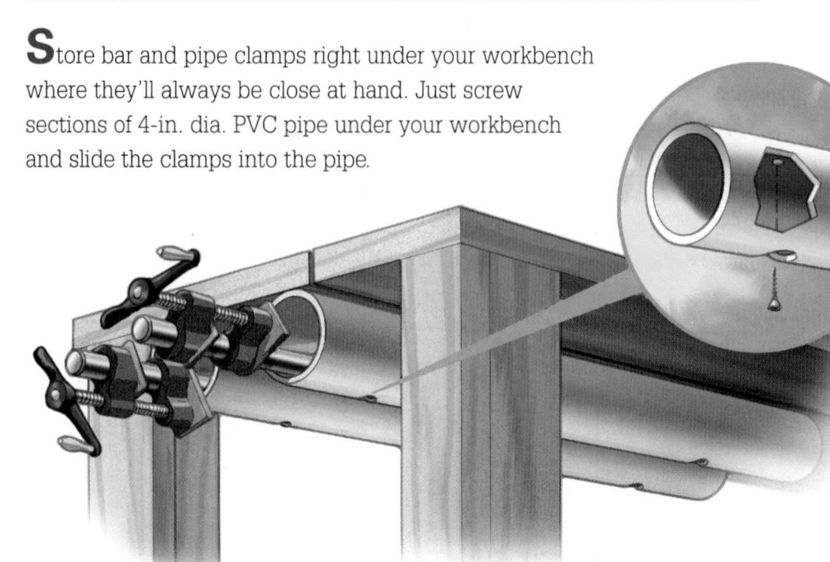

M&M BIT TUBES

Driver and drill bits are a lot easier to find and carry around in a pocket or tool belt if you try this tip. Buy some mini M&Ms in small and megasized tubes, evict the candy bits (mmm good) and load up the tool bits. The shorter tubes are ideal for all styles and lengths of driver bits, and the megasized tubes fit commonly used drill bit sizes.

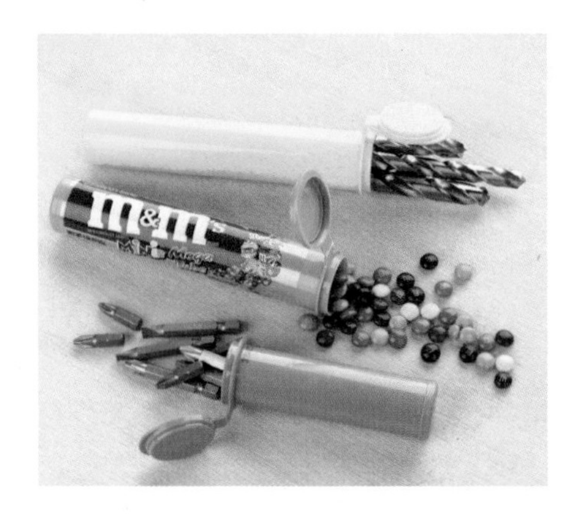

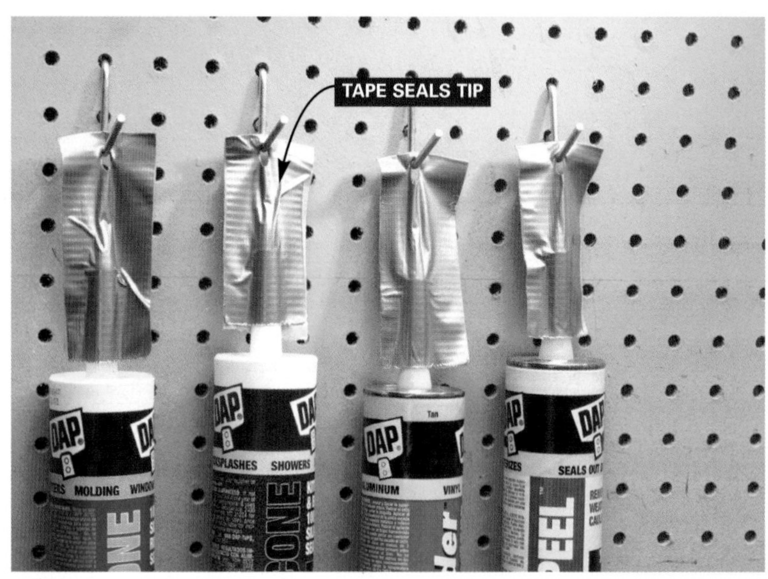

TAPED-UP CAULK TUBES

Here's a slick tip to keep partially used caulk tubes well sealed and at hand. Fold a piece of duct tape over the open tube to seal it, leaving a few inches of extra tape. Drive a nail through the tape and hang the tube on pegboard.

VACUUM ATTACHMENT HOLDER

Take one of your shop vacuum attachments to the home center and find a PVC tee that fits. Drill a hole in the tee large enough to accept a screwdriver, place a small plywood spacer behind it and screw it to the wall.

GUTTER SHELVING

Vinyl rain gutters make great storage shelves for long, thin items such as molding, light lumber, pipe and certain tools. Simply screw the wraparound support bracket to each stud and snap the gutter in place.

TOOL TOTE

Keep all your hand tools within easy reach in a portable 16-in. pine carton. Build one from a 1x8 x 12-ft. pine board, 1/4-in. plywood and a 3/4-in. oak dowel, and you'll never run back to the garage for a bit, blade, wrench or nail. Here's how:

- Cut and screw together the sides and ends with the ends protruding 1 in. beyond the sides. Drill holes in the top of the ends for a 3/4-in. dowel handle and tap it in the holes before assembling the ends and sides. Drill the 3/8-in. storage holes in the top edges of the sides before assembly.

- Saw 1/4-in. x 1-1/2 in. pine strips for the side slats and screw them to the protruding ends.
- Cut and screw on the plywood floor.
- Cut 3/8-in. pine partitions and screw them behind the side slats to create custom-width pockets for the tools.

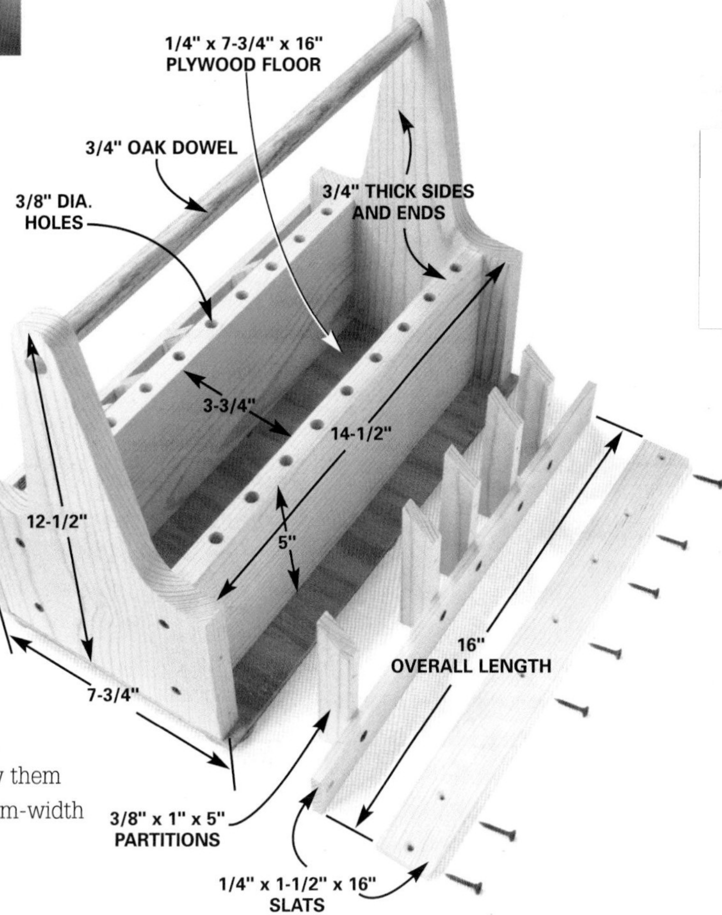

TIPS FOR TOUGH CUTS

Many power saw cuts are difficult to execute, and even downright dangerous if done carelessly. Don't become an emergency room statistic. Master these simple techniques for using circular and miter saws.

by **Jeff Gorton**

REPLACE THAT DULL BLADE

Even the best carpenter can't do good work with a dull blade. And besides making lousy cuts, a dull blade is dangerous. Dull blades can heat up and warp or bind, and they tend to climb out of the cut.

But how do you know if your blade is too dull? Sometimes you can tell just by looking for rounded-over or chipped teeth. But the best indicator is how the blade cuts. If you have to muscle your way through the cut, your blade is dull. A sharp blade will glide through even the toughest wood. Burn marks and rough cuts are other signs of a dull blade.

Many hardware stores offer blade-sharpening services, but I wouldn't waste money sharpening steel blades. High-quality carbide blades are inexpensive and can withstand tons of abuse before they need to be replaced.

A good blade for general circular saw use is a 24-tooth, thin-kerf carbide blade ($8 to $10). To get the most from your miter saw, invest in a 60- or 80-tooth carbide blade ($40 to $80). Use the cheaper blade that came with your saw for general crosscutting, and reserve the good blade for fine work.

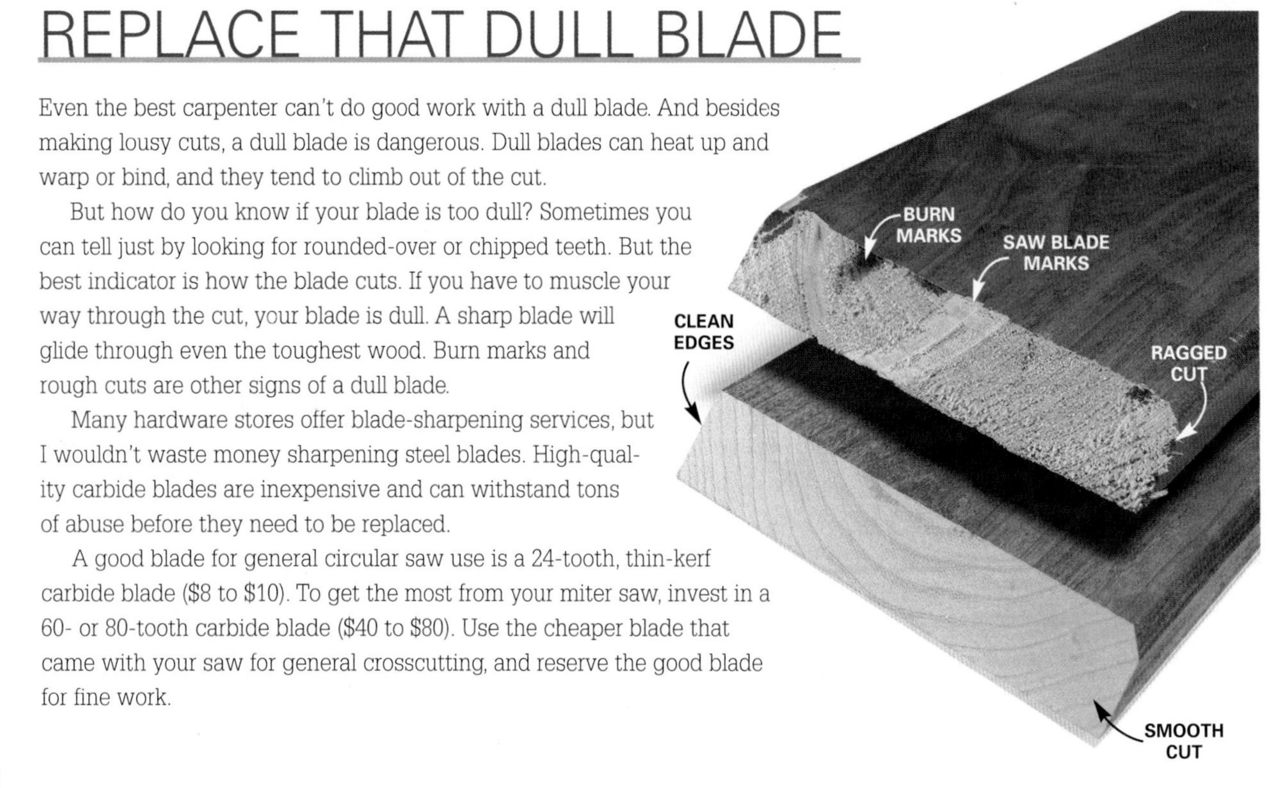

MAKE PLUNGE CUTS SAFELY

Plunge cutting is a useful method for starting a cut when you can't start from an edge. One example is cutting a window opening in a sheet of plywood. But if done with poor technique, this cut is dangerous. The saw will kick back and run back toward you. The photos show good technique. Since you can't see what's under the sheet you're cutting, check before you start to be sure the path of the blade is clear. Never back the saw toward you while it's running. And stand to the side, not directly behind the saw. Set the blade to cut about 1/4 in. deeper than the wood thickness.

1 HOLD the front edge of your saw bed down firmly. Lift the blade guard with one hand and sight down the blade to align it with your line.

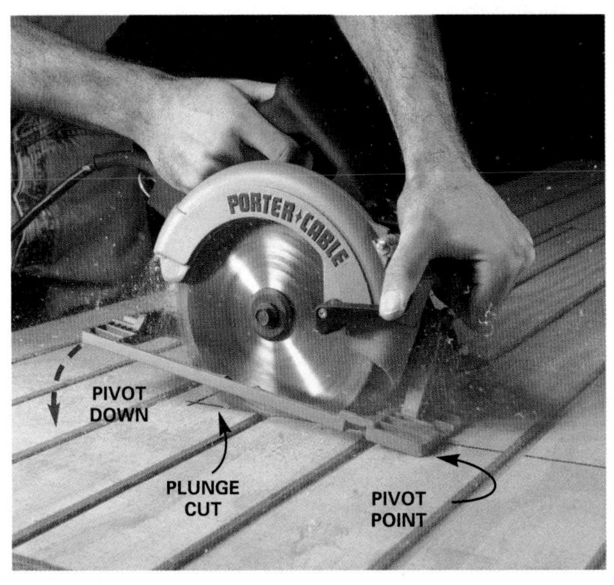

2 START the saw and let it come up to full speed. Gradually pivot the saw down to start the cut. Hold the saw firmly so it doesn't jump back.

3 WHEN the saw bed contacts the work surface, release the blade guard and cut forward. Let the blade fully stop before lifting it from the cut.

Safety tip for circular saws

Your circular saw is one of the most dangerous tools in the shop. Accidents happen quickly and without warning and injuries are usually severe. Binding the blade in a cut is probably the most common and scariest mistake because the saw blade will jump up and run back toward you. It usually happens when you're cutting a long board or large sheet of plywood in half without proper support. To avoid it, make sure the cutoff piece is free to drop or move away from the blade. This will eliminate any chance of binding and make all of your cuts safer.

CUT SMALL PIECES SAFELY

Cutting off small pieces is one of the most challenging and dangerous operations on a power miter saw. You're never sure where the piece will end up. It usually becomes a high-speed projectile when it falls into the spinning blade. But there is a way to avoid this problem. The auxiliary fence helps keep the cutoff from falling back, and stopping the blade keeps the teeth from catching it.

Another trick, not shown here, is to stop just before completing the cut. Let the blade stop. Then remove the molding and complete the cut with a utility knife or coping saw.

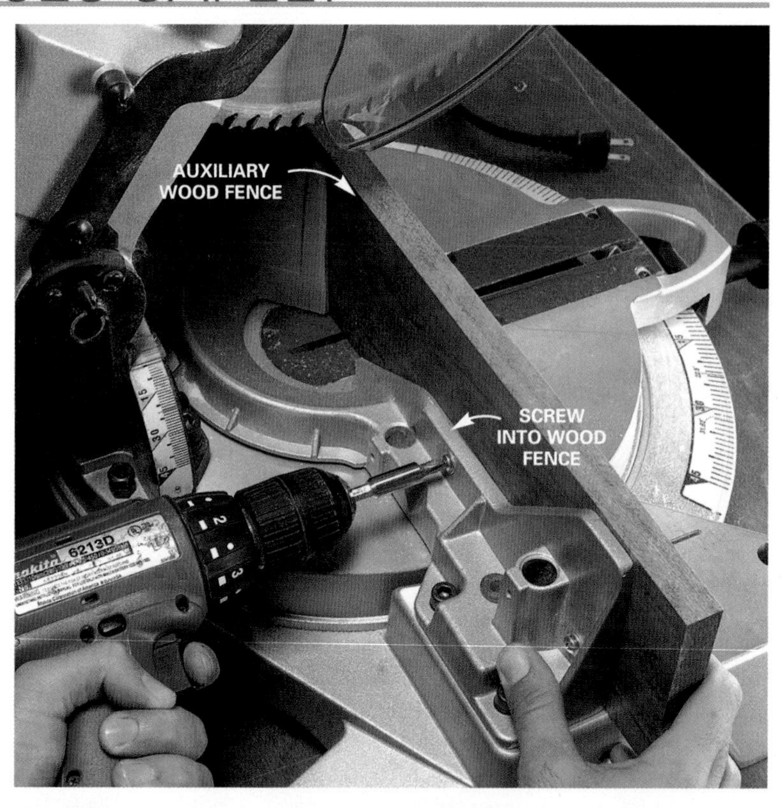

1 SCREW an auxiliary fence to your miter box fence to close the gaps. Make sure it's not too tall or it will restrict the depth of cut.

2 SIGHT down the blade to align the cut. Let the blade come to full speed before you start the cut.

3 COMPLETE the cut and release the switch. Now here's the key: Let the blade come to a complete stop before you raise it.

CLAMP YOUR WORK FOR PRECISE BEVEL CUTS

You can make crisp, accurate bevel or miter cuts with a circular saw but it's tricky. The blade guard can stick, making it tough to get started. And because the blade is angled, it's more difficult to follow a line accurately without twisting the saw and possibly binding the blade.

Two things will help you get a good cut safely. The first is to clamp the board you're cutting. Clamping allows you to use one hand to lift the blade guard out of the way until the cut is started. The second is to use a straightedge guide, like the giant Speed square shown. It allows you to concentrate on moving the saw steadily forward without having to worry about following the line. If possible, cut with the wider part of the bed on the "keeper" side of the board for better control and more accurate bevels. Near the end of the cut, concentrate on a straight-ahead follow-through.

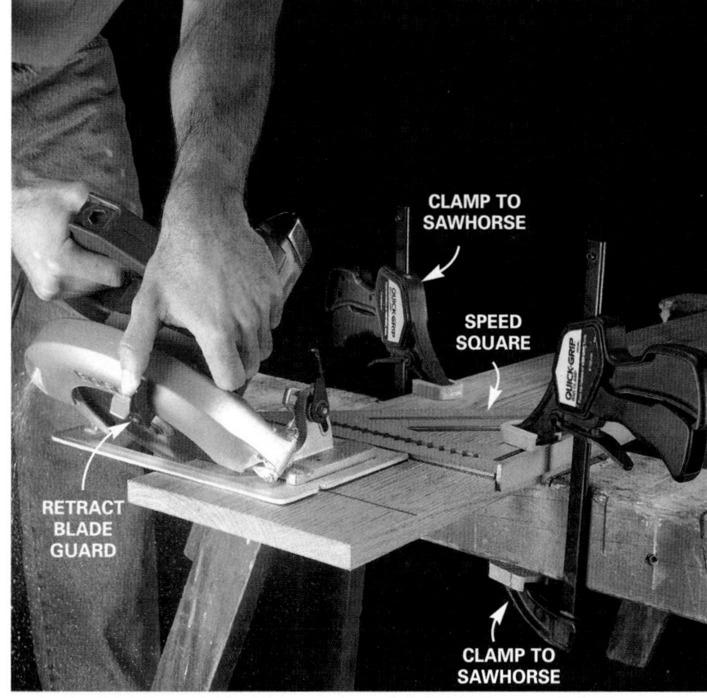

CLAMP your workpiece for bevel cuts. Then retract the blade guard to start the cut. Release it as soon as the blade is fully engaged in the wood.

LET CUTOFFS DROP FREE TO AVOID BINDING THE BLADE

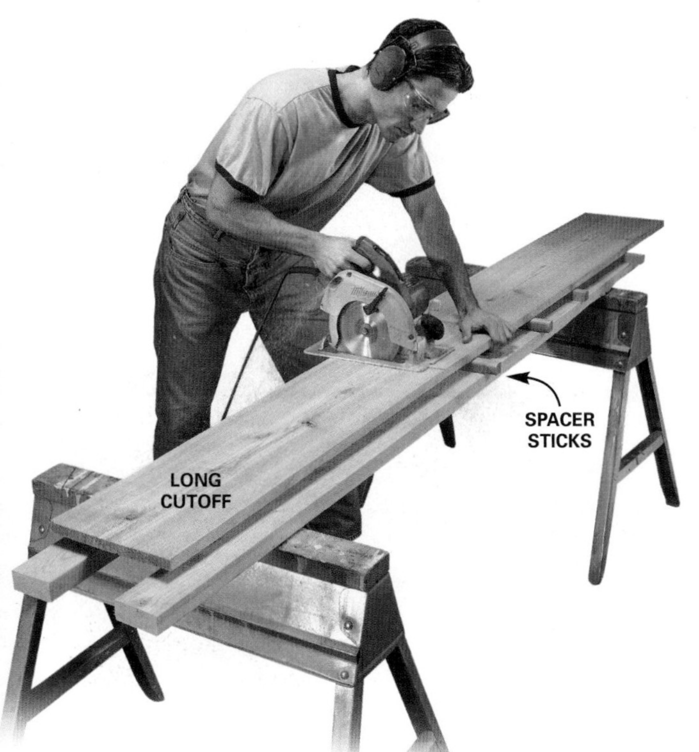

SUPPORT long cutoffs by stacking boards and separating them with strips of wood as shown. Make sure the end of the cutoff is free to drop.

Cutting the end off a board is usually simple. The short cutoff end simply falls away. But cutting a long board in half is different. You can hold one end, but the other must be free to drop or the blade will bind. The trick is to allow the cutoff end to drop slightly, but not so much that it completely snaps off before the cut is complete. One method is to support the board with strips of wood as shown here. You can also support the board continuously by stacking it on an equal-length sacrificial board. Set your blade to cut about 1/4 in. deeper than the wood's thickness. Hold or clamp the keeper side and allow the other side to move freely.

CLAMP SHORT PIECES IN THE "NO HANDS" ZONE

As a reminder to keep hands well away from the blade, most new miter saws have red lines indicating the "no hands" zone. But what if you need to cut a piece that's shorter than the 7- or 8-in. hands-free area? The best solution is to cut short lengths from longer boards whenever possible (p. 174). However, when you have to trim a short piece of molding, use clamps to hold it in place (Photo 2). The auxiliary fence comes in handy for this task by providing a better clamping surface. You'll get better quality miters because the molding can't slide away from the blade. And you'll be assured safer, hands-free cutting.

1 DRAW red lines on the bed and fence of your saw to indicate the "no hands" zone. Draw the lines 7 in. from 10-in. blades and 8 in. from 12-in. blades.

2 CLAMP short pieces of molding. Use strong spring clamps or C-clamps.

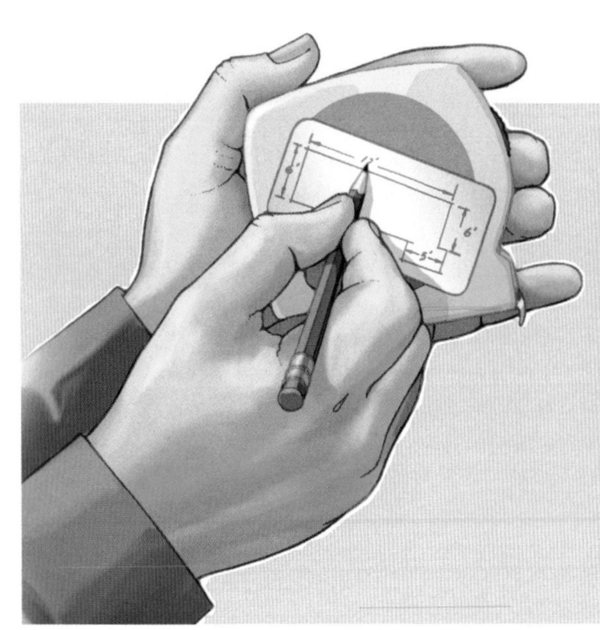

Handy Hints®

MEASURING REMINDER

Place a self-adhesive label on the side of your tape measure for jotting down measurements when you're on a ladder or roof or at the hardware store. The label can be easily erased or replaced as needed.

NO-BOUNCE
BUDGET WORKBENCH

Here's a worktable that takes only an afternoon to build and can absorb a real pounding. It's as rugged as a spendy European-style woodworker's bench, but it's made entirely from 2x4s and only costs about $80. To build it, you'll need:

- Four 33-in. 2x4s (legs A)
- Four 46-in. 2x4s (long stretchers B)
- Four 16-1/2 in. 2x4s (end stretchers C)
- Fifteen 5-ft. 2x4s (bench top D)
- Sixteen 3-1/2 in. x 3/8-in. carriage bolts, nuts and washers
- Sixteen 3-in. x 3/8-in. lag screws
- 2 lbs. of 3-in. deck screws

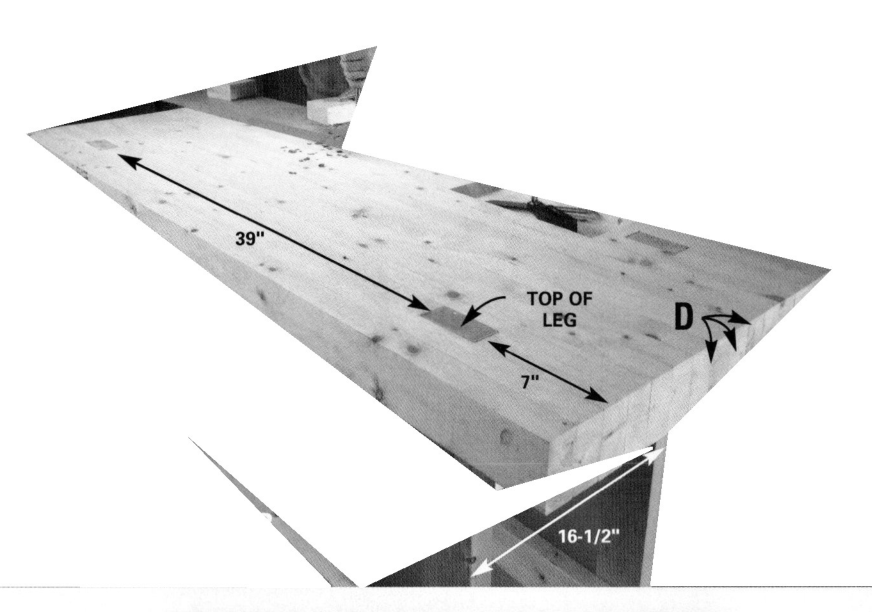

Build the base first

Clamp together the stretchers and legs, then predrill and bolt the base together. Keep the width of the legs from outer edge to outer edge at exactly 16-1/2 in. Use this base as a large sawhorse to assemble the top.

Assemble the top

Cut 15 top boards 5 ft. long and rip them to 3 in. wide with a table saw so the top will glue up flat without the typical rounded edges of 2x4s. For the leg slot, cut two of the top boards into three pieces: a 39-in. middle piece and two 7-in. end pieces. Glue and screw the top together, one board at a time, with 3-in. deck screws, keeping the ripped edge facing up and level with the adjoining boards. Use a corded drill so there's plenty of oomph to drive each screw below the surface. Note that the third glue-up from each end is where each leg notch is inserted. You can also create a nifty tool tray in the top by notching the three top pieces with a jigsaw. Clamp every 8 in. or so before driving in the 3-in. deck screws. Predrill the screw holes near the ends to prevent splitting. When you're screwing on the 7-in. long 2x4s to create the leg slots, use a scrap piece of 2x4 as a spacer.

Final assembly

Before joining the top to the base, loosen the bolts and screws on the lower stretchers to create a little play in the leg posts. Align the top notches with the leg posts and tap the top into place with a hammer and piece of scrap wood, working evenly around the table until all leg posts are level with the tabletop. Tighten the lower stretchers and you're done.

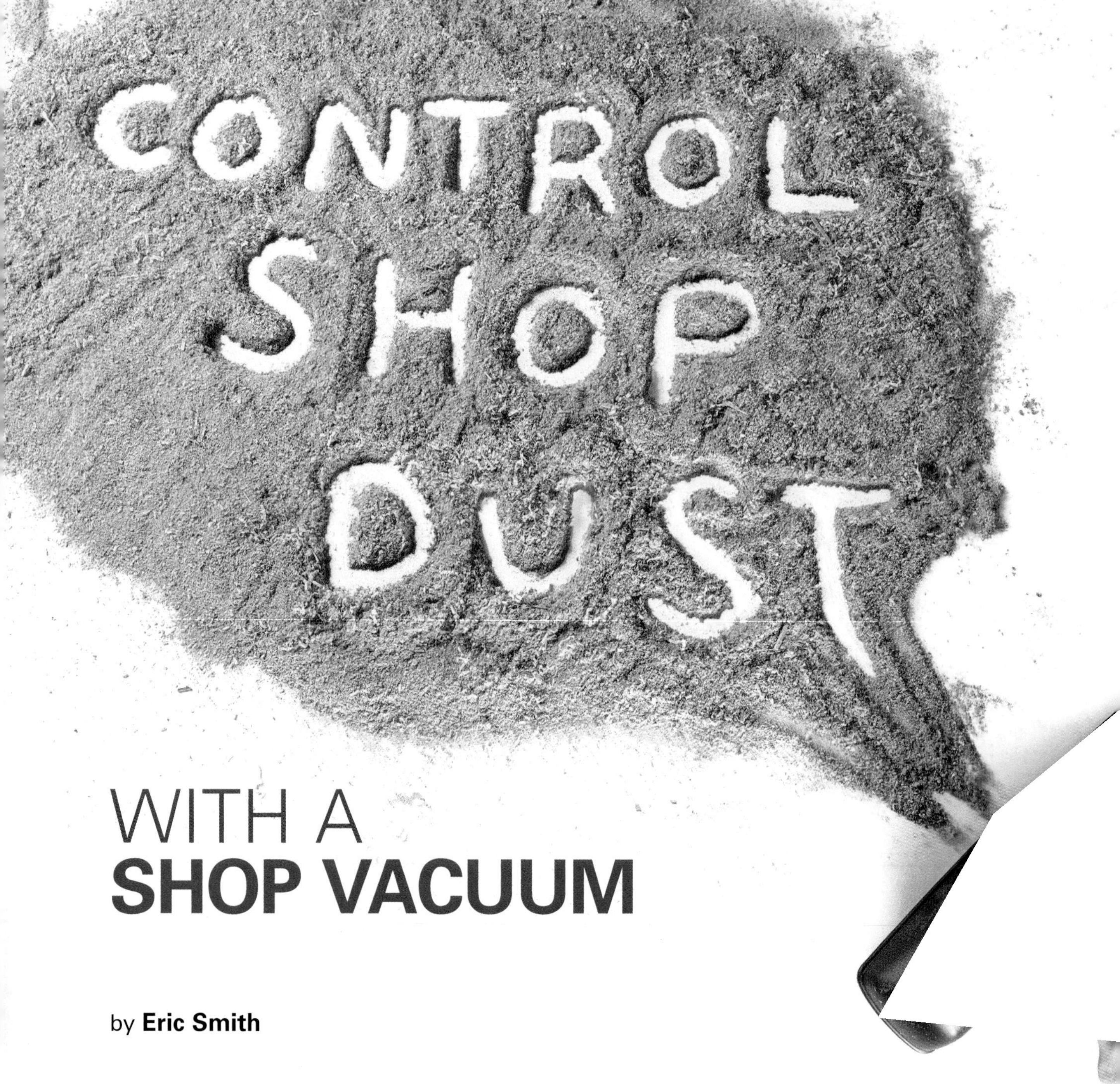

WITH A
SHOP VACUUM

by **Eric Smith**

You don't have to put up with that irritating layer of sawdust that seems to settle throughout the shop, garage or basement every time you cut and sand a few lengths of trim. Nor do you have to shell out the big bucks for a central dust collection system. You can capture most of that nuisance dust with a standard shop vacuum coupled with a few accessories. In this article, we'll show you how to assemble a simple, inexpensive dust control system that'll suck up most of that sawdust before it gets all over the house.

UNIVERSAL ADAPTERS MAKE TRANSITIONS EASY

If you're lucky, you can plug the vacuum hose directly into the dust port of your tool. But that won't happen often, because the size of dust ports on power hand tools varies. The best strategy is to buy a universal adapter ($9), which is available at home centers and other stores that sell shop vacuum accessories. You simply cut the soft rubber with a utility knife to fit the dust port on the tool and the vacuum hose. (We recommend 1-1/4 in. hose for most hand power tools; see below.) However, keep duct tape handy for odd-size dust ports.

ADD A 6-FT. LONG, 1-1/4 IN. HOSE FOR MAXIMUM MANEUVERABILITY

Buy a 6-ft. (or longer) length of 1-1/4 in. hose ($14 and up) to connect directly to hand power tools. Then connect the 1-1/4 in. hose to the standard 2-1/2 in. vacuum hose with a plastic friction fit coupling (**photo** above). The smaller hose is light and flexible compared with the larger hose. No drag, no kinks. You'll barely notice the 1-1/4 in. hose as you move the saw, sander or other tool across the workpiece. (Most sanders have dust ports, but relatively few circular saws and routers have them.)

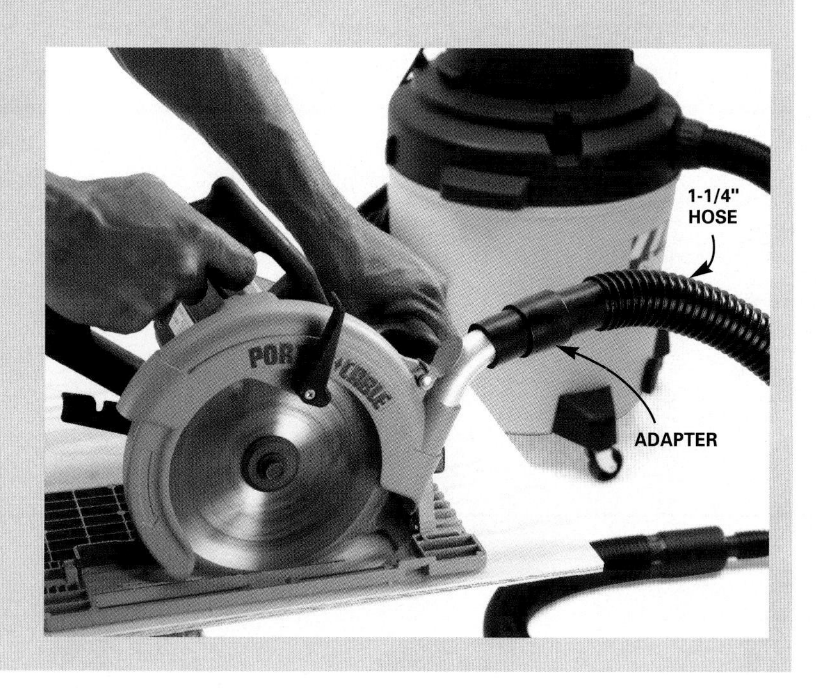

UNIVERSAL adapters and 1-1/4 in. hoses are available at Home Depot, Lowe's and Sears.com/craftsman.

BUY BENCH-TOP TOOLS WITH DUST PORTS WHENEVER POSSIBLE

These days, most bench-top saws and planers have dust ports, and they make a huge difference in controlling dust, even with a shop vacuum. You won't get it all, but even an 80 percent reduction will help a lot. The connections are usually easy. In most cases, the ports are a standard 2-1/2 in., so you can simply push the 2-1/2 in. vacuum hose right into the port as we show here. This works best with larger capacity vacuums, because the sawdust and chips from a table saw or planer build up fast!

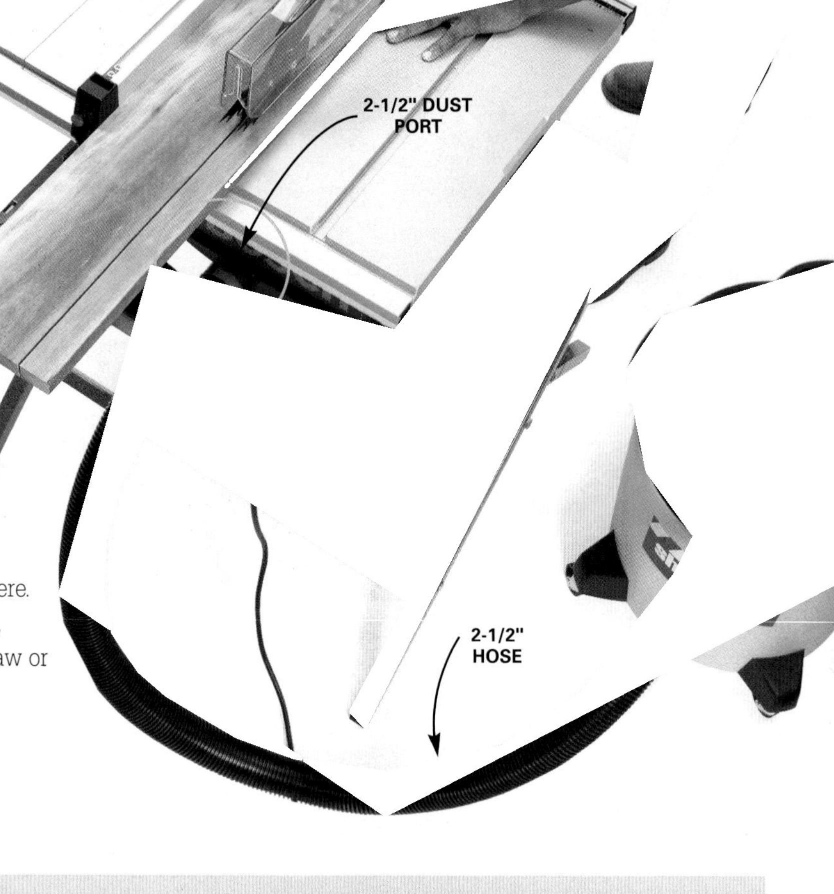

MAKE A PERMANENT ADAPTER FOR FREQUENTLY USED TOOLS

Ideally, tool manufacturers would standardize dust ports so you could swiftly move your hose from one tool to another. But that's not yet the case. In the meantime, save time and frustration by installing an adapter permanently on heavily used tools, such as miter saws. Then you can simply plug in the hose. Note: You'll find that dust collection on miter saws isn't as effective as on other tools, but this will definitely help.

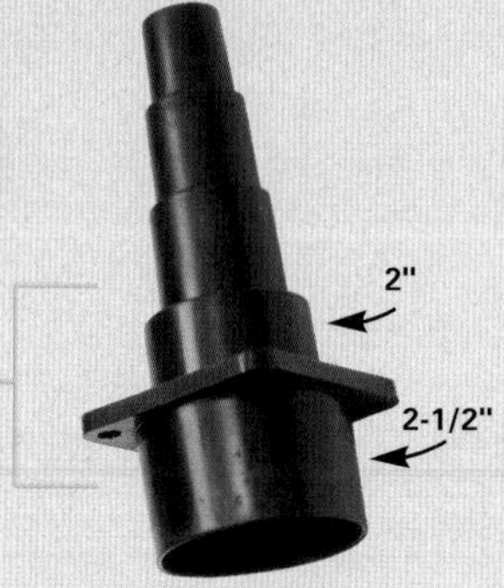

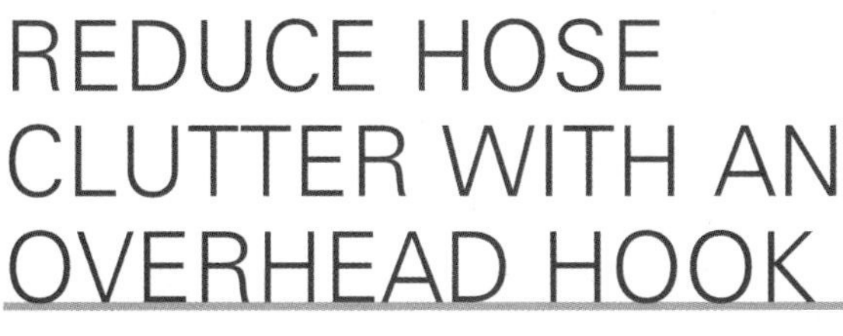

REDUCE HOSE CLUTTER WITH AN OVERHEAD HOOK

Dust collection hoses add to the clutter in a small shop. But if you tend to work in one area, you can eliminate some of the tangle and keep the tool from getting hung up by loosely hanging the vacuum hose from a hook. Or add several in the areas you work in most often.

UPGRADE THE VACUUM FILTER FOR BETTER DUST CONTROL

HEPA FILTER

You may have noticed the cloud of fine dust that blows out the exhaust when you turn on most shop vacuums. Small dust particles flow right through standard shop vacuum dust filters.

To stop this fine dust, buy a high-quality HEPA filter (high-efficiency particulate air filter; $20 to $30) from any store that sells your vacuum brand. They're well worth the price because they last a long time and can be rinsed clean.

USE REMOTE CONTROLS TO SIMPLIFY SWITCH HASSLE

Higher-priced shop vacuums often come with a special switch that turns on the vacuum automatically when the tool starts up. (Fein is one brand.) This is a great feature, because you don't have to walk over to the shop vacuum to turn it on every time you want to make a cut. However, you can also solve this problem in three other ways. One, use a pedal switch ($22) to turn on your vacuum (**near right photo**). Two, buy a remote switch ($40) and turn the vacuum on from anywhere in the room (**far right photo**). Or three, plug your tool and vacuum into a special power box that activates the vacuum when the tool is turned on ($20; **lower right photo**).

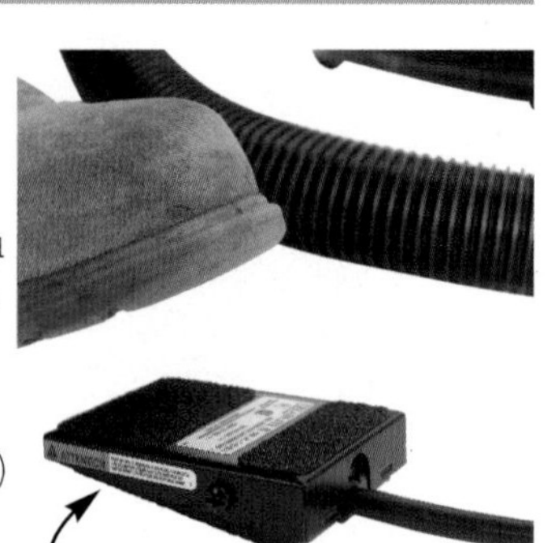

PEDAL SWITCH

THE PEDAL SWITCH we used (No. T-91-SCEA) is available from Linemaster, (860-974-1000, www.linemaster.com). The dust collector remote switch is from Woodstock International. Call (800) 840-8420 to find a dealer. The automatic power switch (No. 24031) is from Sears.com/craftsman.

REMOTE SWITCH (WIRELESS)

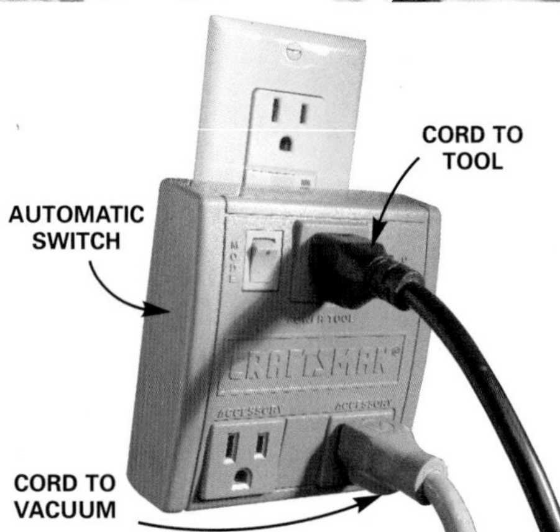

AUTOMATIC SWITCH

CORD TO TOOL

CORD TO VACUUM

NO DUST PORT? USE A PORTABLE DUST HOOD

Many power tools don't have dust ports. But if you're doing a lot of cutting and drilling, you can easily position a portable dust collector nearby. Depending on the system, you may have to fiddle with adapters and metal duct (from home centers) to make the transition to the vacuum hose. You can also rummage through the HVAC aisle at your local home center and put together a less expensive system with stock parts and duct tape.

THIS DUST COLLECTION NOZZLE (D2267; $53) is from Woodstock International. Call (800) 840-8420 to find a dealer.

FOR MORE CONVENIENCE, GET A WHOLE-SHOP DUST SYSTEM

For $70 to $110 and an hour of your time, you can set up a smaller version of a whole-shop dust collection system, complete with enough blast gates and inlets to handle a range of fixed and portable tools. You simply push the parts together (friction-fit them), so you can easily rearrange them as needed. Add an 18-ft. length of 1-1/4 in. hose for hand power tools and a remote control for the vacuum, and you can work virtually dust-free from anywhere in the shop.

THE DUST COLLECTION SYSTEM (No. 801-75-62; $110) we used is made by Shop-Vac and is available at home centers, hardware stores and on-line. Call (570) 326-3557 or visit www.shopvac.com.

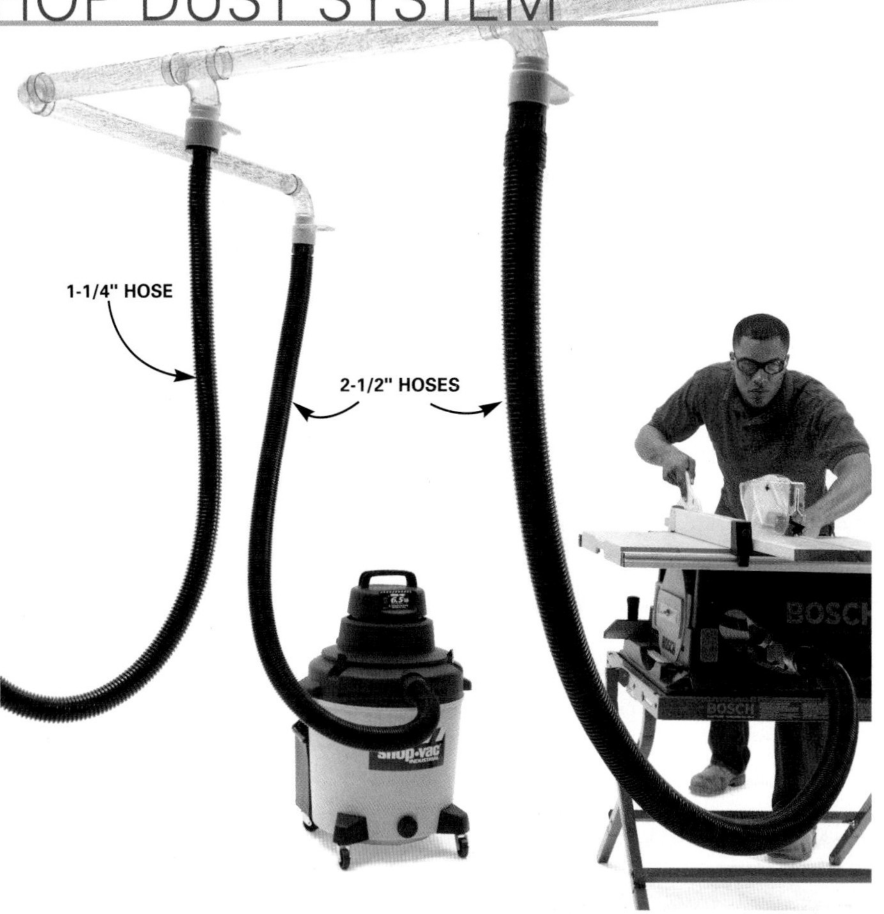

Handy Hints®

AIR NAILER DUST CAP

Keep shop dust out of your air nailer and protect the air hose connector from dents and dings between uses. Cut a 1-in. piece of 1/2-in. plastic plumbing pipe, press on a 1/2-in. pipe cap (no glue required) and stick it on your nailer.

Workshop Tips™

HINGED SAWHORSES

Want more versatility than standard sawhorses can deliver? With these, you can support both long and short lumber at the same time or large sheets of plywood. When you're done, just fold them up for storage.

To build these sawhorses, you'll need five 8-ft. 2x4s, a couple of pieces of scrap 1/2-in. plywood, 2-1/2 in. and 1-5/8 in. drywall screws, and a pair of 3-1/2 in. door hinges ($4 each at a home center).

First, cut the 2x4s into eight 32-in. crosspieces, six 24-in. legs and six 6-1/2 in. pieces for the feet. Cut six triangles from the plywood, making them 6-1/2 in. on two sides.

Next, screw the horizontal pieces into two angle iron–shaped crosspieces, then screw a leg on each end of two crosspieces, positioning the legs on opposite sides so the two crosspieces will meet edge to edge when closed. Finally, screw one leg on the remaining crosspieces, then screw on the feet and triangles and attach the crosspieces with the hinges. That's it. Now you can saw, sand or rout those unwieldy workpieces in comfort.

BUCKET WORKBENCH

Those 5-gallon buckets make great tool carriers, but they can do double duty as a handy, on-the-job sawhorse. Simply cut 3-1/2 in. wide x 1/2-in. deep notches in the rim to hold a 2x4. Works great! See p. 8 for 5-gallon bucket safety warning.

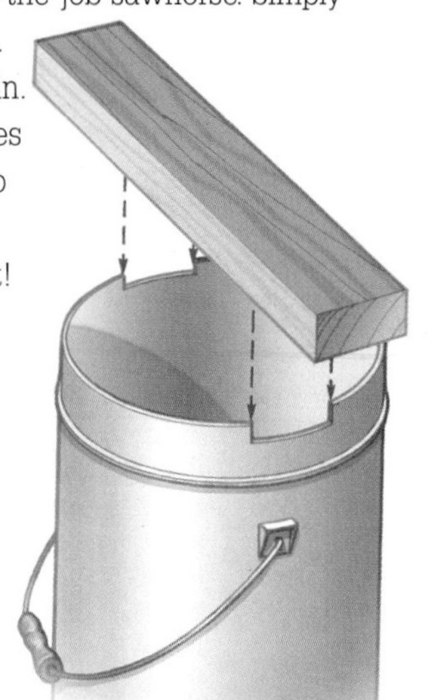

SHARPENING CLUB

Using 3M spray adhesive, apply sandpaper—medium to finer grits—on all four sides of a 12-in. piece of 2x2 hardwood. First cut or sand a 4-in. long handle on one end so you can move through the grits by spinning the handle. You'll grab the club whenever dull utility knives and chisels need resharpening, and it's also handy as a file sander for wood or metalworking. When the sandpaper is used up, just peel it off, respray and apply fresh sandpaper.

ON-A-ROLL HARDWARE HEADQUARTERS

This plywood cabinet keeps all your screws, washers, nuts, nails and bolts in one spot and ready to roll to any project or repair job. It offers 30 drawers and a lower shelf for extra storage. To build it, you'll need:

- A half sheet of 3/4-in. plywood, cut into two 3/4-in. plywood sides, 31-1/2 x 12-1/2 in., and three 3/4-in. plywood shelves, 14-1/2 in. x 12-1/2 in.
- Four 2-1/2 in. swiveling casters
- Two Emplast 15-drawer cabinets ($12 each, 800-445-4117; www.emplast.com)
- Four 1/4-in. x 1-in. x 18-3/4 in. hardwood strips

Screw the sides and shelves together with 1-5/8 in. screws, leaving 7 in. between the lower and middle shelves and 18-3/4 in. between the middle and upper shelves. Slide the plastic cabinets into the frame and screw on the wood strips to secure the cabinets. Add the casters and load the drawers. Your projects and repairs will go much faster with this hardware store on wheels.

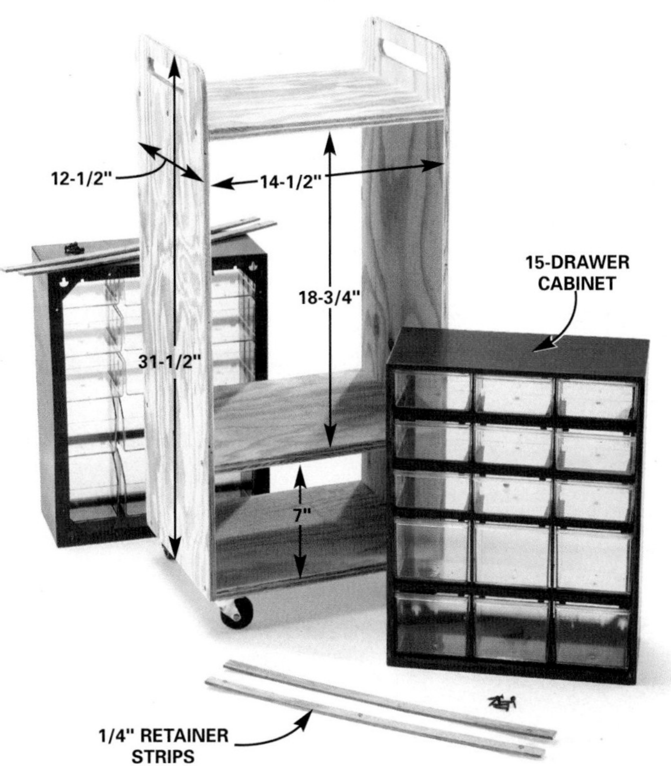

Got your own Workshop Tip?
We now pay $200 for tips we print. Send yours to tfhtips@readersdigest.com or The Family Handyman, 2915 Commers Drive, Suite 700, Eagan, MN 55121.

Workshop Tips™

CAULK TUBE SEAL PUNCHER

Who want to cut the tip off a new caulk tube and then scrounge for a nail or screw to puncture the seal? Drill a small hole in the front lower end of the caulk gun, then slide in a 6-in. piece of coat hanger wire with the end bent to clip on the edge of the gun. Just pull it out to pierce the seal, then stick it back in the hole so it's ready when you need it again.

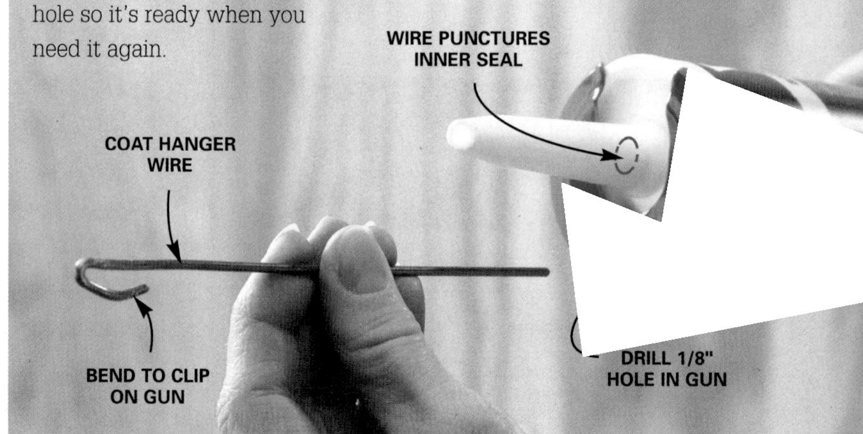

SURE-GRIP BAR CLAMPS

You can tighten and loosen bar clamps with greater comfort and gripping power if you coat the handles with Plasti Dip ($5 a can at a hardware store). It's a flexible rubber coating that's easy to apply and dries in four hours.

To coat the handles, tighten the clamps on the edge of a workbench, using a piece of newspaper on the floor to catch drips. Apply two or three coats for maximum comfort.

STRAW HOLDER

Keep the straw on a spray can from getting lost. Store it in a ball point pen tube taped to the side of the can.

CORDLESS DRILL HOLSTER

Here's a handy way to carry your cordless drill as you work. Cut the bottom and part of one side from a 2-qt. bottle of Pledge Floor Cleaner ($3), then cut parallel belt slits on the other side. The Pledge bottle holds most brands of 12-volt drills, but other bottle styles may work better with your drill. Use a sharp utility knife to cut the holster to conform to and hold your drill so it fits snugly.

NO-MAR HORSES

Meticulous carpenters say you've just got to have a set of sawhorses with carpeted tops for sanding or working with fine pieces of finished wood. Just trim carpeting scraps to size and hot-glue them to the wood tops of your horses. Now you can sand without getting scuff marks on the bottom of the workpiece and assemble prefinished work without leaving marks or scratches.

SPIN-CUT A BOLT

When you need to shorten a bolt, let your drill do the work. Put two nuts on the bolt and tighten them against each other. Then stick the bolt in a drill and hold a hacksaw against the spinning bolt. The nuts help to steady the saw blade and remove burrs when you take them off the bolt.

BETTER BRAD NAILING

Fingers can get in the way when you drive tiny brad nails into delicate projects. Here's the easy solution: Slit the eraser on the end of a pencil, slide in the brad, line it up, and tap it in.

MARKING GAUGE

Here's a nifty way to trace cutting or drilling lines on workpieces. First drill a 1/8-in. pencil hole 1 in. in from the ruler end of a combination square and adjust the square to the desired dimension. Then stick in the pencil and pull the square along the board edge to trace the line. Be careful to drill a hole that's only a smidgen larger than the pencil point.

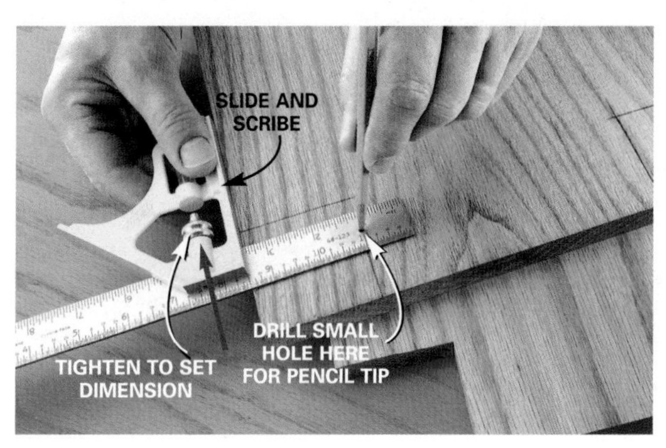

HEIGHT-ADJUSTABLE SAWHORSE

This sawhorse will help you work with longer boards on every power tool in your shop. It's made from good old 1-1/4 in. PVC pipe, a couple of 1-1/4 in. tees and an old sawhorse with a wood cross member you don't mind drilling holes through. Keep in mind that you can substitute 1-1/2 in. pipe and fittings if they aren't available in 1-1/4 in.

Drill the riser holes on the top of a sawhorse with a 1-5/8 in. hole saw, then wrap a strip of adhesive-backed 100-grit sandpaper around the hole saw. Sand the holes to increase the diameter a smidgen so the risers slide up and down with no side-to-side play.

With a hacksaw or bandsaw, cut the top third off the tops of the tees the long way (don't use a table saw). Mount them on the risers and snap in a length of PVC for the horizontal support. Drill 1/2-in. holes in the risers to match the various heights of your power tools, and tap in a 1/2-in. dowel to lock the height adjustment. Now you can put your revitalized horse to work.

So far I've used it with a miter saw, a table saw, a drill press, a planer, a—you get the picture.

Workshop Tips™

SUPER SCREWDRIVER EXTENDER

If you need to reach a screw that's really hidden, try a spade bit extender ($3) with a screwdriver bit in it. For a good fit, you may need to drill out the end of the extender with a 1/4-in. bit.

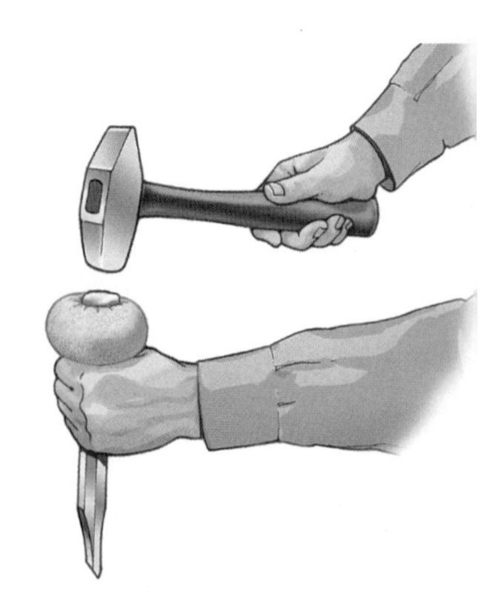

FOAM BALL HAND PROTECTOR

To protect your hand when you're holding a masonry or cold chisel, cut a slit through the center of a soft foam ball and slip it over the shaft of the chisel. Then hammer away.

MITER SAW TABLE

This simple miter saw table has some great advantages and takes less than an hour to make. Just cut a 21-in. x 96-in. piece of 3/4-in. plywood and screw it to a pair of 8-ft. 2x4s as shown for the base. Mount the miter saw to the base with screws or bolts. Next measure the height of the saw's base and make outfeed tables to the right and left of the saw. Then align a fence with the saw's fence and screw it to the back of the outfeed tables.

Here's how to make the table even more efficient. Buy two adhesive-backed measuring tapes (one right and one left) and trim and stick them to the tops of the fence for making cutoffs without fumbling for a tape measure. Then buy another and align it with the end of the large base for measuring and marking miters without a standard tape measure.

You can buy Biesemeyer or Delta 6-ft. left-to-right or right-to-left adhesive-backed measuring tapes at tools.ontheweb.com. The right-to-left (part No. 79-070) and left-to-right (No. 79-069) tapes cost $9.99 plus shipping. They're also available at Ballew Tools. (800-288-7483) for $9.45 plus shipping (same part numbers). You can also buy 12-ft. lengths for long tables.

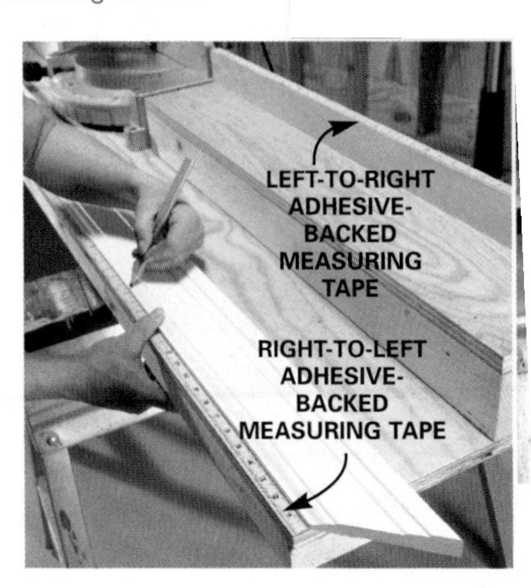

8 Exterior Maintenance & Repairs

IN THIS CHAPTER

Stop Peeling Paint 190

Ask Handyman 196
Painting vinyl siding, repairing concrete and more...

Handy Hints 199
Tips for cleaning gutters, rescuing caulk and bending metal

Pointing Brick 202

Using Tools: Finishing Concrete 206

You Can Fix It 210
Deck Repairs

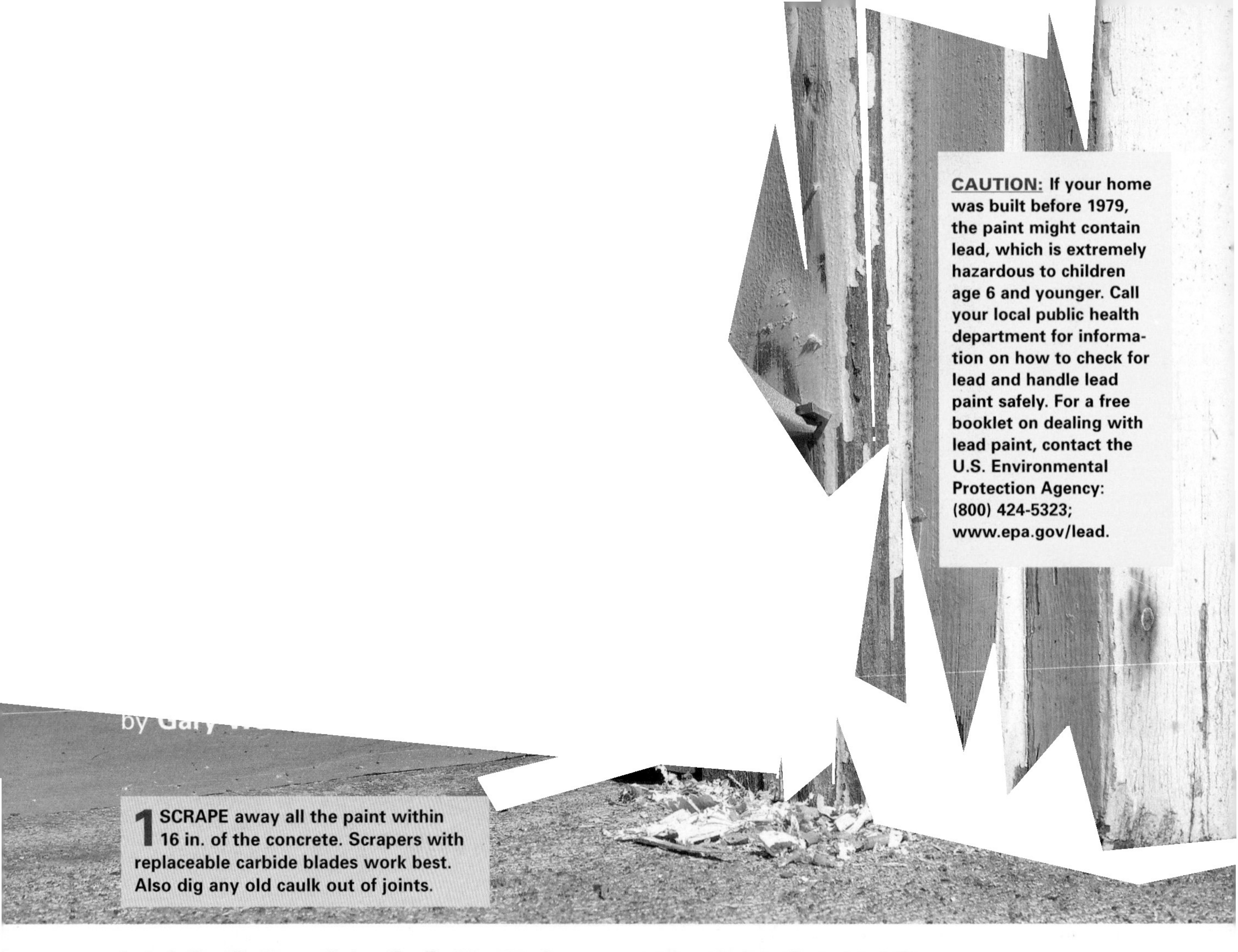

CAUTION: If your home was built before 1979, the paint might contain lead, which is extremely hazardous to children age 6 and younger. Call your local public health department for information on how to check for lead and handle lead paint safely. For a free booklet on dealing with lead paint, contact the U.S. Environmental Protection Agency: (800) 424-5323; www.epa.gov/lead.

1 SCRAPE away all the paint within 16 in. of the concrete. Scrapers with replaceable carbide blades work best. Also dig any old caulk out of joints.

WOOD CLOSE TO THE GROUND

If the lower ends of your garage door trim just won't hold paint, here's why: Concrete soaks up water, then releases moisture slowly. So any wood next to ground-level concrete stays damp, and that constant dampness breaks the wood/paint bond. The same goes for any wood that touches a deck, patio or other surface where water sits.

To correct the problem, create a gap between wood and horizontal surfaces. Then apply water repellent to the bottom 16 in. of the wood.Properly applied repellents add several years to a paint job in areas vulnerable to moisture. (See Buyer's Guide on p. 195 for sources.)

Begin by scraping away all the paint in the peeling area. Two or three coats of paint can usually be removed with a combination of paint scrapers and sandpaper (**Photos 1 and 2**). For heavier buildup, use a heat gun to soften the paint as you scrape. Be careful with a heat gun—it can melt nearby vinyl and weatherstripping. As you scrape, you may find that the wood has turned gray or black in some areas. Check for rot by probing these areas with a nail. Spots that are discolored but firm are simply weathered. Weathered wood doesn't hold paint very well, so sand away the gray surface. If you find soft areas, you've got rot. Small, shallow soft spots can be dug out and repaired with a two-part filler such as Minwax High Performance Wood Filler (800-523-9299). But when rot is deep and widespread, it's best to replace the entire piece.

Next, undercut the trim to create a gap (**Photo 3**). When you're done, scrape dirt or gunk out of the gap with a putty knife and blow out dust using a vacuum or air compressor. To avoid staining concrete, run at least three layers of masking tape under the wood. Apply repellent to all bare wood (**Photo 4**) including the underside (**Photo 5**). Bend a putty knife in a vise to make a tool for reaching into tight areas. Remove the tape right after application.

The label on the repellent will tell you how long to wait before applying a primer. Many repellents require an oil-based primer, so read the label. Apply two coats of paint (**Photo 7**). A single coat may look fine, but two coats form a more durable film that resists moisture better and lasts longer. When using paint and primer, don't ignore the temperature and humidity ranges listed on the label—weather conditions during application really do affect paint longevity.

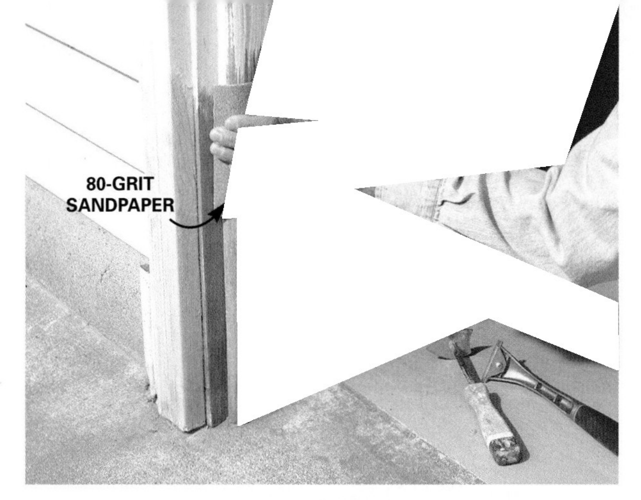

2 **SAND** remaining paint off curves or in corners where scrapers don't reach. Coarse sandpaper, 60 or 80 grit, removes paint quickly and leaves a rough surface for better primer adhesion.

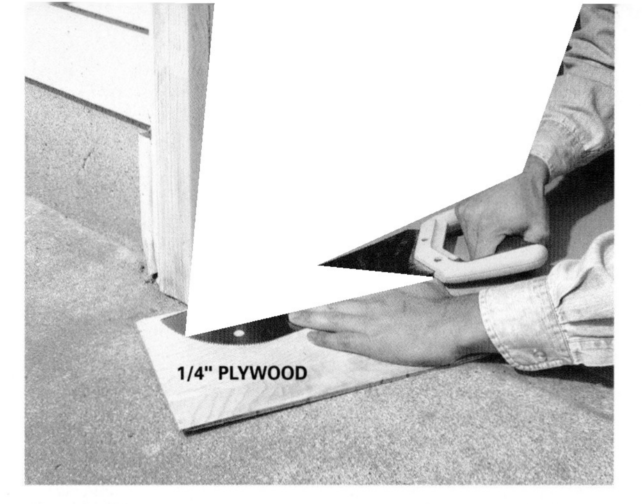

3 **UNDERCUT** the trim to create a gap between the wood and concrete. Use a scrap of 1/4-in. plywood for a saw guide.

4 **BRUSH** the bare wood with paintable water repellent. Keep repellent off existing paint. Wipe off any repellent that doesn't soak in.

5 **SLIP** a folded paper towel underneath the trim, soak the towel with repellent and then squish the towel up with a putty knife to soak the underside. Let dry.

6 **COAT** the underside of the trim with primer using a bent putty knife. When the primer is dry, fill joints and nail craters with acrylic caulk.

7 **PROTECT** the trim with two coats of quality latex paint. Apply paint to the underside of the trim the same way you applied the primer.

A BOARD THAT WON'T HOLD PAINT

Sometimes a piece of wood siding or trim peels while neighboring boards don't, even though they all get the same sun and moisture exposure (Photo 1). In a case like this, the board itself is usually the problem.

Some boards won't hold paint because of "mill glaze," a glossy or waxy surface left when the board was planed at the mill. Cure this problem by sanding glazed areas. Grain pattern can cause a more common and difficult problem (photos below right). Dark bands of grain (called latewood) are less porous and stable than the lighter bands of wood, so paint doesn't stick to them very well. This isn't a problem when those dark bands are narrow and uniform. But when they're wide, paint soon loses its grip. In fact, you can sometimes see a board's grain pattern right through the paint as cracks and peeling develop along the latewood grain lines (Photo 1).

If you have a few bad boards on your house, you can delay peeling by sanding thoroughly with 60-grit paper before priming. That roughens the dark bands so they hold paint better. But the only long-term cure for a bad board is replacement. Before you get started, measure the width and thickness of your siding. Keep in mind that about an inch of the board's face is covered by the board above. Buy matching siding at a lumberyard; most home centers don't carry it. Expect to pay 50¢ to $1 per foot.

To remove a bad piece of siding, you have to pull out two rows of nails: the ones in the bad board itself, and those in the board directly above. Siding is thin and splits easily, so the tricky part of this job is pulling nails without damaging surrounding boards. A cat's paw ($5 at home centers and hardware stores) is the best tool for digging out nails if damage to the surrounding wood doesn't matter (Photo 1).

To get at the nails in the board above, shove a flat pry bar up under it and gently pry the board outward. In most cases, this will pop up the nailhead, so you can pull it with your hammer claw. If you run into a stubborn nail that won't move easily, don't use brute force and risk splitting the good board. Instead, slip a hacksaw blade behind the siding and cut the nail (Photo 2). You can't get the new board in unless you pull the remaining shank of the cut nail (Photo 3).

1 DIG nails out of bad boards by driving a cat's paw under the nailhead and pulling. Then nudge the board above outward with a pry bar.

A BOARD with tight, straight grain holds paint well. Wide bands of darker "latewood" lead to peeling. Regardless of grain, look out for "mill glaze," a wood surface that looks glossy and paint won't stick to.

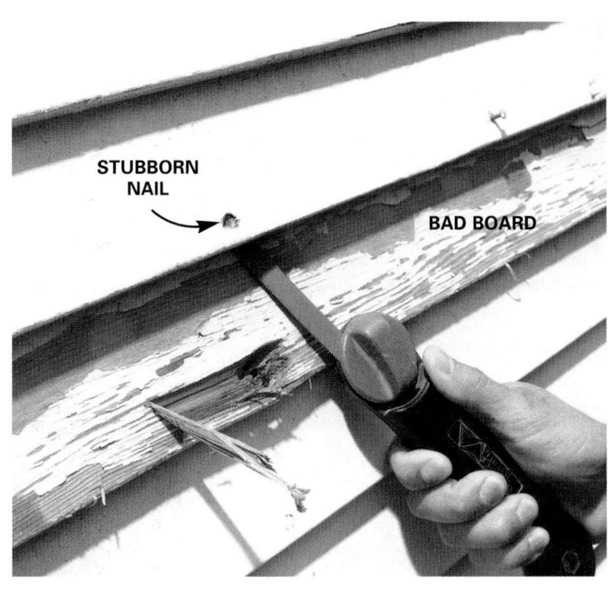

2 PULL the nails in the board above carefully. Slide a hacksaw blade under the siding and cut any stubborn nails. Remove the bad board.

3 BEND the remaining shank of cut nails down with side cutters or needle-nose pliers. Then grab it with nippers or locking pliers and pull it.

4 PRIME the ends and back side of the new board before you install it. Also prime the exposed ends of adjoining siding.

5 SEAL nailheads and craters with primer. Then fill the craters with caulk. You can apply acrylic paint right over acrylic latex caulk—no primer needed.

Before you install the new board, lightly sand it with 80-grit paper. If you come across shiny, glazed areas, sand them thoroughly. Then prime the back side and the ends (Photo 4). Also prime the ends of adjoining boards. This step pays off by slowing the moisture penetration that can lead to peeling at the joints. If the new siding is redwood or cedar, buy a special stain-blocking primer. Both of these woods contain natural chemicals (tannins) that can bleed through paint, causing brownish stains. A stain-blocking primer will seal in the tannins.

Nail the new board into place with 8d galvanized nails. Use a nail set to countersink the nailheads slightly below the wood's surface. Countersinking nails helps to keep the heads from protruding as the wood shrinks and swells. After you prime the sunken nailheads (Photo 5), keep an eye on them for a few minutes; primer may drip out of the craters and leave runs on your siding. When the primer is dry, fill the craters with caulk. Also caulk the ends of the board, where it meets trim or the next piece of siding. Finish the job with two coats of acrylic paint.

SIDING CLOSE TO THE ROOF

Too often, builders install trim and siding right up against shingles and don't bother to seal the ends of the boards. It looks good at first, but trim and siding—whether they're wood or a manufactured material like hardboard—soak up moisture from the wet shingles and before long the paint peels.

The solution is to cut back the siding to leave about a 1-in. gap. This keeps the siding out of contact with the shingles and allows you to seal the ends so they won't absorb moisture. Keep in mind that if the intersection of your roof and siding has been covered with roof cement (a thick, tar-like compound), you may have to deal with roof leaks as well. Chances are you'll have to replace the metal flashing and some shingles after removing the cement. We won't show that process here.

Begin by removing all the paint in the badly peeling area (**Photo 1**). While scraping, you might discover cracked or rotten siding that needs replacing. There's no need to replace an entire board if only a section near the roof is damaged. Instead, cut off the damaged section with a hacksaw (**Photo 3**). Don't install any new boards until you've cut back the bottom edge of the siding. See "A Board That Won't Hold Paint" on p. 192 for help with removing and replacing siding.

Cutting back siding is slow, tedious work. A backsaw or a dovetail saw with an offset handle is the best tool for the job ($10 at home centers and hardware stores). The fine teeth cut slowly but neatly, and the offset handle prevents scraped knuckles (**Photo 4**). Don't cut all the way through the siding or you'll risk dulling the saw teeth and damaging the metal flashing behind the siding. Instead, stop your cut 1/8 in. or so from the flashing and then finish up by making several passes with a sharp utility knife. But be careful—it's pos-

1 SCRAPE and sand to remove all paint from the area that's peeled. Keep a nail set handy so you can reset any protruding nails.

2 TEAR off any cracked or rotted siding, using a cat's paw and pry bar. Cut nails above bad boards using the technique shown in Photo 2, p. 193.

3 **PRY up cracked and rotted ends with shims and cut off the bad ends with a hacksaw. Make sure to stagger cuts on adjacent boards so the joints don't line up.**

4 **CUT the siding back from the shingles using a 3/4-in. thick board to guide your saw. Be careful not to cut into the metal flashing.**

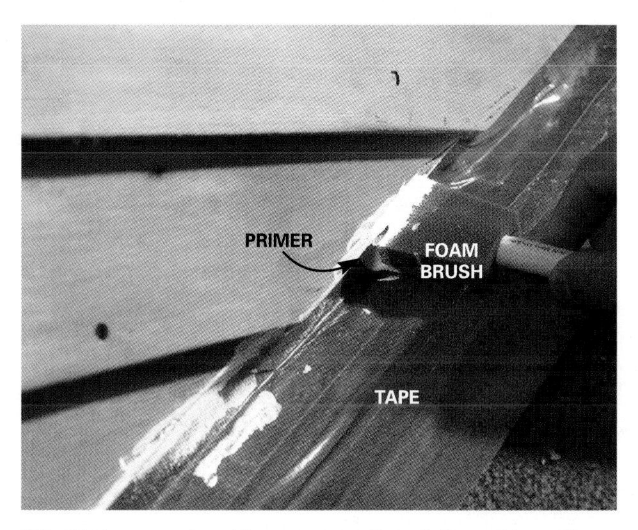

5 **SEAL cut ends with water repellent followed by primer so they can't soak up water. Treat the faces of the siding the same way. Protect flashing and shingles with tape.**

6 **FINISH the primed siding with two coats of paint. Duck down occasionally and check the undersides of the siding—it's easy to miss spots where the boards overlap.**

sible to slice the flashing if you press too hard.

With the siding cut back, take the same steps we covered in "Wood Close to the Ground," p. 191: paintable water repellent followed by primer and two coats of paint on the faces and cut ends of the siding. At each step, use a disposable foam brush to coat the ends of the siding (**Photo 5**). Keep paint off your flashing and shingles with duct tape—masking tape may not stick to them very well.

Buyer's Guide

- Behr No. 2-85 Waterproofing Sealer: (800) 854-0133. www.behr.com
- Cuprinol Clear Deck Wood Seal: (800) 424-5837. www.cuprinol.com
- Penofin Blue Label: (800) 736-6346. www.penofin.com
- Woodlife classic clear wood preservative: (800) 556-7737. www.wolman.com

Water repellents help paint last

Wood that stays dry holds paint longer. Repellents work by penetrating wood and sealing out moisture that works its way through the paint. Some repellents also contain preservatives that fight wood rot.

You have to remove all the paint so the repellent can soak in. Don't apply repellent over old paint; the next coat won't stick. Completely removing paint is slow work. But better paint performance reduces scraping in the future.

Water repellents cost $10 to $30 a gallon. Check the labels carefully: Most water repellents are not paintable. If the label doesn't say how long the product needs to dry before priming, assume it isn't paintable. Wood that's exposed to sunlight for more than a couple of weeks starts to degrade and won't hold paint as well. So avoid repellents with drying times of more than two weeks.

Ask Handyman™

PROPER SHINGLING

I'm going to strip my roof and reroof with new three-tab asphalt shingles, but I'm not sure how to start applying them. Thanks for your help!

Good question, but before you attach your first shingle, make sure you begin with the proper underlayment and roof edging. They're critical elements for a waterproof roof.

After you've obtained a permit (if needed) and safely stripped the roof clean, nail drip edge flashing flush along the eave.

Windblown heavy rain and/or snow can force water up and under even properly installed shingles. Even worse are ice dams (frozen water/snow that builds up on roof edges), which can wreak havoc by allowing water to seep up under lower shingles and then drip into your house. To guard against such seepage, apply self-adhesive waterproof underlayment ("ice barrier"), which adheres tightly to bare roof sheathing and seals around nails driven through it. In severe climate regions, most building codes require applying it 3 to 6 ft. up from the eave (minimum of 2 ft. past the exterior wall). Call your building inspector for details.

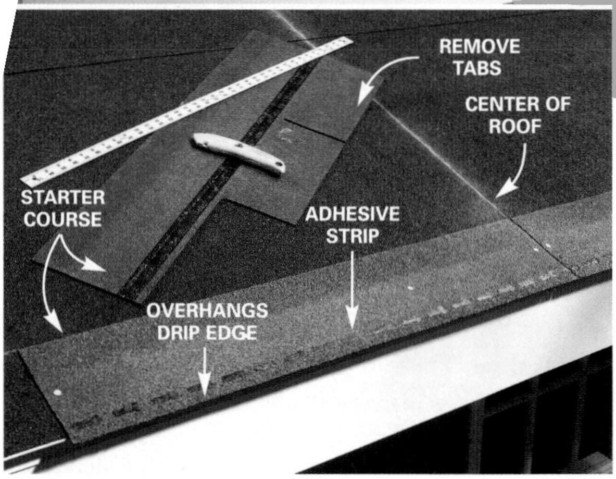

Cover the rest of the roof with No. 15 asphalt-saturated felt underlayment (some codes may require No. 30). Each layer overlaps the lower one by at least 2 in. Follow this step by nailing drip edge along rakes (sides of roof), on top of the underlayment. As you did with the flashing, always lap upper pieces over lower pieces. The felt keeps the roof deck dry before shingles go on, protects against wind-driven rain as shingles fail and increases fire resistance.

Next, find the center of the roof at the top and the eave, then snap a vertical chalk line. Most pros use this line to begin shingling, working left and right toward the rakes. Shingle manufacturers may recommend starting at the left rake edge, so check package recommendations.

For the first row of shingles, called a starter course or strip, you cut the tabs off three-tab shingles (see bottom photo) and apply them with the self-sealing adhesive strip facing up along the eave. Make sure this row has a slight overhang (1/4 to 3/8 in.) beyond the drip edge. The starter course protects the roof by filling in the spaces under the cutouts and joints of the next row of shingles. The adhesive on the starter course seals the tabs of the first full course.

Finally, nail the first course of shingles directly on top of and flush with the starter course. Use four roofing nails per shingle, as indicated on package instructions (six nails in high-wind areas). Once this course is laid, begin snapping horizontal chalk lines up the roof to ensure straight rows. Make sure to expose 5 in. of the shingle tabs where the bottom edge of the tab meets the top of the cutout.

BEST DOOR SCREENING

Between kids and pets, the screen in my door takes a beating. Is there a type of screen that can handle this abuse without tearing?

Aluminum insect screening withstands children and small pets better than fiberglass screening, unless you live in salty air coastal regions where aluminum will corrode. But the downside is it will show bumps, dents and scratches.

To help resist damage by dogs and cats, buy a PVC- or vinyl-coated polyester weave that's also much stronger than fiberglass insect screening. It won't dent or scratch as easily as aluminum screening.

When buying screening, buy a mesh count (number of openings per square inch) that will keep out the smallest flying insects in your area. Standard window/door screen mesh is 18 x 16 (holes per square inch—the larger the number, the smaller the weave). To keep out the smallest of insects, such as no-see-ums (also midges, sand flies and chiggers), go with a 20 x 20 mesh. And if you switch to a different screening material for your door, check to see if it will fit in the spline groove.

Specialty pet-resistant screening will cost about $90 for a 36-in. x 50-ft. roll. Aluminum costs $20 and fiberglass costs $15 for a 36-in. x 25-ft. roll.

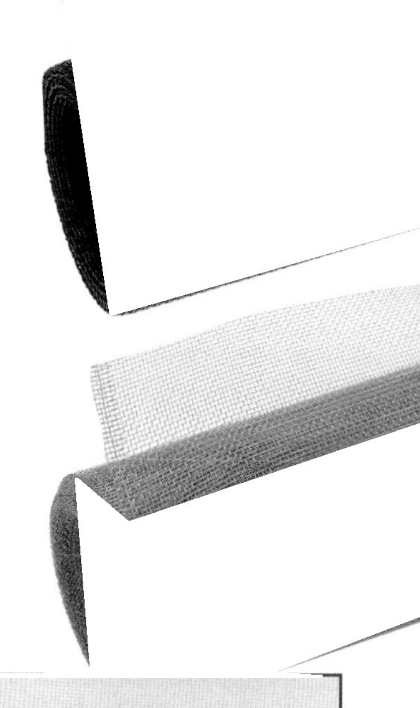

Fiberglass

FIBERGLASS SCREENING costs 30 percent less than aluminum and is easier to install, but it won't hold up as well in high-traffic areas.

Pet screen

PET SCREEN, made of strong vinyl-coated polyester, is much stronger than regular fiberglass screening.

Aluminum

ALUMINUM is the standard traditional screening and is stronger and longer lasting than fiberglass.

Buyer's Guide

- **Bay Mills: (800) 762-6694, www.insectscreen.com**
- **Phifer: (800) 874-3007, www.phifer.com**
- **Prime-line/Elgar: (800) 321-4970, www.elgar-usa.com**
- **StarBrand: (800) 323-5585, www.hanoverwire.com**

PAINT VINYL SIDING?

We bought a house last year that we absolutely love, except for the vinyl siding color. Do we have to spend the bucks to replace the vinyl, or can I paint it instead?

Yes, you can paint it, but you have to choose the right paint and prepare the siding well. Getting paint to stick to vinyl is a challenge because it expands and contracts considerably with temperature changes. So the paint must not only bond tightly but remain flexible as well.

Select a top-quality 100 percent acrylic latex exterior paint that has a blend of urethane and acrylic resins (such as MoorGard Fortified Acrylic from Benjamin Moore). It offers a good combination of flex and adhesive qualities, and also "levels" well. And be sure to buy a color no darker than your current vinyl color. Dark colors absorb more heat and can cause excessive expansion and buckling.

Finally, clean the siding thoroughly to remove all the dirt, grime and especially chalk. Use a pressure washer to knock off the initial layer of grime. Make sure the spray hits the vinyl at a downward angle. An upward angle can force water where it doesn't belong—under the siding. Then take a rag and a bucket of hot water and detergent to scrub the vinyl clean. If you have mildew, add 1 cup of bleach per gallon of water to kill it.

REPAIRING A CONCRETE SIDEWALK

I want to repair my sidewalk where it's chipped and rough. What kind of concrete should I use?

Use vinyl concrete patch. It's available at home centers and hardware stores ($10 for 50 lbs.). It's a fine-powdered cement with vinyl fortifiers and it really sticks to old concrete that's been properly prepared. You can trowel it as thin as 1/16 in.

To prepare the concrete for repair, first remove all the loose material with a chisel and/or steel brush. Then rinse the area well with water. A spray nozzle on a garden hose works great. Make sure to sponge out puddles of water, but leave the area damp. Mix the concrete according to the label directions and apply it with a trowel or putty knife. I've noticed that as you work it, vinyl patching material becomes stickier and harder to smooth, so don't wait long to apply it after you've mixed it. I've had good results and it's held up even in freezing weather.

Ask Handyman™

BUCKLED HARDBOARD SIDING

What causes wavy and buckled hardboard siding, and what can I do about it?

There are three possible causes:

- The siding was too tightly butted. During humid periods, the hardboard expanded slightly, causing buckling. You need about a 7/16-in. gap at the joints.
- Moisture got into the siding from the outside because of flaws in the paint or the siding was left unpainted too long. That doesn't look like the problem here.
- Moisture got in from behind because of roof leaks or inadequate vapor barrier under the siding. This is common, and I suspect it's the problem here, especially if the room directly inside is a bathroom.

Hardboard siding is highly compressed. Any crack, crevice, overdriven nail, butt edge, uncaulked seam or bottom edge that isn't well coated with paint will allow rain or dew to enter the siding. Once the moisture is inside, the siding will swell back up to its normal size and cause warping and buckling. Unfortunately, your best option is to install another type of siding (vinyl or aluminum) unless you can identify the source of the moisture and stop it.

SHINGLE STREAKS

What is causing these dark streaks on my roof? Are they harmful, and how can I get rid of them?

These ugly, dark streaks on an asphalt shingle roof are not a defect in the shingles or a sign of a bad shingling job. It's algae that causes the roof to look bad. Some experts say algae may cause shingles to deteriorate prematurely, but there is no research to support that idea.

This type of hardy, blue-green algae (*Gloeocapsa magma*) thrives in warm, humid climates. In the Midwest, it normally appears on a north slope where shade and moisture support its growth. However, the problem is most severe in the southeast Gulf states, where entire roofs can be covered in as little as four years. The algae feed on inorganic filler materials such as calcium carbonate in asphalt shingles.

Cleaning with a 10 percent bleach solution works for a year or two, but foot traffic and scrubbing during application will damage your asphalt shingles, and the solution can harm plants and surfaces below. The best option is to replace your shingles with algae-resistant shingles, with copper granules in them (look for the 3M Algae Block label).

Zinc also prevents the growth of algae, so another option is to install a zinc strip along the ridge of the roof. Rain hits it and carries zinc carbonate down the roof. It won't wipe out algae that already has a foothold, but it'll stop new growth from forming. Check out Shingle Shields (800-942-3004, www.shingleshield.com) or Z-Stop strips (800-845-5863, www.z-stop.com).

Handy Hints® from our readers

SHEET METAL BENDER

Bending sheet metal and flashing into crisp angles is easy with this two-board bending tool. To build one, you need a couple of short boards, a few screws and access to a table saw. Set the table saw fence far enough away from the blade to slice off a 1/16-in. wide x 2-in. deep notch, then push one board edgewise through the saw to create the thin notch. Now screw the boards together face to face with the notched edge in the middle, clamp them to a bench, slide the sheet metal into the opening to the desired depth and press down to bend. To bend angles other than 90 degrees, cut the desired angle on the unnotched board edge, then press the metal until it's flat on the angled edge.

BEND TO 90 DEGREES

CREATE A 1/16" CUTAWAY ON TABLE SAW

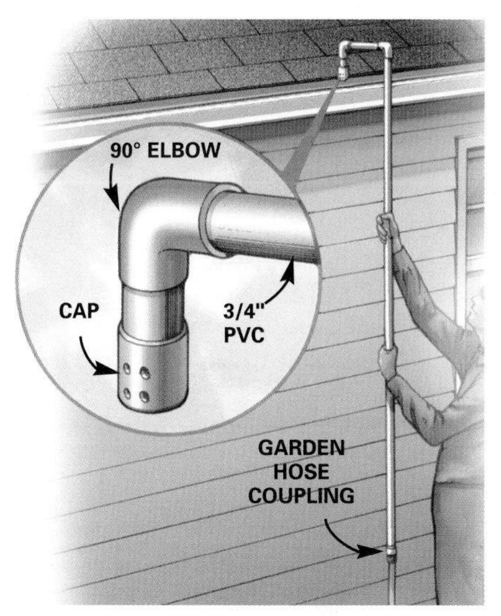

GUTTER CLEANER

This gutter cleaner takes about 10 minutes to make, costs about $5 and will help you avoid ladder climbing. Buy 3/4-in. PVC pipe, two elbows, a garden hose coupling and a cap at a local home center. Drill 1/16-in. holes in the cap as shown. Make the handle long enough to comfortably reach your gutters, and cement the parts together with PVC glue.

LADDER BALANCING ACT

Use spray paint to mark the center of your long ladder. That way, you'll know just where to pick it up for easy balancing.

Handy Hints® from our readers

SHINGLE-SAVING ROOF RAKE

An aluminum roof rake really cleans the snow off a roof, but it scrapes off some of the granules at the same time. To solve this problem, attach a vinyl door-bottom sweep ($5 at home centers) to the rake. It still removes the snow, but it's much gentler on the shingles.

HANDY LADDER PAINT BUCKET

Recycle mouthwash bottles for use as disposable paint buckets. Cut out the center of the used container as shown, and hang the bucket from a ladder rung.

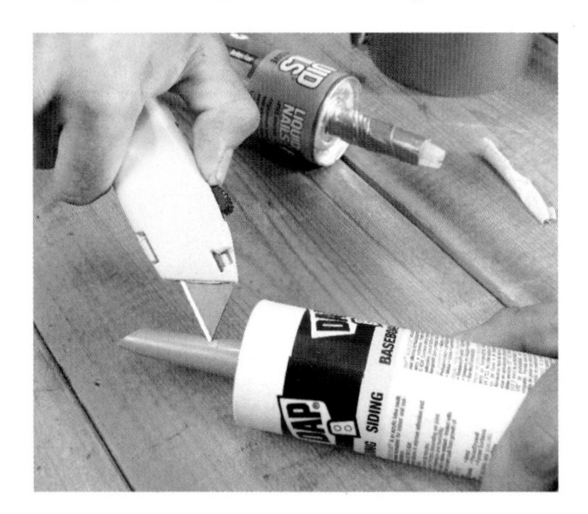

REUSABLE CAULK TUBE

How often do you have dry caulk stuck in the tip of the tube but know that there's a lot of fresh stuff behind it? Get to the fresh stuff by first cutting two slits along the tube, on opposite sides, with a sharp utility knife. Pry out the dried plug of caulk. Then wrap the tip with duct tape, put the tube back in the gun and use up that caulk.

ROUGH-PAINT SCRAPER

When you need to scrape down very rough areas of peeling paint, wrap a piece of old metal window screening around a block of wood and use it like a sanding block. It smooths quickly and without damaging the wood.

MILK JUG TARP WEIGHTS

Here's a classic hint: Use milk jugs partially filled with water or sand to weight the edges of a tarp. It looks weird, but for awkwardly shaped stuff it works better than trying to tie the tarp down.

I-SPY RAIN GUTTER

Here's a quick and easy way to eyeball rain gutters for possible clogs—before the next downpour causes an overflow. Cut a 60-degree angle on the end of a piece of PVC pipe and tape a hand mirror to the angled end. Hoist the mirror above the gutter to spot leaves and mini jams.

INSTANT WORKTABLE

Tired of bending down to dip your paint brush or pick up tools? Make an instant worktable from a plastic garbage can with the lid upside down. Tools and small parts can't fall off, spills can't run over, and it's light and easy to move.

HOW MUCH GAS IS LEFT?

Grab the bathroom scale and weigh your propane tank to calculate how much cooking time remains. A normal-size tank with a 20-lb. capacity weights about 17 to 18 lbs. empty and about 37 to 38 lbs. when full of propane. A full-size grill (35,000 Btu) will cook for 30 minutes per pound of propane. The tank shown tipped the scale at 21 lbs., so it contains about 4 lbs. or approximately two hours of grilling time (4 lbs. x 30 min.)

SLICK GUTTER SCOOP

You can make a great gutter-cleaning scoop by cutting away the bottom portion of a rectangular motor oil container. It's just the right width to fit into the gutter, and the spout gives you a handy grip.

POINTING **BRICK**

Restore crumbling mortar joints with a chisel, grinder and a lot of patience

by **Bruce Clark**

Brick is one of the most prized exteriors for homes because it's so attractive and easy to maintain. Yet over the years, water, ice and seasonal expansion and contraction all attack the solid mass of a brick wall at its most elastic (and weakest) point: the mortar joints.

Mortar joints deteriorate wherever water can soak them—under windows and walls, around chimneys, behind downspouts, at ground level and at any exposed wall top.

Repairing eroding and cracked mortar joints is called pointing, repointing or tuckpointing. We'll show you the proper tools and techniques to repair and restore cracked and worn-away mortar joints to make them solid, durable and good looking. To keep them that way for the long run, you have to stop water from getting into your bricks and foundation.

Is this a job for you?

Repointing brick is slow, painstaking work that requires few special skills but a lot of patience. Using the steps we

1 **CUT grooves 3/4 to 1 in. deep in cracked or deteriorating mortar using a 4-1/2 in. angle grinder fitted with a diamond blade. Push the blade into the joint until the grinder head contacts the brick, and make a single pass along the center of the joints.**

2 **POSITION a flat utility chisel at the edge of the brick and drive it toward the relief cut to fracture and remove the mortar.**

3 **CLEAN out all the loose dust from the brick cavity using a whisk broom or compressed air. Moisten the cleaned cavity with a garden hose.**

show in Photos 1 – 8, you can expect to repoint about 20 sq. ft. of brickwork a day. However, if you rush and do careless work on a highly visible area, the results will stick out like graffiti. Brick is durable; bad results will bother you for a long time! If you don't have pointing experience, consider hiring a pro for:

- Larger-scale pointing jobs, such as a whole wall that needs repair
- Chimney and wall repair requiring setting up and moving scaffolding
- Areas with a lot of loose or missing brick requiring rebuilding walls or corners
- Color-matching new mortar to existing mortar in highly visible areas

Tools and materials

Home centers and well-stocked hardware stores carry the tools and materials needed for pointing brick. Anything they don't have can be bought from retailers that sell to contractors. Look in the Yellow Pages under "Brick."

Cleaning out old mortar joints requires basic tools: hammer, flat utility chisel (Photo 2), safety glasses, dust mask and whisk broom. Filling the cleaned-out joints requires masonry tools: brick trowel (Photo 5), 3/8-in. pointing trowel (Photo 5), a special tool for contouring the joints (Photo 7) and waterproof gloves.

If you do tackle larger jobs or encounter hard mortar that can't be easily chiseled out, rent or buy an angle grinder (about $15 rental a day or $85 purchased) fitted with a diamond blade (Photo 1). Select a grinder with a 4-1/2 in. blade diameter; larger grinders are harder to control and cut the mortar too deep.

Break out the old mortar

Break out old mortar using a hammer and cold chisel or a flat utility chisel that's narrow enough to fit into the joints (Photo 2). Wear safety glasses and a dust mask and remove 3/4 to 1 in. of old mortar (more if needed) until you reach a solid base for bonding the new mortar. If the mortar is so soft that the bricks are loosening up, you'll have to remove and properly reset them. If the cracked mortar is harder, make a relief cut down the center of the mortar joint using the pointed edge of the chisel and then gently chip out the mortar that contacts the brick.

If the removal work is going really slowly, use an angle grinder to make the relief cuts (Photos 1 and 2). Exercise care here; the grinder can easily nick and chip the bricks, so don't use it to clean out the mortar contacting the brick. To avoid nicking the bricks, cut the vertical joints before cutting the horizontal joints.

Once the old mortar is removed, dust out the joints (Photo 3). Prepare the joints to receive new mortar by misting them lightly with a garden hose sprayer.

Mix the mortar just right

Using only the amount of water specified by the manufacturer, mix the mortar until it's the consistency of peanut butter and sticky enough to cling to an overturned trowel (Photo 4). It should be stiff but not crumbly.

Allow the mortar to "rest" for 10 minutes as it absorbs the water, then remix it using your brick trowel. Don't try to revive mortar that's drying out by adding more water to it. Mix a fresh batch instead.

Filling the mortar joints

Follow the pointing techniques shown in Photos 5 and 6 and these additional tips:

- Pack the mortar tightly with no voids for strong, water-resistant joints.
- Fill deeper joints (those greater than 3/4 in.) in two stages. Allow the first layer to partially harden (until a thumbprint barely leaves an indentation) before adding the second layer.
- In hot weather, work in shaded areas first (if possible) so the sun won't dry the mortar too fast. Mix smaller batches of mortar.
- Don't work in temperatures below 40 degrees F.

4 DUMP mortar mix into a cement "boat" and gradually add the specified amount of water while mixing with a brick trowel. Allow the mortar to "rest" for 10 minutes, then remix it before using. The mix is right when it sticks to an overturned trowel.

5 LOAD mortar onto an overturned brick trowel, hold the trowel under the horizontal joint—tight to the brick—and sweep 1/4-in. slivers of mortar into the cavity using a 3/8-in. wide pointing trowel. Fill the horizontal joints first. Avoid getting mortar on the brick face.

6 LOAD smaller amounts of mortar onto the back of the brick trowel, hold the trowel tip along the vertical joints and above the horizontal joints—tight to the brick—then sweep and pack the mortar into the cavity using the pointing trowel.

7 DRIVE a 6d box nail into a short 1x2 board so that it matches the depth of the existing joints. To "rake" joints, hold the board perpendicular to the bricks and move it back and forth, first along the vertical joints and then the horizontal joints. Other joint profiles require other shaping tools.

8 SWEEP the loose mortar from the finished joints and brick faces using a soft-bristle brush. Mist the new mortar twice a day for two days using a hand pump sprayer or a light mist from a garden hose to help it harden.

Match new joints with the old

Buy the mortar finishing tool you need to match the contour and depth of your existing mortar joints (**Figure A**). We recommend that you repoint brick sills (**Photo 1**) and other horizontal brick surfaces (ledges, wall tops, etc.) with flush joints (**Figure A**) to promote drainage—regardless of the type of mortar joint in your vertical walls. Allow the mortar to cure to "thumbprint" hardness before you finish the joint. Shape the vertical joints before working the long horizontal joints.

Use a soft-bristle brush as shown in **Photo 8** to remove mortar chunks on the brick face before they harden. The brush keeps the mortar from smearing. If you do smear mortar onto the brick, you'll have to go back later and use a chemical cleaner.

Prevent water from entering and damaging your brickwork by applying color-matched polyurethane caulk where stucco, wood and other materials meet brick.

Figure A: Common mortar joint profiles

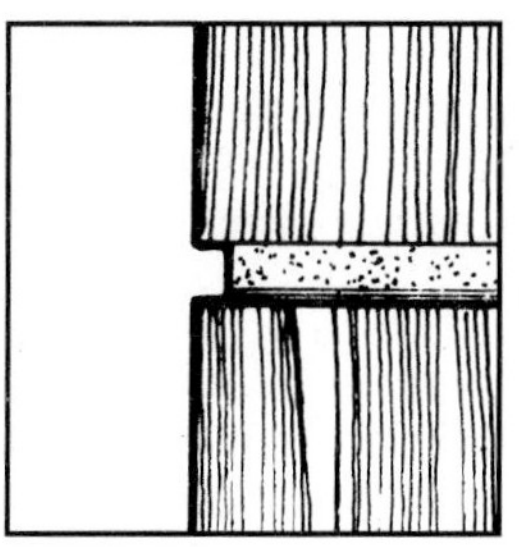

RAKED JOINT
Formed by removing mortar to 1/4 in. deep with a raking block (Photo 7).

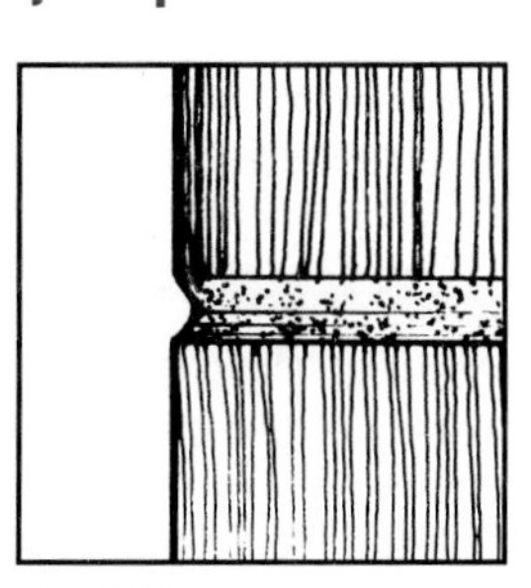

V-JOINT
Formed by a brick jointer, it has a concave, "V" look.

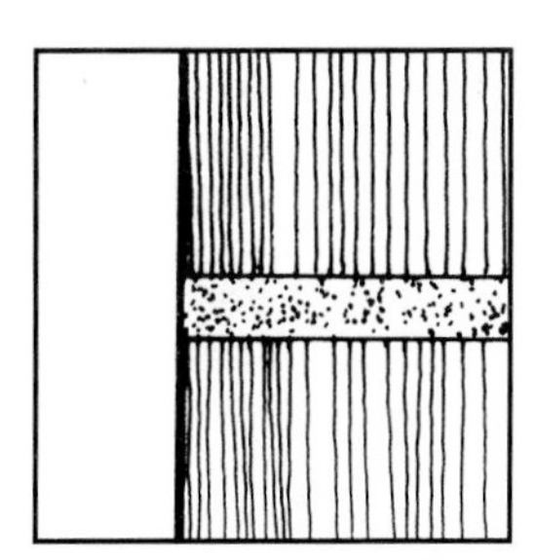

FLUSH JOINT
Formed by cutting off the mortar with the edge of a brick trowel.

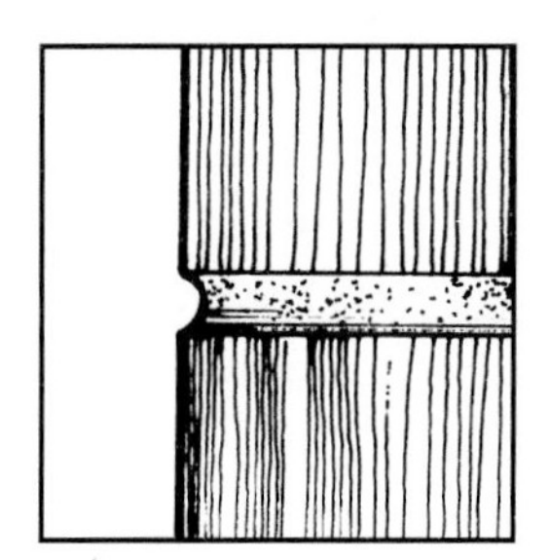

CONCAVE JOINT
Formed by the curved end of a brick jointer.

Using Tools™

FINISHING CONCRETE

by **Jeff Gorton**

Putting a smooth, durable finish on concrete is a skill you can only master with the proper set of tools and practice. We'll show you the tools and how to use them for each step of the process. And equally important, we'll help you determine when the concrete is ready for the next finishing step.

But you really can't practice these techniques except on real concrete. So it's smart to start with a small project like this garbage can pad. When you get the hang of it, you can move up to a larger slab. But keep in mind that finishing larger slabs (more than about 100 sq. ft.) is trickier because the concrete may set up too fast.

In this article, we'll show you how to level the concrete in the forms, round over the edges and make a progressively smoother finish.

Each step in the process requires a different tool. You can make the screed (**Photo 1**) and darby (**Photo 2**) from scraps of wood. The rest you'll have to rent or buy. You'll need a magnesium float ($15 to $25), an edger ($5 to $20), a grooving tool ($10 to $30) and a steel trowel ($8 to $40). Pros buy expensive top-quality tools that will stand up to the rigors of daily use, but less expensive versions are available at home centers and hardware stores and will work fine for occasional home use.

Concrete is a blend of Portland cement, sand, aggregate (gravel) and water that harden when mixed. While there are additives that can slow down or speed up the process, and special bagged mixes that set fast, in general, the speed of the process largely depends on the temperature and humidity. Hot, dry weather accelerates the hardening process, sometimes so much that it's nearly impossible to complete all the finishing steps in time. Work while your project is in shade if possible. On cool days, you may spend a lot of time waiting for the concrete to reach the next stage. That's why we can't give you exact waiting times. But we'll show you how to tell when the concrete is ready for each finishing step.

Screed and darby the concrete right away

Screeding levels the concrete with the top of the forms and begins the process of forcing the larger aggregate below the surface. Use any 2x4 that overlaps the forms by at least 6 in., but make sure it's straight (**Photo 1**).

Follow screeding immediately with the darby (**Photo 2**). Your goal is to level out marks and fill small holes left by screeding. In the process, you'll force larger aggregate down, leaving a slurry of cement and sand to fill the surface. The darby should be large enough to reach a little more than halfway across the slab. Make a darby by screwing a handle (we cut a 2x4 with a jigsaw to make a

1 **PUSH OR PULL the screed board across the forms with a back-and-forth sawing motion. Shove concrete into low spots in front of the screed board. Repeat to remove excess concrete.**

2 **SWEEP the darby across the concrete in overlapping arcs to flatten the surface, push down lumps and fill voids. Lift the leading edge slightly but keep the darby level with the surface. Make two passes.**

3 **WAIT. Water will appear on the surface. Wait until this "bleed" water and sheen disappear entirely before edging, grooving or floating the concrete.**

handle) onto a straight piece of 1x4. Longer darbies may require two handles for better control. If you can't reach the entire slab from the edges with a darby, rent a bull float and handle to use instead. Two passes over the surface with the darby are enough. Overworking the concrete will draw too much cement and fine sand to the top and create a weak surface.

Edge, groove and float the slab when the sheen is gone

After smoothing the slab with the darby, water will "bleed" out of the concrete and sit on the surface (Photo 3). This is temporary. It'll soon reabsorb into the concrete. However, it's critical to wait until it disappears. Working the concrete before the surface "bleed" water disappears will weaken the surface of the slab when it dries. When all traces of the water are gone and the concrete starts to harden, you can resume finishing activities. Test by pressing your gloved thumb onto the surface near the perimeter. The concrete is ready when pressing hard only leaves a 1/4-in. deep impression.

Start by running the edger around the perimeter to round and compact the corner (Photo 4). Sometimes it's a little tough at first as you push larger aggregate back into the concrete and round over the edge. If the edger is leaving a path deeper than about 1/8 in., wait for the concrete to set a little longer and apply less downward pressure.

Next divide the slab into equal parts with a straightedge and groover (Photo 5).

CAUTION: It might be hard to believe that concrete can be dangerous. But the strong alkalinity of cement can cause chemical burns just like a strong acid. By the time you realize you're being burned, you may already have skin damage. That's why it's essential to prevent prolonged skin exposure to wet concrete. And why you should be extra careful to keep wet concrete from getting in your eyes. Wear rubber gloves, a long-sleeve shirt, long pants and safety glasses. Wear rubber boots if you'll be wading in concrete. Rinse wet concrete from your skin immediately and remove clothes that have become saturated with concrete.

Sidewalks and small slabs need grooves about every 4 ft. Add grooves every 10 or 12 ft. on driveways and garage slabs. Dividing slabs with grooves looks nice, but the real reason is to control cracking. Drying and soil movement cause concrete to crack. The groove creates a weakened spot for the crack to form where it won't be seen. To be effective, the groove must be at least one-fourth the depth of the slab.

Float and trowel the surface to smooth and compact it

Float the concrete when you're done grooving and edging (Photo 6). Floating removes the marks left by edging and brings the surface one step closer to a final finish. You may have to bear down on the float if the concrete is starting to harden. You'll be surprised that with enough scrubbing you'll be able to bring a slurry to the surface of even a fairly hard slab. If you're happy with the look of your floated slab, you don't need to do any more finishing. Repeat the edging and grooving steps after floating and after troweling to refine the groove and edges. For a decorative border effect similar to what's shown in the inset to Photo 4, run the edger around each section of slab after a final broom finish.

In Photo 7, we show how to put an even, smooth finish on the slab with a steel trowel. Troweling is one of the trickier steps in concrete finishing. You'll have to practice to develop a feel for it. For a really smooth finish, repeat the troweling step two or three times, letting the concrete harden a bit between each pass. At first, hold the trowel almost flat, elevating the leading edge just enough to avoid gouging the surface. On each successive pass, lift the leading edge of the trowel a

4 WORK the edging tool back and forth, using the edge of the form as a guide. Lift the leading edge slightly. Use long strokes, working the aggregate back until you have smooth, round edges.

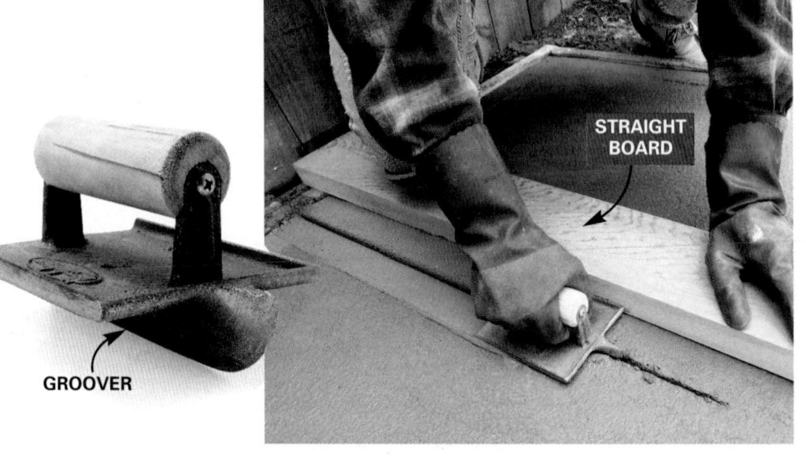

5 SET a straight board along predetermined marks for control joints. Run the groover back and forth against the straightedge until the bed of the tool is riding on the concrete surface.

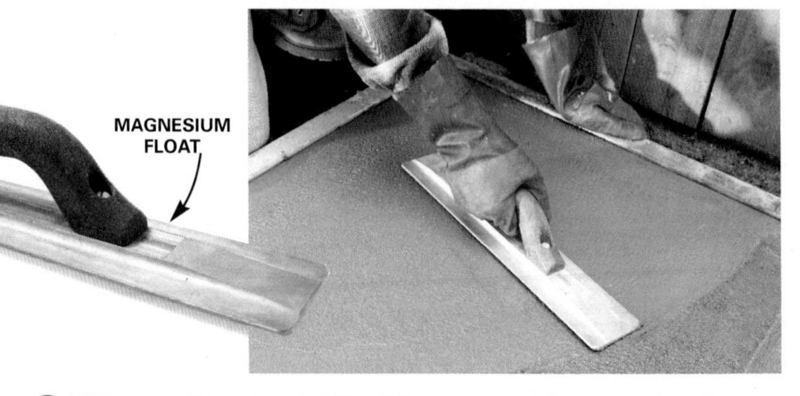

6 LIFT the leading edge slightly while you sweep the magnesium float over the concrete in large arcs to compact the surface. Blend in the marks left by the edges of the edger and groover.

7 SMOOTH the surface with a steel trowel after it's partially hardened. Hold the trowel almost flat and swing it in large overlapping arcs while applying pressure.

8 DRAG a broom across the concrete after floating it with the magnesium float to create a non-slip surface. Adjust the downward pressure to create the desired amount of texture.

little more. If you want a rougher, non-slip surface, you can skip this step and do a broom finish (Photo 8). Also, if you order air-entrained concrete delivered, don't trowel the surface.

Broom finish for better footing

Dragging a broom across partially hardened concrete leaves a rough texture that gives better traction in slippery conditions (Photo 8). Special concrete brooms are available, but a regular push broom will work too. Just remember to wash off the bristles as soon as you finish brooming. As with all the other finishing steps, the key to a successful broom finish is to wait until the concrete surface is just right. If concrete starts to pile up in front of the bristles as you drag the broom across, resmooth the broomed area with a float or trowel and then wait a little longer before trying again.

When you're done finishing the concrete, cover it with plastic or keep it moist by sprinkling it several times a day for about a week. This slows the curing process and results in a stronger, more durable slab.

Handy Hints®

DISGUISING CAULK ON CONCRETE

If you're caulking concrete, either to fill a crack or to seal it around the edge, you can make the caulk almost invisible. Simply dust the caulk with dry concrete mix while it's still wet. When it's dry, brush away the excess, and the caulk will virtually disappear.

You Can Fix It™

DECK REPAIRS

Replace broken deck boards

You don't have to let a split, rotted or otherwise ugly deck board ruin the appearance of your deck. Simply replace it and in a year or so the replacement will blend right in.

You usually don't have to replace an entire board. Just make sure to cut out a piece that spans at least three joists. The remainder should be at least that long. And don't hesitate to cut out a little extra to keep adjacent decking joints staggered for better appearance.

The most difficult part is cutting out the damaged section cleanly (**Photo 1**). . Don't try to cut directly over a joist. Instead, cut to one side and screw on a cleat to support the new decking. It's a fairly hefty cut for a jigsaw, so use a sharp, stiff blade to keep your cuts as straight and smooth as possible.

Predrill screw holes in the cleats so they pull tight to the joists (**Photo 2**). Also pull up on them so they butt tightly against the decking on each side as you screw them in.

Cut the new deck board from matching material, both in thickness and wood type. It'll look different initially, but it'll blend in after a year or so, especially if you clean and reseal or stain your deck. Cut the new deck board to fit snugly, then screw or nail it into place (**Photo 3**).

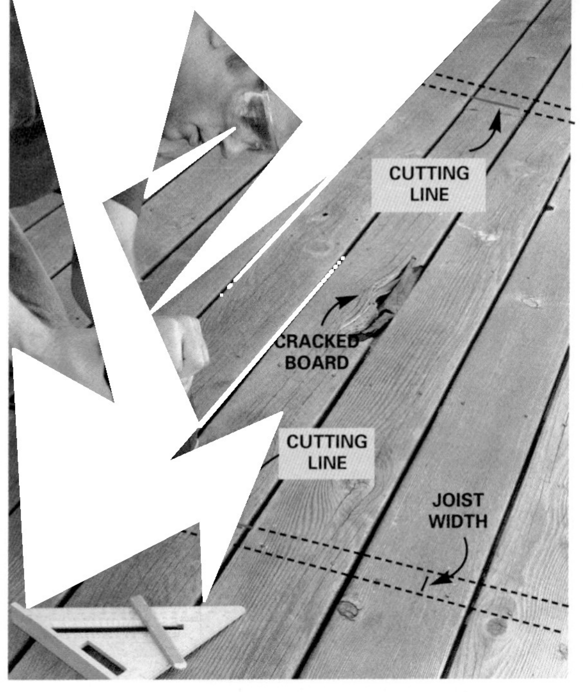

1 DRAW a square line on the decking to one side of a joist below. Cut the deck board with a jigsaw. Pull the decking nails with a cat's paw.

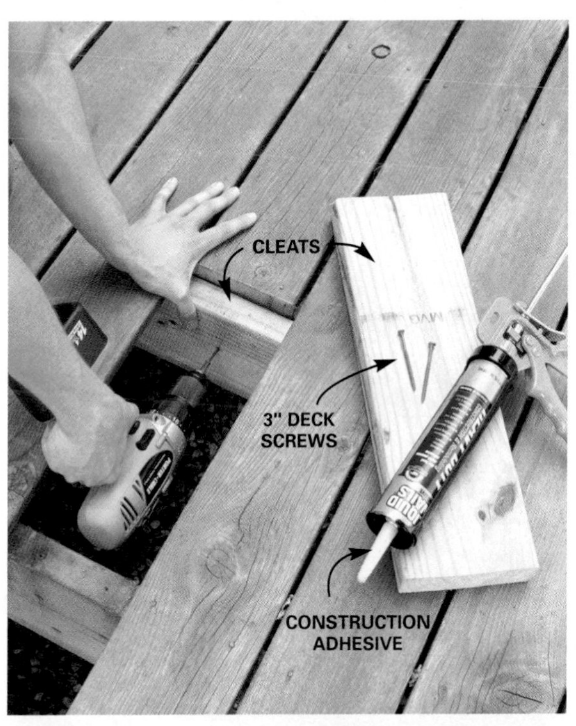

2 PREDRILL three clearance holes in two 16-in. treated wood cleats. Apply construction adhesive, hold each cleat tight to neighboring deck boards, and screw one to the joists at each end of the repair.

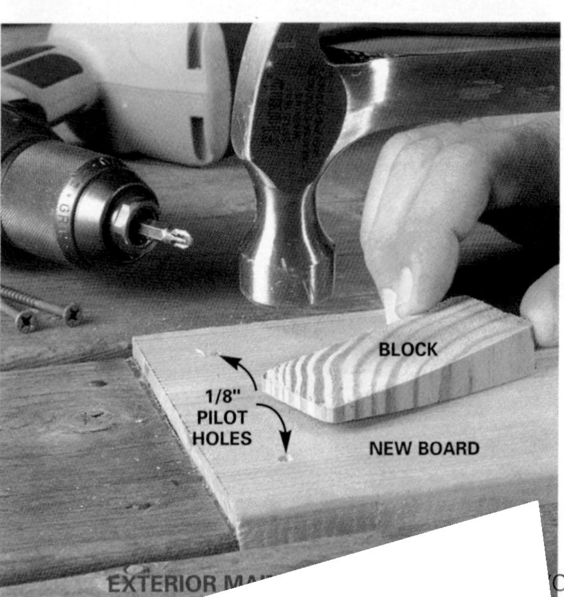

3 CUT the replacement board to length. Then tap it into place with a hammer and a wood block. Predrill pilot holes and drive a pair of 2-1/2 in. deck screws (or galvanized nails) into each cleat. Fasten at all other joists as well.

You Can Fix It™

Strengthen wobbly posts

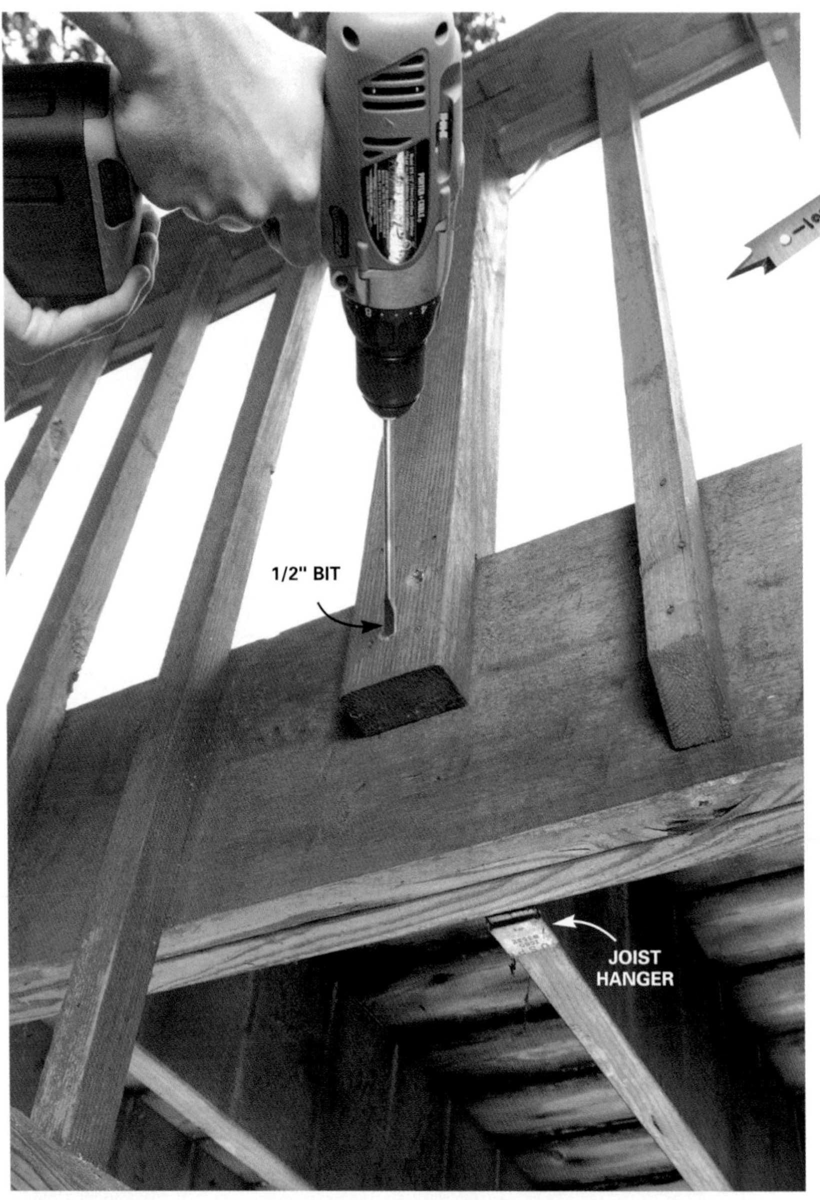

1 DRILL two 1/2-in. clearance holes through the post and framing. Offset the holes to prevent splitting the post. Angle the hole to avoid joist hangers.

You don't have to live with loose, wobbly railing posts when a couple of bolts will make them safe and solid. Measure the thickness of the post/framing assembly, add 1 in. and buy 1/2-in. diameter galvanized carriage bolts that length (plus a nut and washer for each) from any hardware store or home center.

Drill the 1/2-in. clearance holes well apart, one about 1-1/2 in. from the top of the framing and one about 1-1/2 in. up from the bottom of the post (Photo 1). You may have to angle the holes slightly to avoid joists, framing anchors or other obstructions. If your drill bit isn't long enough to go through the post and framing, get a long spade bit. Versions up to 16 in. long are available for $8 at home centers and hardware stores.

Most posts are held fairly plumb by the railing, but check them anyway with a level and tap in shims to straighten them if necessary. Don't overtighten the bolts; the heads will sink deep into soft wood without much effort.

2 TAP in 1/2-in. carriage bolts, shim if necessary to plumb the post, and install washers and nuts. Tighten the nuts until the bolt heads are set flush to the post.

Stiffen a bouncy deck

A deck that bounces when you walk across it won't feel strong and solid, even if it meets structural requirements. The cause is usually long joist spans between beams or between a beam and the house.

To stiffen a deck, you have to be able to get to the framing underneath. You can add another beam, along with posts, to support the joists. However, this is a big job. We recommend that you first add rows of solid blocking every 3 to 4 ft. along the span (**Photo 1**). Run the first row down the middle of the span, check the deck for bounce, then add rows to further reduce it.

Use treated lumber blocking that's the same size as the joists (usually 2x8 or 2x10). Install the blocking in rows along a chalk line snapped at a right angle to the joists. You'll have to measure and cut each block separately to get a snug fit, since the joists are never exactly the same distance apart. Staggering the blocking in a step pattern (**Photo 2**) allows you to easily drive nails from both sides, rather than having to toenail.

1 SNAP lines for blocks every 3 to 4 ft. along the joist span. Measure and cut the blocks to fit tightly. Tap them into place in a staggered pattern.

2 SQUARE each block to the joist and drive three 16d galvanized box nails through the joists into each end of the block. Repeat for each row.

Take out the sway with an angle brace

Some otherwise solid decks tend to sway or wobble as you walk across them, especially decks resting on tall posts 4 or more feet above the ground. Angle-bracing the posts is one good solution to this problem, but the braces often look tacky. Instead, install an angle brace underneath your deck. It's a virtually invisible fix that all but eliminates sway.

If your longest 2x4 doesn't span the entire distance, don't worry. Add a second one starting from the other corner and run it back alongside the first, nailing it to at least two of the same joists. Have a helper hold the 2x4 in place while you drive the first nails. Driving 16d galvanized nails upward will give your hammer arm a workout!

1 CUT AND NAIL a treated 2x4 diagonally from corner to corner under your deck. Drive two 16d galvanized nails at each joist.

You Can Fix It™

Replace loose, popped nails

Decking swells and shrinks as it goes through repeated cycles of wet and dry seasons. This frequently causes nails to loosen and pop up above the deck boards. You can drive them down again, but chances are that's only a short-term solution. They'll probably pop up again after a few years. The long-term solution is to remove the popped nails and replace them with deck screws.

The trick is to pull the old nails without marring the decking. Always use a block under your prying tool (**Photos 1 and 2**). And work on tough-to-get-out nails using several steps. A diagonal cutter works well for nails that only protrude slightly (**Photo 1**). The slim jaws can slip under the head. You'll only raise the nail a slight amount, so you may have to repeat this process two or three times. Once the nailhead is high enough, you can grip it with a cat's paw or hammer claw without marring the deck board (**Photo 2**). Be sure to use thin wood blocks to protect the decking. Minor dents will disappear when the wood swells after the next rain.

There's no need to drill a pilot hole if you send the screw down the old nail hole. However, one drawback of screws is that their heads are larger than nailheads and can be unsightly. We recommend that you buy deck screws in a color that most closely matches the aged decking.

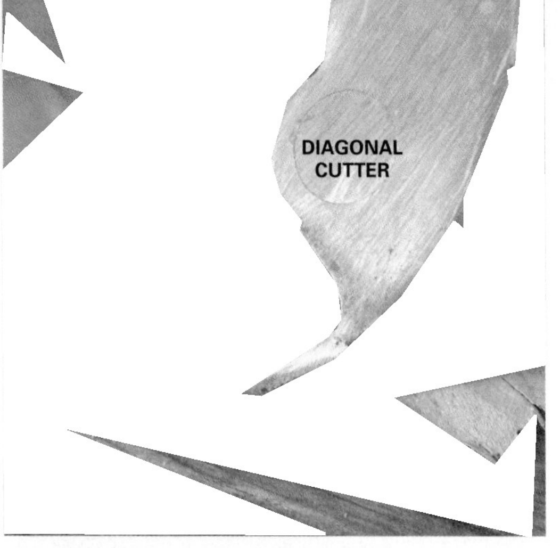

1 GRAB slightly protruding nails directly under the head with a diagonal cutter. Roll the cutter back onto thin blocking to pry the nail up slightly.

2 TAP the claw of a cat's paw under the nailhead and lever the nail up. Finish pulling with a hammer or pry bar. Protect the deck board with a shim or thin block.

3 STAND ON the deck board to hold it down. Then drive a 2-1/2 in. deck screw down into the old nail hole. Set the screwhead flush to the surface.

Solutions for stubborn nails

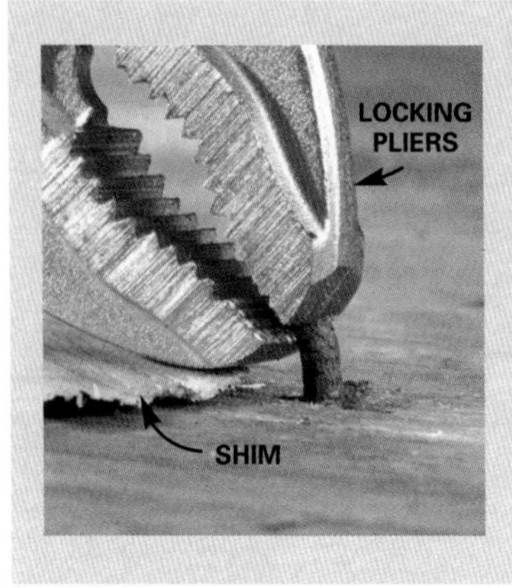

If the head breaks off a stubborn nail and you can't get it with a pry bar, try pulling it with a locking pliers. Grip the nail tip and roll the pliers over to get it going (**photo left**). If the nail shank breaks off, don't worry. Just drill a pilot hole beside the nail and drive a screw. The screwhead will cover the nail (**photo right**).

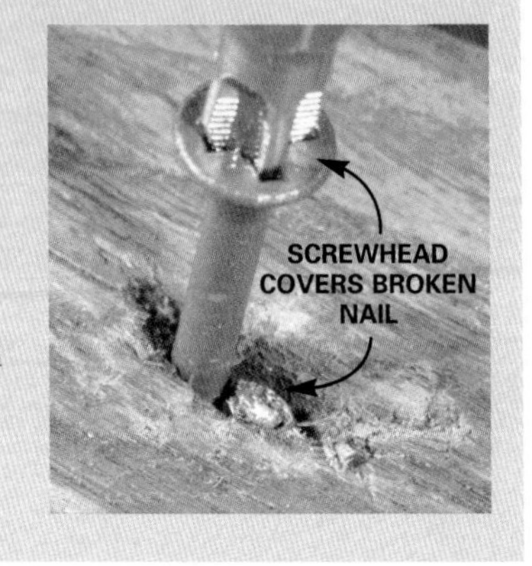

9 Outdoor Structures & Landscaping

IN THIS CHAPTER

7 Steps to a Lush, Green Lawn 216

Ask Handyman 224
Treated-wood safety, stop hose kinks, efficient sprinklers and more ...

Retaining Walls 226

Handy Hints 232
Garden gear caddy, brush hauler, patio paver puller and more ...

Backyard Stream & Waterfalls 234

Gallery of Ideas 240
Timber-frame garden arbor, brick and stone path, barbecue island, dream deck, outdoor light and outlet, copper trellis, yard shed, cedar and glass rail, patio privacy screen

You Can Fix It 246
Fixing pond leaks

Low-Maintenance Garden Borders 248

Wordless Workshop 252

7 SIMPLE STEPS
TO A LUSH, GREEN LAWN

A healthy lawn takes a bit of extra effort in the first two years but saves work and money later

by **Travis Larson**

Having the best lawn possible doesn't mean you have to sweat and fret all summer long. Establishing and maintaining a nice yard are mostly just a matter of quenching your lawn's thirst with long drinks of water, feeding it three or four times a year and mowing it at the right height. If your lawn's been neglected, it may take up to two years of extra work to rejuvenate it. But once you get it going, a healthy, lush lawn largely takes care of itself. Weeds can't get a foothold, the soil retains moisture better, and insects and disease have a harder time getting established.

In this article, we'll tell you the seven simple steps for a healthy, low-maintenance lawn. None of these are difficult, expensive or particularly time-consuming. But several require timing (fertilizing) and a watchful eye (when to mow and water). And several may ask you to follow through on simple tasks you've never done (pH test, soil moisture check). The results will be worth it.

Following our recommendations won't necessarily guarantee you the best lawn in the neighborhood. There are simply too many variables in soil quality, sun exposure and grass types to say that. But we can promise this: If you follow our general advice, soon your lawn will be in the best shape ever and it'll stay that way with very little effort.

STEP 1

Identify your grass and its growing cycle

You need to know what type of grass you have to determine the best care regimen for your lawn. Different grasses have different cutting heights and watering and fertilizer needs, and all can be harmed by certain herbicides.

There are dozens of varieties of grasses, but they break down into two broad categories: warm and cool climate grasses. **Warm climate grasses** are found mainly in the Southern United States where hot (and sometimes humid) conditions predominate during the summer and the winter is mild. They grow most rapidly before and after the hottest summer period. **Cool climate grasses** are found nearly everywhere else with the exception of the desert regions. They thrive just before and after the hot summer months and go dormant in the dead of winter. In the transitional zone, both types can be found.

Cool climate grasses
Transitional zone
Warm climate grasses

To identify your grass type, simply pull a plug of the most dominant variety (or varieties; most lawns have a combination of species) and show it to experts at a local garden center. They will be a wellspring of regional advice and be able to recommend the timing and application of the lawn care products that work best with your grass and in your local climate and soil conditions. They'll also know how to deal with local garden pests, weeds and soil conditions.

Can't find professional help? Become your own lawn expert. It's easier than you think. In "For More Information," p. 223, we list a few of our favorite resources for advice on identifying and treating pests and weeds. You can also figure out what type of grass you have and find mowing and special care information.

Growth calendar for warm climate grasses

WARM climate grasses grow slower during the summer months when the temperatures are above 95 degrees F. When the weather cools down (below 80 degrees F), the growing rate speeds up. It slows down again when temperatures fall below 55 degrees F.

Growth calendar for cool climate grasses

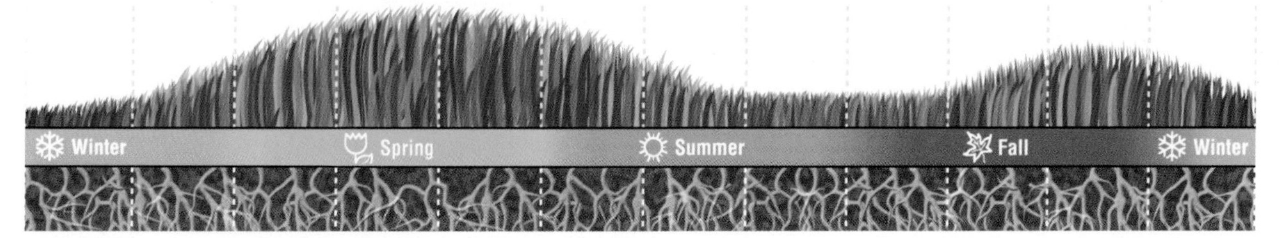

COOL climate grasses have two distinct growing periods, the main one being in the spring and a shorter one in the fall. During the hot, stressful summer months, growth slows.

STEP 2

Feed your lawn four times a year

If you were fed only sporadically, you probably wouldn't feel or look too healthy. The same goes for grass. It hungers for four "meals" during specific periods throughout the season. Feeding (fertilizing) means supplying your grass with three basic nutrients: nitrogen (N), phosphorus (P) and potassium (K). In general, the many other trace nutrients your grass may need occur naturally in the soil. All fertilizers have a label detailing the proportions of N-P-K they contain. Most lawns are content with a 4-1-2 mixture. Some grasses need more nitrogen and some soils need more of one or more ingredients (or trace nutrients) at least until they become balanced. A soil test (p. 221) will let you know of any deficiencies. Advice from the garden center will help you tailor a fertilizer mixture for your soil and grass type.

Four lawn feedings each season are needed for healthy grass:

First feeding: Fertilize your lawn in the spring after it's up, green, growing and has been mowed at least twice. This feeding picks up where the last feeding in the fall leaves off. And the grass is vigorous enough to absorb the nutrients. If you fertilize before the grass is able to use it, you're just wasting time and money.

Second feeding: Just before the hot weather starts, fertilize the grass to keep it nourished during the stressful summer months. In most parts of the country, that's early June, but in the Sunbelt states, it can even be early May.

Third feeding: Apply this treatment later in the fall when dew starts forming on the grass in the morning. That's after the hot weather subsides and the temperature generally stays below 80 degrees F. This feeding replenishes the nutrients used up during the summer and helps the root structure begin regenerating.

Fourth feeding: Apply the fourth feeding (sometimes called a "winterizer") about three weeks before the last expected mowing. This is the most important treatment because the roots are multiplying and storing food for the winter. Then, when the grass comes out of dormancy in the spring, it'll have a bellyful of food for that initial growth spurt.

Tips on fertilizing

- Select fertilizers that are a combination of "slow" and "fast" release. They give the grass both immediate and longer-term nutrients.
- Never fertilize wet or damp grass; wait until it's completely dry. Otherwise, the fertilizer will stick to the blades and could damage them. An exception to this rule is combination fertilizer/herbicides. They should be applied to damp grass, when no rain is forecast (and no watering) for 48 hours. Water after that.
- We prefer a "broadcast" spreader to distribute the fertilizer because it spews out the granules, distributing them faster and more evenly than a "drop" spreader.
- Fill the spreader on a hard surface like a driveway, patio or sidewalk—never on the grass. You'll be able to reclaim any spills and keep them from damaging the grass. Use a shop vacuum to pick up spills. You'll never be able to sweep up fine granules.
- Water thoroughly after fertilizing to dissolve and drive the fertilizer into the soil.
- If you aerate (see p. 223) in the fall, apply the fertilizer afterward so the fertilizer will drop into the aeration holes for better soil penetration.
- Never fertilize when the ground is frozen because it won't penetrate the soil. Instead the fertilizer will run off and find its way into streams and waterways.

STEP 3

Water thoroughly but only when it's needed

The key to a good watering regimen and a healthy lawn is to water not only when the grass needs it but also enough to penetrate the soil to a depth of 3 to 4 in. That encourages healthy, deep root growth and gives the soil moisture reserves, so it'll need less frequent watering. Moist soil also helps the roots absorb and metabolize nutrients and keeps the grass cooler in hot weather. But keep in mind that different parts of your yard need more or less water. Sunny and hilly areas will need more water than shady or low areas.

To develop a sound watering strategy, perform this experiment (after a dry spell) in any of these areas your lawn may have: flat, sunny, shady, on a slope, and a couple of feet from the street/driveway (or sidewalk) intersection. Shove a spade into the grass about 6 in. and pull the shovel back and forth until you can see a cross section of the soil. Look for a level of moister, darker soil at some point below the surface. It indicates how deep the soil moisture penetrates. Your lawn needs watering any time the top 3/4 to 1 in. of soil is dry. Water and keep track of the watering time until repeated tests indicate a moisture depth of about 3 to 4 in. at each location. That'll tell you how long to water specific areas each time.

Perform the shovel test once a week for three to four weeks, keeping track of watering duration. After that testing period, you'll have a good feel for the water retention of your soil and intuitively know how much to water and when without performing the digging test. Sounds like a lot of work, right? The results will save you big on water and you'll have a healthier lawn to boot.

Digging soil-moisture inspection slits

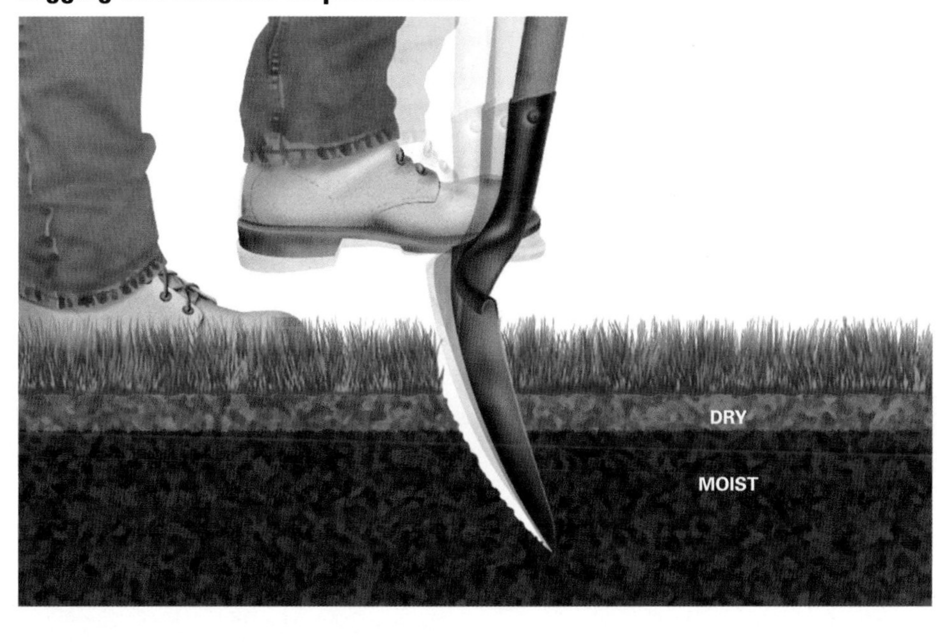

SHOVE a spade into the ground about 6 in. and wiggle it back and forth to create a slit. You'll be able to see or feel the soil to determine soil moisture depth.

Tips on watering

- The morning hours are the optimal watering time because the grass blades will dry before nighttime. Lawns that stay moist at night encourage harmful mold and fungal growth. Quit watering one to two hours before sunset. You'll also lose more water to evaporation if you water during hot afternoons.
- An impact (or impulse) sprinkler will lose 20 percent less of its water to evaporation than the types of sprinklers that send thin streams of water into the air. But oscillating sprinklers do work better on smaller, rectangular yards.
- Never give your yard just a "sip" of water, thinking that's better than nothing. That encourages shallow rather than healthier deep roots.
- Don't overwater, either. If water puddles or is streaming off the yard, you're simply wasting water.
- Attach a water timer ($20 to $40) to your hose, and set it each time you water. Once you know how long to water, a water timer will do the thinking for you. You won't have to worry about shutting off the water at the right time.

STEP 4

Mow your grass to its ideal height and don't wait too long between cuttings

Each type of grass has an ideal height range for cutting, where you leave enough blade length to sustain the health of the plant and keep the grass thick enough to crowd out weeds. Two mistakes are to cut the grass too low and to let it grow too long before cutting. The chart below shows the cutting range for each grass type. Pick a height within that range that's suitable for your terrain. Then set your mowing height by placing the mower on a flat, hard surface, measuring to the bottom of the mowing deck and adjusting the wheels accordingly. Your grass needs mowing when it's 1-1/2 times the ideal cutting height. That means if the cutting height is 2 in., cut the grass when it's about 3 in. high.

Use a mulching blade instead of a standard blade in your lawn mower. It chops up the grass more finely so it can fall in between the grass blades and decompose easier. The clippings are a free source of nitrogen for your lawn and help retain soil moisture.

Ideal mowing height ranges

COOL CLIMATE GRASSES	
Bent grass	1/4 to 3/4 in.
Chewing hard or red fescue	1-1/2 to 2-1/2 in.
Tall fescue	1-1/2 to 3 in.
Kentucky bluegrass	1-1/2 to 3 in.
Perennial ryegrass	1-1/2 to 3 in.

WARM CLIMATE GRASSES	
Bahia grass	2 to 3 in.
Bermuda grass	1/2 to 1 in.
Blue grama grass	2 to 3 in.
Buffalo grass	2 to 3 in.
Carpetgrass	1 to 2 in.
Centipedegrass	1 to 2 in.
St. Augustinegrass	1 to 3 in.
Zoysia grass	1/2 to 1 in.

Tips on mowing

- Change mowing directions each time you mow to lessen soil compaction (from you with a walk-behind mower or the tires from a riding mower).
- Mow with a sharp cutting blade. A dull blade rips off the blades rather than cutting them. That stresses the grass and leaves a brown shredded end on each blade, which detracts from a lush, healthy look. It's not a bad idea to have two blades on hand so you'll always have a sharp one when the other's at the sharpening shop.
- Rake or catch clippings if it's necessary. Long grass should be removed if it's so long that it clumps when it's discharged. Those clumps can smother or even kill underlying grass and encourage fungi and molds.
- In climates that receive snow, reduce the first and last seasonal mowing to 1-1/2 to 1-3/4 in. That will discourage snow mold and reduce shrew and vole damage during the winter, especially with fescues and bluegrass.
- If you've neglected your lawn and the grass is long, just cut off the top one-third of it on the first mowing. Let it recuperate from the stress for a few days before mowing again. This time, too, cut off no more than one-third until you reach the right height (see left).

STEP 5

Test the soil pH and adjust if necessary

Soil pH is often overlooked but is one of the key ingredients to a healthy lawn. If you've watered, mowed and fertilized properly and still have a sickly lawn, overly acidic or alkaline soil could well be the problem. Grass is most content in a soil that's slightly acidic. If you've never checked your lawn's soil pH, it's a great idea to take soil samples and have them tested. Don't be intimidated; it's a simple process both to test and to correct any problems.

Check your soil pH by calling a garden center or a university or county extension service that tests soil samples (for $3 to $10). They'll tell you how to collect and submit samples. Different parts of the yard can vary significantly. The best way to collect samples is to follow the grid shown.

Once you know the pH, the garden center will help you determine the best treatment to achieve a more grass-friendly pH. It's inexpensive and just a matter of applying the specified amounts with a spreader.

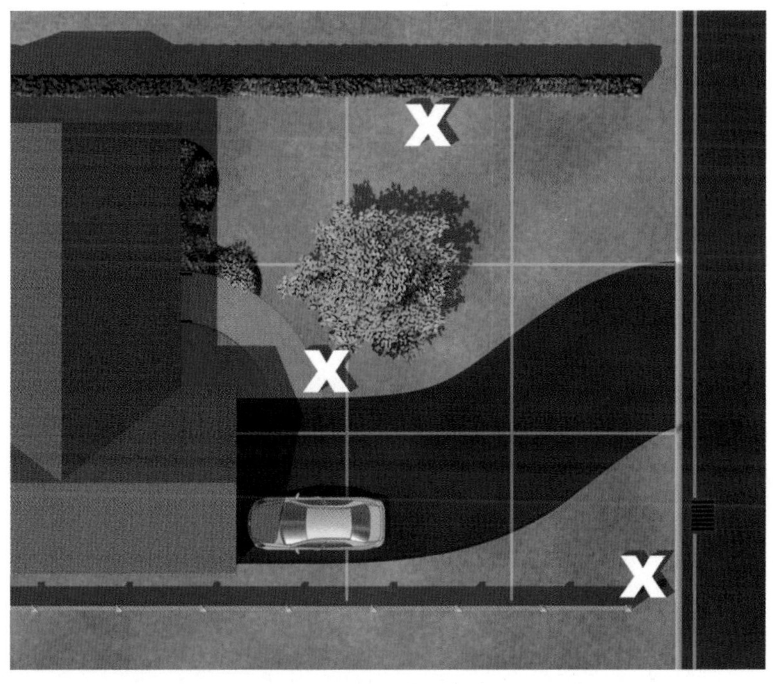

MIX together samples from the center of the yard near the house and at spots at opposite sides of the yard. Use the same sampling pattern for the back yard and have the two mixed samples tested separately.

Tips on pH

- Once you adjust your lawn's pH, test it again in four months to see if it has maintained the correct pH range. Treat it again if necessary. Once you've established a consistent level, retest and adjust it (if necessary) every three years.
- Inexpensive, do-it-yourself test kits for pH testing are available at garden centers but aren't very accurate. For reliable results, get a professional analysis.
- Don't mix the front and back yard samples. The whole idea is to tell which areas need treatment. Pay to have them tested separately.
- Pelletized limestone is the best way to raise pH levels. Iron sulphate or sulphur is generally used to lower pH. Applied incorrectly, however, this treatment is potentially damaging to your lawn, so be sure to follow the directions.
- Grasses in soils with high or low pH values won't make the best use of naturally occurring or added fertilizers.

The best pH level for grass

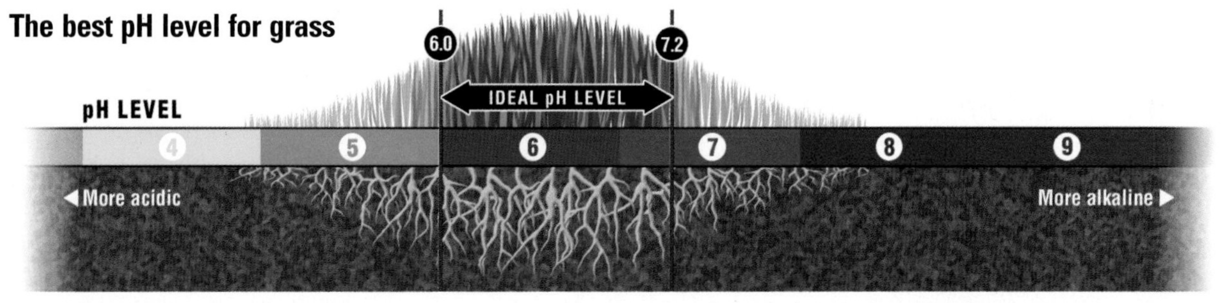

THE ACIDITY level is gauged on the pH scale. A pH of 7 is neutral. Below that is acidic and above it is alkaline. Soil that has a pH of between 6 and 7.2 is best for grass. Above or below that range can be highly detrimental to root development and leaves grass susceptible to heat stress and disease.

STEP 6

Identify the weed before choosing a weedkiller

The real key to a weed-free lawn is to nurture a healthy one. When the turf is dense, weed seeds have a hard time getting through to the soil. And once there, they can't get the sun they need to germinate and grow. But if you already have weeds, it's easy to eliminate them, provided you use the correct weedkiller at the proper time of year and within the temperature parameters called for in the directions.

Lawn weeds fall into three simple categories and require different treatment strategies. If you don't know the weed category, take a sample to a garden center for identification.

Broadleaf weeds

Dandelions, clover, creeping charlie and plantain are all examples of broadleaf weeds. They not only survive the winter but also go to seed, propagating new generations the following spring. Kill broadleaf weeds with either liquid sprays or granular herbicides (weedkillers) distributed with a spreader while the weeds are growing heartily. That's usually when the lawn is growing well too.

Liquid herbicides should be applied to dry or slightly damp lawns, but only apply granular herbicides when the weeds are wet, either after you water or when they're still damp from dew or rain. When the leaves are wet, the chemical sticks to the leaves, where it will be absorbed and sent to the roots to kill the plant. It's usually best to apply herbicides when the temperature will remain below 80 degrees F (preferably even lower), and it's not expected to rain for at least 48 hours. Hot days cause liquid herbicides to vaporize before the weed can absorb it. And if it rains too soon, the granules will wash off the leaves and be ineffective.

Perennial weedy grasses

Perennial weedy grasses are ones that, like your lawn itself, survive the winter and reappear every spring. Quack grass and Dallis grass are common examples. Perennial weedy grasses have to be killed one by one with carefully applied general weedkillers like Roundup or Kills-All, either by spraying individual weeds or simply by wiping the concentrated herbicide (10 percent or higher) on the blades of grass. Be careful when spot-killing. General plant killers kill your yard grass just as easily as they kill weeds.

Replace clumps of dead weeds by raking fresh seed through the dead grass into the soil below after the weeds turn brown. Then water daily until the grass is established.

Tips on weed-killing

- Don't waste your money or time applying herbicides (except pre-emergence treatments) when there aren't any weeds. No weeds? Just fertilize.
- Use a pump-up type sprayer to spot-treat weeds that are limited to specific areas. Only mix the amount of liquids you need that day. They have a very short shelf life once mixed with water.
- The soil should be moist and the grass growing before you apply any herbicides.
- Apply liquid herbicides only on calm, windless mornings. When the wind's blowing, you'll not only waste material but also possibly kill nearby shrubs and flowers.
- Water your lawn thoroughly before any weed treatment.
- Granular herbicides work poorly on viney broadleafs like clover or creeping Charlie. Use liquid herbicides on those. Some work better on hard-to-kill broadleaf weeds. Ask for advice at the garden center.
- Buy concentrated liquid herbicides; they're cheaper than premixed solutions.

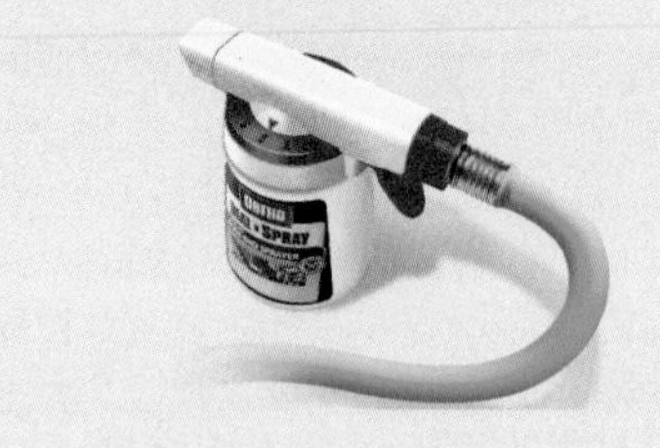

Annual weedy grasses

Annual weedy grasses like crab grass or foxtail die at the end of every growing season after seeding the yard for the following spring. While they too can be spot-killed, the best remedy is to apply a pre-emergence herbicide in the early spring right after the first or second mowing. A pre-emergent works by preventing the weed seeds from sprouting. Talk to a local expert to help nail down the timing; it's the difference between success and failure.

Some types of weed grasses can be killed with specific herbicides without harming your grass. One example is a post-emergence crab grass spray, which will kill some other annual weedy grasses as well. For more details on these, bring a sample plant to the garden center for advice or check out the books or Web sites we recommend for help.

STEP 7

Aerate to eliminate compacted soil under your lawn

Grass roots need "friable" (crumbly) rather than dense, compacted soil so they can spread and have access to the water, nutrients and oxygen they need to thrive. Soil can be compacted because it has too much clay or simply because of too much foot or mower traffic. To test for compaction, shove a large screwdriver into the soil after watering. If it doesn't easily penetrate a couple of inches, you should aerate.

An engine-driven machine called an aerator is the easiest way to aerate your yard. It pulls out thousands of plugs of soil and grass and drops them on the yard, where they eventually break down. Aerating loosens the soil and helps oxygen and water penetrate to augment deeper root development.

Aerate in the fall once dew begins forming regularly but stop at least three weeks before frost in the snowbelt. Plan to aerate heavily compacted soils three years in a row and after that, whenever the screwdriver test calls for it. Aerating in the spring will encourage weedy grass seeds to sprout in the aeration holes. If you aerate then, apply a pre-emergence herbicide to reduce germination.

RENT an aerator at the rental shop or garden center for about $35 per half day. It's heavy, so you'll need a strong back to help you unload it.

Tips on aerating

- Aerate only during cool weather. The exposed roots surrounding holes will dry out on hot summer days.
- Wait two years before aerating newly seeded yards and one year before aerating newly sodded yards.
- Make two passes at 90-degree angles. In heavily compacted soils, make a third diagonal pass for thorough aeration or before seeding.
- Don't bother aerating lawns growing in sand unless there is a buildup of thatch.
- The soil should be moist 3 to 4 in. deep before aerating. Otherwise the tines won't penetrate and extract the necessary 1 to 1-1/2 in. plugs.

Benefits of aeration

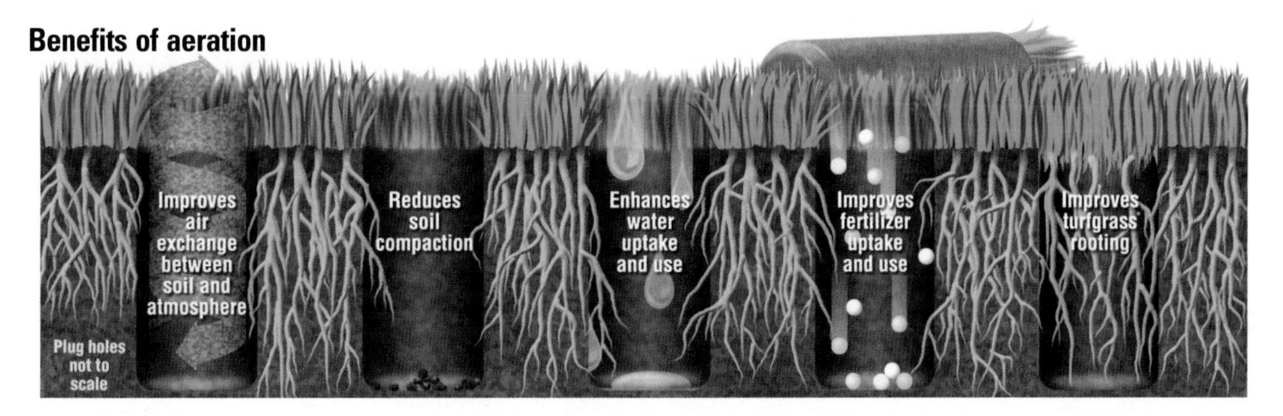

For More Information

- **"Lawns, Your Guide to a Beautiful Yard," The Scotts Co. $20. Available at bookstores, garden centers and home centers.**
- **"All About Lawns," Ortho Co. $10. Available at bookstores, garden centers and home centers.**
- **www.scotts.com**

Handy Hints® from our readers

Stay-together landscape edging

Here's a way to keep your edging strong and looking good. When you install it, cut off about 1-1/2 in. of the tubular portion at the end of each section, and allow the flat portions of the edging to overlap about 3 in. Drill small holes in the overlaps and secure them with aluminum Pop rivets or small sheet metal screws.

Ask Handyman™

TREATED-WOOD SAFETY

I've read that arsenic is no longer used in treated wood. Is the treated-wood play structure I built several years ago safe for my kids?

There's no need to panic or tear down your play structure, since the health risk from the arsenic is low, according to the Environmental Protection Agency. However, the EPA has taken the precaution of eliminating any exposure to the arsenic found in chromated copper arsenate (CCA) treated wood. It banned the use of this wood preservative by the end of 2003 in materials commonly found around the home.

If this low risk still concerns you, you can apply an oil-based penetrating stain every couple of years to seal the wood. Instruct your kids to keep their hands out of their mouth during play, and then to wash their hands with soap when they're finished playing.

Two common arsenic-free preservatives that will replace CCA are alkaline copper quaternary (ACQ) and copper azole (CBA or CA-B). Both appear to resist bugs, mold and rot as effectively as CCA. The downside is that, since these preservatives contain more copper, the wood will be more corrosive to nails, screws and other hardware.

Always follow the handling precautions on the label: Wear a dust mask and goggles when cutting or sanding, wear gloves when working with treated wood, and toss scraps for regular trash collection. Also, do not burn treated wood.

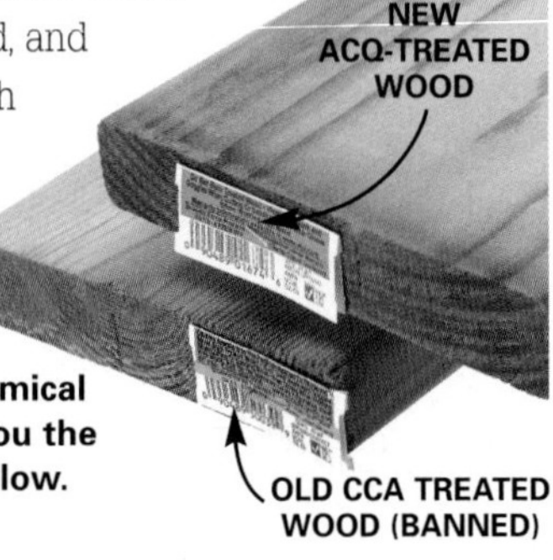

CHECK the labels on treated wood (or ask the retailer) for the type of chemical used. The label also tells you the handling precautions to follow.

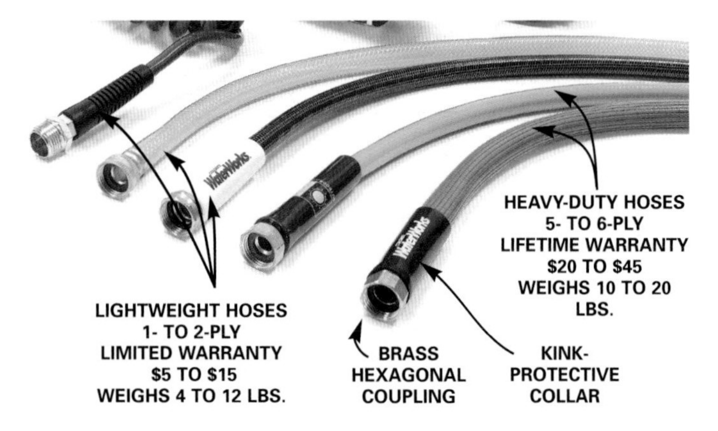

STOP HOSE KINKS

Last summer my dad teased me about my cheap garden hoses that kept kinking up as I moved the sprinkler. He swears by the heavy-duty, expensive hoses. Is an expensive hose worth it?

There is something to be said for inexpensive hoses. If your hoses are seldom used, you may be satisfied with a basic vinyl hose that's lightweight, making it easy to handle. But they are more prone to kinking and become stiffer with time. Lightweight coiled hoses look nice and work well when new, but they should be stored on trays so they stay tightly coiled, and some models lose their recoil rather quickly.

Serious gardeners and lawn pros opt for high quality over low price. Hoses that contain more rubber and tire cord reinforcement are stronger and more durable, but they're heavier, making them harder to handle.

To buy a hose that will kink less, select a larger diameter (like 5/8 in.). Also read the packaging to find a 5- or 6-ply rubber or rubber/vinyl hose with cord reinforcement that offers kink-resistant construction with a lifetime warranty/guarantee. If you can't find it on the packaging, check the company's Web site. In addition, look for a protective collar that extends 3 to 4 in. from the coupling to prevent kinks. Other quality components include brass hose couplings and swivels (which should be hexagonal, not round, for attachment ease) and perhaps a "drinking water safe" designation or bacteria inhibitor inside if you plan to drink from the hose.

And to improve hose longevity:

- Keep the hose in a shaded area as much as possible.
- Shut the water off at the spigot when you're done using it to reduce pressure on the hose.
- Protect the hose from accidental cuts or punctures.
- Mount a hose hanger or hose reel in a shaded place next to the spigot or purchase a mobile hose reel caddy or cart.
- Drain the hose after use and protect it from freezing.
- Don't run hot water through the hose unless it is specified to carry hot water.
- Don't drive over it.

EFFICIENT SPRINKLERS

I understand that watering my garden with an oscillating sprinkler and its 12-ft. tall fountain wastes water. What type of sprinkler is best for my square garden?

When it comes to saving water, you have two great choices: a rotary sprinkler with a fairly square pattern that matches your garden size, and a rotary impact sprinkler with a circular pattern larger than your square garden (see photos below).

You are correct to say that the oscillating sprinkler (not shown) isn't water efficient. Any sprinkler that produces a fine mist or launches water skyward will cause water to evaporate as well as be blown off target. Oscillating sprinklers also lack uniform coverage because the water delivery rate tends to be much heavier at the sides than at the center of the pattern.

I like a good rotary sprinkler (shown above) for your application because it will deliver a fairly square pattern and water your garden evenly. Check the box to determine its maximum coverage size. This sprinkler type will be suitable for more soil types. You can reduce the water volume for slower watering of poorly absorbing, heavy clay soils, or increase the volume for faster absorbing sand or loam soils. The goal is to make sure all the water is absorbed, not running away from the garden.

PULSATING (ROTARY IMPACT) SPRINKLERS
- **Fairly uniform water coverage**
- **Highly adjustable pattern**

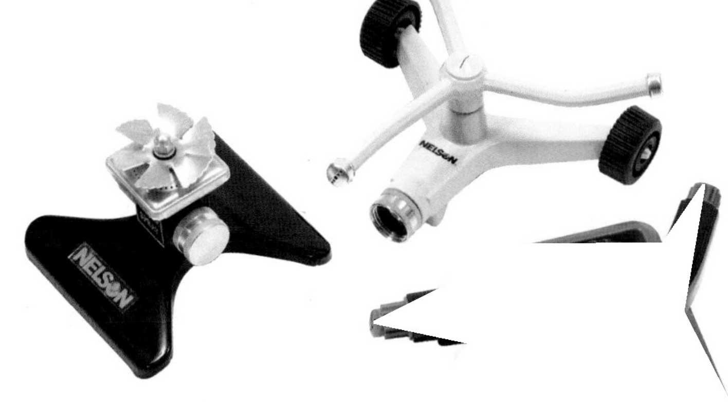

ROTARY SPRINKLERS
- **Uniform water coverage**
- **Irrigation speed adapts to soil types**

While reducing water volume does reduce coverage, it adds versatility beyond your garden. Your sprinkler will fit smaller flower beds or limited landscaped areas. Wheels on the sprinkler help when moving it.

Your second choice, a rotary impact or pulsating sprinkler (shown below), uses a water-driven flapper that hits an anvil and drives the nozzles in a circular pattern. Most models are highly adjustable, from changing the circle diameter, to watering a portion of a circle, to changing droplet size. You'll have some water waste covering a square garden with a larger circle, and coverage isn't as uniform as it is with the rotary sprinkler. However, they do a good job of keeping water close to the ground to minimize drift and reduce evaporation.

A 72-in. tall pulsating sprinkler (not shown) is very useful for large gardens as plants grow and become tall enough to interfere with sprinkler patterns. Buying an elevated sprinkler is more costly (the Nelson model 222RC model is $60), but you can always build a platform or use a bucket to elevate your sprinkler above your tall tomatoes.

Finally, it's smart to measure the amount of water you apply. A good rule of thumb is to make sure your garden gets an inch of rainfall or irrigation per week, wetting the top 3 to 5 in. of soil. And it's always best to water in the morning, giving plants the rest of the day to dry so leaf diseases won't develop.

For more information, contact LR Nelson Corp., (800) 635-7668, www. lrnelson.com; and Gilmour Group., (800) 458-0107, www.gilmour.com.

REMOVING MORTAR STAINS

I just completed my first masonry project: a tree ring constructed of masonry block. How do I remove the mortar stains along each of the joints?

To clean fresh mortar stains, use a solution of muriatic acid ($3 at home centers) and water. Start with 1 part acid to 4 parts water. Always pour the acid into the water, never the water into the acid. Apply it to the stained areas with a stiff-bristle brush, then rinse well. If the mortar stain remains, double the proportion of acid and reapply. Rinse well.

CAUTION: Acid can burn your skin and eyes. Wear rubber gloves, long pants and sleeves and goggles.

RETAINING **WALLS**

Wood , stone or concrete block?

by **Jeff Timm**

You covet the stone wall your neighbors built, but wood walls may be cheaper and easier to build. Then your contractor said that a concrete block wall is the only one that will last. Which do you choose?

CONCRETE BLOCKS

Modern concrete block walls are fairly sophisticated systems designed for strength as well as for fast, easy assembly. You simply stack the blocks on top of one another and secure them with pins, clips or interlocking edges. They're designed to be set on a compacted gravel base. This allows them to flex slightly with ground movement and still remain strong. They're available in a wide variety of styles and sizes (see next page).

The garden wall size is the most common. These are relatively small (about 12 in. long x 4 in. high) and work best for accent walls around the yard and garden up to about 30 in. high. They're perfect for terracing or building a raised planter. They're lightweight (less than 25 lbs.), quick to install and widely available at home centers, nurseries and landscape supply outlets. You can usually build a wall with this size block in a weekend.

For heavy-duty walls up to 30 ft. tall, go with full-size blocks (shown below). They're 16 to 18 in. long x 6 to 8 in. high and weigh 50 to 75 lbs. You'll typically find them at landscape supply yards. Working with these blocks is a big job best left to pros. Big walls usually entail excavating and moving tons of soil and gravel as well as the heavy block itself. Walls over 4 ft. tall must be designed by a licensed engineer to ensure adequate strength.

Photo from VERSA-LOK

Styles of block

If you think concrete block walls look cold and commercial, look again. You now have a wide variety of shapes, textures and colors to choose from. Select one that blends well with your yard, gardens and home. If possible, look at a completed wall to get the best idea of the appearance. Most manufacturers produce these four main styles.

Three-way split

Photo from Handy-Stone

Three-way split: This is the block style that started it all. The corners are split off the face of this block, leaving a highly textured, rounded surface. These are usually the best choice for tighter curves (see "Design Issues," p. 229).
Cost: $7 to $10 per sq. ft.

Flat Face

Photo from Handy-Stone

Flat face: This style of block has an even-textured face. When stacked, they have the classical look of chiseled stone. The uniform texture provides a good backdrop for a garden or a visual base to a house. Its muted appearance will look in style for years to come. The size of block varies. As a general rule, use the small sizes for smaller walls.
Cost: $7 to $10 per sq. ft.

Tumbled

Photo from VERSA-LOK

Tumbled or weathered: This is a hybrid of the flat face block. The edges are rounded to soften its appearance and make it look more weathered and natural. Different length blocks can be mixed to further vary the look.
Cost: $8 to $11 per sq. ft.

Mosaics

Photo from VERSA-LOK

Mosaics or ashlars: This handsome variation of tumbled and weathered block integrates different sizes to give a varied, custom-fitted look to the wall. This block works best for straight walls. Curved walls in this style require more building experience and block cutting. This type also requires more expert advice for planning curves, corners, stairs and other details.
Cost: $8 to $11 per sq. ft.

Stacking Systems

Almost every style of block is made in two weights and in one of several stacking systems, depending on the manufacturer. The stacking system evenly spaces the blocks, holds them in place and allows the flexibility required for corners, curves, steps and other design features. Pick the weight and stacking system that best handles the design details of your wall. (See the next page for key wall planning details.)

Solid

Solid and semi-solid blocks are heavy (up to 75 lbs.) but are also the most versatile. You can simply split them to form 90-degree corners or any other angle, rather than having to order special blocks. However, you'll have to rent a splitter ($85 per day) or have the landscape yard split the blocks for you. You can also order special corners if you don't want to split them. Some types won't require special cap blocks, although cap blocks look better.

Hollow core

Hollow-core blocks are about half the weight of their solid counterparts. After you set each course, you fill the cores with gravel, making the wall every bit as strong as a solid-block wall. However, they're less versatile. You'll have to order special blocks for corners and caps. They're a good choice if you want to ease back strain.

Lip System

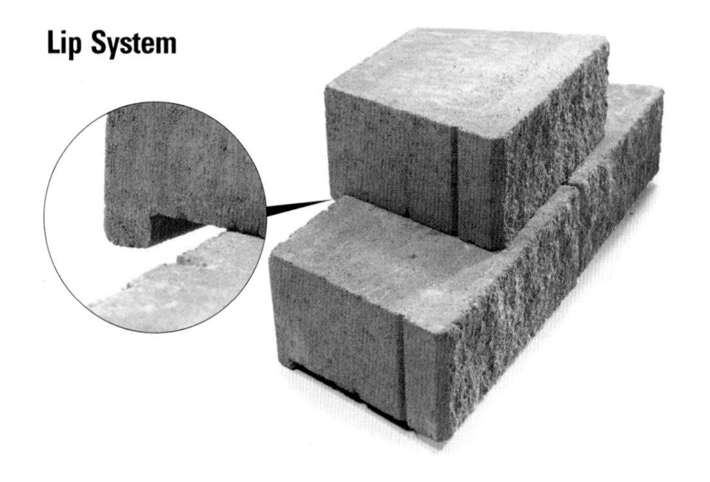

The integral lip or tongue-and-groove system interlocks the blocks and makes the installation fast and easy. You simply drop the blocks in place. Just be sure to stagger the vertical joints between rows. However, it isn't quite as versatile because you can't vary the setback. (See p. 229.)

Pin System

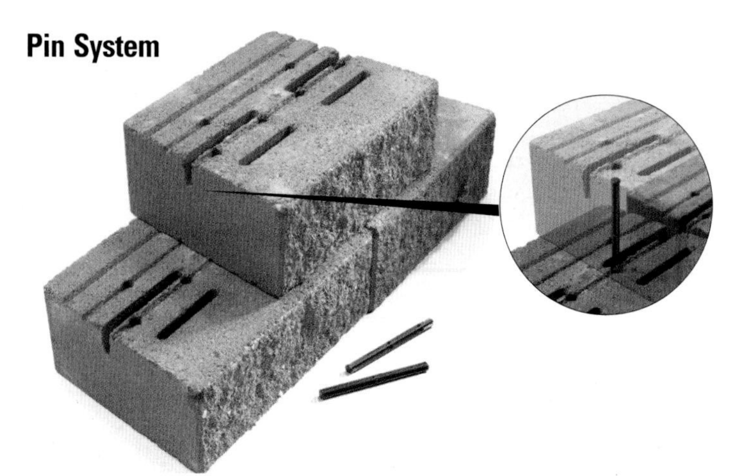

A pin or a clip system, made from tough plastic or fiberglass, anchors each row of blocks to the ones below. These systems are more fussy. You may have to cut blocks to fit some curves to get the pins to fit. And the pins are tough to get in if you've spilled gravel or dirt in the pinholes. However, some pinned systems will let you slide the block forward (no setback) if you need a more vertical wall.

Design issues

Begin your planning by making a sketch of your proposed wall, including curves, corners, stairs, junctions with the house and any other details. Add dimensions to the drawing so you (or the staff at the landscape yard) can estimate the number of blocks you need and which special blocks to order. These details will also help you decide which block system to choose. Don't skip this step; it'll save you hours during construction and prevent big headaches. Be sure to note the following details:

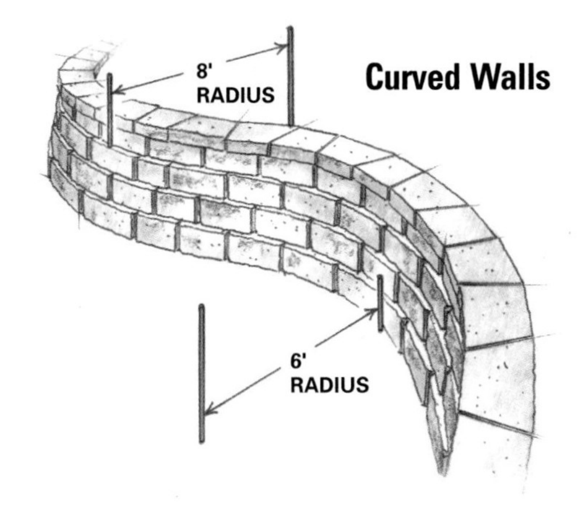

Curves: With a tape measure and helper, examine the site and measure the tightest radius you envision, for both inside and outside curves. All block systems have limits as to how tight a curve they can cover without cutting. This information is on the spec sheet for each system. Review the spec sheets with the dealer and use this as one factor in your final decision. **Tip:** Don't plan to build the smallest radius a system can handle. Leave yourself wiggle room for minor changes.

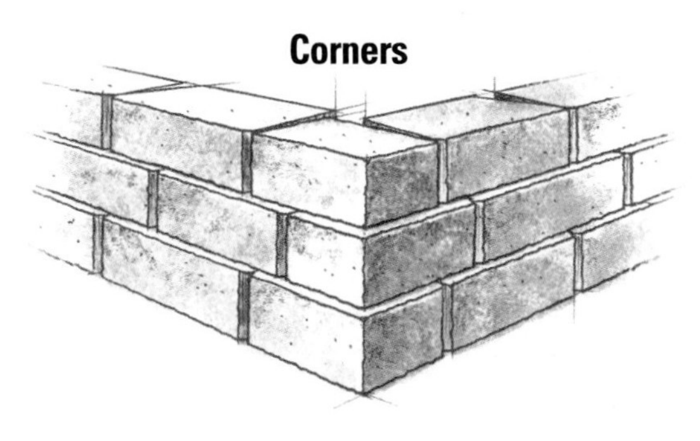

Corners: Study the corner details on the manufacturer's spec sheets. The blocks they require vary. Sometimes you can split blocks for outside corners and sometimes you have to order special ones. Inside corners don't require any special blocks. Chances are, you'll have to rent a diamond-blade saw for special cuts if you have more than two corners in your plan.

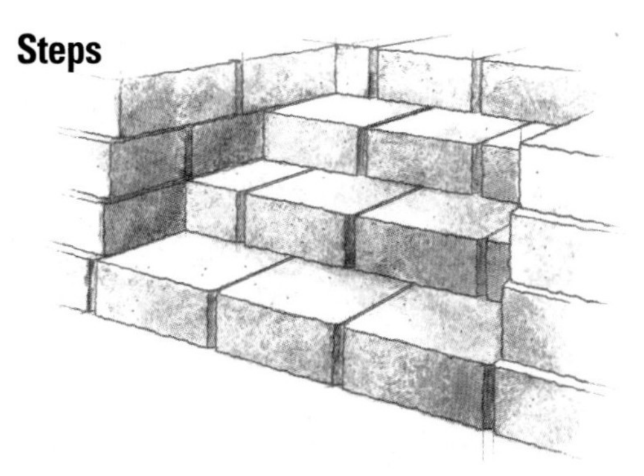

Steps: Almost all systems are designed to incorporate steps. Measure the total height of the steps, and using the spec sheet, the dealer will help you order the special blocks needed.

Cap blocks: Cap blocks seal the last row of blocks for an attractive appearance. With most systems, you order enough to cover the top of your wall. Check the system's versatility. Some types handle both curves and straight sections easily. Others may require more cutting.

Cap Blocks

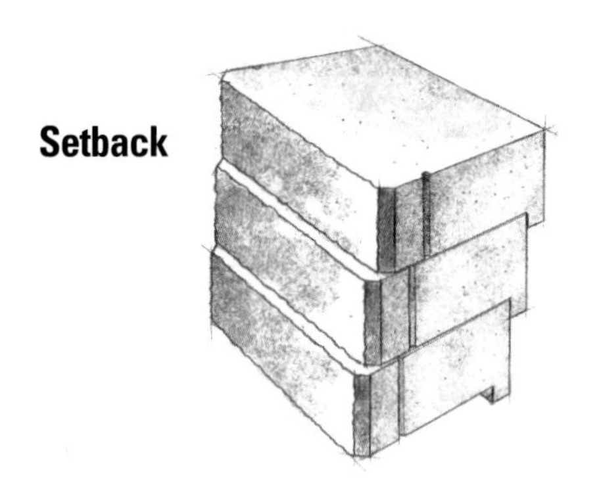

Setback: Setback is the amount each course of wall steps back into the slope. Each block system has one or a range of possible setbacks, varying from zero to 1-1/4 in. per row. Sometimes you don't want much setback, especially where a wall meets the corner of a house. But keep in mind that the setback helps strengthen the wall, so use minimum setback only when absolutely necessary.

NATURAL STONE

Stone makes the nicest-looking walls of all. You have a wide variety of choices that will fit just about any style of yard and garden. On the downside, stone is usually more expensive, and the walls require more skill and more time to build. They'll give your creative skills a workout, as well as your shoulder muscles! Limit your efforts to walls up to 3 ft. high. Pros can build higher stone walls, but typically they require engineering expertise. Stone walls fall into three main types:

Photo by Ramon Moreno

Cut stone:

The stone is split at the quarry either 8 in. or 12 in. wide and at several lengths and heights. They weigh 40 to 100 lbs. apiece. Simply stack them in rows or mix heights within a row for a random look. You don't need mortar. As with a concrete block wall, build a firm gravel base and ensure good drainage. Step each row back into the slope about 1-1/2 in. per foot of wall height.

Cost: $12 to $20 per sq. ft.

Rubble wall:

A rubble wall is made of stone of random sizes and shapes fitted tightly together when stacked. Blends of various colors and/or types of stone make these walls attractive and unique. While it's creative, building this type of wall is time consuming. It takes a while to find the stone that fits just right. Start with a wide base and step the stone back slightly, narrowing the wall at the top. Carefully compact gravel into the joints behind the wall to eliminate voids that could settle later.

Cost: $12 to $30 per sq. ft.

Boulder walls:

Photo from Yardscapes

Boulder walls consist of larger stones, typically 8 in. and larger, that are fitted and stacked. The larger the rocks, the larger the wall you can build. Figure on using 8- to 18-in. diameter stones for a 3-ft. high wall. The one big drawback is weight. Even the smaller stones weigh at least 80 lbs. The gaps between stones will also be larger. Place landscape fabric behind the wall to prevent soil from washing through, or fill the gaps with plants.

Cost: $5 to $12 per sq. ft.

WOOD/TIMBER

Although fading in popularity, wood walls complement some yards and homes, especially if the home has a rustic appearance (such as stained wood and stone). It's also a good choice when cost is an issue. You can use either standard lumber (2x4s, 2x6s, 2x8s, etc.) like we show on the top of page 226, or timbers (4x6s, 6x6s) as in the photo above. You can easily incorporate multiple angles and steps. And they're a great project if you're a carpenter at heart.

PERPENDICULAR 6x6

The timber style, which is the most common, gets most of its strength from 6x6s set perpendicular to the face of the wall. A crossed 6x6 at the rear adds additional support as shown above. As with other types of walls, set the timbers on a gravel base and provide good drainage behind the wall. Fasten the timbers with long spikes or screws. Choose timbers that have a .40 treatment rating (suitable for ground contact) and seal any cut ends with preservative to prevent rotting. Timbers are usually available in green and brown. Cost: $5 to $10 per sq. ft.

New Product

MOTORIZED WHEELBARROW

Ever try to muscle a wheelbarrow full of retaining wall blocks up an incline? Over uneven terrain? Or through mud? Forget it! Until now, that is. Check out the battery-powered Cargomaxx wheelbarrow. A slight squeeze on the thumb switch lets you negotiate a load over rough terrain at a snail's pace. Give it a full squeeze and you'll be off at a brisk walk down the driveway. The Cargomaxx tirelessly hauls loads up to 400 lbs. over nearly any terrain for up to five hours between recharges.

At $400, it's not for the once-a-year wheelbarrow pusher. Contact Country Home Products, (800) 687-6575, www.countryhomeproducts.com for shipping costs.

Handy Hints® from our readers

GARDEN GEAR CADDY

An old golf bag—especially one on a cart—is perfect for storing and hauling garden tools. Get them all to the garden in one trip and park them in the caddy shack when you're done. Fore!

RECYCLED SPREADER

Save those Parmesan cheese containers when they've completed their dinner duty. Load 'em up with grass seed, ice melting chemicals, fertilizer and other products for easy spreading. Just make sure the can is clearly marked and out of the reach of children.

MINI GREENHOUSE

Give vegetable and flower seedlings an early growth spurt this spring. Place seedling trays in a mini greenhouse—an upside-down transparent storage container ($3 at discount stores). Just lay down the lid in a warm, sunny location, load it with trays, then snap on the container. For greater air circulation, drill a few 3/8-in. holes in the sides of the box or let it rest loosely on the lid.

HOMEMADE PLUMB BOB

Can't find your level when you have to plumb a new fence post? Tape heavy washers to the ends of two 20-in. lengths of string, then crisscross the strings over the top of the post so the washers hang down on each side. The post is plumb when all four washers lie flat against the wood! The washers will hang best if you tape the string on the outer rim of the washer. This technique works great for plumbing both cylindrical and four-sided posts.

SNAP-IN, SNAP-OUT FLAGPOLE

Fly your colors in a second with two spring-grip tool holders ($2 at a home center) mounted to a solid post. First snap the holders on the flagpole a couple of inches apart, then hold the whole thing up at your desired angle and mark the post for the screws. Remove the holders and screw them to the post. That's it—raise your banner!

PATIO PAVER PULLER

After a winter of freezing and thawing, some individual bricks or pavers in your sand-based patio may need releveling. How do you get the bricks or pavers out? Make these pullers from two pieces of coat-hanger wire. Slip the wires down both sides of the offending paver, turn them a quarter turn and pull up the paver. For large patio blocks, make four pullers and get a second person to help.

FOOT-FRIENDLY SPADE

Give your shovel-shoving foot a more comfortable pushing surface. Saw a slit in a scrap of 1-in. PVC pipe and slip it over your shovel's flange. If it won't stay put, add a bead of hot-melt glue.

PORTABLE SHOE SCRAPER

This simple shoe scraper is portable but won't slide around when you use it. Screw a large stiff-bristle scrub brush upside down to a piece of plywood about 12 in. wide and 16 in. long. Your weight on the plywood base keeps it stationary while you scrape each shoe. Rinse the scraper off with a garden hose and store it out of sight between uses.

BACKYARD **STREAM & WATERFALLS**

This cascading stream flows into a gravel bed, not a pond, so it stays clean with little maintenance

by **Kurt Lawton**

We've all stopped, gazed and listened upon encountering a rippling brook or waterfall—to soak up the serenity that nature provides. But where is that spot when we need it most?

Since you probably can't drive and hike to a tranquil location after a hard day's work, you can use this project to help you re-create these all-too-fleeting moments in your back yard. And you can build your stream in two weekends.

We designed this stream to eliminate the filtering and cleaning maintenance that comes with ponds. The trick to low maintenance is to let nature (layers of gravel and stone) filter the water, using an underground sump at the lower end to catch the filtered water before pumping it back up to the top of the stream. All you have to do is occasionally add water to replace what evaporates—and rainfall may handle this task for you.

In this story, we'll show you how to slope the stream, lay the liner and install the pump and the catch basin as well as landscape the stream. We'll help you plan the ideal location and size of your stream, and tell you how to select liners, pumps and stone. We won't get into kits that are available either on-line or at home centers. We chose to build our system with parts and components that are readily available and less expensive than kits. They'll give you more flexibility to design the stream that best fits your yard.

You can complete this project successfully even if it's your first water feature. But it's heavy work. The only special tools you'll need are a strong wheelbarrow (one with pneumatic tires is best) and a two-wheel ball cart ($18 per day to rent) for moving and placing heavy boulders.

What's my investment?

For the basic materials (pump, plumbing, tools, sealant—see the list below), plan to spend about $300, not including the liners. Add in the underlayment and liner cost at about $1.20 per sq. ft. of stream (we used 120 sq. ft.). We purchased all materials from a home center, except for black expanding-foam sealant made for ponds and waterfalls and the EPDM rubber liner, which we bought from a local pond supplies dealer (www.aquascapedesigns.com). Aquascape guarantees its liners; other suppliers may void the guarantee once you trim the liner to size.

The largest additional cost of the project is the stone. The amount of stone and gravel will depend on your stream design. Take your plan to the stone and gravel retailer to get help with estimates. All told, our "deluxe" stream used 8 tons of stone and gravel, which came to $725, plus tax and delivery. One could easily reduce stone costs to $350 for this 15-ft. stream with fewer specialty boulders. You could save even more if you dig the entire

Materials List

Large waterfall pump	$150
Hose kit and connections	$15
PVC primer and cement	$9
Ball valve and clamps	$10
Sewage basin (18" x 30") and lid	$55
Two hole saw bits (2" and 1")	$10
EPDM pond liner	$1 per sq. ft.
Underlayment fabric	$1 per lin. ft.
Waterfall foam sealant	$12 per can
Gravel	$30 per ton
Field boulders	$85 per ton
Decorative boulders	$200 to $300 per ton
Bagging and delivery	$100 to $200

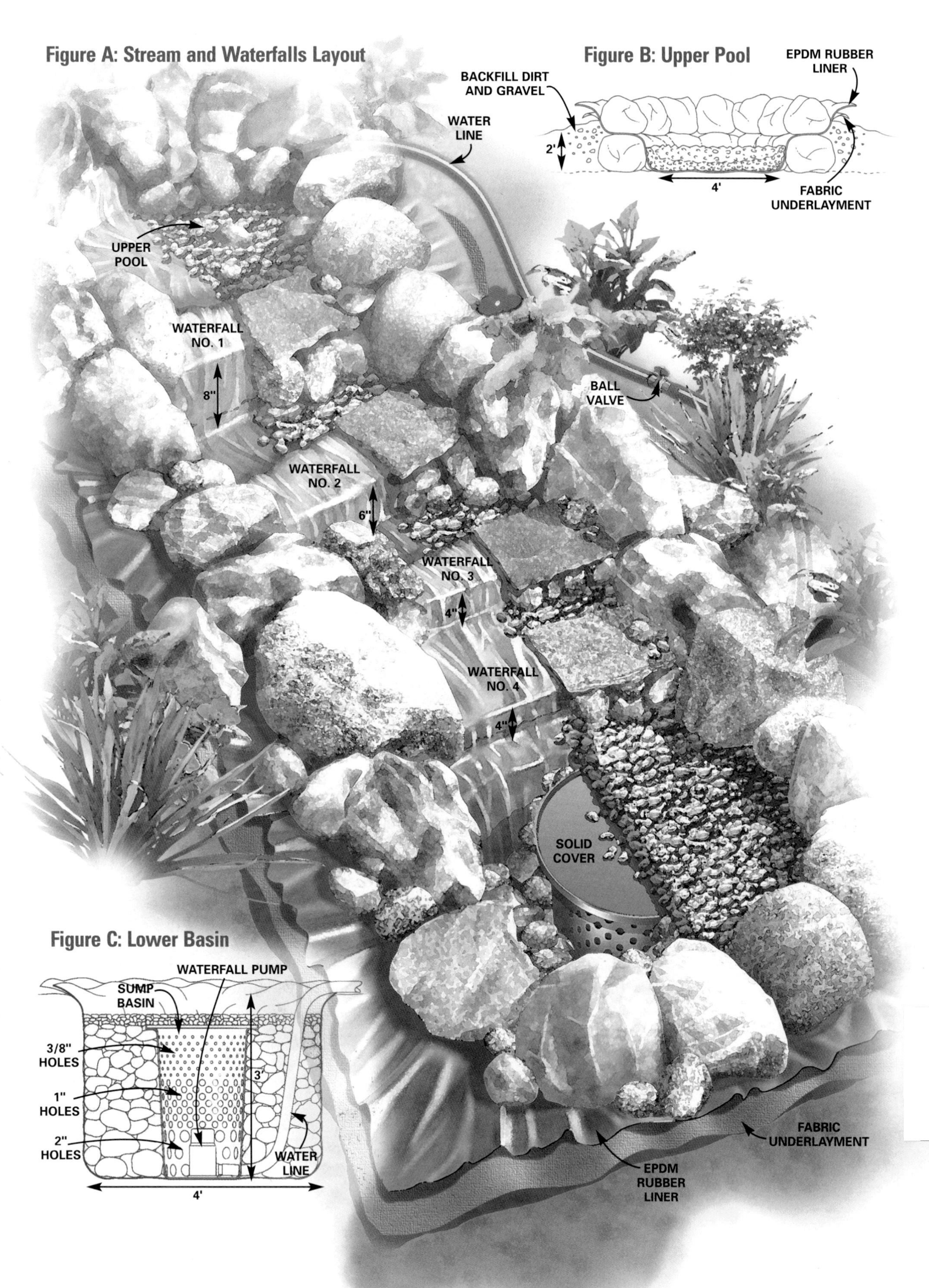
Figure A: Stream and Waterfalls Layout
WATER LINE
UPPER POOL
WATERFALL NO. 1
8"
BALL VALVE
WATERFALL NO. 2
6"
WATERFALL NO. 3
4"
WATERFALL NO. 4
4"
SOLID COVER
FABRIC UNDERLAYMENT
EPDM RUBBER LINER
Figure B: Upper Pool
BACKFILL DIRT AND GRAVEL
EPDM RUBBER LINER
2'
4'
FABRIC UNDERLAYMENT
Figure C: Lower Basin
WATERFALL PUMP
SUMP BASIN
3/8" HOLES
1" HOLES
2" HOLES
3'
WATER LINE
4'

stream into the ground rather than building the upper section higher.

Plan by ear

Sit in a favorite spot and visualize where a stream with waterfalls would fit into your landscape—perhaps near a patio or deck.

Planning elements to consider:

■ **Foundation.** If your soil is easy to dig, then excavate the entire project. If digging is difficult, build your stream above ground with stones for the base.

■ **Slope.** Very little slope is needed (minimum 2 in. drop per 10 ft. of stream). For faster-moving water or taller waterfalls, make the grade steeper (which also adds more sound).

■ **Size.** Plan your stream size first to determine how much water the lower basin and upper pool must hold when the pump is off. Plan on five gallons per linear foot of flowing stream (2-1/2 ft. wide x 3 in. deep). Our lower basin (40 gallons) and upper pool (240 gallons) easily held our 75-gallon stream capacity.

■ **Sound.** For a babbling brook sound, use a waterfall height of 2 to 4 in. To drown out street noise, use 10-in. and greater waterfall drops. More waterfalls equals more sound.

■ **Location.** Waterfalls should be visible from your favorite deck, patio or inside-the-home chair. Consider a location near the bedroom if you like the sound of running water at night; you can always turn it off if it's too loud or distracting. Make sure your pump location (lower basin) is close to an electrical source, and that you can reach the stream with a garden hose to add water as needed.

For our site, we wrapped an S-shaped stream next to a ground-level deck built into an existing perennial garden. We varied the height of the four waterfalls and the width of the stream to give it a more natural look and sound. Plus we added a ball valve to the return water line so we could speed or slow the flow rate, and control the sound level.

If you need to add a GFCI outlet, see "Outdoor Light and Outlet, p. 243.

Order stone

When you start your stone search, look under "Rock," "Quarries" or "Sand & Gravel" in the Yellow Pages. Call to check prices and types of stone available. Go visit dealers to get exactly what you want, plus you can select specific

CAUTION: Although these pools are shallow, they can be a drowning hazard for small children. Check with your local building department for local regulations. And be watchful of toddlers.

1 HAUL in your boulders and stones and place them around the worksite. Outline the location of your stream with a garden hose, then paint a line around it. Also use paint to mark waterfall locations and ideal spots for large decorative boulders.

2 DIG the hole for the lower basin so it sits below the level of the streambed. Place boulders to build up the sides of the upper pool and upper portion of the stream, which are above the original grade (Figure A). Pack dirt and gravel to hold all stones in place.

3 DRILL holes in the basin using three different size hole saw bits (see Figure C). Prime, cement and attach the hose adapter to the pump.

4 **LAY the fabric underlayment and rubber liner in the basin hole, then add the pump basin with pump. Attach the hose. Then add stone layers (Figure C) and the basin lid.**

5 **CARVE a winding streambed 6 to 8 in. deep, 2 to 3-1/2 ft. wide. Dig the channel so it stair-steps down at waterfall No. 3, and dig 3- to 4-in. deep pools below waterfalls No. 2 and 3 (Figure A).**

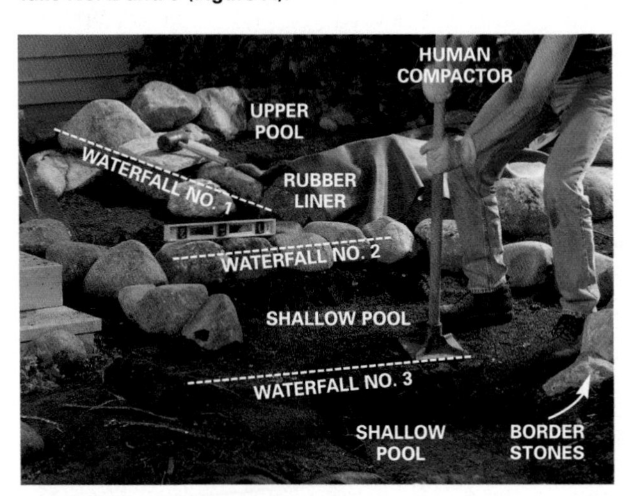

6 **PACK dirt and gravel around the border stones to build waterfalls No. 1 and 2 above the existing grade. Level the rows. Inspect the entire streambed and remove anything sharp. Tamp down the entire stream, banks and upper pool area.**

colorful accent boulders and flat stones for the waterfalls—then have it all delivered (for a $100 to $200 fee). Some quarries will even bag the stone by type and size (for a fee), and these palleted bags take up less space on a driveway, as opposed to piles of gravel and boulders.

For gravel (3/4-in. to 2-in. stones), figure you'll need 1/2 ton per 10 ft. of stream, plus we used 1 to 1-1/2 tons for the upper pool and lower basin. For basic field boulders (6 in. to 24 in.) to line the stream banks, figure 3/4 ton per 10 ft. of stream. Add 1-1/2 to 2 tons more of larger 12-in. to 24-in. boulders for the upper pool and lower basin. Because we built the top half of the stream above ground, we used 3-1/2 tons of extra boulders.

If you want specialty colorful accent boulders, expect to pay premium prices—about $200 to $300 per ton. The flat waterfall stones cost about $3 per sq. ft. Avoid limestone, as it can encourage algae growth.

Map the stream and start digging

After all the stone and gravel arrive, map out your design and mark it with spray paint (Photo 1).

We built the upper half of the stream and two waterfalls above the ground, then carved the lower half of this 15-ft. stream out of the soil (Figure A). Pick whichever technique works with your soil and go with it. Either way, keep the ibuprofen handy to soothe those sore lifting and digging muscles!

Next, dig the lower basin for the sump basin and surrounding stone and gravel. Dig a square hole at least 2 ft. wider than the basin diameter and 6 in. deeper than the height. It should be at least a foot wider than the stream.

Simultaneously, build a ring of stone for the upper pool foundation and the stream banks (Photo 2). Place 12-in. tall stones flat side up (if possible) so the next layer of stone will fit more securely on top (Figure B). Use a rubber mallet to pack dirt and gravel tightly around the stones to hold them in place.

Complete the lower basin first

Use a 2-in. hole saw bit and drill holes every 4 in. in the bottom third of the pump basin (Figure C and Photo 3). Repeat the process with a 1-in. hole saw bit for the middle third, then use a 3/8-in. bit for the top third.

Remove sharp objects from the bottom of the basin, then lay in the underlayment and liner. Calculate the size

CAUTION: A few days before you plan to dig for your stream, call (888) 258-0808 to have underground utilities in the area located and marked.

carefully and cut the underlayment first. Then cut and fit the liner so it is tucked in all corners and extends about 2 ft. out of the hole in all directions. With the pump basin in place, insert the pump, connect the water line and lay it in place to ensure it will reach the top of the upper pool. Add layers of stone around the basin and top with the lid (Figure C and Photo 4).

Dig out (or build) a long staircase

First, at each waterfall location, dig down to the approximate depth of the drop you desire or build up the fall if you're working above grade. This gives you a streambed depth target. Now move to the bottom of the stream and carve a 2 to 3-1/2 ft. wide streambed 6 to 8 in. deep, sloping upward as you dig upstream to meet that streambed depth target at each waterfall (Photo 5). Then dig out shallow pools below waterfalls as needed (Figure A) to slow the water flow.

Since we built above ground for the upper section of the stream, we next added a level row of stones for waterfalls No. 1 and 2 (Photo 6). Pick the height you desire. Use 6-in. tall stones to frame the banks. Also finish compacting a gravel and dirt mixture to the inside and outside of the upper pool stones. Then tamp down the upper pool area and the streambed.

Lay the liner and position waterfall stones

Position the fabric underlayment and liner to extend from the lower basin to the upper pool, with slack at the base of each waterfall, because placing boulders can stretch and rip a tight liner (Photo 7). Place decorative boulders at the side of each waterfall, and add an extra piece of rubber liner underneath each heavy stone to protect the base liner.

Tip

If you live in a freezing climate, make sure the pump and hose are easy to blow out or remove.

For stable, above-ground stream edges, backfill the edging stones with a gravel and dirt mixture and compact it (Photo 8). Next, lay the final piece of underlayment and liner in the upper pool so it tucks in at all corners and extends 2 ft. out in all directions. There's no need to tape the liners to each other; just make sure the top liner overlaps the liner underneath it by 1-1/2 to 2 ft. Then add the top layer of stones around the upper pool.

7 **LAY the underlayment and a rubber liner into the streambed. Leave 3 to 4 in. of slack in the liner at the base of the waterfalls, extend about 2 ft. up each bank and overlap the basin liner by 2 ft. Place decorative boulders at waterfall locations.**

8 **LAY the underlayment and liner over the upper pool, overlapping the built-up boulder edges. Overlap the lower liner by about 2 ft. Backfill stream edging boulders for stability.**

9 **SET decorative boulders at each side of waterfalls No. 1 and 2. Then coat the bottom of the flat spill stones with foam sealant so they adhere to the liner. Wedge stones into cracks between the spill stones and the sides of the stream bank.**

10 **FORCE gravel along all sides and under spill stones, then apply foam sealant in the gaps so water flows only over the top of all spill stones.**

11 **ADD a top layer of small boulders to complete the upper pool and streambed. Place steppingstones in the middle of the stream and the stones below the waterfalls. Cover the rest of the streambed liner with gravel.**

12 **FILL the bottom basin with water and plug in the pump. Spray down all stones and the stream until the water from the pump runs clear. Place the hose from the pump into the upper pool. Trim off remaining exposed liner and adjust stream flow by moving rocks and adjusting the ball valve.**

Add spill stones and foam the gaps

Once you place the decorative boulders at the waterfall locations, place all the flat spill stones. Apply black expanding foam sealant, designed for ponds and waterfalls, to the underside to adhere them to the rubber liner. Now fill all gaps with stones to force water to go only over the waterfall (**Photo 9**). Then apply foam sealant to all sides and to the underneath of each spill stone to create a good seal (**Photo 10**).

After the foam has dried for 30 minutes, take your garden hose and run water down the stream. Look for any water trails (leaks) along the spill stone edges and underneath. Fill any leaks with more foam and repeat until all water goes over the top of the spill stones.

Add gravel and clean the stream

The final construction step is to place steppingstones in the middle of the stream to make it inviting for people, birds and pets. Then carefully layer in gravel to cover any exposed liner (**Photo 11**).

Spray down the entire stream area with a garden hose nozzle until the water level rises above the gravel in the bottom basin. Now power up the pump and direct the pump hose away from the stream. Keep washing down the stream and rock until the water from the pump hose runs clear. Then insert the pump hose into the upper pool (make sure it is hidden), and finish your stream by trimming and covering any rubber liner that shows (**Photo 12**).

Now it's time to take that favorite seat, with a cold beverage in hand, and relax to the soothing sounds of your new stream.

Tip Choose stones with fractures and broken edges to place under waterfalls for more water sound and movement.

PUMP SIZING

Submersible pumps are rated by gph (gallons per hour) at a specific discharge height (known as head or lift). To calculate the gph you need, figure 150 gph for each inch of your widest waterfall. Next, to figure the head/lift you need, calculate the distance your water line travels from the pump to the upper pool (measure vertical and horizontal; 10 ft. of horizontal distance = 1 ft. of vertical rise). Look for a high-quality pump (bronze, brass or stainless steel; not a cheap sump pump) that can exceed the gph and lift you need.

Gallery of Ideas

TIMBER-FRAME GARDEN ARBOR

This timber garden arbor can serve as your place to get away for a quiet retreat or as a delightful entrance to a side yard, backyard or garden. Building it is enjoyable too. The main structure goes together like an old-fashioned timber frame with tenons and notches you cut into 6x6s with your circular saw and handsaw. It's an attractive feature that will age gracefully, while lasting a lifetime.

FROM MARCH, 2004, p. 34

Project Facts

Cost: $450
Skill level: Intermediate carpentry skills
Time: 3 to 4 days

Skill Builders

As you build this structure, you'll also learn how to:

- **Build a mini timber-frame structure**
- **Precisely notch posts and beams**
- **Create curved brackets and rafter tails**

BRICK AND STONE PATH

This project is constructed the same basic way a standard brick or paver patio walkway would be—but the natural stone accents add a unique decorative dimension. And if you're concerned about strength and stability, don't worry. It will stay flat and smooth, even under heavy use, and, unlike concrete, it won't crack.

FROM MARCH, 2004, p. 56

Project Facts

Cost: About $12 per square foot for materials, plus tool rental costs
Skill level: Intermediate do-it-yourself skills; heavy lifting
Time: At least 3 days, depending on size of project

BARBECUE ISLAND

FROM JUNE, 2004, p. 65

If you want to transform an everyday patio into an attractive gathering and cooking spot for family and friends, check out this barbecue island. The built-in stainless-steel grill and doors create the cooking center, while the tile top provides a place for preparing and dining. The stone veneer surround ties the whole barbecue island together.

Project Facts

Cost: $3,700, as shown
Skill: Advanced carpentry and tile-laying skills
Time: 6 to 8 days

To order photocopies of complete articles for the projects shown here, call (715) 246-4521, email familyhandyman@nrmsinc.com or write to: Copies, The Family Handyman, P.O. Box 83695, Stillwater, MN 55083-0695. Many public libraries also carry back issues of *The Family Handyman* magazine.

FROM MAY, 2004, p. 38

DREAM DECK

A dream deck can mean different things to different people. To some it means low maintenance, to some it means a shady retreat and for others it means a showplace for entertaining. This deck fulfills all three dreams. It's built using composite decking, which means lower maintenance than a wooden deck. Its multi-level design provides an upper deck for eating and gathering, and a lower deck for sunning. The pergola provides plenty of shade and the cascading stairs give you access to every part of your yard. There are even built-in planters for those who love to garden.

Project Facts

Cost: $7,000 for materials
Skill level: Advanced carpentry skills
Time: 2 to 3 solid weeks for two people

Skill Builders

When you tackle this project, you'll not only wind up with a handsome deck, but also many skills you can apply to other projects down the road. During this project you'll learn how to:

- **Square up a deck and other large structures**
- **Install composite decking**
- **Build a copper-tubing rail, and make it look older and more natural using an aging solution**
- **Construct "stacked platform"-type stairs**
- **Craft a simple pergola**

OUTDOOR LIGHT AND OUTLET

If you need a bright light in the far reaches of your backyard, or a remote outlet to power a pond pump or tools, this project will take care of both needs. It combines a 120-volt light with a combination switch/outlet mounted on an attractive post. The most difficult part may well be rolling up your sleeves and digging the long, deep trench required for burying the wire.

Project Facts

Cost: About $100
Skill level: Basic carpentry and electrical wiring skills
Time: 2 days

COPPER TRELLIS

If you need a place for your plants to hang out or just want an attractive accent piece in your garden, consider this copper trellis. Copper is an ideal material for garden structures. It has a warm natural look, whether shiny or tarnished, and lasts for years without upkeep. Plus it's easy to work with and relatively inexpensive.

Project Facts

Cost: About $50 for materials, plus the cost of the tools required if you don't already own them
Skill level: Beginner do-it-yourself skills
Time: 1 weekend or less

FROM APRIL, 2004, p. 105

To order photocopies of complete articles for the projects shown here, call (715) 246-4521, email familyhandyman@nrmsinc.com or write to: Copies, The Family Handyman, P.O. Box 83695, Stillwater, MN 55083-0695. Many public libraries also carry back issues of *The Family Handyman* magazine.

YARD SHED

FROM JULY/AUGUST, 2004, p. 40

If your garage is overrun with bikes, wheelbarrows, lawn mowers and other lawn and garden supplies, this yard shed will help free up enough space so you can actually fit a car inside. The basic 2x4 construction, prefabricated roof trusses and straightforward design help simplify this project. And the wide front and side overhangs provide plenty of extra room for storing more stuff—or even for relaxing in the shade.

Project Facts

Cost: $3,500 (not including concrete work)
Skill level: Intermediate to advanced carpentry skills
Time: All summer long

Skill Builders

Tackle this project and you'll learn how to:

- **Lay out and build basic 2x4 walls**
- **Install factory-built trusses**
- **Install lap siding, plus door and window trim**
- **Build and install a simple sliding door**

FROM JULY/AUGUST, 2004, p. 79

CEDAR AND GLASS RAIL

Whether you're trying to keep an eye on your kids in the backyard, or simply enjoying the view, most deck rails tend to get in the way. This cedar and tinted glass railing is not only strong and safe, but maximizes the view and adds a distinctive touch to your outdoor living area as well.

Project Facts

Cost: About $50/lin. ft. for cedar/glass sections; $8/lin. ft. for cedar spindle railing sections
Skill level: Basic carpentry experience
Time: Varies greatly according to size of project

PATIO PRIVACY SCREEN

If you feel as if you're living in a fishbowl when you lounge outside, build this simple, airy screen. It will block prying eyes and create a buffer for heavy winds, while still allowing sunlight and gentle breezes through. This cedar privacy screen is 12 ft. long and 7 ft. tall, but you can adapt the length and height to meet your own needs.

Project Facts

Cost: About $400 (less, if using treated wood)
Skill level: Intermediate carpentry skills
Time: 1 weekend

FROM SEPTEMBER, 2004, p. 76

To order photocopies of complete articles for the projects shown here, call (715) 246-4521, email familyhandyman@nrmsinc.com or write to: Copies, The Family Handyman, P.O. Box 83695, Stillwater, MN 55083-0695. Many public libraries also carry back issues of *The Family Handyman* magazine.

You Can Fix It™

FIXING POND LEAKS

Every pond occasionally needs water added to make up for evaporation. But if you're topping off your pond more often than you used to, chances are it has developed a leak. There are four basic types of pond leaks: plumbing leaks, a sagging liner, water wicking and a punctured liner. In this article, we'll show you how to find these leaks and fix them.

Plumbing leaks

Plumbing leaks usually aren't hard to find. A close inspection of the soil along tubing and around connections should yield the source of a leak. After a period of dry weather, look for moist soil. When you find a damp spot, start digging and follow the dampness until you find plumbing. Dig carefully with a small shovel so you don't damage the plumbing.

With the pump running, examine the hoses as you uncover them. If the leak is large enough, you may actually see dripping water, but a slow leak won't be visible. To find an invisible leak, clean the tubing and connections with a paper towel. Then take a dry paper towel and wipe the tubing. When you've found the spot that wets the towel, you've found the leak.

The repair can be as simple as tightening a hose clamp or replacing a rubber washer. Or you may have to replace a fitting or section of hose. When you're done with the repair, let the pump run for a few minutes and repeat the paper towel test to make sure you've solved the problem.

You can find replacement parts and repair materials at pond dealers and nurseries that sell pond equipment.

A sagging liner

If you don't find any plumbing leaks, inspect the perimeter of the pond for wet spots where water is seeping over the liner. This is common around stream beds or at waterfalls where sections of liner overlap, but it also occurs around the edges of a pond. Leaks like these are easy to see once you've uncovered the edge of the liner. Uncovering the liner's edge can be a real pain, though; you'll have to move rocks, soil and even plants. Readjusting and raising the liner is usually all it takes to keep the water inside.

1 INSPECT the pond edges for signs of leakage. Prop up the sagging liner with soil and then secure the edge with a covering of stones.

2 CHECK for water flowing over the liner at waterfalls and along stream beds. Raise the liner so that it holds water in. Reposition any rocks that channel water outside the liner.

Water wicking

Soil, sand or plants that cover the edge of the liner can draw water up and over the liner. The evidence of this wicking is wet soil around the pond.

The solution is to remove plants, soil and sand from the water's edge. Rocks and gravel won't wick out water, but as a preventive measure, occasionally clean out the sand and soil that washes into the spaces between the rocks that surround the pond. If you prefer to let plants spread over the liner's edge and into the water, you'll just have to live with a pond that frequently needs water added.

STOP water from wicking out of the pond by removing any plants, sand or soil in contact with the water. Be careful not to damage the liner as you dig.

A punctured liner

A hole in the liner is the toughest problem to locate. Begin your investigation by letting the water level drop. The draining will stop at the level of the leak (this can take days). This gives you only the level of the leak, not an exact location. You'll still have to move rocks and carefully inspect the liner all around the water line. If the leaking stops at the level where the water flows over a waterfall or into a stream, suspect a hole in the stream liner or waterfall basin.

Repairing a puncture is as easy as fixing a bicycle inner tube. A repair kit costs about $10 at garden centers and other pond supply dealers. Some kits are meant for all liners; others work only with specific types. If you don't know whether your liner is made from vinyl or a synthetic rubber like EPDM, cut off a small piece and take it with you to the garden center, where you can find out which patching materials to use.

1 LET the water level stabilize, then examine the liner around the water's edge. When you find the hole, drain more water so you can make the repair.

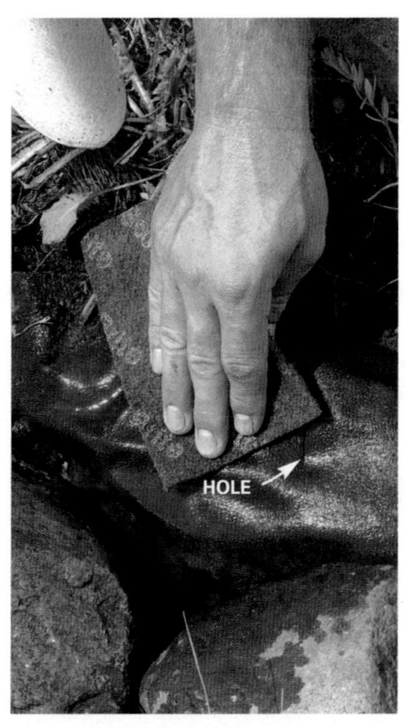

2 SCRUB the repair area with a scouring pad, then let it dry. The area has to be clean and dry for the patch to adhere well.

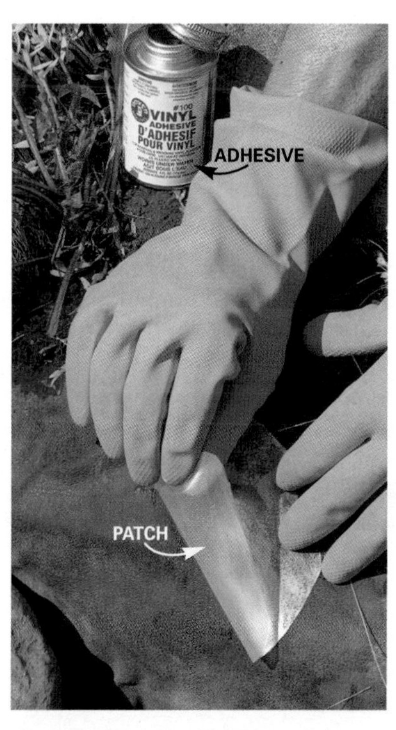

3 APPLY repair adhesive and then the patching material. Let it set according to the repair kit directions.

2 LOW-MAINTENANCE **GARDEN BORDERS**

These simple, attractive borders will keep your grass from invading the garden and eliminate the need for edge trimming

by **Marcia Williston**

METAL—A NEARLY INVISIBLE BORDER

The simplest and most subtle borders that effectively separate your lawn from a garden are 4-in. deep strips of steel, aluminum or plastic. They all bend easily into smooth, graceful curves and stop the spread of grass roots. However, painted aluminum and steel offer the sleekest, most refined look because they almost disappear against the grass and garden bed (photo below). The plastic types have a prominent black bulge along the top edge. All work best on fairly even terrain; if you have a lot of dips and rises, it's easier to install a border more like the paver one shown on p. 250.

Although aluminum and steel cost about the same, we chose aluminum because it was much lighter. It weighs about 41 lbs. per 100 ft., while steel weighs about 225. With aluminum, you get a professional look without the heavy lifting. (See "Buying Edging," right, for more details.)

Plan to set the border with the top edge about 1/2 in. above the soil level to maintain the lawn/garden separation and keep roots from crossing over the top. This makes the border almost invisible and, in many situations, allows you to mow right over the top. However, be aware that the thin top edge can hurt bare feet. After cutting it, make sure you round off any sharp edges with a file.

Follow the photos for the basic installation techniques. The key to setting this border is to cut a clean vertical edge along the grass with a square spade (Photo 1). Then you can lay the border tightly against the edge when you stake and backfill it. There's no rule for shaping the edge. Simply follow the edges of your garden, making smooth, gradual curves. To make smooth, sharp curves, bend the edging around a circular form.

Buying edging

Steel edging is the most common metal edging, although you might not find it at local nurseries. Look for it at larger garden centers or at landscape suppliers, which is where most pros get it. (Look under "Landscape Equipment and Supplies" in your Yellow Pages.) Steel edging comes in 4-in. wide by 10-ft. long strips in a variety of colors. Keep in mind that it'll eventually rust, especially in a salt environment. It's heavy, floppy stuff and needs almost full support when you transport it.

Aluminum edging, besides being lighter and stiffer, won't rust and is also available in a wide variety of colors. Look for it through landscaping suppliers, although it might be difficult to find. You might have to order it. One source is Permaloc Corp., (800-356-9660, permaloc.com); call to find a nearby dealer or order direct. Both aluminum and steel edging cost from $1.60 to $2.30 per ft. (delivery included). Be sure stakes are included with your purchase.

You'll find black plastic edging at every garden center and home center, sometimes in both regular and heavy-duty thicknesses. Buy the thicker material. It better withstands those inevitable bumps and hard knocks that go with lawn mowing. It costs about $1.70 per ft.

CAUTION: **Call your local utilities to locate underground lines before you dig and install all edging.**

1 CUT a narrow, 4-in. deep trench with one vertical side along the lawn edge. Shave the vertical edge to smooth out curves. Follow a string line for straight edges.

2 SNAP together the 8-ft. border sections, drop the edging into the trench and lay it against the vertical edge. Cut the final section to length with a hacksaw.

3 DRIVE stakes to set the depth at about 1/2 in. above the soil level of the lawn. If the edging drops too low, pry it up with the tip of your shovel.

4 BACKFILL with soil from the garden bed and compress it firmly. Leave room on top for mulch.

A PAVER BORDER

Both concrete and brick pavers make a simple, handsome border and work well as edging material too. They're ideal when you want a wide border that keeps grass out of the garden, yet allows flowers and other plants to spill over without intruding onto the grass. You're less likely to chop them up with the lawn mower. The paver design shown here also provides a nice, flat surface for the lawn mower wheel to roll along and make a clean cut. You shouldn't have to trim the edges after mowing.

Concrete pavers (55¢ each) are designed for rugged outdoor use. Brick pavers ($1 each) are too, but don't confuse them with regular bricks, which are typically softer and more likely to break down. Set the pavers in a bed of sand for easier positioning and leveling (**Photo 3**). The sand bed that you lay over landscape fabric keeps most grass types from sending roots under the edging and getting into the garden.

Paver borders work well for straight, formal gardens but even better for informal yards with gradual curves and varying slopes. You can easily adjust them to follow the contours of an uneven yard. But they won't fit as well on tighter curves unless you alter the design and are willing to cut them to fit with a diamond blade saw.

Use a garden hose to mark the best-looking border shape and to make gradual curves (**Photo 1**). Don't hesitate to trim the trench a bit here or there as you cut the edge to smooth curves or alter the garden bed shape. For straight borders, follow a tightly stretched string line.

Follow the photos for installing the pavers. It's important to set the front edge of the pavers about 1/2 in. above the soil in the lawn so the lawn mower can cut the grass cleanly. We also leveled our pavers from front to back to keep the row from dipping and rising, but it's not necessary and on slopes might look better if set on an angle. Just make sure the top of each paver sits flush with its neighbor and that the front edges create a smooth line. You can go back later and whack them perfectly flush with a block of wood and a hammer or a rubber mallet. The pavers we set on edge are primarily decorative, but they also raise the garden bed slightly and help retain mulch. Set them higher or lower to fit the needs of your garden.

1 LAY out the edge of the border with a garden hose, using the brick pattern as a spacer. Make curves gradual and smooth.

2 DIG a 4-in. deep trench about an inch wider than the brick pattern, using a square spade. Cut the edge along the grass smooth and square.

3 CUT landscape fabric to fit the bottom and sides of the trench and dump in about 2 in. of sand. Smooth and flatten the sand with a block of wood.

4 SET the bricks tightly together so the tops and front edges are even and about 1/2 in. above the soil. Sweep sand into gaps and pack soil against the back side.

Wordless Workshop™

by **Roy Doty**

SWING-OUT BIRD FEEDER

10 Auto & Garage

IN THIS CHAPTER

Clear Your Garage Floor 254
4 Storage Projects

Handy Hints 259

Auto Fast Fixes 260
Emergency heater hose repair, body side molding fix, flat tire hints and tips

Ask Handyman 266

Great Goofs 268

Handy Hints 269
Garage wall tool holder, hang-it-all hooks, under-joist shelf and more...

CLEAR YOUR GARAGE FLOOR **4 STORAGE PROJECTS**

Simple, quick, inexpensive solutions

by **Kurt Lawton**

So you're finally ready to organize your garage because the clutter is mountainous. (Or maybe you were motivated by Spousus eruptus.) But now you're stumped by how and where to begin. We can help you jump-start your garage storage quest by tackling some big stuff.

In this article, we'll show you our favorite way to get heavy bicycles, a long extension ladder, a wheelbarrow and small clutter off that garage floor. The good news is, all of these projects can be built using 2x4s, plywood and readily available hardware.

WHEELBARROW ON THE WALL

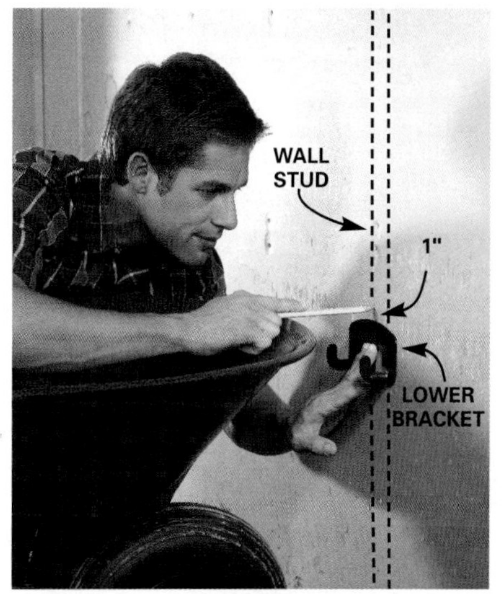

1 **MARK the wall at the height of the front wheelbarrow lip, then screw the lower bracket into a stud 1 in. below that mark.**

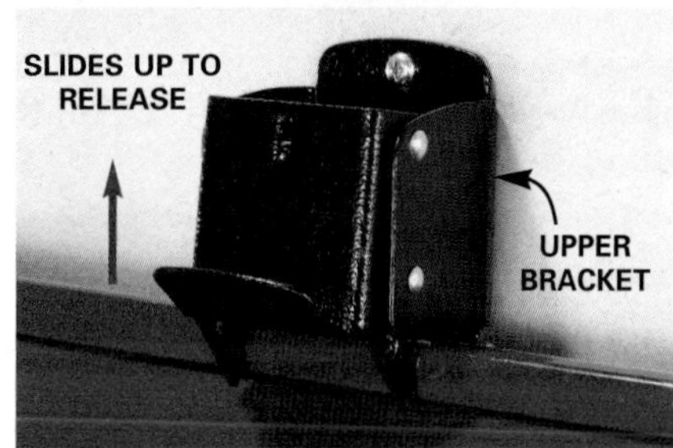

2 **SWING the wheelbarrow up, mark the position of the upper bracket and screw it into place.**

Wheelbarrows are fairly heavy and awkward. The trick to storing them is to get them up off the floor but not so high that you can't lift them down easily. We've designed simple wall storage brackets in the past, but it's tough to beat the nifty $4 wheelbarrow holder bracket we found at Home Depot (see Buyer's Guide).

With this bracket, you simply set the front lip of the wheelbarrow into the lower bracket and swing the back up and into a latching upper bracket. To get the wheelbarrow down, just unlatch the upper bracket and swing it down. Keep in mind that the metal legs will stick out and can cause a nasty bump or bruise. Hang your wheelbarrow along a little-traveled wall or cover the legs with something soft.

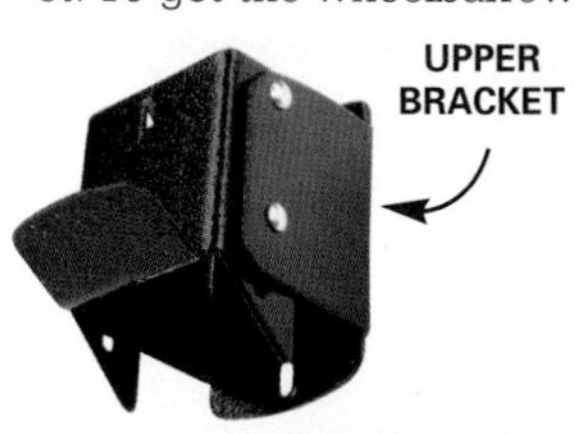

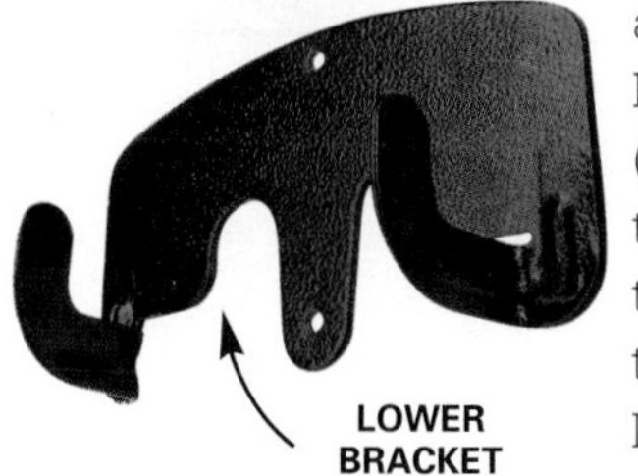

Push the wheelbarrow next to a wall stud and mark its height (Photo 1). Attach the lower bracket to the stud with wood screws (provided), 1 in. below the mark. Next, push the wheelbarrow up so the front lip drops into the lower bracket, then raise the handles to the wall (Photo 2). Mark the upper bracket location, then attach the bracket to the stud.

Buyer's Guide

- **All shelf and ladder bracket materials can be found in home centers and full-service hardware stores. Other products mentioned are listed below.**
- **Shelf support corner brace (also called an L-bracket): 1-in. x 5-in. Stanley corner brace, (800) 622-4393, www.stanleyhardware.com. (Home Depot SKU No. 243078, $2.19).**
- **Bicycle hoist: ProStor PBH-1 Hoist Monster: (800) 783-7725, www.racorinc.com. $25 to $30 plus shipping. Also available at Ace, TrueValue, Target and other stores.**
- **Wheelbarrow holder: Crawford No. WBH, (800) 523-9382. www.lehigh-group.com. $3.97 at The Home Depot; also available at other home centers and many hardware stores.**

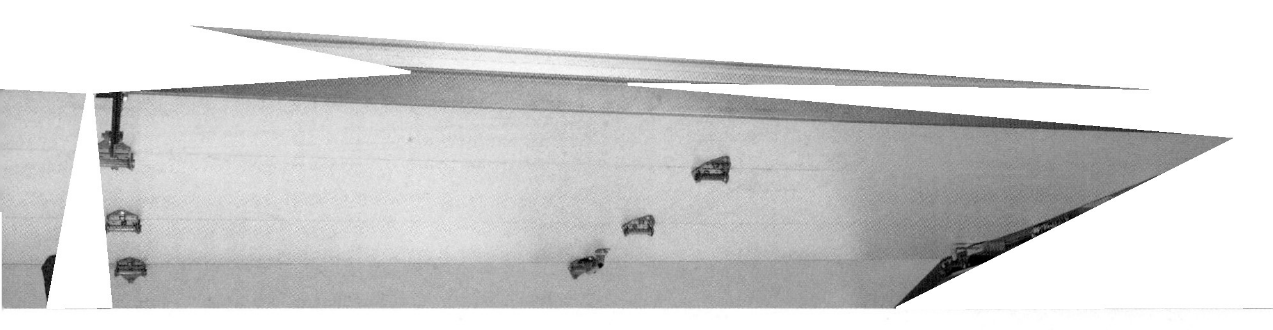

SUSPENDED SHELVING

1 MEASURE from the ceiling to the top of the raised garage door. Subtract 1 in. to determine the height of the side 2x4s.

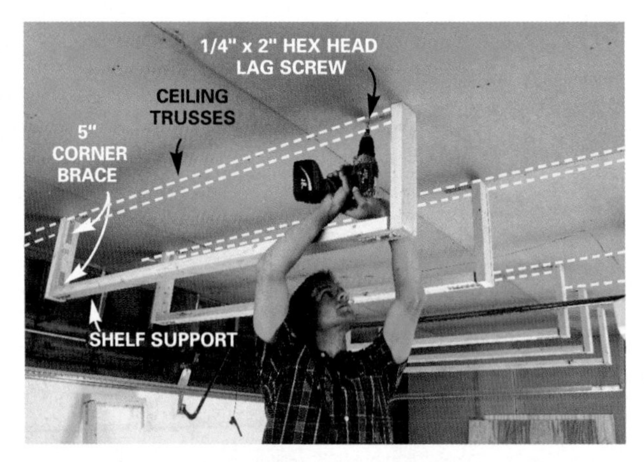

2 BUILD three identical shelf supports, align the side supports, and predrill and lag-screw each into the center of the ceiling trusses/joists.

3 CUT 3/8-in. plywood for the shelf base and attach it to the 2x4 shelf supports with 1-in. wood screws.

Tuck medium and lightweight stuff onto shelves suspended from the ceiling. The shelves are designed to fit into that unused space above the garage doors (you need 16 in. of clearance to fit a shelf and standard 12-1/2 in. high plastic bins). However, you can adjust the shelf height and put them anywhere. The only limitation is weight. We designed this 4 x 6-ft. shelf to hold about 160 lbs., a load that typical ceiling framing can safely support. It's best to save the shelf for "deep storage," using labeled bins with lids, because you'll need a stepladder to reach stuff.

First, find which way the joists run, then plan to hang one shelf support from three adjacent joists (Photo 2). Our joists are 24 in. apart; if yours are spaced at 16 in., skip one intermediate joist. We built ours to hold plastic bins, but if you put loose stuff up there, add 1x4 sides to keep things from falling off.

Assemble the 2x4s as shown (Figure A, p. 257), using 5-in. corner braces ($2 each; see Buyer's Guide) and 1/4-in. x 1-in. hex head lag screws (drill pilot holes first).

Now attach the corner braces on both ends of a shelf support to the center of a joist/truss by drilling pilot holes

One shelf holds all this!

Each shelf holds eight containers 16 in. wide x 24 in. long x 12-1/2 in. high.

and using 1/4-in. x 2-in. hex head lag screws (Photo 2). The only challenge is finding the center of joists through a drywall ceiling (if your ceiling is finished) to attach the shelf supports. Tap a small nail through the drywall until you locate both edges of the joist. Measure to find the center of the adjacent joists, and measure to keep the three supports in alignment with one another. Finish the shelf unit by attaching a 3/8-in. x 4-ft. x 6-ft. plywood floor (Photo 3).

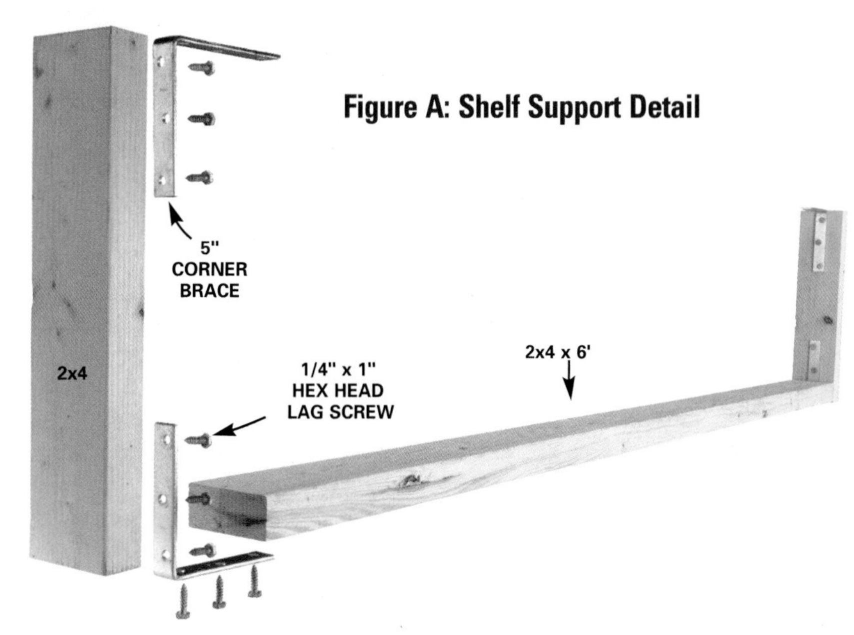

HEAVY-BICYCLE LIFT

ATTACH the lift assembly hardware to the center of the ceiling joists with the screws provided.

Hanging bikes by one or both wheels on bicycle storage hooks is the quickest and cheapest way to get them off the floor and out of the way. But the hooks won't always work if your bike is too heavy to lift easily. Then the best solution is a convenient pulley system that allows you to quickly and easily raise the bike out of the way.

We couldn't design a system much cheaper or better than a purchased system like the Hoist Monster from ProStor (about $30; see Buyer's Guide, p. 255). It can lift up to 100 lbs. with its quality mechanical system of pulleys and hooks, and its dual safety design (locking mechanism and rope tie-down cleat) keeps the bike secure.

Attach the pulley brackets to a ceiling joist with wood screws. Position the hooks the same distance apart as the distance from the handlebar to the seat rear. Choose a location that's convenient yet doesn't interfere with vehicles or people, since the bike will hang down about 4 ft. from the ceiling. If the joists aren't spaced right, lag-screw 2x4s to them, then screw the brackets to the 2x4s.

Mount the safety rope cleat to a garage wall stud, out of a child's reach. Wrap the cord around the cleat to secure the bike.

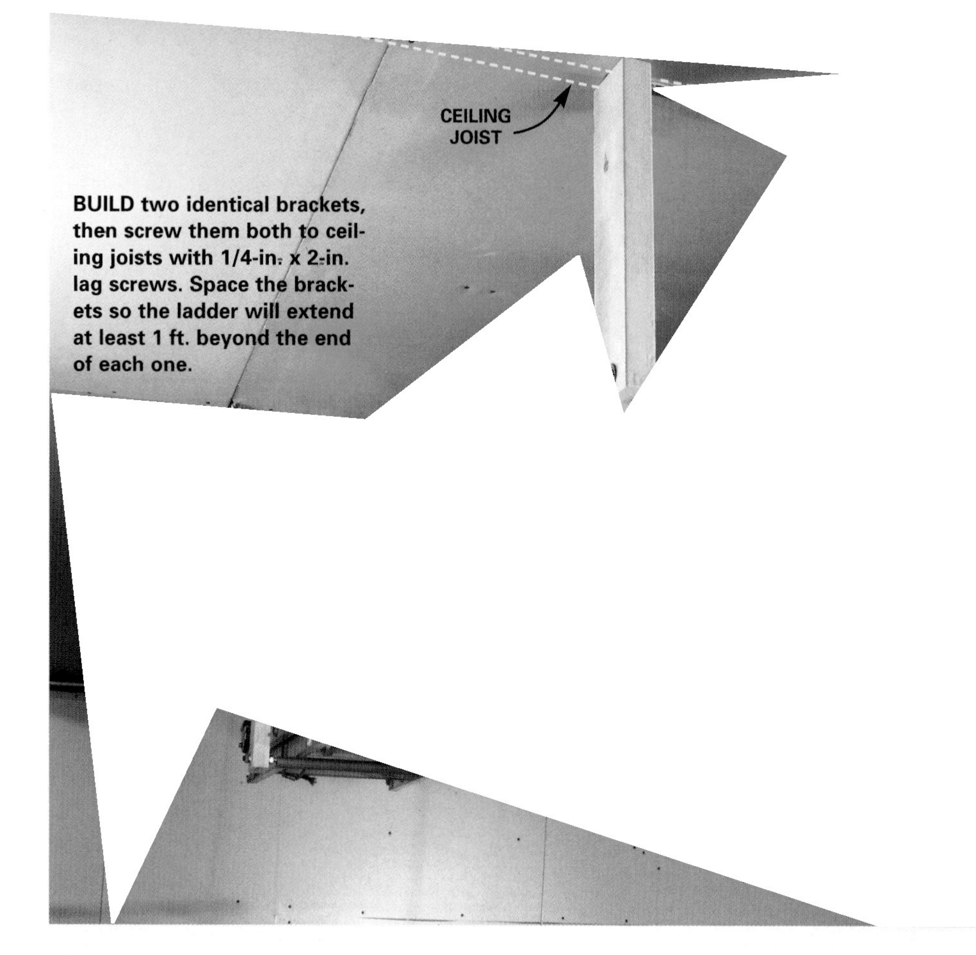

SUSPENDED EXTENSION LADDER

It's always most convenient to hang an extension ladder on brackets on a wall. But unfortunately that wipes out all other storage potential for that wall. To save that valuable wall space, we designed a pair of 2x4 suspended brackets so a ladder can be stored flat along the ceiling.

Simply slide one end of the ladder into one bracket, then lift and slide the other end into the other bracket. Most people will need to stand on something solid to reach the second bracket. The 2x4 bracket sides are 16 in. long with 5-in. corner braces lag-screwed (like the shelf unit) into the top for attachment to the ceiling joist (Figure B).

The bracket base is a 1/2-in. x 24-in. threaded steel rod ($2.75) that extends through 5/8-in. drilled holes on the bracket sides. It's held in place with flat/lock washers and a nut on each side of both 2x4 uprights. A 3/4-in. x 18-in. long piece of PVC conduit pipe surrounds the rod for smooth rolling action when you slide the ladder in and out.

Figure B: Ladder Support Detail

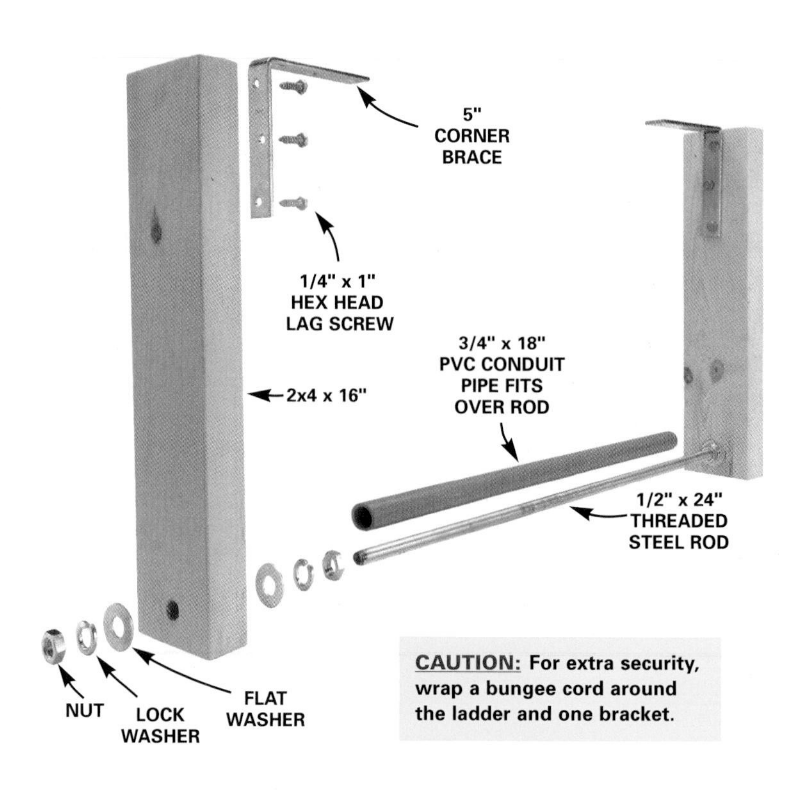

CAUTION: For extra security, wrap a bungee cord around the ladder and one bracket.

from our readers

GARAGE DOOR FOUL LINE

Here's the straight solution for keeping bikes, trikes, garden tools and car bumpers from being squashed by a descending garage door (or keep them from triggering the electric eye). Close the garage door and press down a strip of 2-in. wide masking tape along the inside edge. Lay another strip of tape 1-1/2 in. to the outside of the first. Spray on the line, pull the tape and let dry. Now when you close the door, glance at the line to be sure the door will seal on concrete, not on a tool or the tail of your sleeping cat.

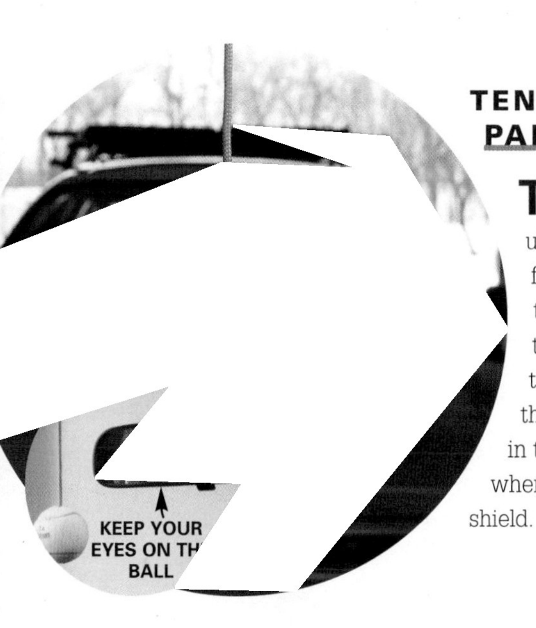

TENNIS BALL PARKING GUIDE

This could be the most popular handy hint ever! For perfect parking every time, thread a string through a tennis ball and hang it from the garage ceiling. Position the ball so your vehicle lands in the center of the garage when the ball touches the windshield.

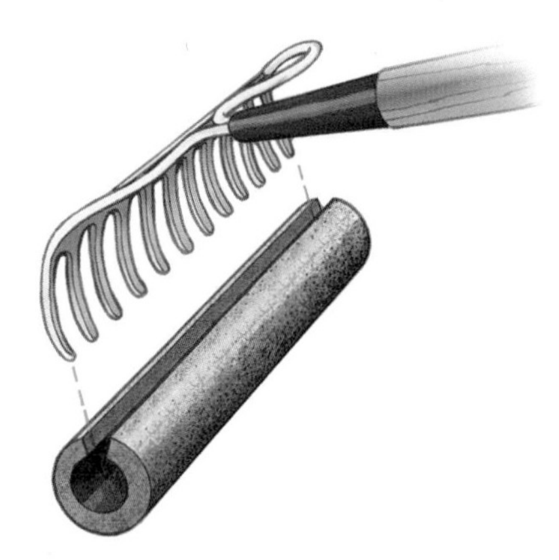

SUPER-FAST FLOOR SQUEEGEE

When you need to round up water on your garage or basement floor, assemble this simple squeegee. Slip a piece of foam pipe insulation over the tines of an ordinary garden rake to push the water to a drain or out the door.

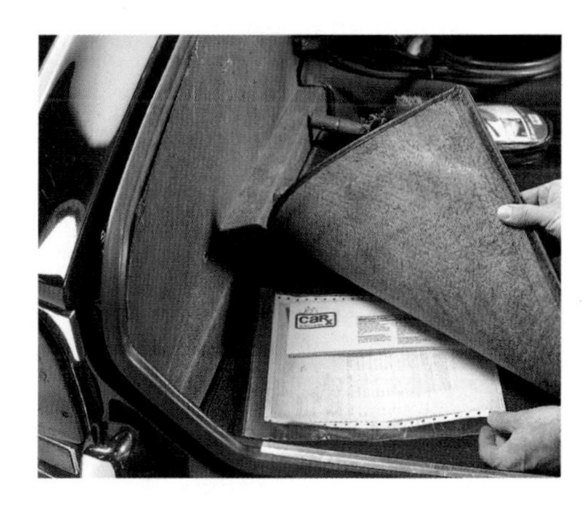

CAR-CARE FILE IN THE TRUNK

Keep your car's maintenance records in the car itself and you'll never have to ransack your house looking for them. Just put them in a locking plastic bag and slip them under the carpet in the trunk.

AUTO
FAST FIXES

by **Bob Lacivita and David Radtke**

EMERGENCY HEATER HOSE REPAIR

You're driving along running just a bit late for an appointment when steam starts belching up through the edges of the hood. Your car has just blown a heater hose and the coolant is vaporizing as it drains onto the hot engine. Well, we can't make you feel any better about what just happened, but we can help you get back on the road in a reasonable amount of time.

If your car is more than 6 years old, no doubt your radiator and heater hoses have seen better days. Next time you're in the auto supply store, pick up a kit containing a heater hose coupling like the one shown and a pair of clamps. The kit costs less than $5 and is a good insurance policy. Just be sure you also carry a flashlight, a pocketknife and a set of screwdrivers (essential tools to always have on board).

Open your hood and let everything cool down

1 DON'T MESS with the radiator cap or anything yet! Don't touch anything until you can do so comfortably. You could get a serious burn. You might have to wait as long as 45 minutes. As the engine cools, look for splits or tears in the hoses. The telltale signs of a blown hose will be coolant splashed over the engine and under the hood. This alone doesn't mean you have a blown hose, however. It could be a faulty thermostat that caused the radiator cap to release. If the cap has a pressure-release flap that's released, your engine may have only overheated, but if the cap is intact and you can see a leak in the heater hose, you'll be able to fix it. Once the engine is cool, remove the radiator cap. Put the cap back on after the fix.

Look for a leak along the length of your heater hose

2 CAREFULLY EXAMINE the hose from the water pump back to the heater core inlet and outlet near the firewall (backside of the engine compartment).

Cut out the bad section of hose

3 THE LEAK may be at a fitting on the water pump or even at the heater core. If this is the case, you won't need to use the coupling; just cut the bad end off the hose, stretch the hose and reclamp it to the fitting. If the leak is along the hose, cut it at the leak and remove the bad section.

NOTE: Hose couplings come in several sizes. Check your hose before buying.

Push the hose firmly onto the coupling

4 APPLY coolant to the coupling as a lubricant. Insert one end and tighten the clamp on it. Then slip the second clamp over the hose and push the other end of the coupling into the hose.

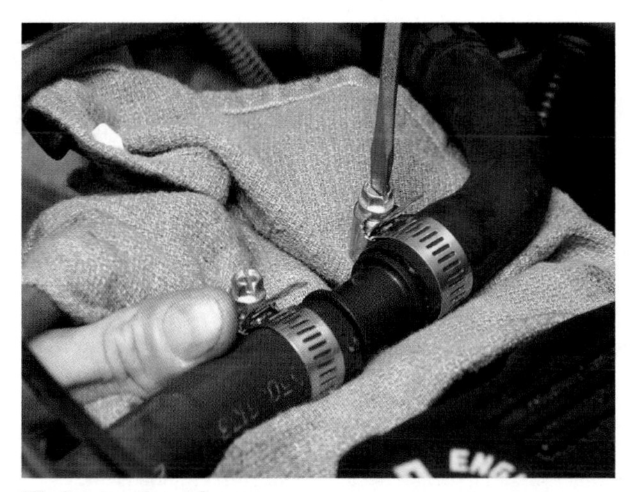

Tighten the clamps

5 MAKE SURE the hose is slipped onto the coupling and tighten both clamps. Don't cowboy the hoses; they may be fragile and in need of replacement. Add water to your reservoir or radiator, or drive (no longer than 10 minutes!) to the nearest place you can get coolant. This fix isn't permanent, so make an appointment to have your hoses and coolant checked.

Handy Hints®

IRONING BOARD BUTLER

Bolt 1/2-in. plywood to the top of an old ironing board for an instant worktable. The height's adjustable, so whether you're standing or kneeling, it'll nose right in to put a catchall surface close at hand. After the job's done, it stores flat against the wall. Customize the top with a 3/4-in. wood border to corral loose parts.

BODY SIDE MOLDING FIX

Maybe you're one of those people driving down the road with your rubber or vinyl side molding flapping in the wind. Well, for less than $15, you can fix this problem once and for all before your $50 molding strip ends up in the back of the highway cleanup crew's truck. At the auto parts store, pick up adhesive remover and molding tape (see Buyer's Guide, p. 263). Then all you'll need is denatured alcohol, a plastic putty knife and clean rags.

1 SATURATE a cotton rag with adhesive remover and clean the old adhesive off the door. Do this in a well-ventilated area, preferably outside on the driveway. Scrape the old adhesive with a plastic putty knife and continue applying remover and wiping until the old adhesive is gone. Then further clean the surface with denatured alcohol to remove residue. Don't use abrasives. What you want is a smooth, blemish-free surface for the mounting tape.

2 THOROUGHLY CLEAN the backside of the molding by saturating it with adhesive remover and rubbing and scraping the old adhesive away. This can be a stubborn job, but take your time and stick with it. When the surface is free of adhesive, wipe it with a clean cloth dampened with denatured alcohol.

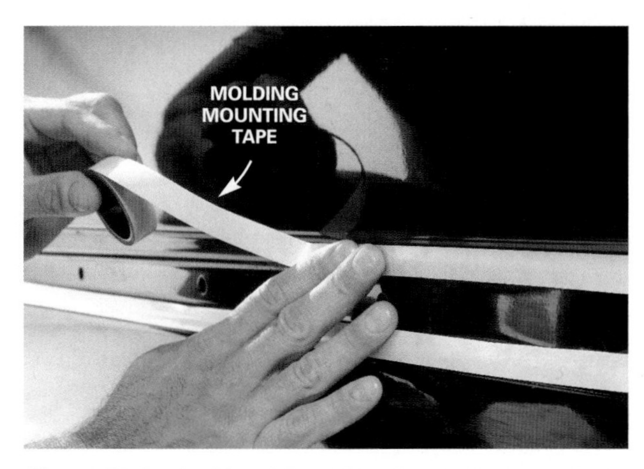

3 APPLY the double-stick molding tape to the areas that will contact the molding. Press the tape firmly along the length. For wide trim, use two strips as shown.

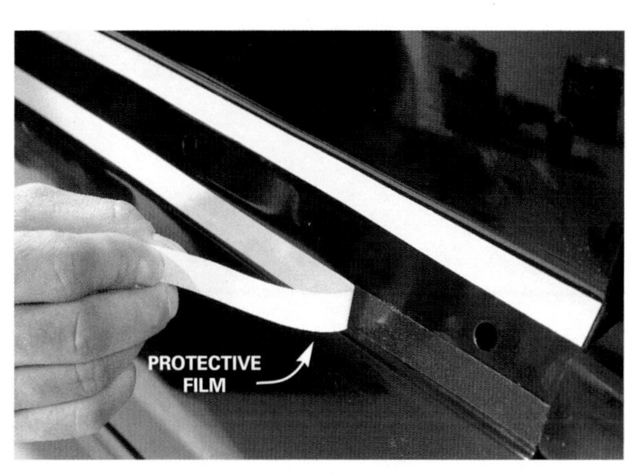

4 PEEL the protective film off the tape to expose the sticky surface. Be careful not to touch it with your fingers or let any debris get on the tape.

5 CAREFULLY POSITION the molding at one end, and then slowly push it onto the tape. The tape grabs firmly, so take your time. Once the molding is in place, push it firmly with a rag. Use a back-and-forth motion across the molding to bond the entire length.

Buyer's Guide

- You can find the adhesive remover and molding tape at most auto parts stores. You can also find them on-line at www.midwayautosupply.com. Or call (866) 643-9291.
- Adhesive remover, No. MMM-03607. $7.21.
- Adhesive molding tape, No. MMM-03609. $4.

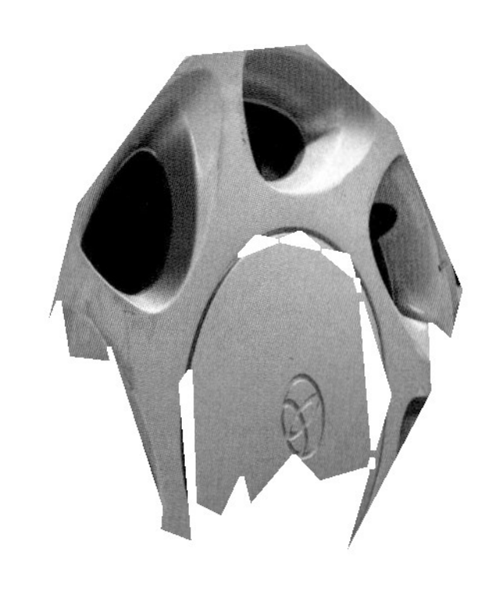

FLAT TIRE TIPS AND HINTS

Getting a flat tire is always a bummer, but the hassle is compounded when the lug nuts won't turn, the car's on a slope or the hubcap won't come loose. The owner's manual won't help here. The following special tools and techniques will solve most common complications and quickly and safely get you back on your way.

Block the opposite wheel before jacking

Make a wheel chock out of a scrap piece of 4x4, cut with a 45-degree angle on it. Then store it in your trunk and use it to keep your vehicle from rolling when you jack it up. Always use it on the wheel opposite the one you're changing. Analyze the lay of the land. If the car is pointing downhill, you may have to block the front side of the opposite wheel instead of the back side.

Use leverage to pop off stubborn wheel covers

When you're trying to remove stubborn wheel covers, grab a tool handle as shown or use a block of wood as a fulcrum to get some leverage. To get it free, you'll need to work your way around as if you were opening a paint can.

Lift the wheel off—don't jerk it from the rotor or drum

Remember, your vehicle is on a jack and you're right next to it. If the wheel sticks to the drum or rotor, give a sharp jab near the outer edge of the tire with the heel of your hand. Pull the wheel and tire free from the lugs and set it behind your vehicle. Lift the spare onto the lugs and snug it with your wrench. Lower the jack so the spare is resting firmly on the ground.

Tighten the lugs in an opposite pattern

If you have five lug nuts, choose a star pattern. Get the lugs good and tight with your wrench. Pick up your tools, flat tire, hubcap and wheel chock. Look out for traffic and head home.

Buy a telescoping lug wrench

I'm sure the folks who designed my short factory lug wrench never tried to change a tire that's gone through years of road salt and was torqued down to about 100 ft.-lbs. by an overzealous mechanic. Get some mechanical advantage with this nifty telescoping lug wrench (see the Buyer's Guide, right). Loosen each lug nut (lefty loosey, righty tighty) one-half turn only! Some like to lift up on the wrench from the other side, but if your back is like mine, you'll push down.

And remember:

Carry a roadside flare

Get a reflector or a roadside flare and stick it in the spare tire well so next time you'll be prepared. When you get a flat or any roadside emergency, set up the reflector or flare 20 ft. behind the vehicle to warn oncoming motorists. I'm sure you've heard this advice before, but it can save your life on a dark, winding road.

Don't make your spare a permanent replacement

Remember that you no longer have a spare. Make an appointment to get the tire fixed. Most small spares are rated for less than 50 miles.

Check your spare regularly

Check your spare regularly to make sure it has enough air pressure to get you back on the road when you get a flat. The only reminder that seems to work for me is that every time I change the oil, I check the pressure of the spare tire. It's a simple pairing that seems to work.

Buyer's Guide

If you can't get a telescoping lug wrench at your local auto store, go to www.tirerack.com (or call 888-541-1777) to order the Gorilla wrench for $13.99. It's also available from www.stylinconcepts.com (for $14.95) or by calling (800) 586-9713.

Ask Handyman™

FORCED-AIR HEATER

HEATING A GARAGE

To keep from going stir crazy this winter, I plan to heat my attached garage so I can work on various projects. I plan to run natural gas from the house to the garage. What's the best way to heat my two-car garage?

There are two types of natural gas heaters to consider: a forced-air garage heater (shown above) that blows warm air like a conventional furnace, and a "low-intensity" infrared tube heater **(top photo, opposite page)** that radiates heat. (Avoid "high-intensity" infrared heaters—which visibly glow red—because most aren't approved for residential use.)

Both will burn natural gas (your most economical choice) or LP gas, and both are available in several sizes, so you can choose the one that best heats your space. As you can see, both require an electrical hook-up, and both require venting to the outside as well. But the similarities of the two types end there (see chart).

We'll assume your garage walls and ceiling are already insulated (minimum of 4 in. thick in the walls, 6 in. thick in the ceiling); otherwise you'll waste energy and money. The basic differences are how the heaters perform and how they feel in terms of comfort.

Since you plan to work on projects in the garage, presumably with wood, an infrared heater may work better because it doesn't raise dust or keep dust airborne. A forced-air heater will stir up sawdust which is a big problem when your painting or staining.

You won't feel warm as quickly with an infrared heater because it heats objects first, then the air.However, once your concrete floor warms, you'll feel more comfortable because infrared heat is more uniform. But you must keep all objects 3 to 4 ft. away or they'll overheat—and so will you. With forced-air heat, the air is warmer at the ceiling and cooler at your feet. And a forced-air heater will take longer to reheat the space after the garage door has been opened and shut.

Another big difference is the initial cost. Most forced-air units cost half as much as low-intensity infrared tube heaters. We paid $611 (not including the vent kit and thermostat) for the 60,000-Btu Modine Hot Dawg forced-air unit, and $995 (including the vent kit) for the 30,000-Btu Caribe infrared unit shown. However, it's usually less expensive to run the infrared unit, so the cost difference will decrease with frequent use. Check with the manufacturers or a local heating pro for a more exact estimate.

Installation is markedly different too. Infrared heaters must be installed a minimum of 7 ft. above the floor, and must hang down a minimum of 4 in. from the ceiling (check the manufacturer's instructions, as these measurements vary with the size of the heater). It's critical that you make sure objects below are not too close. The 30,000 Btu unit shown requires a minimum 3-ft. distance from heater to objects below. Most infrared heaters are installed at the back of a garage pointed toward the garage door, then aimed downward at a 45-degree angle. They can also be installed between car bays if the garage door opener rail allows and you don't have a tall vehicle.

With a forced-air heater, the installation details aren't as exacting. Most are placed in a corner, near a gas line and an electrical outlet (needed to power the blower). The instructions will indicate the exact spacing required between the unit and the sidewalls or ceiling.

How many Btu you need depends on variables such as the garage size, your climate zone and the temperature you want to work in. A basic rule of thumb for forced-air heaters is 45,000 Btu to heat a two- to 2-1/2 car garage, and 60,000 for a three-car garage. The makers of low-intensity infrared tube heaters say that 30,000 Btu can heat a two- to 2-1/2 car garage, and suggest 50,000 for a three-car garage. Check with a local heating pro or the heater manufacturer for a specific recommendation to fit your needs.

Both heater types need to be vented if powered by natural gas or LP gas. Check the instructions for specific vent pipe sizes and lengths (some models include a vent kit, or you can purchase components separately). Most can be routed either through sidewalls or through the attic and roof.

One other option, if venting or gas-powered heat isn't what you want, is an electric infrared heater. Granted, electric heat may cost you more to run, but check with your local electrical utility to see if it offers any type of rebate or off-peak rates that would make this option more cost efficient.

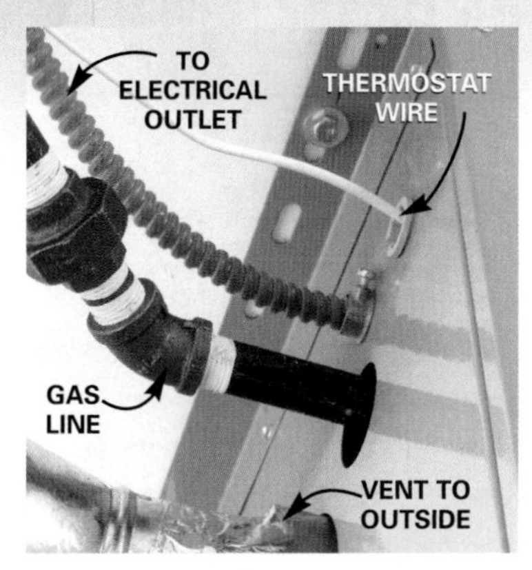

Forced-air heater connections (rear)

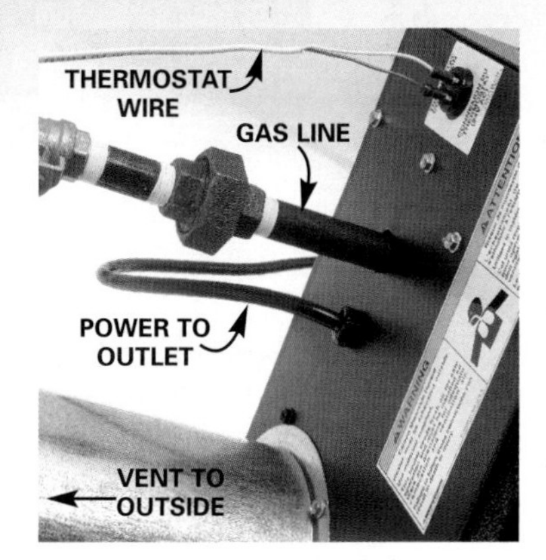

Infrared heater connections (rear)

Buyer's Guide

- **Hot Dawg model HD60 from Modine Mfg., (800) 828-4328 (to locate dealer).**
- **Caribe model CGTH-30, Roberts Gordon, (800) 828-7450 (to locate dealer).**

Forced-air heater:

PROS

- **Less expensive initial cost (50 percent less than comparable infrared heater)**

CONS

- **Noisy**
- **Loses heat quickly if garage door is opened (longer recovery time)**
- **Heat rises and stratifies (the air is warmer at ceiling, cooler near floor), but you won't notice it with a 7- or 8-ft. ceiling**
- **Air movement tends to blow airborne dust around (woodworkers will have to shut down unit before staining and finishing projects)**

Low-intensity infrared tube heater:

PROS

- **Little noise**
- **No air movement (dust settles)**
- **Lower cost to operate**
- **More uniform heat distribution (no stratification)**
- **Quicker heat recovery if door is opened/closed (floor and objects retain heat)**

CONS

- **Higher initial cost (50 percent more than forced-air)**
- **Correct location of heater is critical (minimum 7 ft. from floor, 3 ft. from objects). Adequate headroom is also critical, because you can overheat if you're working near the unit.**

Great Goofs™

Bungee shrub

The shrubs along the front of our house were getting overgrown and needed a good pruning. After a couple of hours of aggressive shearing, the shrubs looked worse than ever, so I decided to pull them out and get new ones. After digging around the trunks to free the roots, I tied a heavy rope to the base of one of the shrubs and fastened the other end of the rope to the back of my 4x4 pickup. I slowly drove the pickup forward to tighten the rope and then accelerated quickly, hoping to jerk the bush free of the soil. Well, it worked. What I didn't expect was the rubber-band effect of the nylon rope. It catapulted the bush right through the back window of my truck. Sitting in the cab with glass strewn all over the interior, I regretfully remembered that my dad always used a heavy chain for this task!

Auto accident

A good friend of mine decided it was time to clean up the garage and get rid of all those boxes on the floor so he could get the car in. He installed a big shelf just high enough so he could get the front end of his wife's car under it. He picked up some plastic anchors, screws and brackets at the hardware store and got to work anchoring the brackets into the plaster walls. When the shelf was hung, he loaded it up with all the boxes and a bunch of clay pots. Soon after he pulled the car in, there was a loud crash. His wife came out to see all the contents of the shelf on top of her shiny hood. Gerald doesn't do shelves anymore.

Pretty in pink?

To spruce up the house and give it some curb appeal, we decided to add red shutters around the windows. Painting shutters with a brush can be slow, so we decided to rent a paint sprayer and paint them assembly-line style in the garage. We laid down dropcloths, opened the doors and windows for ventilation and sprayed on primer and two coats of paint. After finishing up for the day, I closed the overhead garage door and saw that our nice white door was now a uniform pink! The overspray from the sprayer had risen and settled on top of the door while it was open for ventilation. The next day was taken by still another painting project—the garage door!

Handy Hints® for garage storage

HEAVYWEIGHT CORD AND TOOL HANGER

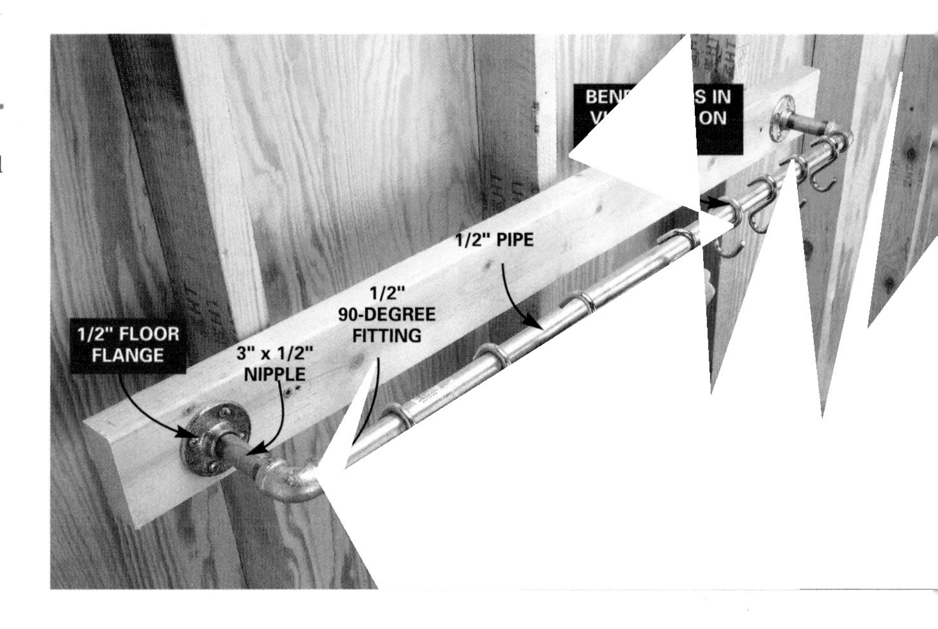

Store a load of cords, air hoses, ropes and tools on this rugged rack. To build one, you'll need:

- One 3- or 4-ft. x 1/2-in. iron pipe threaded on both ends
- Two 3-in. x 1/2-in. pipe nipples
- Two 1/2-in. 90-degree pipe fittings
- Two 1/2-in. floor flanges
- Several 3-in. S-hooks
- Cable Clamps ($25 for a 20-pack of medium-size clamps at home centers; www.cableclamp.com; 727-528-1000). Or you can just use leftover strips of plastic-sheathed electrical cable.

Assemble the pipe, elbows, nipples and floor flanges, then screw through the flanges to a horizontal 2x4 set at shoulder height on a shop wall. Attach your S-hooks. If yours don't fit, clamp the hooks in a vise and bend open one end just enough to fit on the pipe after assembly. Now snap Cable Clamps on all your coils and hang 'em from the S-hooks.

GARAGE-WALL TOOL HOLDER

If you have lots of rakes, shovels, brooms and garden tools cluttering your garage, but not a lot of wall to hang them on, try this. Cut two 16 x 16-in. pieces from 1/2-in. plywood and screw them to a wall stud at a slight upward angle. Then slide in your tools.

HOOK AND CHAIN CORD HANGER

A length of chain and a wall-mounted coat hook provide a secure hangout for bulky electrical cords, ropes or other cumbersome coils. Hang one end of the chain on the lower hook, then loop the chain around the coiled cord and attach the other end of the chain to the upper hook.

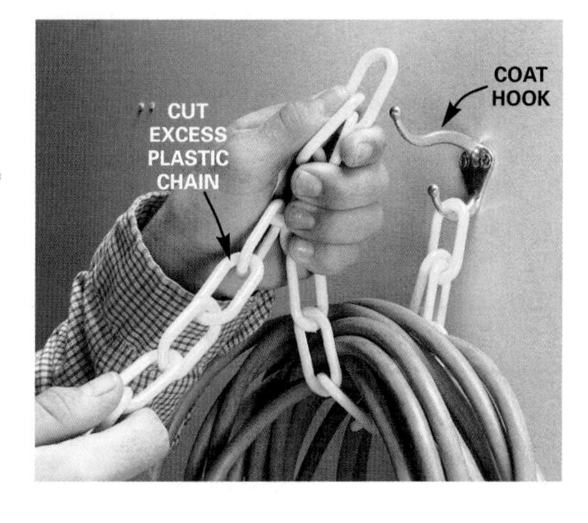

Handy Hints® for garage storage

HANG-IT-ALL HOOKS

Those plastic hooks that plumbers use to support pipes make convenient hangers for just about anything. They're strong, cheap (25¢ to $1 each) and come in a range of sizes. Find them in the plumbing aisle at home centers and hardware stores.

WHEELBARROW RACK

Hang your wheelbarrow on the garage wall to free up floor space. Center a 2-ft. 1x4 across two studs, 2 ft. above the floor. Tack it into place, then drive 3-in. screws through metal mending plates and the 1x4, into the studs. Leave about 3/4 in. of the plate sticking above the 1x4 to catch the rim. Rest the wheelbarrow on the 1x4 as shown, and mark the studs 1 in. above the wheelbarrow bucket. Drill pilot holes and screw ceiling hooks into the studs. Twist the hooks so they catch on the wheelbarrow lip and hold it in place.

BOTTOM BRACKET

EASY STORAGE RACK

Use this storage rack for lumber and other long stuff. Simply drill a line of 3/4-in. holes about 1-1/2 in. deep in adjacent studs, angling the holes slightly downward. Then insert 15-in. long sections of 1/2-in. galvanized pipe. Keep the lowest pipes at least 6 ft. above the floor so you won't crack your skull on them.

UNDER-JOIST SHELF

Create extra storage space by screwing wire closet shelving to joists in your garage or basement. Wire shelving is see-through, so you can easily tell what's up there. Depending on the width, wire shelves cost from $1 to $3 per foot at home centers.

HARDWARE OIL-GANIZER

Save up 12 plastic oil quart bottles, cut away one side with a utility knife, scrub out the oil residue and load them with nails and screws. Build a carrying case from scrap 1/2-in. and 1/4-in. plywood. Then label the bottle caps and slide in the bottles. Add a handle and tote it to your next project.

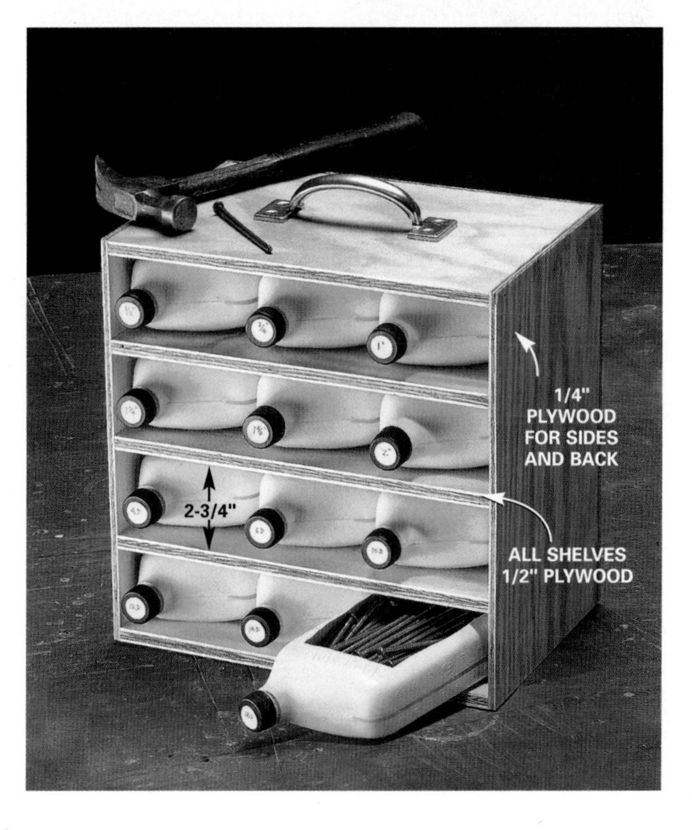

Handy Hints® Hall of Fame

Handy Hints has been the most popular department in The Family Handyman magazine since it was launched in 1951. It's the way our ingenious readers show their ingenious solutions to everyday problems. Here are the best of the best:

BEST HANDY HINT FOR **RETIRED BOWLERS**

STRIKING TIP FOR STORING CIRCULAR SAWS

An old bowling-ball bag makes a great portable home for your circular saw. The saw slides in easily and it's easy to lug around. There's plenty of extra room for spare blades, a rip guide and blade-changing wrenches, too. Keep your eyes peeled for yard and garage sale bargains.

BEST HANDY HINT FOR **MEASURING IN A PINCH**

THE ONE-DOLLAR TAPE MEASURE

The next time you need to measure a piece of furniture, some building materials or the distance from point A to point B, but find yourself without a tape measure, reach for your billfold. A dollar bill is about 6-1/8 in. long. Fold it in half or thirds for shorter measurements.

BEST HANDY HINT FOR **YARD CLEANUP**

DIVE INTO YOUR YARD WORK

Don't banish that leaky plastic wading pool to the trash. Put it to work as a mega-container for cleaningup and hauling leaves, brush and litter. Bore small holes through the side and a block of wood as shown, then slide a rope through both holes and haul away.

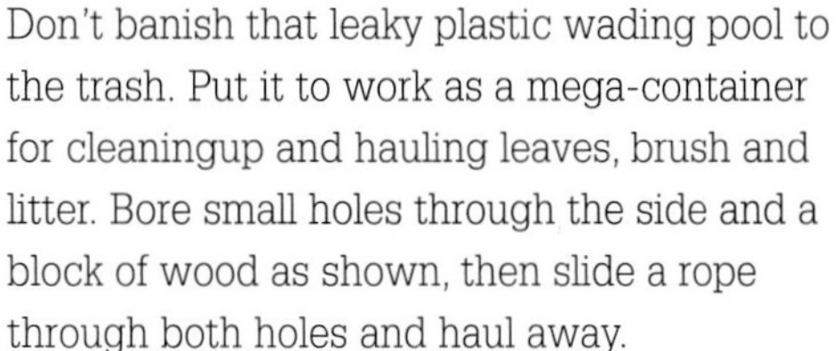

Got your own Handy Hint?
See how your hint can be worth $100 at
www.familyhandyman.com

BEST HANDY HINT FOR **SAVING SPACE**

CREATE SPACE WITH A SHOP VACUUM

Those seldom-used, billowy comforters, pillows and blankets take up lots of storage space in your closet. To save space, toss those puffy items into heavy-duty plastic bags, at least 2 mil thick, and then use your shop vacuum to remove as much air as possible before tying off the bag. To keep the items fresh, toss in a fabric-softener sheet before you use the vacuum.

BEST HANDY HINT FOR **HOME SAFETY**

BURGLAR BUSTER

It doesn't take much to jimmy and slide open a sliding glass door, unless the culprit encounters this sturdy lock. Cut a 2x3 to fit between the edge of the sliding panel and door frame, then cut and hinge a small section and add a handle. When you need the door secured in the closed position, leave it fully extended. When you need to open it a bit, flip the short block back.

BEST HANDY HINT FOR **USING UP OLD CDs**

A SIMPLE SPOTLIGHT

Like a surgeon using one of those Dr. Kildare–type silver forehead discs, you can use a CD to look into tight places—like inside of appliances, wall cavities or your kid's sore throat. Just peer through the little hole in the middle while you light up the area by reflecting light off the silvery surface.

SECOND BEST HANDY HINT FOR **USING UP OLD CDs**

DIGITAL SCARECROWS

If you've got piles of old, unusable or promotional CDs, here's a tip that's for the birds. Drill a hole in the edge of each disc, thread some dental floss or wire through it and hang them from your fruit trees or tall plant stakes. The silvery, flashy surface will scare the birds away.

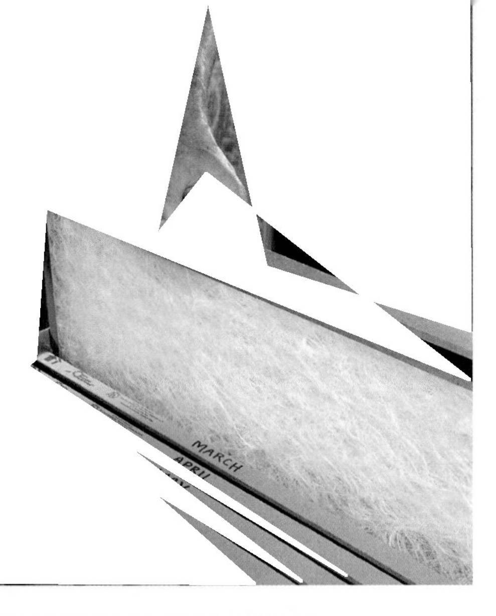

BEST HANDY HINT FOR **HOME MAINTENANCE**

FURNACE FILTER REMINDER

Whenever you buy a new box of furnace filters, write the months of the year on the individual filters. That way, you'll always know when you last changed the filter.

BEST HANDY HINT FOR **IMPERSONATING THE GOVERNOR OF A LARGE WESTERN STATE**

SUPER-DUPER WINDOW WASHER

If you'd just as soon terminate having to climb ladders for your window washing chores, try this. Load a super soaker with water, squirt the windows, and then scrub and squeegee them clean. NEVER put bleach or soap in the water shooter; you never know who might use it next.

BEST HANDY HINT FOR **PEOPLE WHO SELL STUFF ON EBAY**

ULTRA-SAFE PACKING

If you're sending a fragile item, protect it with expanding foam sealant. Double wrap the item in plastic bags, and then cover the bottom of the box with 2 to 3 in. of foam. After the foam has expanded and begun to harden, nestle the item into the box. Cover the item and sides of box with more plastic, then partially fill the box with more foam and let it set overnight. If the foam expands beyond the top of the box, cut away the excess with a knife.

BEST HANDY HINT FOR **PEOPLE WHO LOVE MONSTER TRUCK RALLIES**

SOUPED-UP NONSLIP MOWER TREAD

You can retread old, worn mower tires with a knobby bicycle tire to prolong their life or for extra traction on hilly terrain. Cut four strips long enough to wrap around your tires. Remove the sidewall with a scissors and secure the new tread every 2 in. with a pair of 1-in. sheet-metal screws.

BEST HANDY HINT FOR **GETTING YOU OUT OF A JAM**

NARROW TILE SNAPPING JIG

If you have trouble making the cut when you need narrow pieces of tile, make this simple jig. Cut two 12-in. pieces from a 1x6, and then sandwich a piece of wood slightly thicker than the tile between them. Score the tile, and then slide it into the jig so the line falls on the edge of the 1x6s. Clamp the jig down and apply pressure to the tile until it snaps.

BEST HANDY HINT FOR **VERTICALLY CHALLENGED DIYERS**

A LONG HELPING HAND

If you need a really long screwdriver or drill bit, try this simple trick: Buy a length of 5/16-in. threaded rod and a 5/16-in. coupling nut from the hardware store. Pound the hex end of a bit driver into the coupling nut, and then screw the coupling nut onto the end of the threaded rod. Chuck the rod into your drill, stick a screw bit (or a hex-drive drill bit) into the driver and go to work.

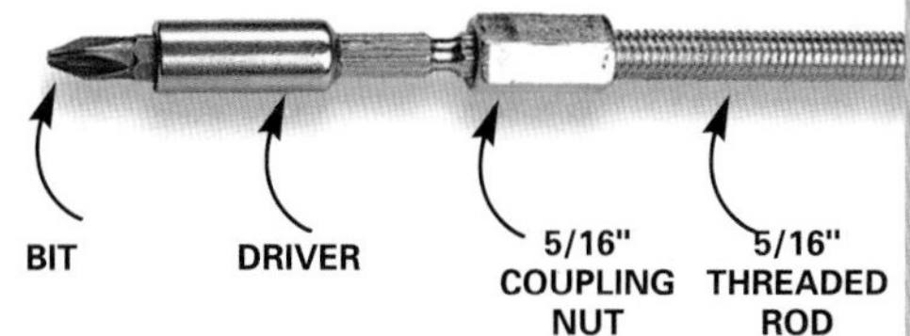

BEST HANDY HINT FOR **MARTHA STEWART WANNABES**

MICROWAVE CLEANER

It's easy to clean baked-on food and spills from your microwave. Partially fill a measuring or coffee cup with water and add a slice of lemon. Boil the water for a minute, and then leave the door closed and let the steam loosen the mess. After 10 minutes, open the door and wipe away the grime.

BEST HANDY HINT FOR **PAINT CLEANUP**

A KINDER, GENTLER HAND CLEANER

You can clean oil-based paint or stain off your hands (or out of your hair) with vegetable oil. Pour a small amount of oil on the area while the paint is still wet and rub away. It's safer, gentler and less stinky than mineral spirits.

BEST HANDY HINT FOR **WORKING ALONE**

SOLO PLYWOOD CARRIER

To make carrying those cumbersome 4x8 ft. sheets of plywood easier, make this sling from a towel and a tie-down strap. Set the plywood on its long edge and attach one tie-down hook on each end. Adjust the length, then wrap a towel around the middle of the strap and loop it over your shoulder. Use your free arm to steady the plywood as you carry it.

5 SIMPLE "ONE-HOUR" GIFTS

CHINESE CHECKERS

This classic doesn't take long to make and you'll never have to change the batteries!

What it takes: A 17-in. x 21-in. piece of plywood or wood panel, a 1/2-in.-dia. countersink bit, a ruler, and sandpaper or router.

Here's how:

1. Glue boards together (or buy plywood or an already-glued-together panel) and cut it into a 17 in. x 21-in. panel. (Eventually it gets cut to 17 in. square, but the extra length makes it easier to center the game design.)

2. Use a pencil and ruler to mark a center line, then lay out two intersecting, equal-sided triangles with 12-in. sides, as shown in **photo 1.**

3. Mark off 1-in. spaces along each side of the triangles and draw parallel lines inside the triangles to mark centers for the marble holes.

4. Cut the panel into a 17-in. square, and then bevel the top edges with a router or sandpaper.

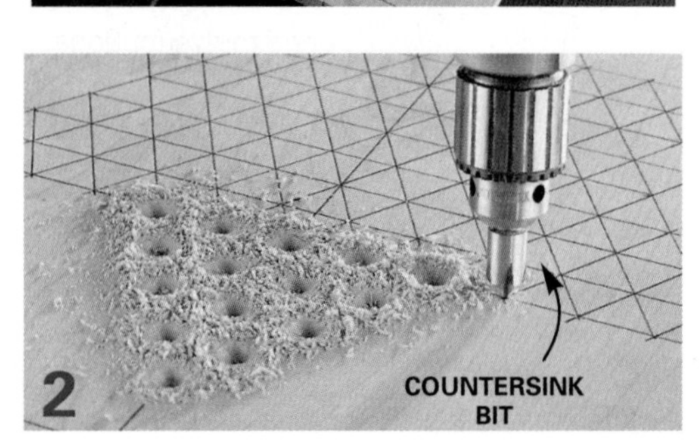

5. Drill the marble holes with a 1/2-in.-dia. countersink bit (**Photo 2**).

6. Sand, finish with Danish oil, add marbles and it's ready to wrap.

PERSONAL STEPPINGSTONES

If you're in search of a unique gift for a yard-and-garden lover, make some of these custom concrete stepping-stones. The key is to keep the shapes simple, since small detailed edges tend to break off when you remove the forms or walk on them. The project only takes one-hour and costs less than $20.

What it takes: One sheet of 2-in. x 4-ft. x 8-ft. rigid polystyrene insulation, bagged cement, concrete dye (optional), a jigsaw, and a concrete edging trowel.

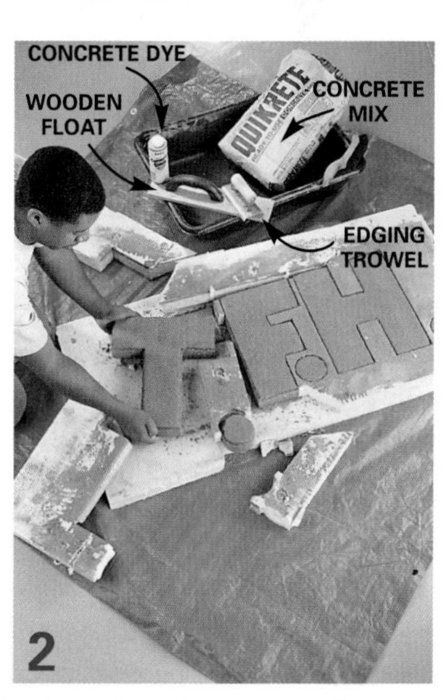

Here's how:

1. Mark out and cut the desired shape in the polystyrene with a jigsaw (**Photo 1**), then place the form on a flat, plastic-covered surface.
2. Mix the concrete mix (adding dye concentrate if you want color), and then fill the forms.
3. While it's wet, slightly round the edges of the concrete with a 1/2-in. edging trowel, and then run a fine bristle broom across the surface to provide texture and hide minor imperfections.
4. After the concrete has dried for a few days, remove the form (**Photo 2**). Since the form isn't reusable, it's easiest to just break it away.
5. Install the steppingstones on a 2-in. bed of sand to support and level them.

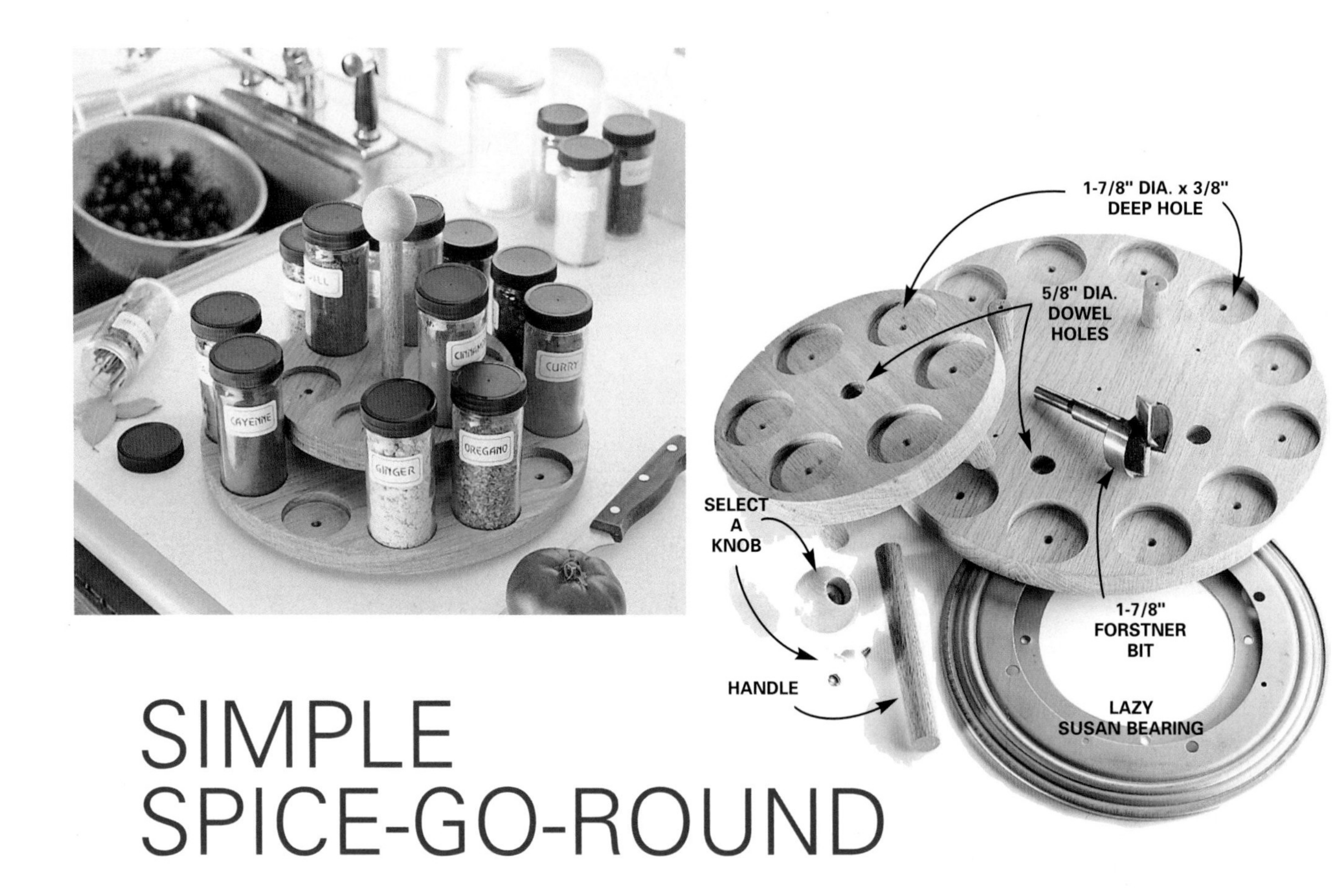

SIMPLE SPICE-GO-ROUND

This spinning spice rack is a great gift for those who love to cook. It keeps 18 spices organized and easy to locate and grab. It's a project easily tackled by someone with intermediate woodworking skills, but it's a good "step up" project for beginners too. The completed rack can be stored on the counter or in a wall cabinet.

What it takes: An 11-1/2 and a 7-1/4-in. dia. wood disc, lazy Susan hardware, 5/8-in. dowel, dowel centers, a 1-7/8-in. Forstner bit and 5/8-in. spade or brad point bit, a drill press, and a wood ball or knob.

Here's how:

1. With a pencil and protractor, divide the larger disc into 30-degree wedges; you'll wind up with 12 center lines.

2. Center and trace the smaller disc on top of the larger disc. Then drill 3/8-in.-deep holes with the Forstner bit and drill press, spacing them between the large disc's outer edge and the just-traced circle.

3. Divide the smaller disc into 60-degree wedges, and then drill six more 3/8-in.-deep holes with the 1-7/8-in.-dia. Forstner bit.

4. Drill four 5/8-in.-dia. holes, 1/2 in. deep in the large disc, just inside the traced circle. Then use dowel centers to transfer marks to the underside of the small disc. Drill those holes 1/2 in. deep and secure the two discs together using glue and 1-5/8-in.-long dowels.

5. Drill the 5/8-in. hole for the handle, then glue and insert a 5-1/4 in. length of dowel. Add a wood or ceramic knob.

6. Apply a finish, and then center and screw the lazy Susan bearing under the large disc.

TRIVET GIFT

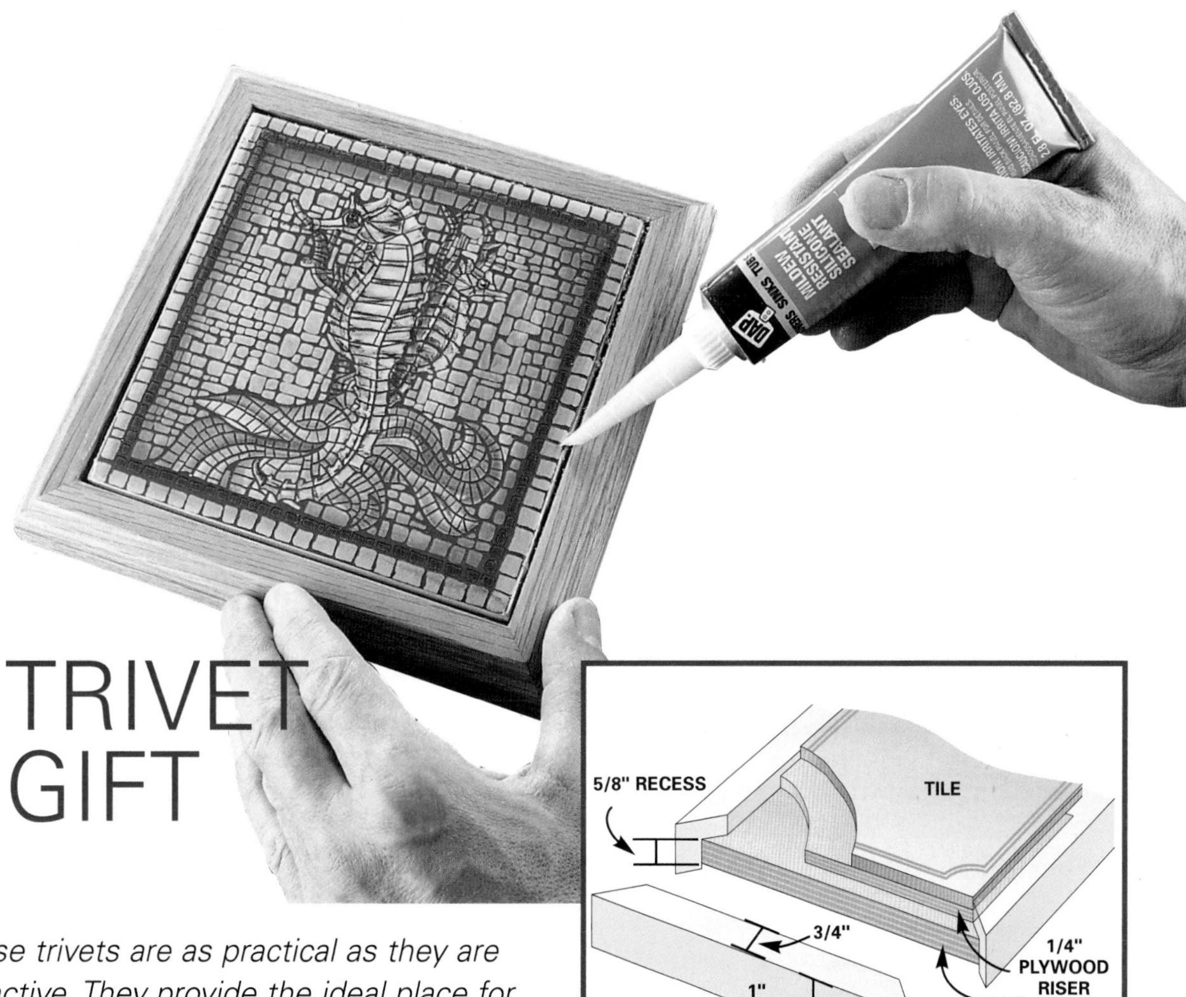

These trivets are as practical as they are attractive. They provide the ideal place for setting those piping hot casseroles and dishes, and when they're not in use they provide an attractive tabletop or countertop decoration.

What it takes: 6- or 8-in. tiles, 1-in. x 3/4-in. wood strips for frame, 1/2- and 1/4-in. plywood, a router, and silicone sealant.

Here's how:

1. Cut four frame pieces with 45-degree miters across the 3/4-in. width, so the finished trivet will be 1 in. high. The final inside dimensions should be about 1/8 in. larger than the actual tile.
2. Glue the frame together using wood glue and clamps or masking tape.
3. Use a handheld router to rout a 5/8-in.-deep recess on the inside edge of the bottom. You can also rout a decorative profile on the outer edge of the top side.
4. Sand and apply a finish.
5. Cut the 1/2-in. plywood "floor" for your tile to rest on and glue it into the recess on the bottom.
6. Cut the 1/4-in. plywood riser to size and glue it to the top of the "floor." Run a crisscross bead of silicone on the riser, and then set and center the tile. Apply a bead of clear silicone to seal the gap between the outer edge of the tile and the frame.

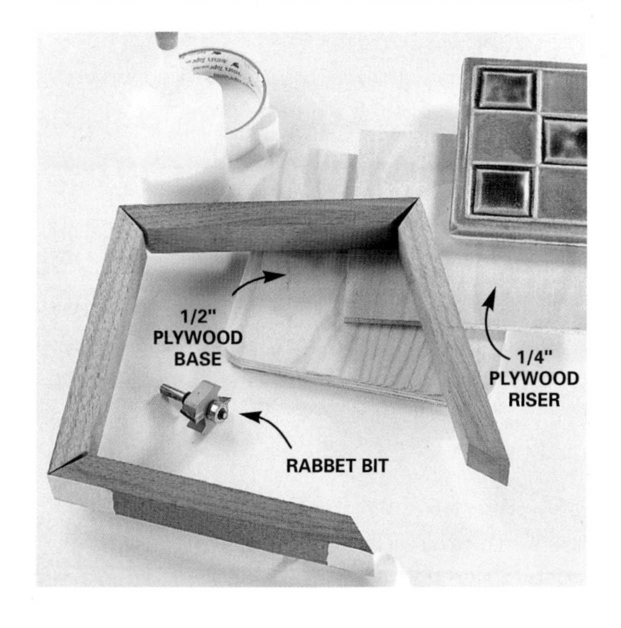

SWEDISH BOOT SCRAPER

Those who like to garden, hike or work outside are bound to pick up a little of Mother Nature's finest while they're walking about. This Swedish boot scraper will help keep that mess outside where it belongs. And when the scraper gets too dirty, just hose it off, let it air-dry and put it right back in place again.

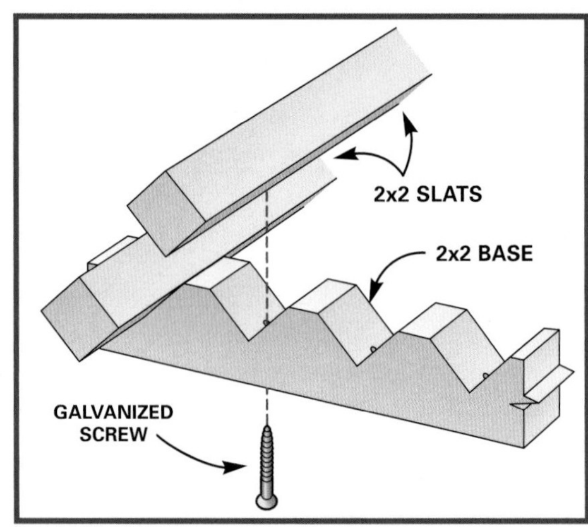

What it takes: A circular saw, 2x2s, 1-5/8-in. galvanized all-purpose screws and a drill.

Here's how:

1. Create the base pieces by placing two 18- to 24-in. 2x2s side by side, and mark the location of the Vs that will hold the cross slats. You can make the spacing as close or as far apart as you want. The top of each V should be about 1-1/2 in. wide.

2. Set your circular saw to cut about 7/8 in. deep at a 45-degree angle. Keeping the base pieces side by side, cut both legs of the Vs. Little triangles of wood should separate cleanly from the base pieces.

3. Cut the correct number of 2x2 slats to the desired length. These can be anywhere from 24 to 32 in. long.

4. Predrill holes, and then attach the slats from underneath using 1-5/8-in. galvanized screws.

15 Amazing PVC Pipe Tips and Tricks

PVC pipe is cheap, readily available and easy to work with. In other words—next to duct tape—it's one of the most versatile materials around. Here are a few ideas:

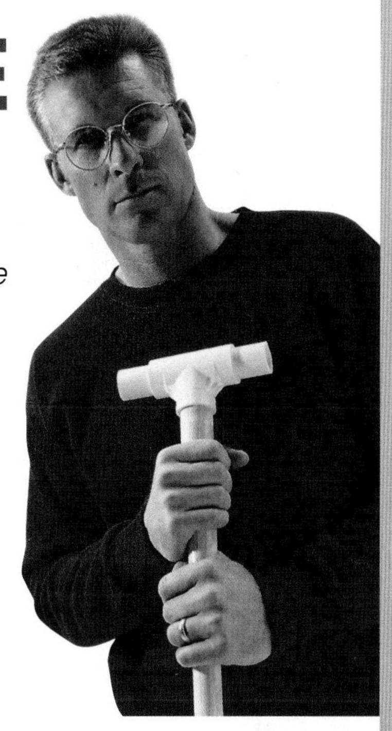

PVC Shovel Handle

Need a little more leverage while shoveling? Add this simple PVC grip to the end of a shovel to increase gripping power. You can install it on shovels that never had a handle, or use it to replace a broken handle on an older shovel.

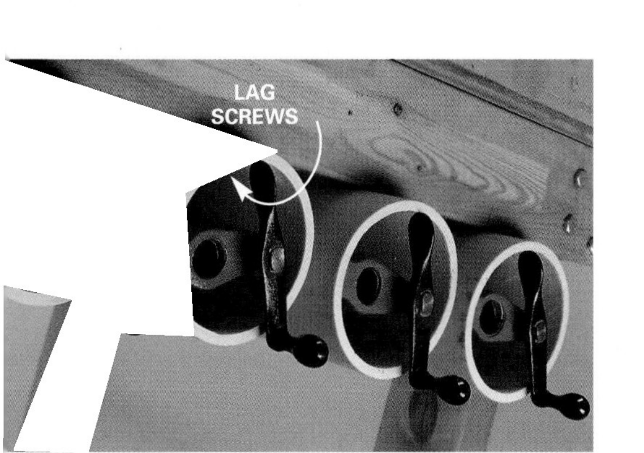

Pipe-Clamp Quivers

A great way to store pipe clamps up and out of the way is inside pieces of 4-in. dia. PVC pipe screwed under your workbench. To secure the pipes, use 2-in. lag screws and a socket wrench with a ratchet drive to allow you to reach in the end of the pipes and tighten them.

PVC Organizers

Here's a great way to use up even the shortest leftover pieces of PVC pipe. Glue them to a 1x4 or 1x6 with construction adhesive, then attach this platform to the wall with L-brackets. You can bend the brackets down slightly so you can see and access the contents more easily. Long sections are great for holding glues, spray paint, pencils and paintbrushes. Short sections are convenient for holding nails, screws and even that cup of coffee you keep knocking off the workbench.

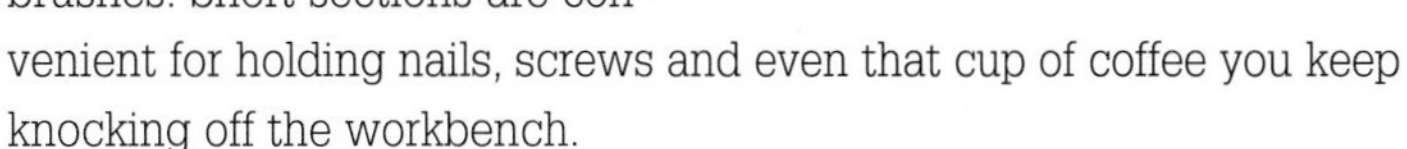

Pencils at the Ready

Sometimes it's the little things that count—like a convenient place to stash your pencils as you work. Build this simple, dust-free pencil holder by securing a small piece of screen to a small length of PVC pipe with Super Glue, then screw the pipe to your workbench.

Cord Holders

You can temporarily hang extension cords on ceiling joists or along the edge of your workbench with these holders made of 1-in. dia. PVC pipe. Cut a slot in a length of pipe, cut the pipe into 1-in. lengths, and then drill pilot holes. Screw the "clips" in place and then run your extension cord through them. They'll work for supporting air-compressor hoses, too.

HANDSAW BLADE SAVER

Letting a handsaw rattle loose in your toolbox has two strikes against it—the teeth can damage the cords and tools they rub against, and the teeth themselves get dull and harder to cut with. Make this handy dandy saw sheath by placing a section of 1/2-in. PVC pipe in a vise and sawing a slit down the middle. Slide it over your saw blade to keep the teeth sharp.

PVC BUNGEE-CORD ORGANIZER

If the bungee cords you keep in your trunk, pickup truck or garage are a tangled mess, take five minutes to make this simple organizer. Cut a piece of PVC pipe just a little bit longer than your longest cord, and drill a series of 1-in. holes along its length. When you're done hauling, simply stretch the cords between the end of the pipe and one of the holes.

PVC FURNITURE ANYONE?

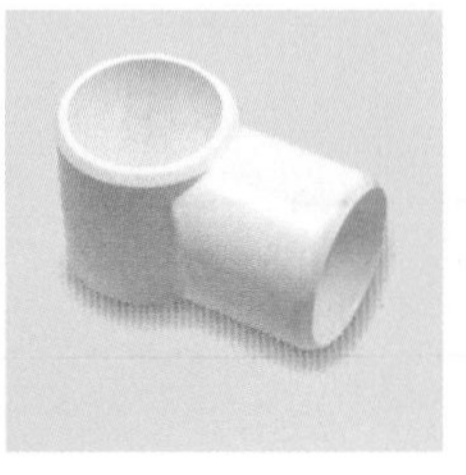

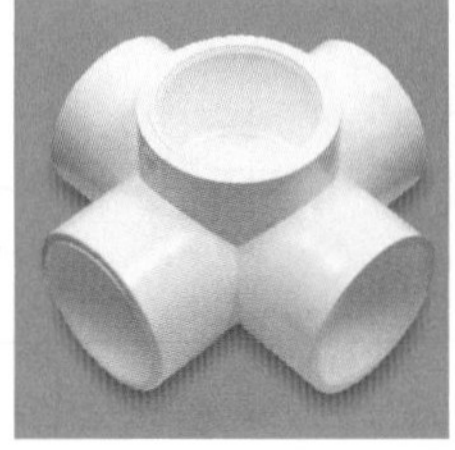

You can build patio furniture from standard PVC pipe and fittings, but the type used for plumbing is brittle, can't stand up to the sun and has printing emblazoned across it. So consider investing in specially formulated, furniture-grade pipe and fittings. They're sleeker, impact resistant, and available in colorfast white, beige and gray. The company Patios To Go (www.patiostogo.com; 352-243-3220) offers PVC materials and plans.

DUST COLLECTOR

Capture the dust that flies off a sanding drum or other tool before it fills your workshop (or lungs). Bolt a pot magnet to a 3 in. x 2 in. PVC reducing coupling and slide the coupling over the end of the vacuum hose. (A 2-1/4-in.-dia. shop vacuum hose fits snugly inside the coupling without clamps or glue.) Then set the magnet and hose on the tool's metal table and have your vacuum eat the dust.

CURVY SANDERS

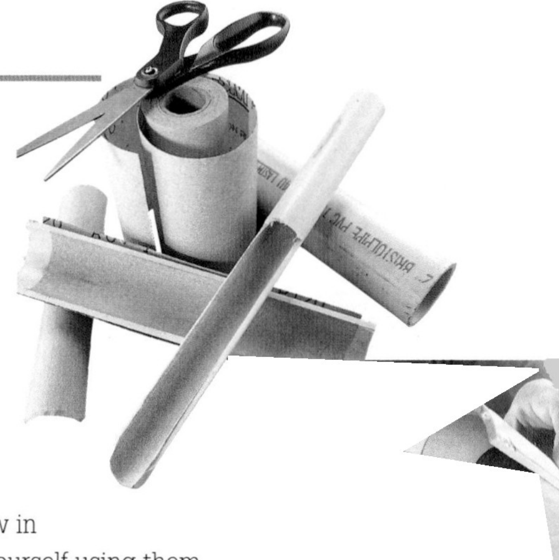

You can cut short pieces of PVC lengthwise with a handsaw or jigsaw to make contour sanders for convex andconcave surfaces and edges. Leave a section uncut to create a handle, if you want. You can apply adhesive-backed sandpaper to inner or outer diameters or spray photo-mount adhesive on the pipe and use regular sand-paper. Make a few in various diameters and you'll find yourself using them for all sorts of filing, fitting and smoothing tasks.

REACH HIGH FLY AND DUST SUCKER-UPPER

If you've got cobwebs, dust or bothersome bugs lurking in the upper reaches of a skylight or ceiling, simply duct tape a length of PVC pipe to the nozzle of your vacuum cleaner nozzle, then clean away.

FAST $40 TABLE

If you need an easy-to-build, easy-to-store, easy-to-pay-for table, just turn to our old friend—PVC pipe. Buy a hollow-core door slab 28 to 36 in. wide at a lumberyard or home center (usually around $30). Screw 3-in. toilet flanges at each corner, then cut four sections of 3-in. PVC pipe about 27 in. long and insert them in the flanges. Flip the assembly over and you have a table for working, dining or crafting. To store it, just pull out the legs and stash the pieces in the garage or basement.

PVC GARDEN TOOL HOLDER

Organize that avalanche of garden tools in your garage with this little tool holder. Use a jigsaw to cut a 1-1/4-in. channel along the length of a 2-in. PVC pipe. Cut several 3-1/2-in.-long sections with a hacksaw or miter saw, and drill a pair of 1/8-in. holes behind the notch. Use 1-1/4-in. drywall screws to attach the pieces to a 2x4 screwed to the wall and fill it up with rakes, shovels, brooms and other tools.

FISHING ROD ORGANIZER

To keep your fishing rods organized and tangle-free, build this simple rack. Screw a length of 1x4 to the wall about 1 ft. off the floor, and another right above it about 6 ft. off the floor. Predrill holes and screw 1-1/4-in. PVC end caps, spaced about 4 in. apart, to the bottom 1x4. Mount 1-1/4-in. PVC couplings directly above these on the upper 1x4. To stow a rod, slide the tip up through the coupling and let the handle rest in the cap.

QUICK-DRAW DRILL

Make a nifty cordless drill holster by screwing a 45-degree 4-in. PVC pipe elbow to the side of your workbench; this will accommodate most drills. When you're ready for action, just quick-draw the drill.

INDEX

For a complete 5-year index visit us at www.familyhandyman.com

A

Additions, heat for, 104
Air conditioners, cleaning, 103
Appliances
- gas, lighters for, 107
- manuals for, storing, 58, 132

Arbors, timber-frame, 240
Automobiles
- heater-hose repair for, 260-61
- manual storage for, 259
- molding repair for, 262-63
- tire-change hints for, 265-65

Bits
- concrete, 165
- extender for, 188, 275
- storage for, 168

Blinds, cord holders for, 133
Bolts, cutting, 187
Bookcases
- built-in, 156
- cherry, 155
- *See also* Shelves.

Bootscraper, making, 280
Brass, protecting, 95
Brickwork
- pointing, 202-5
- *See also* Mortar.

Brush, large container for, 233

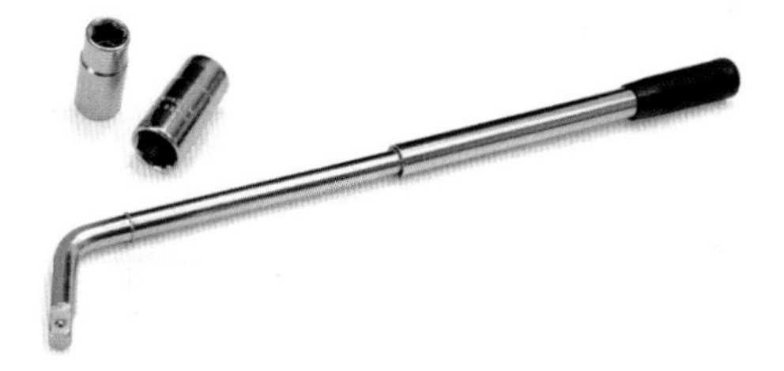

B

Backsplashes
- laminate, 68
- tile, 60

Baking sheets, storing, 57
Baseboards
- above carpet, 36
- around bad walls, 34-39
- protecting, 116

Basements, framing, 130
Bathrooms
- tiling, 63
- *See also* Septic systems.

Bicycles, storage for, 256
Biscuit joinery, strength of, 158

Brushes
- cleaning, 26
- making, 132

C

Cabinets, painting, 62
Carpet
- for basements, 21
- paint on, cleaning, 43
- restretching, 129

Caulk
- for concrete, 209
- neat, 108
- seal puncher for, 186
- storage for, 169, 170
- for trim, 35

CDs, uses for, 273
Ceilings, panels in, fitting, 14
Chains, racks for, 269-70
Chair rail, urethane, applying, 18-19
Chairs
- Adirondack, making, 142-47
- repairing, 160-61

Chisels, hand protector for, 188
Chinese checkers, building, 276
Circular saws
- bevels with, 175
- blades for, 172
- cutoff supports for, 175
- guides for, 149
- plunge cuts with, 173
- safety with, 173
- small pieces with, 174, 176
- storage for, 272, 281

Clamps
- extenders for, 149
- pipe, 148
- storage for, 169, 170, 186

Closets, built-in, 157
Combination square, marking with, 187
Concrete
- caulking, invisibly, 209
- edging, 208
- finishing, 206-9
- moisture from, 190
- repairing, 197
- screws in, 164-67

Countertops, laminate, 64-68

Cracks
- major, 121
- repairing, 159
- *See also* Drywall: repairs in.

Curtains, no-hole holders for, 133
Cutting boards, cleaning, 51

D

Decks
- composite multi-level, 242
- repairing, 210-14
- stiffening, 213

Dishwashers, touching up, 107
Doors
- bifold, sticking, 118-19
- bumpers for, 49
- hinges on, adjusting, 49
- latches for, 49
- metal, frozen, 121
- painting, 28
- screens for, 197
- security of, upgrading, 134-38
- stands for, 132

Doorways, protecting, 116
Drawers
- fixing, 50
- lubricating, 50
- slides for, replacing, 50

Drill presses, plugs with, 148
Drills
- hammer, 166, 170
- holster for, 186, 283

Dryers, shelves for, 58

Drywall
cutouts in, 23
lifting, 24
lifts for, using, 22-23, 25
marking, with lipstick, 14
nailers for, adding, 25
by oneself, 22-25
repairs in, 10-13
sanding, 44-46
See also Joint compound; Plaster: Venetian.
Dust
collector for, 282
reduction strategies for, 114-15
See also Shop vacuums.

E

Electrical. *See* Wiring.

F

Fans
bathroom, motors for, 72
ceiling, sizing, 20
for dust removal, 114
quieting, 95
Faucets
kitchen, installing, 69-71
repairing, 98-101
Fertilizer, spreader for, 232
Finishes
excess, blowing away, 148
exterior, 147
Flagpoles, holder for, 233
Floors
basement, carpeting, 21
protecting, 117
from paint, 40-41
squeak removal for, 30-33
Foam sealant, packing with, 274
Foundations, cracked, 121
Furnace filters, storage for, 274

G

Garages
car markers for, 259
heaters for, 267
squeegee for, 259
storage for, 254-59
Garbage disposers, jacking up, 58
Gardens, edging for, 248-51
Gas torches, self-igniting, 110
Gloves
as paint-can sealers, 28
plumber's, 59
Glues
choosing, 162
excess, removing, 149
working with, 158-62
Greenhouses, mini-, 232
Gutters, cleaning, 199, 201

H

Hardware, storage for, 271
Heating systems
extending, 104
for garages, 266-67
Hinges, adjusting, 49
Holes
filling, 51
plugs for, making, 148
See also Drywall: repairs in.
Home theaters, designing, 126-27
Hoses, cheap *vs.* quality, 224
Hutches, garden, 157

I

Insulation, cutting, 133
Irons, refilling, 57
Islands, exterior cook-out, 241

J

Joint compound
fast-setting, 11
patching, 25
See also Plaster: Venetian.

K

Kitchens
See Backsplashes; Cabinets; Countertops.
Knives
drywall, adapting, 14
utility, renewing, 14
Knobs. *See* Pulls.

L

Ladders
balance-point mark for, 199
bucket holders for, 133, 200
Lamps
fixing, 74-77
See also Light bulbs.
Latches, adjusting, 49
Lawns
aerating, 223
installing, 216-21
weeds in, 222
See also Sprinklers.
Levels
laser, 123
testing, 125
using, 122-25
Light bulbs, fluorescent, choosing, 79
Light fixtures
exterior, 243
protecting, 43
Locks, security of, upgrading, 134-38
Love seats, Adirondack, making, 142-47
Lumber, treated, toxicity of, 224

M

Masking tape
dispenser for, 132
large, 27
removing, 26
using, 115
Measurements
inside, 168
on tape measures, 176
Metal, bending, 199
Miters, adjusting, 38
Miter saws, fence for, 188
Moldings
coping, 14
crown, 128
See also Chair rail.
Mortar, stains from, removing, 226

N

Nailers, for trim, 39
Nails
presetting, 23, 187
replacing, 214

P

Paint
  mixing, in bags, 26
  pads for, clean-up, 26
  peeling, stopping, 190-91
  preparation for, 40-41
  rollers for, storing, 27, 228
  scrapers for, 26, 201
  storing, in jars, 28
  water repellents for, 195
  and wet wood, 190, 194-95
  worktable for, 201
Paint removers, gentle, 27
Parts, sources for, 53, 103
Paths, masonry, 241
Patio door, security, 273
Pavers
  borders of, 250-51
  lifter for, 233
Pictures, hanging, 131
Pipe, sloping, 124
Plaster, Venetian, applying, 15-18
Pliers, soft jaws for, 108
Plumb bobs, using, 124
Plumbing
  pipes for
  cutting, 106
  quieting, 106
  shutoff valves in, 106
  soldering, 110-12
Plywood, carrying, 275
Ponds, repairing leaks in, 246-47
Pulls
  gluing, 51
  replacing, 120
PVC pipe
  tips for, 281
  furniture from, 282
  organizers from, 281, 283
  table made from, 283
  bungee organizer from, 282
  clamp storage from, 281
  cord holder, 281
  vacuum cleaner extension, 282

R

Radon, discussed, 20
Railings
  strengthening, 212
  wood-and-glass, 245
Refrigerators
  ice makers in, repairing, 54
  leakage from, repairing, 55
  moving, 56
  parts for, 53
  plumbing for, 105
  quieting, 52
  temperature repairs for, 53
Remodeling
  appreciation priority for, 62
  See also Additions.
Roofs
  mildew on, 198
  snow rake for, 200
Rope, racks for, 269-70

S

Sanders
  coping with, 14
  curved, 282
Sawhorses
  adjustable, 187
  no-mar, 186
Scrapers, shoe, 233
Scratches, repairing, 51
Screens, for patios, 245
Screws
  anchors for, 165
  inconcrete, 164-67
Scribing, process of, 65, 67
Seeds, spreader for, 232
Septic systems, explained, 102
Sheds, plans for, 244
Sheet goods
  panel lifers for, 24
  panel rollers for, 24
  stabilizers for, 149

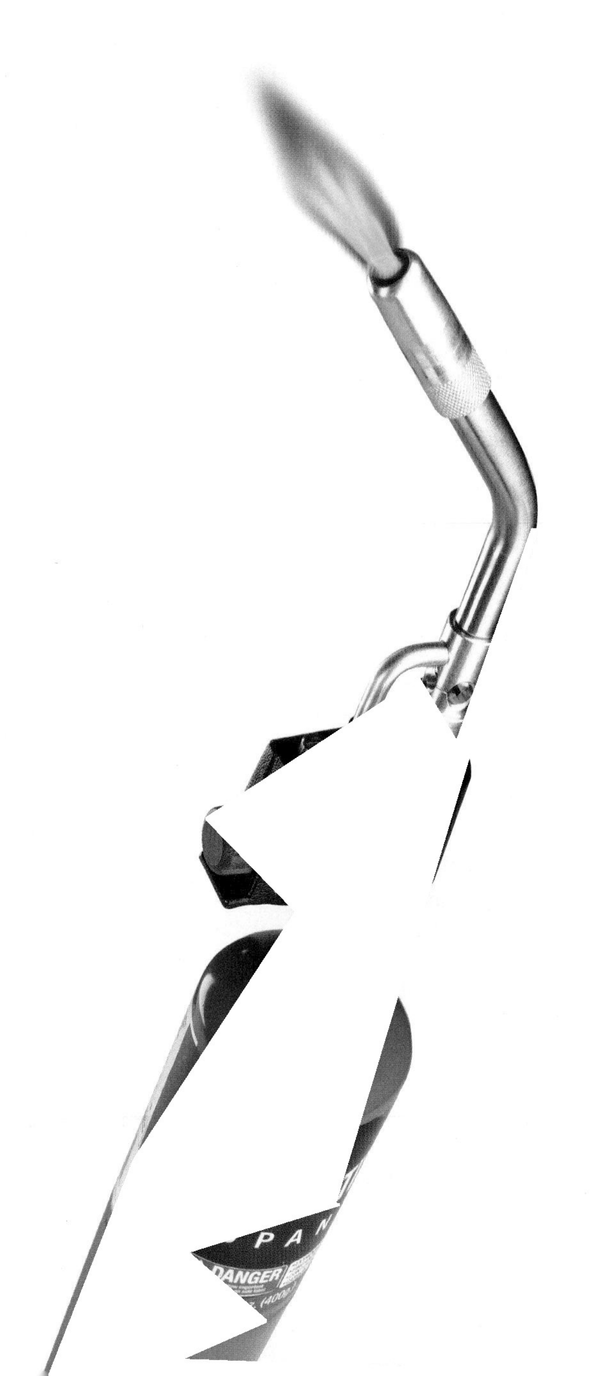

Shelves
over appliances, 58
wall-leaning, 150-54
wire, in showers, 59
Shingles, installing, 196
Shop vacuums
adaptors for, 179
dust ports for, 180
filters for, 181
hoses for, 179, 181
storage for, 171
Sidewalks, repairing, 197
Siding
hardboard, buckled, 198
replacing, 192-95
vinyl, painting, 197
Sinks
chipped, fixing, 103
kitchen, installing, 69-71
quieting, 57
sprayers of, freeing, 59
wall-hung, 61
Soldering, process of, 110-12
Spades, foot-friendly, 233
Speakers, wires from, hiding, 80
Spice rack, making, 278
Sprinklers, best, 225
Staircases, railing for, 129
Stairs, protecting, 117
Steppingstones, making, 277
Storage
air-tight, 14
in ceilings, 254-57, 271
garage, 254-59
from guttering, 171
pegboard, corner holders for, 169
racks for, 269-70
for small parts, 107
Streams, adding, 234-39

T

Tables, quick work, 201
Tape, storage for, 168
Tarpaulins, weights for, 200
Tilework, over vinyl, 63
Tile trivet, making, 279
Toilets
mounting, 108
snakes for, 107
Tool holders
plastic, 169
between studs, 170
wooden, 171
Tools
dust ports of, 180
garden caddy for, 232
storage for, 269
Trellises, copper, 243
Trim
around bad walls, 34-39
caulking, 35
exterior, replacing, 192-93
nailers for, 39
splicing, 39
touchups for, 133

V

Vacuums, for dust removal, 114

W

Walls, retaining
masonry, 226-30
wood, 231
Washing machines, shelves for, 58
Water features, adding, 234-39
Wheelbarrows, storage for, 258, 270
Window seats, built-in, 156
Wire strippers, choosing, 93, 95
Wiring
aluminum, danger of, 91
boxes for adjustable, 78
airtight, 79
breakers for, 83
conduit for, 88-89
fuses for, 82
hiding, 80
joining, 92-93, 94
loose, 84-85
organizing, 95
outlets of
checking of, 82-83
protecting, 42
quality, 94
plugs for, replacing, 75
raceways for, 81
stripping, 93
surface-mounted, 81, 86-89
See also Light bulbs.
Wood, storage for, 270
Workbenches, making, 177

ACKNOWLEDGMENTS

FOR THE FAMILY HANDYMAN

Editor in Chief	Ken Collier
Editor	Duane Johnson
Executive Editor	Spike Carlsen
Senior Editor	Dave Radtke
Associate Editors	Jeff Gorton
	Kurt Lawton
	Travis Larson
	Gary Wentz
Senior Copy Editor	Donna Bierbach
Design Director	Sara Koehler
Senior Art Director	Bob Ungar
Art Directors	Becky Pfluger
	Marcia Wright Roepke
Office Administrative Manager	Alice Garrett
Technical Manager	Shannon Hooge
Reader Service Specialist	Roxie Filipkowski
Office Administrative Assistant	Shelly Jacobsen
Administrative Assistant	Lori Callister
Production Manager	Judy Rodriguez
Production Artist	Lisa Pahl Knecht

CONTRIBUTING EDITORS

Eric Smith
Bruce Wiebe
Jeff Timm

FREELANCE ART DIRECTORS

David Farr
Barb Pederson
Mark Jacobson
Gregg Weigand
Rick Dupre

PHOTOGRAPHERS

Mike Habermann, Mike Habermann Photography
Mike Krivit, Krivit Photography
Phil Leisenheimer, LA Studios
Shawn Nielsen, Nielsen Photography
Ramon Moreno
Bill Zuehlke

ILLUSTRATORS

Steve Björkman
Gabe De Matteis
Roy Doty
John Keely
Bruce Kieffer
Don Mannes
Doug Oudekerk
Frank Rohrbach
Eugene Thompson

OTHER CONSULTANTS

Charles Avoles, plumbing
Al Hildenbrand, electrical
Kathryn Hillbrand, interior design
Dave MacDonald, structural engineer
Jon Jensen, carpentry
Bob Lacivita, automotive
Mary Jane Pappas, kitchen and bath design
Ron Pearson, environmental issues
Tom Schultz, drywall
Dean Sorem, tile
Costas Stavrou, appliance repair
John Williamson, electrical
Ron Zeien, appliance repair
Les Zell, plumbing